Play Therapy Treatment Planning and Intervent

The Ecosystemic Model and Workbook

Play Therapy Treatment Planning and Interventions

The Ecosystemic Model and Workbook

Kevin John O'Connor

California School of Professional Psychology
Fresno, California

Sue Ammen

California School of Professional Psychology
Fresno, California

ACADEMIC PRESS

San Diego London Boston New York Sydney Tokyo Toronto

Copyright © 1997 by ACADEMIC PRESS

Academic Press
a division of Harcourt Brace & Company
525 B Street, Suite 1900, San Diego, California 92101-4495, USA
http://www.apnet.com

Academic Press Limited
24-28 Oval Road, London NW1 7DX, UK
http://www.hbuk.co.uk/ap/

Library of Congress Cataloging-in-Publication Data

O'Connor, Kevin J.
    Play therapy treatment planning and interventions : the
ecosystemic model and workbook / by Kevin John O'Connor, Sue Ammen.
        p.   cm.
    Includes index.
    ISBN 0-12-524135-6 (alk. paper)
    1. Play therapy.   2. Ecopsychiatry.   I. Ammen, Sue.   II. Title.
RJ505.P60264   1997
618.92'891653--dc21   97-25959
                                                           CIP

PRINTED IN THE UNITED STATES OF AMERICA
97   98   99   00   01   02   EB   9   8   7   6   5   4   3   2   1

For Ryan, Matthew, and Kayli
with special thanks to Bob and Gail

◆ Contents ◆

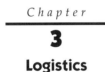

◆ Preface ◆

Play therapy is an interactive process that goes on between the child, the play therapist, and the systems in which the child is involved. Its success depends on the attitudes, knowledge, and skills of the play therapist, the child's capacity for change, and the ability of the systems in which that child is embedded to support or at least not resist change.

In Ecosystemic Play Therapy, we emphasize the effect of each of the systems in which a person is embedded on the course, and the ups and downs, of that person's life. One of the systems we talk about is Historical Time, referring to the way things in the world change as time passes. The impact of this system can be directly seen in a fortuitous coincidence between our thinking and the evolution of the mental health field in the past 5 to 10 years. As managed care has come to have a progressively stronger foothold in the management of mental health service provisions, it has brought with it both negative and positive changes. While the miserly approach to dispensing services seems to have had a very negative effect on clients and their families, the outcome focus of these programs has pushed mental health professionals to begin thinking in terms of accountability. Therapists now actively consider the goals to be pursued in treatment, strategies for accomplishing those goals cost effectively, and ways to measure and document those changes. While the therapy process should not become mechanical or recipe driven, this does not mean it cannot be organized, focused, and highly efficient. This cannot help but improve the quality of the services that clients are able to access.

This text and Workbook were designed specifically to help play therapists meet the increasing demands made by various regulating agencies for specific treatment goals and even more specific treatment plans that can be used to assess the need for service and the effectiveness of the outcome. The very notion of such specific planning often runs counter to the training that play therapists receive. After all, allowing the child to lead the way and to work at his or her own pace are the cornerstone principles of the Axlinian model in which most therapists were trained. The Ecosystemic model shifts responsibility for the forward progress of the sessions onto therapists and, so that they can meet that responsibility, it also shifts more of the control of the direction and content of the session to them. This is not to say that the Ecosystemic Play therapist runs roughshod over the feelings and experiences of any child client. Quite the contrary. The Ecosystemic Play therapist's entire focus is on helping children learn behaviors that will lead to their needs being met effectively in ways that do not substantially interfere with the ability of those around them to also have their needs met.

The purpose of the Workbook is to provide the play therapist with a format for conceptualizing a case in a manner consistent with Ecosystemic Play Therapy Theory as it is presented in Chapter 1, "Theoretical Foundations." The model encourages the play therapist to define goals for each of the systems in which the child is embedded and then to make decisions about his or her role in addressing each of those goals. Some goals will be suited to individual play therapy, some to family or group work, some to case consultation or education, and still others to an advocacy approach. The value and pitfalls of the play therapist's entering any or all of these roles are also discussed in Chapter 8.

Having described the theoretical base, we go on to discuss the impact of diversity issues on the practice of Ecosystemic Play Therapy in Chapter 2, "Recognizing, Addressing, and Celebrating Diversity." Because these issues are considered central to the practice of competent and ethical play therapy, they are also discussed throughout the text. The primary issues addressed are rooted in phenomenology; namely, the way each of us perceives, experiences, and interacts with the world is unique and, in part, a reflection of the groups in which we are members. This uniqueness is a gift that is critical to the creativity and survival of both the individual and the human race as a whole.

The remainder of the text takes the reader through the process of completing and using the Workbook. In Chapter 3, "Logistics," Chapter 4, "Data Collection: Intake and Mental Status," and Chapter 5, "Assessment," we have attempted to include most of the knowledge we have acquired over the years about how to gather case information effectively using a combination of interview and assessment strategies. We have attempted to provide the reader with a fairly extensive, though not exhaustive, list of data that might be appropriately gathered in the course of an intake and pretreatment assessment. All of these data are organized in a manner consistent with the Ecosystemic Play Therapy Theory, moving from information about the smallest systems (internal to the child) to the largest (historical time).

Having gathered the data, the Ecosystemic Play therapist then invests considerable time and energy into organizing those data into a comprehensive description of the child, as described in Chapter 6, "Case Conceptualization," and then developing a systematic treatment plan as described in Chapter 7, "Treatment Planning." This treatment plan is then enhanced with specific session plans for both experiential and cognitive/verbal activities and interventions. The core elements of good Ecosystemic Play Therapy are presented in Chapter 8, "Interventions." This chapter is one of the most comprehensive attempts in the existing literature, of which we are aware, to describe what play therapists actually do in session to address the child's problems over the course of the treatment process. In Chapter 9, "Session Activities," a sample of 25 different session activities geared toward children at different developmental levels with a wide variety of presenting problems is described. We hope this chapter shows the creativity and variety that are possible within well-planned play therapy sessions, as opposed to creating a sense of a cookbook for session planning.

In Chapter 10, "Jennifer M.," a complete case example of the use of the Workbook in developing an Ecosystemic Play Therapy treatment plan is presented without interruption. The reader may choose to work along with the play therapist on the case by using a blank copy of the Workbook provided at the end of the book.

Psychiatrists, psychologists, social workers, nurses, and counselors at all levels of training and experience should find this text informative, thought provoking, and clinically useful.

Kevin John O'Connor
Sue Ammen

◆ About the Authors ◆

Kevin John O'Connor, PhD, RPT-S, is a Clinical Psychologist and Professor in the Ecosystemic Clinical Child Psychology Program at the California School of Professional Psychology in Fresno, California. He is the cofounder and Executive Director of the Association for Play Therapy. He also maintains a small private practice treating children and adults recovering from childhood trauma. Dr. O'Connor is the coeditor of the *Handbook of Play Therapy, Volumes I & II* and *Play Therapy Theory and Practice,* and the author of the *Play Therapy Primer* and numerous articles on child psychotherapy and professional practice. Currently, he is writing a second edition of the *Primer.* Dr. O'Connor is also currently researching the personal and professional issues and struggles faced by gay and lesbian psychotherapists who choose to work with children and families. He presents regularly such topics as Play Therapy Assessment and Treatment Planning, Increasing Children's Verbalizations in Play Therapy, Structured Group Play Therapy, and others, across the United States and abroad.

Sue Ammen, PhD, RPT-S, is a Clinical Psychologist and an Associate Professor and Director of the Ecosystemic Clinical Child Psychology Program at the California School of Professional Psychology in Fresno, California. Dr. Ammen frequently presents workshops and classes on play therapy, attachment issues, and child abuse treatment. She is presently conducting research specific to attachment and attachment-related problems. She authored a chapter, "The Good Feeling–Bad Feeling Game," in the *Handbook of Play Therapy, Volume II.* Her private practice focuses on the treatment of issues related to trauma, attachment, and the family.

· 1 ·

THEORETICAL FOUNDATIONS

It must be remembered that the object of the world of ideas as a whole (the map or model) is not the portrayal of reality—this would be an utterly impossible task—but rather to provide us with an instrument for finding our way about more easily in the world.

H. Vaihinger, *The Philosophy of As If* [1]

A MAP OF PLAY THERAPY TREATMENT

This book is our map for finding our way through the process of play therapy treatment planning and implementation. It is a map based on Ecosystemic[2] Play Therapy Theory as it was first presented in *The Play Therapy Primer* (O'Connor, 1991) and later expanded in the *Handbook of Play Therapy, Volume 2* (O'Connor, 1993b), and in *Play Therapy Theory and Practice: A Comparative Presentation* (O'Connor & Braverman, 1997).[3] Ecosystemic Play Therapy Theory is a systems theory that addresses intrapsychic, interactional, develop-

mental, and historical processes. The relevance of the term "*eco*systemic" as opposed to "systemic" for capturing the integration of temporal and systemic variables is found in the definition of ecology. Ecology comes from the Greek root, *oik*, for house or living place. Ernest Haeckel, a German zoologist, first proposed the term "oekologie" in 1873 to represent the study of the individual as a "product of cooperation between the environment and organismal heredity" (Bubolz & Sontag, 1993, p. 419). Contained within this idea is the importance of studying the developing individual over time in interaction with the multilevel systems that make up that individual's living place or ecosystem. Thus, the term ecosystemic captures not only the importance of the systemic interactions between a child and that child's ecosystem, but also the developmental and historical processes that are embedded in the child and the child's ecosystemic context.

Each of the authors in this book brings to Ecosystemic Play Therapy his or her own experiences and understandings. For Kevin O'Connor, this understanding began with the integration of several existing theories of both general and play therapy into a comprehensive theory and treatment approach that is consistent with and informed by his experience as a play therapist.

[A] broadly systemic perspective called **ecological** or **ecosystemic** was the filter for determining which elements of the the-

---

[1] Quote taken from Bandler & Grinder (1975, p. 7), in which they modified Vaihinger's (1924, p. 15) quote by adding the words in brackets.

[2] The term "ecosystemic" has been used by different writers in the social sciences (e.g., Belsky, 1980; Bronfenbrenner, 1979) to conceptualize the importance of the larger systemic context. Although O'Connor (1991) developed Ecosystemic Play Therapy Theory independently of these writers, we acknowledge the presence of these overlapping ideas.

[3] Throughout the rest of this chapter any reference to Ecosystemic Play Therapy Theory and practice refers to the ideas presented in these three texts.

ories or techniques of play therapy that were reviewed should be retained or discarded. . . . The integrated model described in this volume focuses, as the term **ecology** suggests, on "the totality or pattern of relations between organisms and their environment" (*Webster's Seventh New Collegiate Dictionary,* 1967). This emphasis is unique to the extent that the play therapist is forced to consider the multiple systems of which the child is a part from the point of intake until termination. (O'Connor, 1991, p. vii)

O'Connor has defined Ecosystemic Play Therapy as a hybrid model that integrates biological science concepts, multiple models of child psychotherapy, and developmental theory. This model is not eclectic. Instead, it is an integration of multiple models to create a freestanding model that is different from the sum of its parts. It differs from most models of family or systemic therapy because the basic unit under consideration is the individual rather than the family or some other system. At the same time, Ecosystemic Play Therapy differs from most models of play therapy because it does not focus solely on the functioning of the child client. Rather, the focus is on optimizing the child's functioning in the context of that child's ecosystem or world. Finally, Ecosystemic Play Therapy Theory is developed from a phenomenological philosophical perspective, as opposed to the more traditional natural science perspective. Within the phenomenological perspective, absolute truth does not exist; rather, our understanding of events is always the result of the interaction between our internal processes and our experiences in the world.

For Sue Ammen, this theoretical journey started with a search to understand the systemic theoretical roots of the family therapy field, particularly to unravel the implications of Maturana's biological systems theory (Ammen, 1990). The best known sources of systems theory used in family therapy theory are general systems theory (e.g., Bertalanffy, 1968) and cybernetics (Ashby, 1956; Wiener, 1961). A second generation of systems theories entered the family therapy field in the early 1980s. The most significant impact came from the works of Humberto Maturana, both alone and with Francisco Varela (e.g., Maturana, 1978; Maturana & Varela, 1973/1980, 1987).[4] Ammen concluded that Maturana's biological systems theory radically changed and expanded many of the theoretical assumptions of the earlier systems theories. Perhaps what was most exciting about Maturana's theory was its incorporation of individual intrapsychic experience and historical–developmental processes into a comprehensive systems theory.

Maturana's theory contains many elements that co-incide with and complement Ecosystemic Play Therapy Theory:

- Individuals are identified as the basic systemic unit relative to the family system or other social systems;
- Behavior is always defined as being adaptive relative to the environment;
- Developmental and historical processes are thoroughly integrated; and
- The human experience is defined as including biological, intrapsychic, and interactional experiences that are complementary and interdependent ways of being.

In addition, Maturana (1978) identified the way we know and operate in our world as always subject-dependent.[5] This means that everything we experience and understand about our world is always from the perspective of ourselves as participants in and observers of our experience in that world. This idea is consistent with the phenomenological philosophical perspective used by O'Connor in developing Ecosystemic Play Therapy Theory. The difference between Maturana's concept of subject dependence and the phenomenological perspective is that the concept of subject dependence came directly out of Maturana's research which led to his systems theory, whereas the phenomenological perspective is a philosophical position.

As Ammen's practice and teaching became more focused on play therapy, she integrated her systemic model based on Maturana's theory with her understanding of Ecosystemic Play Therapy. She also incorporated insights from Bowlby's attachment theory (e.g., Bowlby, 1973, 1980, 1982, 1988; Bretherton, 1987, 1993; Karen, 1994) and Stern's (1995) synthesis of psychoanalytic and interpersonal dynamics in infant psychiatry to provide a more direct understanding of caregiver–child relationships and of the clinical situation.

Rather than simply repeating all of the details of Ecosystemic Play Therapy Theory as they have been presented elsewhere (O'Connor, 1991, 1993b; O'Connor & Braverman, 1997), the purpose of this chapter is to summarize the main points of the theory and to expand portions of it through the integration of ideas derived from both Maturana's work and attachment theory. In the previous writings, O'Connor's Ecosystemic Play Therapy Theory combined biological, individual, intrapsychic, developmental, and historical concepts with systemic concepts to create an integrated theory, even though the traditional systemic theories could not fully incorporate all of these concepts. Maturana's sys-

---

[4]See Ammen (1990) for a description and interpretation of Maturana's work, particularly as it applies to family therapy.

[5]See Maturana (1980) or Ammen (1990) for discussion of Maturana's biological research that led him to this conclusion.

tems theory provides a way to anchor the integrated Ecosystemic Play Therapy Theory within a systems theoretical context. We apply Ecosystemic Play Therapy Theory to the critical elements of any psychotherapeutic theory of play therapy, identified by O'Connor (1993b) as (a) the concept of personality, (b) the concept of psychopathology, and (c) treatment goals and curative elements of play therapy, and link the theory of Ecosystemic Play Therapy directly to the practice of Ecosystemic Play Therapy, setting the stage for the rest of the book.

PHILOSOPHICAL PERSPECTIVE

Theories are cognitive models that we, as human beings, use to describe or explain events or phenomena in our world. We make assumptions about the nature of the phenomena that we want to explain (i.e., the nature of reality) and assumptions about *how we know* what we know about that reality. These assumptions define the philosophical context of a theory. Interestingly, many play therapists would probably have difficulty describing the theoretical model they use in any detail and even more difficulty describing the philosophical context of that theoretical model. Typically, this difficulty arises because people in general tend to think more about what they do than why they do it. In spite of this, understanding one's philosophical context is critical because different philosophical contexts can lead to different theoretical conclusions that, in turn, result in differences in clinical practice. There are two general philosophical approaches to the study of human behavior: the natural science perspective and the phenomenological perspective.[6] The philosophical context from which we approach our theorizing is phenomenological.

The central assumption of the natural science perspective is that a clearly identifiable, objective reality exists, independent and external to humans, that can be discovered, described, explained, or controlled. This is the dominant view in Western society. From this perspective, the purpose of a theory is to accurately describe some external reality or phenomenon. When we, as therapists, operate from this perspective, we assume our theory is providing a description about what is real external to us (e.g., an emotionally disturbed child) and we use this description to plan our interventions, often

[6]The terms *natural science* and *phenomenological* were chosen to emphasize the dichotomy between the traditional scientific approaches in psychology based on the natural sciences that have their roots in logical empiricism/logical positivism (e.g., Hempel, 1966) and the alternative approaches that have their roots in Husserl's phenomenological philosophy (e.g., Giorgi, 1985).

with the goal of "fixing" or correcting the situation.

The phenomenological perspective, in contrast to the natural science perspective, assumes that objective reality is not determined by an absolute external phenomenon, nor is it arbitrarily determined by the observer's internal processes. Rather, reality is the result of an interaction of both the observer and the observed (Giorgi, 1983). In particular, we do not see the intake process as gathering information about an objective problem that can be targeted and corrected. Instead, the "observational focus is the evolving psychological field constituted by the interplay between the differently organized subjectivities of child and caretaker [or other relevant participants in the child's ecosystem]" (Atwood & Stolorow, 1984, p. 65). This also means that as therapists, we must understand that our internal models and beliefs and our participation in the client–therapist system will have an effect on the therapy we conduct. Using this model, we can no longer see ourselves as being outside the client's experience while we attempt to discover his or her truth so that we can correct it and provide relief. We are an integral, inseparable part of the system.

We view Ecosystemic Play Therapy Theory as a map that guides us rather than as a description of an actual reality. It is not an arbitrary theory built solely of our isolated subjective experiences. Rather, it is influenced by our professional, cultural, and social contexts as well as by our many experiences and our internal understanding of those experiences. In particular, this theory is informed by our many interactions with children and families both in our daily lives and in the context of therapy, and it continues to be modified and deepened by those experiences.

This raises a question as to how we can evaluate the validity of our theoretical model. From the natural science perspective, validity refers to the accuracy or correctness of a theory. In contrast, validity of a theory from the phenomenological perspective is evaluated in terms of its general usefulness and its effectiveness in changing the experiences of the participants in directions that they experience as positive. The following criteria for evaluating a theory from the phenomenological perspective have been adapted from Valdés (1987): (a) It is coherent; (b) it has accomplished the goal of the theorist to increase his or her understanding; and (c) it is of consequence to those who will put it to use. With respect to the first two criteria, this model of play therapy is particularly useful in organizing our understanding of the needs of the children with whom we work so as to develop a consistent and focused treatment plan. With respect to the last criterion, the practitioner will be the judge. We believe that the Ecosystemic Model of Play Therapy facilitates the collection and organization of case data and enhances one's ability to develop a comprehensive case conceptualization and list of treatment goals and to use these to practice highly effective play therapy.

ECOSYSTEMIC PLAY THERAPY THEORY AS A SYSTEMIC THEORY

A "bit" of information is definable as a difference which makes a difference.

Gregory Bateson, *Steps to an Ecology of Mind*[7]

Following Bateson's idea that information is a "difference which makes a difference," we now identify how Ecosystemic Play Therapy Theory is different from the traditional systems theoretical views and use these differences to highlight key aspects of this theory. Ecosystemic Play Therapy differs from most models of play therapy in that it does not focus solely on the functioning of the child client. Rather, the focus is on optimizing the functioning of the child in the context of that child's ecosystem or world (O'Connor, 1993b). The influence of the child's ecosystem is thought to be critical, both as a source of support for the child and as having the potential to interfere with the child's movement toward more optimal functioning. As a result of this focus on how the child functions in his or her ecosystemic context, Ecosystemic Play Therapy qualifies as a systemic theory. How the child's ecosystem is addressed in the therapy varies. This may mean any of the following: the content of individual play therapy interventions specifically addresses the child's functioning in relationships in his or her ecosystem; the therapist is involved in consultation and advocacy roles with different systems in addition to the play therapy component of treatment; the play therapy interventions themselves include other people from the child's ecosystem, such as parents, siblings, or teachers; or, most likely, the treatment involves some combination of individual, dyadic, family, consultation, and advocacy roles with the other systems.

Ecosystemic Play Therapy differs from most systemic models of therapy in three significant ways. First, when compared conceptually with family therapy, the basic systemic unit in Ecosystemic Play Therapy is the individual child, not the family system. Second, the child's ecosystem includes both the child's interactional systems (e.g., family, peers, etc.) and the child's intrapsychic system as interdependent ways of being in the world. Third, as previously discussed, the term ecosystemic incorporates developmental and historical phenomena as relevant to the child's functioning in his

or her ecosystem. Although these ideas differ from traditional systems theory approaches, they are consistent with Maturana's systems theory. In the following paragraphs, each difference is discussed in some detail using the theoretical constructs from Maturana's systems theory.[8] This is followed by a brief description of the ecosystemic model.

The Child as the Basic Systemic Unit

One of the core assumptions of traditional systemic approaches to the treatment of children and families is that the family (or larger social system) is the basic systemic unit for intervention:

> People are products of their natural contexts, the most significant of which is the family; *psychological disorders are therefore not individual problems, but family problems* [emphasis added]. Although these disorders seem to be handicaps they are actually part of the family's attempt to maintain a viable and cohesive structure. Families may be understood as systems, operating not as collections of individuals, but as emergent, whole entities. (Nichols, 1984, pp. 117–118)

With Bertalannfy's general systems theory (e.g., Bertalanffy, 1968; Davidson, 1983) as its map, family therapy used living organisms as the metaphor for family systems. Because living organisms are made up of components (e.g., cells), which they subordinate to their functioning as a whole, the same rationale was applied to families. Individuals were seen as components of the family system whose functioning is subordinated to the functioning of the system as a whole. As a result, the focus of treatment was the family system as a whole.

Maturana's systems theory challenges this assumption because it defines the organization of living organisms (i.e., living systems such as individual human beings) as being different from the organization of social systems (such as families). He called the organization of a living organism the *autopoietic organization*. Thus, it is inappropriate to use a living organism as a metaphor for the family system because the organization of the family as a social system is different from the organization of an individual as a living system.

Maturana's systems theory developed out of his search as a biologist to answer the question, What is it about living organisms (e.g., living systems, including human beings) that makes them living rather than nonliving? General systems theory defined the unique characteristic of living organisms as something that

---

[7]Bateson, G. (1972). Steps to an Ecology of Mind, p. 315. New York: Ballantine Books.

[8]The following descriptions of Maturana's systems theory are drawn from the second author's dissertation (Ammen, 1990) in which she interpreted all of Maturana's English-language publications through 1988 (13 articles and books). No attempt is made here to identify the specific Maturana references from which these ideas were derived except when directly quoting material.

emerges out of their operation as a whole as a consequence of being open systems. That is, living organisms were defined as living because they were open systems that exchanged energy, matter, and information with their environment, which allowed them to develop toward states of higher order and differentiation. Thus, whether or not something was living was defined by its relationship with its environment.

Maturana concluded that this definition did not account for the autonomy (self-definition, self-direction) of living organisms. Biology has long recognized that living organisms seem to function according to their own rules and purposes; that is, they seem to be autonomous. To account for this autonomy, Maturana identified living organisms as autopoietic, which means self-creating or self-defining. In other words, what makes a living organism living is that its way of being in the world is always organized around maintaining its own being, or it dies.

This definition of living as autopoietic creates a systems theory that differs dramatically from the traditional systems theories. In particular, Maturana's systems theory defines the individual human being as primary relative to the systems created by those individuals, such as families. Individual human beings are autopoietic systems that subordinate the functioning of their cells to their functioning as a whole. In fact, once cells combine to create a living organism, they cannot exist on their own. However, the same is *not* true for families and other social systems. Although it might be painful, it is possible for a person to no longer be part of a family and still exist.

> It is only the individual who is able to process matter, energy, and information. The comparison of the individual with a cell in an organism is wrong, as cells are not able to decide whether and to what extent they will participate in a suprasystem. (Willi, 1987, p. 433)

Although it is true that individuals in a family create a system of relationships that in turn have a powerful effect on the individuals within that family, the autonomy of each individual is still maintained. Maturana defined the individual as always operating from a *subject-dependent perspective* because of the nature of the autopoietic organization that maintains this autonomy. Basically, this means that we do not directly receive outside information about our world; rather, we experience an interaction with our world and create some meaning internally as a result of that interaction. As we create meaning, we create our reality.

> Biologically, there is no "transmitted information" in communication. . . . The phenomenon of communication depends on not what is transmitted, but on what happens to the person who receives it. And this is a very different matter from "transmitting information." (Maturana & Varela, 1987, p. 196)

Subject-dependent knowledge is a middle ground through which we understand the regularity of the world as a result of our history of interactions and current interactions, without any point of reference independent of ourselves.

This means that to understand the child's current functioning within the system, we must understand the child's individual perception of how he or she gets needs met within the context of that system, which may or may not coincide with the perceptions of the other members of the system who are relating to each other according to their own needs and perceptions. Note that an individual's needs may be systemic, such as the need to be in a relationship (attachment) or the need to protect a child (caretaking). These perceptions are based in part on the individual's histories with other members of the family system, which influences the current pattern of interactions. Even though the child's behaviors may be in response to the family system dynamics, the child's behaviors reflect that child's attempts to get his or her needs met most effectively as he or she understands and experiences life at that moment. Clinically, this suggests that we need to look for the adaptive meaning of a child's dysfunctional behaviors from that child's subject-dependent perspective within his or her current ecosystemic context. This provides a systemic rationale for viewing the individual, and in the case of play therapy, specifically the *child, as the basic systemic unit* instead of the family or another larger system. The resulting *treatment unit* may, in fact, be the family, because it is the most effective way to intervene in an ongoing pattern of interactions that are adversely affecting the ways in which the individuals perceive they can get their needs met.

Interdependence of Intrapsychic and Interactional Systems

Although Maturana's concept of autopoietic organization clarifies the centrality of the individual's functioning within his or her ecosystemic context, it does not clarify the nature of the relationship within the ecosystem. As living human beings, we are drawn to engage in interactions with others and to use language to develop meaning systems about our experiences. Maturana introduced the term *structural coupling* to address this process.

A living organism becomes structurally coupled with its environment when it interacts with that environment over time. During this interaction, there will be changes in both organism and environment as a result of their reciprocal responses to each other. At the same time, the changes each undergoes are independently determined by their own unique structures.

When this structural coupling occurs between two living organisms, the ongoing interaction results in a coordination of behaviors that take on meaning between the involved organisms. If these living organisms are human beings, with the neurological capacity to develop and engage in language, this structural coupling results in two interdependent phenomena: (a) the emergence of interpersonal (social) systems (such as families, religious groups, and so forth), and (b) the emergence in the individual of an intrapsychic symbolic system in which the individual becomes an observer of his or her experiences (including behavior, affect, and thoughts) and, as an observer, develops internal models of self, others, relationships, and the world. Thus, children are structurally coupled both to their interactional systems (e.g., family, peers) and to their intrapsychic system as two interdependent ways of being in the world.

The development of our intrapsychic systems cannot emerge independent of interactions with others in our interpersonal systems. Although we are biologically wired to develop language, the actual language–meaning system is created in an interpersonal context and includes nonverbal, verbal, and affective communication. As we develop language in this interpersonal context, our self-referential nature (i.e., autopoietic organization) results in the creation of an internal meaning system and an everchanging cycle begins. Our intrapsychic reality affects how we behave interpersonally, and the ongoing interactive patterns and meanings created in this interpersonal context affect the meanings we create in our intrapsychic reality, which in turn feeds back into our interpersonal behavior.

As we interact through language, we develop an intrapsychic representational system that includes our concepts of ourselves and our world. These concepts are called internal working models by Bowlby (1973, 1980; Bretherton, 1987), and schemas by Stern (1995). These internal representational systems derive from our history of interactions with others, particularly with our primary caretakers.

> According to attachment theory, as patterns of interaction and affective response are repeated in close relationships over time, children build expectations about future interactions with caregivers and others that guide their interpretations and behaviors in new situations. As these expectations and interpretations become elaborated and organized, they are termed "internal working models" of relations. These working models of self and others tend to perpetuate themselves in the absence of specific influences for change, and to become incorporated as stable interpersonal tendencies that endure over time. (Lyons-Ruth & Zeanah, 1993, pp. 16–17)

Hinde (1979) notes that an interaction is not a relationship. Rather, a relationship is the remembered history of previous interactions. Thus, history is embedded in each participant's intrapsychic model of his or her interactional past and through this process the present relationship is influenced.

Over time, we develop the ability to observe our own conceptual systems, that is, to think about our thinking. Maturana describes this as becoming a self-observing system through which self-consciousness is generated. In clinical terms, this refers to the ability to reflect on our feelings, thoughts, and experiences. This ability, in turn, allows us to imagine other ways of being with ourselves and others and, thereby, to choose different ways of behaving. In children, prior to the development of abstract thinking at about age 12, this reflective process is greatly facilitated by representing the events in their lives concretely or metaphorically through play.

Relevance of Developmental and Historical Phenomena

Maturana's systems theory incorporates historical phenomena at three levels. The intrapsychic system level, where the individual generates internal working models based on his or her history of experiences and interactions, has just been discussed. The other two levels lie, metaphorically, on either side of the intrapsychic system. The more fundamental level is the biological level, where history is conceptualized as the normal maturational processes of the physical body (development). The more general or abstract level is that of the social systems in the environment created by the establishment of rules, expectations, and so forth (culture) that may be passed across generations. These three levels of historical phenomena are interdependent, in that changes in each of these domains influences and is influenced by changes in the other domains.

Although the biological domain defines the initial constitutional abilities of the child, *development* occurs through the interaction of the child's internal states (both biological and intrapsychic) with each other and with the environment (including other people). This is a critical point. Development is not a static, predetermined process. The child's biological maturation influences and is influenced by the child's intrapsychic development and changing sociocultural context. As a result of the structural coupling that takes place during such a process, history becomes embodied both in the structure of the living system and in the structure of the environment (including social systems).

When working with children, it is impossible to deny the effect of maturational variables on a child's functioning. The younger the child, the more these variables must be taken into account, both because the developmental process is more pronounced and because deviations from normal development have the potential to affect significantly the child's subsequent biological, intrapsychic, and interpersonal functioning.

Cultural behavior refers to the transgenerational stability of behavior patterns acquired in the communicative dynamics of a social environment. We are usually unaware of the historical texture behind the simplest of actions of our social life. Cultural behaviors refer to the whole body of communicative interactions that give a certain continuity to the history of a group, beyond the particular histories of the participating individuals. By this definition, culture occurs in any group that has a history together. Thus, the communicative meanings that exist in a family represent that family's unique "culture." At the same time, the family is embedded in local cultural systems, such as religious or ethnic communities, and in larger cultural contexts, such as the dominant political system. The definition of culture and its effect on our day-to-day lives and on the practice of play therapy are discussed in detail in the next chapter.

Temporal phenomena influence the individual's behavior indirectly. Past experience is involved indirectly in current behavior and interactions in the sense that the meanings of these past experiences have become embedded in the individual's intrapsychic system and in the interactional and cultural context in which that individual is involved. For example, if a child was abused when he was 3 years old by a sibling, this experience will have meaning for that child based on that child's developmental level and the other systems' responses to this event. Developmentally, at age 3, he would have expected his parents to know what was going on, even if they did not. Culturally, if he told them about the abuse, they may not have believed him or may have defined the abuse as normal sibling behavior. This response on the part of the others in the child's ecosystem may be embedded in their own histories of abuse, which may make it difficult for them to acknowledge that their child is being abused. Or their responses to him may be affected by the culture's failure, in large part, to acknowledge the reality and significance of sibling abuse. Thus, it is not the historical event per se that has an impact on current functioning, but the interaction of that event with the child's development, the child's intrapsychic understandings, the response of interactional systems in which that child is embedded, the meaning the child ascribes to those responses, and the cultural context which influences both the responses and the meanings. Obviously, in this theory even simple human behaviors are seen as the result of complex interactive processes.

Description of Ecosystemic Model

At this point we have all of the components of the Ecosystemic Play Therapy Theory. The following discussion is brief because the components of the theory have been described in detail in O'Connor (1993b) and in O'Connor and Braverman (1997) and because the discussion of the workbook structure in the rest of the book is organized around these components. Figure 1.1 presents a way of representing the different components of the Ecosystemic Play Therapy Theory from the perspective of the child, but no diagram can truly capture the complexity and richness of this process.

No system beyond a certain level of complexity can be completely known (i.e., modeled in all of its detail). To develop a working model, we must select a portion of the ecosystemic universe for consideration. In the description that follows, an attempt is made to identify those aspects of a child's ecosystem most relevant to planning effective play therapy. This model is not all inclusive, and additional points of view may need to be incorporated or emphasized to meet the needs of any particular client.

The basic unit of this ecosystemic model is the individual child. The child is seen as operating in three critical domains: (a) as a physical body, (b) as a child engaging in behavior with his or her world, particularly in interpersonal relationships, and (c) representationally through his or her internal working models (IWM) of the world.

The model starts with the child's individual functioning, then targets the child's functioning in dyadic relationships, family relationships, peer and other social relationships, and in the other systems in which the child may be directly involved, such as school, church, legal system, medical system, mental health system, and so on. It is important to understand that all of these systems influence the child, both directly through interactional experiences and indirectly through the meanings that the child places on these experiences.

Ecosystemic Play Therapy defines the sociocultural and sociohistorical contexts as metasystemic influences. Bronfenbrenner (1977) used the term *macrosystem* to refer to the social–cultural influences on a child. He described macrosystems as "carriers of information and ideology that, both explicitly and implicitly, endow meaning and motivation to particular agencies, social networks, roles, activities, and their interrelations" (p. 515). This is similar to the meaning of metasystem in Ecosystemic Play Therapy, but we prefer the term *meta*—which means beyond, transcending, more comprehensive—to *macro*—which means large, inclusive. Metasystem seems to capture the idea that this level of involvement is not just a larger system, but one that

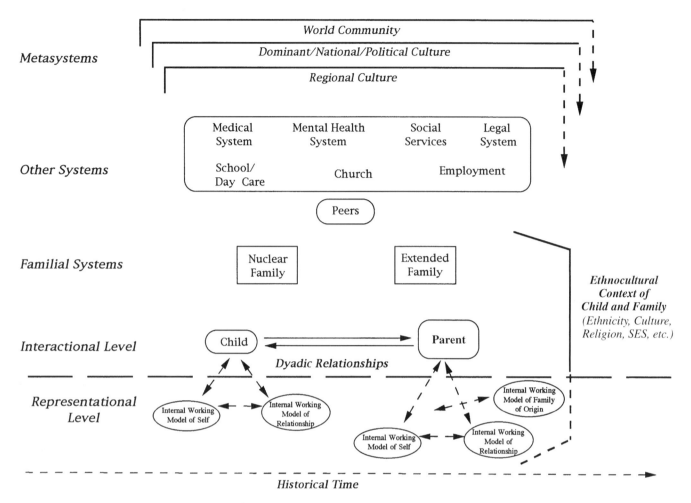

FIGURE 1.1 Ecosystemic model of play therapy.

represents a qualitatively different type of systemic influence. These are not necessarily systems with defined boundaries and membership. Metasystems influence the child (and family, and therapist, and so forth) indirectly through their influence on the representational understandings of the culture's expectations, beliefs, and values. But this also directly affects the child when these representational understandings determine the behaviors of people in systems in which the child is involved. The metasystemic level refers to both the current sociocultural context and the recognition that this context evolves over time and is affected by its history.

For example, in California there was a movement in the late 1980s and early 1990s for both partners in lesbian couples to be able to obtain legal rights with respect to a child adopted by or born to one of them through a process of second-caregiver adoption. At that point in time, the sociocultural context tended to value providing children with two legal caregivers. As the

gay rights movement gained momentum, there was a reactionary movement to stop this momentum, so that by 1995, California's governor issued a policy that essentially stopped any further second-caregiver adoptions by lesbian caregivers. For children in lesbian families, their lesbian parents will continue to function as their psychological caregivers even though only one of the parents has legal custody. But the child's experience may be dramatically affected if, for example, the lesbian parent with legal custody dies and the child is removed from the second parent by biological relatives who have a stronger legal claim to the child in some courts. The result in such cases is that the child loses not one but both psychological caregivers. These events may trigger political actions in support of the psychological welfare of children such that second-caregiver adoptions will again be allowed. The sociocultural context changed and will continue to change, in part, in response to the past changes.

To summarize, children and their behavior exist within the context of multiple interacting systems, including physical, interpersonal, intrapsychic, and metasystemic systems, which change over time. Ecosystemic Play Therapy treatment takes all of these systems into account when conceptualizing the presenting problem and formulating a treatment plan.

CRITICAL ELEMENTS OF ECOSYSTEMIC PLAY THERAPY THEORY

Personality

As we are using the term here, *personality* refers to the sum total of an individual's intrapsychic functioning. O'Connor (1991, 1993b; O'Connor & Braverman, 1997) has described three essential elements of the Ecosystemic Play Therapy Theory of personality: first, that the basic drive motivating human behavior is a derivative of the biologically based survival instinct; second, that the structure and function of personality is inextricably linked to the process of development; and last, that personality derives from the accretion of the residual of one's interactions with the many systems in which one is embedded, that is, one's ecosystem.

As we described earlier, intrapsychic functioning does not develop in a vacuum, but develops as a result of the meaning systems created in the interpersonal domain. Maintaining a relationship with a caregiver is a basic survival need that begins in infancy, as was so dramatically demonstrated by Spitz's 1947 classic movie about infants in foundling homes who died from lack of an attachment relationship in spite of excellent physical care (Karen, 1994). Children have a fundamental need for a relationship with a caregiver, regardless of the quality of that relationship. In the language of Maturana, when two people meet and spend time together, they develop structural coupling in their actions and language that, to an observer, will appear as a remarkably congruent dance of intercoordinated behaviors. The first dance in our lives is the caregiver–infant attachment relationship, which becomes a template for all subsequent dances. It also becomes a template for the therapeutic relationship.

In the 1950s, psychoanalysts like Bowlby (1973, 1980, 1982, 1988) and Winnicott (1965) identified the critical importance of the caregiver–infant interaction; in particular, the communicative system that developed between caregiver and child. However, these ideas were not well accepted in either behaviorist or psychoanalytic camps. Starting in the 1970s, developmental researchers such as psychoanalyst Daniel Stern (1985, 1995) and psychologist Edward Tronick (1989) demon-

strated the incredible importance of this "structural dance in the choreography of coexistence" (Maturana & Varela, 1987, p. 248). Microanalysis of films and videos of infants and mothers engaged in ordinary, everyday interactions repeatedly showed that they:

> continually engage in lengthy reciprocal exchanges, with the mother matching the infant's intensity and tempo, adding variations to elaborate the communication, and attending to the infant's cues, such as the desire to initiate an exchange with a coo or a gaze or the wish to terminate it when he feels he's had enough, often by turning away. (Karen, 1994, p. 349)

Infants bring to this relationship innate social interest and capabilities that facilitate the development of a relationship with a caregiver. During the first hour or so after birth, the infant's vision and hearing are more acute than they will be for several days and weeks afterward. It is as if nature has arranged for the infant to make the most of this initial meeting with his or her caregivers, and by being in this very alert state, helps the caregivers to fall in love with him or her. Even as a newborn, an infant can demonstrate through sucking on an electronically rigged pacifier a preference for a recording of the mother's voice. Infants are particularly attuned to the human face and the human voice and will seek out these stimuli over others in their environment. Within a few weeks to months, they will identify one or two people in their caretaking network as their primary attachment figure(s) and will prefer this person to all others, particularly when tired, hungry, scared, hurt, and so forth. All of these behaviors promote the development of a relationship with a primary attachment figure.

Even young infants typically have innate communicative behaviors, such as making eye contact and cooing, or turning the head away to signal readiness for or a desire to avoid engagement. They are able to decode communicative behaviors in others, including misattunement if a caregiver's body language does not match the experience of the infant. This innate communicative language is modified and enriched by the familial and cultural influences in the child's interpersonal context (Stern, 1995).

Optimally, the primary caregiver brings to the relationship the ability to be attuned to the infant's emotional states and needs and to respond in a consistent and appropriate manner to those needs (Ainsworth, Blehar, Waters, & Wall, 1978). Winnicott (1965) identified the mother's ability to be tuned into her baby as central to every aspect of the child's psychological development.

> In timing with her baby, Winnicott believed, the mother (or primary caregiver) struggles to bring the world to him in understandable form. She gives him a sense of achieving what he is incapable of achieving on his own. By knowing what he

wants and responding to it, she gives meaning to his cries and other signals, so that eventually he knows what he wants and learns to signal with intent. She puts words to his feelings. . . . A long period of intense and harmonious involvement with a sensitively attuned mother is, thus, essential to the baby's emotional health. (Karen, 1994, pp. 348–349)

Tronick (1989) described this as an affective communication system through which infant and adult engage in mutually coordinated interactions. In normal interactions, the infant will experience periods of positive affect, periods of negative affect, and frequent transformations of the negative affect into positive affect such that the overall experience of negative emotions is brief. It is the role of the caregiver to help the infant (and child) to learn to cope with the negative affective experiences such that the infant does not feel overwhelmed and begins to develop the ability to tolerate and cope with frustrations. The infant begins to perceive of himself or herself as effective and the caretaker as reliable. This facilitates the infant's (and child's) ability to explore the world, engage with others, and regulate as well as communicate his or her emotional states. Affective communication and the reparation of negative affective experiences within interactive relationships contribute to the development of the intrapsychic representational systems (internal working models of self, others, relationships, the world) through which the individual creates meaning about the current situations in which he or she is involved. From that meaning, the individual engages in interaction with other people and with the environment in ways that are uniquely shaped by that individual's biological, developmental, and interpersonal history and which, to observers, appear to have a stable structure that we refer to as personality.

Psychopathology

Throughout his writing on Ecosystemic Play Therapy, O'Connor (1991, 1993b; O'Connor & Braverman, 1997) has defined psychopathology in a somewhat idiosyncratic way. Specifically, he states that psychopathology can only be said to exist when a person is unable to get his or her needs met consistently and in ways that do not substantially interfere with the ability of others to get their needs met. This last phrase embeds Ecosystemic Play Therapy in a moral and sociocultural context. The therapist (and the child) is faced with a constant struggle to balance the child's needs against the needs of others in the child's ecosystem. This is rarely an easy task and it is discussed at some length in Chapter 2, "Recognizing, Addressing, and Celebrating Diversity." Psychopathology, as just defined, may be the result of a problem inherent in the individual, the

interaction of the individual with one or more other persons (interactional), or the interaction of the individual with a larger system (systemic).

All behavior is the child's best attempt at getting his or her needs met. Examining Maturana's definition of adaptive behavior helps to clarify this relationship between the child and the family system (or other participants in the child's ecosystemic). Behavior is always adaptive in the moment relative to the child's internal organization, history, and environmental context. Maturana's definition of the individual as "maintaining his or her autonomy" does not refer to that person becoming independent or autonomous from the other people in the environment. Everyone exists within an environment. It is not possible for us to exist in a vacuum. We are always in some sort of relationship with other people. However, this relationship must be adaptive; that is, it must not be destructive to the basic organization of the individual, as experienced or defined by that individual, or the individual may choose to remove or distance himself or herself from the problematic system.

Clinically, this suggests that we need to look for the subject-dependent, adaptive meaning that a behavior has for a child when that behavior appears dysfunctional from an outside perspective. In what ways does the child's behavior meet some current need or some need perceived by the child as a result of the child's history? For example, children with learning problems become very adept at avoiding having to perform academic tasks by engaging in disruptive or distracting behaviors. Even though these may trigger many negative responses from others, including teachers, caregivers, and peers, the behavior still satisfies a need that is experienced by the child as being more important than the immediate negative consequences. The child may in fact be able to accomplish the current academic task, but if the child's past experience leads him or her to *believe* that the result will be failure, the adaptive response on the part of that child is to avoid the task.

It is important to differentiate Maturana's use of the term adaptive from the typical use of this term in psychotherapy. In psychotherapy the term *adaptive* tends to imply a healthy or positive response to a problem or difficulty, as evaluated from the perspective of the therapist. In Maturana's theory adaptiveness is considered from the perspective of the individual. That is, the goal of the individual's behavior is always to maintain his or her own functioning given his or her experiences, intrapsychic understanding, and the current environmental context. However, from the perspective of an observer, a child's behavior may not appear adaptive, because it compromises too many of the child's other needs. James (1994) addresses this phenomenon in her discussion of children in dysfunctional and abusive families:

> Children of all ages—infants to adolescents—alter their behavior in service of preserving attachment relationships when their parenting needs are not met. Such alterations are *necessary* [emphasis added] for their survival and are often wise and creative but not necessarily healthy. . . . Children's adaptive roles include being overly compliant with abusive parents, being entertainers with distracted parents, being mini-caregivers with needy parents, being demanding bullies with nonresponsive parents, or being manipulators with neglectful, withholding parents. (p. 6)

From the perspective of the therapist, the child's denial of his or her authentic thoughts and feelings in exchange for parental care and attention does not seem adaptive, because it is not the most healthy way (from the therapist's perspective) for that child to get his or her needs met. From the child's perspective, it *is* adaptive because it is the *only* way the child can identify to preserve the attachment relationship which the child experiences as necessary for survival.

We must recognize that the client's reasons for behaving in a particular way are embedded in the client's history of interactions and current experience of his or her world rather than some objective, discoverable reality. Furthermore, the client is engaged in relationships with others, including the caregiver–child dyad, the family, the school, and so forth. The participants in each of these systems hold their own subject-dependent understanding about why the child is behaving in a particular way, and these influence how they respond to the child's behavior. To make matters even more complicated, it is common for the perceptions of the child and those of the other participants in the child's ecosystem to be divergent. To work effectively with children and their ecosystems, we must understand the subject-dependent perceptions of all of the relevant participants.

It is important to differentiate the etiology or origin of the problem from what maintains the problem, because these may often be different. Attachment-related difficulties illustrate this issue. As previously discussed, the caregiver–infant dance ideally is interactively coordinated with respect to the child's needs and affective experience. When the caregiver–infant dance is not coordinated, problems with tantrums, impulse control, and acting out may arise out of the child's experience of a breakdown in mutual regulation, leading to his or her inability to self-regulate. Alternatively, these children may become emotionally constricted and depressed in an effort to regulate themselves. Both the infant and the caregiver are active participants in this attachment relationship and problems with the child or the caregiver, or even just a mismatch between

them, may contribute to a lack of coordination in their attachment dance.

Infants may bring to the interaction deficits in their neurological functioning that make it difficult for them to tolerate much stimulation from the environment, such that they turn away from normal attempts of the caregiver to engage. The caregiver experiences failure and incompetence and begins to withdraw from active engagement in the dance. Some caregivers have unresolved emotional issues that make it difficult for them to interact with the infant around negative emotions, or even to be emotionally available at all. Or children may bring to the relationship the history of a prior abusive relationship that leads them to distrust the current attempts of a new caregiver to engage them. The new caregiver may bring to this relationship expectations that the child will be grateful for the good caregiving and be angered by the child's attempts to rebuff the relationship. This takes us back to the importance of understanding the perspective of the child and of the other relevant participants in the child's ecosystem, because these perspectives influence the ongoing interactive patterns that develop between the child and other members of his or her ecosystem.

Treatment Goals and Curative Elements of Ecosystemic Play Therapy

The primary goal of Ecosystemic Play Therapy is to resolve children's psychopathology, that is, to enable children to get their needs met consistently and in ways that do not interfere with the ability of others to get their needs met. A secondary goal is to facilitate the assumption or resumption of optimal developmental functioning and growth. The determination of specific treatment goals is discussed in detail in Chapter 7, "Treatment Planning."

There are two elements of the Ecosystemic Play Therapy process that can be viewed as fostering the resolution of psychopathology. One is the nature of the relationship between the child and the therapist. The other is the ability of the therapist to engage the child in developing problem-solving strategies that enable the child to get his or her needs met effectively and appropriately. Simply put, the role of the Ecosystemic Play therapist is to create a context in which the therapeutic or curative elements of Ecosystemic Play Therapy take place. To accomplish this, the therapist provides children with experiences and cognitive/verbal explanations that alter their understanding of their life situation. With this new understanding children are able to engage in alternative problem solving and to discover more effective and appropriate ways of getting their needs met. The alternative experiences are provided through the context of the relationship between child and therapist and through play. The alternative cognitive/verbal explanations are provided through interpretation and by engaging the child in active, overt problem solving. It is not so much the specific solutions to problems or changes in a person's perception or experience of reality that matters, although these can have a relevant influence, it is the very process of experiencing something differently or understanding different possibilities for getting needs met that can have a profound positive effect on clients (Elliott, 1984). This is a basis of the solution-focused and constructivist techniques that emphasize helping people change the meanings they attribute to their experiences (e.g., Anderson & Goolishian, 1992; Eron & Lund, 1996). "Therapists need simply to help clients talk differently about their lives and to notice their own successes" (Eron & Lund, 1996, p. 31). Children not only need to talk differently, they need to experience different meanings through interactive and symbolic play. Chapter 8, "Interventions," addresses these issues in more detail.

ECOSYSTEMIC PLAY THERAPY PRACTICE

Ecosystemic Play Therapy differs from most play therapy and systemic therapy models in its emphasis on both the interactional, experiential world and the internal, representational world of the child. Although most play therapy models recognize both the representational and experiential aspects of the child's experience, the tendency is to emphasize either one or the other. For example, psychoanalytic play therapy approaches view the experiential aspects of play therapy as the pathway to understanding and communicating about the representational world of the child, which is where healing is believed to occur (O'Connor, 1991). Developmental play therapy approaches such as Theraplay (Jernberg, 1979) and humanistic play therapy approaches (Axiline, 1947; Moustakas, 1959) emphasize the therapist's interaction with the child and place minimal emphasis on the representational meanings of the child play and behavior (O'Connor, 1991). Systemic therapies present with a similar dichotomy, either emphasizing the interactional aspects in treatment (e.g., structural and systemic approaches) or the representational aspects (e.g., constructivist approaches), with little integration between them (Ammen, 1990).

As previously stated, we are both actors and spectators in the drama of existence (Folse, 1985). At the actor level, we engage in interactions with other human beings that over time develop into relationship systems, such as caregiver–child, family, or friends. At the spectator level, we observe our interactions and relationships and describe these experiences through language that creates internal, representational systems. One of the implications of being subject-dependent is that information is not received directly from the environment. Instead, each individual person involved in the child's ecosystem, including the child and the therapist, operates out of his or her own subject-dependent reality. As the people involved interact with each other through language and actions, they establish a degree of congruence between their separate understandings that leads to a consensual system of meaning, that is, a relationship. But the greater the confusion, lack of communication, or miscommunication, the greater the likelihood that the parties involved will be experiencing vastly different realities based on their interpretations of their experiences.

Ecosystemic Play Therapy intervenes both at the actor level through corrective experiences/behavior (interactional, experiential level) and at the spectator level through shifts in cognitive/emotional understanding (intrapsychic, representational level). These two levels are complementary domains that are related but cannot be reduced to each other and are both important in understanding a child's experience and in helping the child to change that experience. Once the individual has developed the capacity to be reflective about his or her participation in the patterns of behavior that generate relationship systems, it is possible for that individual to choose different ways of behaving within those relationships. For a child, this reflective process is facilitated through symbolic play and interpretation.

The process of becoming self-conscious through reflection allows us to choose different ways of interacting. If we choose to interact differently, we may change the way in which others interact with us. This is the rationale for intervening at the internal representational level through education and interpretation. If we experience interactions that disconfirm our representational system about ourselves and the world, we may come to change our internal models. This is the rationale for intervening at the system level (e.g., family therapy) or at the experiential level (e.g., humanistic play therapy).

This is consistent with Stern's (1995) definition of the nature of the clinical system itself as being made up of the interactive behaviors between the participants, the internal representational systems of each of the participants, and the dynamic mutual influence of these different systems on each other. The therapist's interactional behaviors and internal representations are also part of this clinical system.

> If therapy alters any one element, it will have an impact on all the elements within the system because of the dynamic interdependence of the elements. It is this property of the system

that leads me to suggest that the nature of the system itself is such that it will distribute throughout all its parts any influence that impinges at any one point, regardless of where that point is. (Stern, 1995, pp. 147–148)

There is an exciting outcome study comparing clinical interventions with mother–baby dyads that supports this notion (Cramer et al., 1990). A psychoanalytically inspired brief therapy approach was used to target the internal representational systems of one group, and a nonpsychodynamic behavioral approach to target the overt maternal behaviors in caregiver–child interactions was used with the second group. The therapists for each clinical condition were highly trained in and believed in the superiority of their particular approach. The researchers predicted changes in both groups, but greater representational changes in the group in which this aspect of the clinical system was targeted and greater behavioral changes in the group in which the maternal behavior was targeted. The results: Both treatments worked and they worked equally well at changing both the interactional behaviors and the internal representations.

Finally, when considering the practice of Ecosystemic Play Therapy, we must remember that as therapists, we are also human beings who operate out of a subject-dependent position that is determined by our own history of experiences and learning, and we must be aware of the degree to which we impose our own subject-dependent perceptions onto the therapeutic situation. This is not to suggest that we should not ever impose our perceptions, because that would be impossible. The only way we can interact with our world is from our subject-dependent position. But the more we become conscious of the subject dependence of our own knowledge as well as the subject-dependent knowledge of the other participants, the more we can adjust our interactions and interventions to take these multiple perspectives into account.

In summary, Ecosystemic Play Therapy can be seen as an integrative theory incorporating developmental (individual and family), systemic (dyadic, familial, social, and other systems), contextual (sociocultural metasystems), and representational (intrapsychic) variables from the perspective of the child's functioning in his or her ecosystemic world.

· **2** ·

RECOGNIZING, ADDRESSING, AND CELEBRATING DIVERSITY

Issues of diversity are integral to all discussions of Ecosystemic Play Therapy. The role of individual, group, and systems differences in the onset and eventual resolution of psychopathology is pervasive in the model. This chapter introduces some of the general issues and concepts that are central to integrating diversity effectively into play therapy practice. However, because we believe these issues are so much more than peripheral, we have kept this chapter fairly short and have included additional discussions of these issues throughout the remaining chapters. The reader is referred to the following sources for additional reading: *A Handbook for Developing Multicultural Awareness* (Pedersen, 1988), *Counseling the Culturally Different: Theory and Practice (2nd edition)* (Sue & Sue, 1990), *Ethnocultural Issues in Child Mental Health* (Solomon, 1993), *Children's Play in Diverse Cultures* (Roopnarine, Johnson, and Hooper, 1994), *Culturally Diverse Children and Adolescents: Assessment, Diagnosis, and Treatment* (Canino and Spurlock, 1994), and the *Family Therapy Networker* special issue on Multiculturalism (July/August, 1994).

DEFINITION OF TERMS

One of the immediate problems faced by anyone who attempts to discuss issues of diversity is the variability and emotional and political nature of the terms used in both formal and casual discussions of diversi-ty. Indeed, language and terminology have a major impact on the nature and quality of the discourse. The use of the term diversity is, in itself, somewhat awkward in that it is so general that it may lose some of its relevance. There is also a tendency to use the phrase "diverse groups" as a subtle way of referring to any group that is different from the dominant group. The diversity categories listed in the *Ethical Principles of Psychologists* and the *Code of Conduct* (American Psychological Association, 1992) are age, gender, race, ethnicity, national origin, religion, sexual orientation, physical status, language, and socioeconomic status. Rather than attempt to address each of these areas separately, we have loosely grouped them under the heading of culture and will refer to cultural differences as inclusive of all of these.

In this context, culture refers to a set of behavioral and social norms passed across generations that are characteristic of a particular group. Although one might argue that any one of the groups previously mentioned does not represent a culture per se, it is difficult to argue that these and most other societal groups do not have certain expectations for the behavioral, social, and even emotional actions of their members. The elderly are expected to behave in certain ways and, in fact, these expectations are passed across generations and are often adhered to within groups of elderly persons. Similarly, gays and lesbians are expected by others to behave in certain ways and have rather defined expectations for behavior within their community. Each of these groups even tends to develop specialized language with which to communicate among themselves. In addition to focusing on behavioral aspects of any given group, the term culture also carries with it a positive connotation and a sense of inherent value. For these reasons it is a term particularly well suited to this discussion.

In addition to the overall definition of culture, three other variables must be considered when discussing any group or specific client: objective culture, subjective culture, and oppression. *Objective culture* is the cultural group to which one is assigned by others. This assignment may be made for many reasons, valid or not, and appearance is often the most dominant of these. "Funny, you don't look _____," is a phrase that reflects objective culture as it can negatively affect a person regularly assigned to a group with which he or she does not identify. These people continually find themselves in the position of having to undo the assumptions that others make about them. The counterpart to objective culture is *subjective culture.* This refers to the client's self-identification regardless of external signs or factors. Objective and subjective culture may often differ, and when they do, the difference may produce a special stress for those experiencing it. This conflict is often quite salient in the lives of people who belong to so-called "invisible" groups, such as those who have been oppressed for reasons of religion or sexual orientation. Persons in these groups are often aware of the benefits they enjoy by being able to blend in when necessary. At the same time, however, blending into the dominant culture is often experienced by the individual as a betrayal of both the self and the group. A powerful example of this was seen in some Holocaust survivors, especially those who escaped by "passing" for Aryan Germans. One woman survived the concentration camp solely because, being blonde, she caught the attention of the commandant at the concentration camp who discovered that besides appearing Aryan she also had musical talent. He kept her alive to entertain him "even though she was Jewish." On the one hand, she survived; on the other hand, it caused her to spend the rest of her life finding ways to assert and value her Jewishness.

Yet another example of the clinical implications of objective and subjective culture can be seen in the experience of a family we recently treated in which the primary caretaker (not a biological caregiver) was African-American. All but one of the children were of mixed African-American and Anglo-American parentage. One child was of mixed Anglo-American and Asian-American parentage and was a half-sibling to the other children. Not only did the primary caretaker

refuse to acknowledge that the one child was not a full sibling, she refused to recognize that the child was of a different racial mix. At the time of referral the child believed herself to be African-American and was distressed because she was being teased by both Anglo-American and African-American peers at school. The child believed she was being teased because she was African American and, therefore, did not know why she was being teased by the African-American children. The reality was that she was being teased because she appeared to be Asian. In her peer setting, Southeast Asians tended to have lower social status than African-Americans. Needless to say, the child in this situation was unable to develop a stable sense of identity, unable to access a viable social support system, and was, subsequently, unable to cope with the reactions of her peers.

When considering issues related to culture, one must also consider the degree to which the client's cultural group has been or is oppressed. The degree to which culture becomes a salient factor in play therapy is often directly proportional to the level of oppression that a group experiences. In the United States in the 1990s, being 10th-generation English-American may have very little meaning in the client's day-to-day life. On the other hand, being a recent Southeast Asian immigrant or being gay/lesbian or bisexual is likely to be experienced as an every day stress by most clients.

Related to the issue of oppression, it is interesting to note that the groups that are usually included in a discussion of diversity exclude those who make up the dominant culture, namely young, white, heterosexual males. There are pros and cons to limiting a discussion of diversity in this way.

One advantage to limiting a discussion of diversity to those groups that have typically been neglected or oppressed by the dominant culture is that it tends to focus the discussion on the issue of oppression. This prevents us from minimizing the reality that for some groups the world is experienced as a hostile and dangerous place. Like it or not, girls grow up in a world that places them at greater risk for victimization than boys. Similarly, African-American children grow up knowing that the potential for experiencing verbal and even physical aggression is ever present. Gay adolescents kill themselves at an astonishingly high rate to avoid the devastating social sanctions they see imposed on others like themselves. This is such a pervasive reality that parents in some groups, such as African-Americans, Jews, and gays and lesbians, actively prepare their children for possible oppression as a coping strategy. However, focusing on the reality of oppression also tends to diminish a group both in the eyes of its own members and in society's eyes. The group comes to exist only as victims of the dominant culture.

Unfortunately, being identified as the one who is different tends to include being identified as the one who is not as good as the members of the not-different group. Humans seem to have a difficult time seeing objects that are substantially different as equal. Furthermore, we tend to base the value of an object largely on its appearance. For example, we often prefer to buy produce that looks good, according to some arbitrary criteria, even if it does not taste that good. Grocery stores stock those beautiful, tasteless tomatoes because customers will not buy blemished ones, no matter how good they might taste. The more something differs from the standard we value the more we tend to reject it. The same seems to apply to people. If we value ourselves we seem prone to minimize the value of those who are substantially different from us. The irony of this system of values is its incredible instability. One can become different on the whim of fashion (fatness or thinness), as the result of relocation (immigration), a twist of fate (homelessness subsequent to a natural disaster), or inevitable biologic processes (aging). Should one's relative human value suffer accordingly? Logic says, of course not, but reality seems to be rarely based on logic.

To be identified as a victim is a dual-edged sword. Victim status allows victims to externalize the blame for their situation and preserve their self-esteem. It also entitles them to certain protections. However, victim status is the opposite of empowerment and tends to decrease rather than increase the victim group's ability to get their needs met consistently and appropriately. Suddenly, the victim group is dependent on the dominant group for protection and benevolence. Victims do not make demands, they accept what they are given. Furthermore, once victimized, the need for safety becomes dominant. Safety is such a basic need that seeking it will supplant any attempts to get higher-order needs met. A child who is afraid of being attacked will be unable to seek out, much less establish, interpersonal intimacy, for example. Therefore, victims may become stuck in a relationship with the dominant group that prevents them from progressing.

Failing to include dominant groups in discussions of diversity blinds both sides to the characteristics of those groups and their impact on the ecosystem. Typically, the majority of any social group's higher-order systems are created by the dominant culture. That is, the medical, legal, and educational systems, among others, will all have been designed by the dominant group, and these will have a powerful impact on members of every other group. Furthermore, when the dominant group is not included in diversity discussions, its dominant role is reinforced and there is a tendency to accept that group's behavior as normative and even normal. Including the dominant culture in discussions of diversity means accepting that culture as just one more perspective from which the world can be viewed—a view that is no more or less accurate and no more or less valuable than any other world view.

Whether or not one accepts the definition of culture as delineated in this chapter, it is impossible to deny the ever-increasing diversity of the populations within most countries of the world. In the 21st century, diversity is certain to become more, not less, of an issue, in psychology as well as in all other service professions. This leads us to consider the value of diversity and multiculturalism. For all the problems living in a diverse society sometimes entails, the reality is that diversity enriches all of our lives and is worth maintaining rather than attempting to eliminate it just to fix the problems we associate with it.

VALUE OF MULTICULTURALISM

In the past there has been a tendency to evaluate other cultures from the perspective of either cultural deviance or cultural relativism (Abney, 1996). The cultural deviance perspective imposes the judgment that anything that differs from one's own culture is bad or threatening. Although most mental health professionals have managed to give up this perspective, many have compensated for it by becoming cultural relativists. In cultural relativism all behavior is accepted because it is attributed to cultural differences. The actual impact of the behavior is not considered. Both perspectives are dangerous. Viewing all other cultures as deviant fosters aggression and actively attempts to alter the behavior of others to conform with the views of the play therapist. Cultural relativism fosters the acceptance of all behavior, no matter how destructive. An excellent example of how these two positions can effect one's judgment is found in the way U.S. child abuse workers often react to nonwestern medical practices. In Central California many Southeast Asian families use treatments consistent with their culture. Two of these include coining and burning. Coining involves rubbing a coin over the affected part of the body until a red welt is raised which later will turn into a long, purplish bruise. Although the marks appear painful the process is actually not that distressing. Burning involves touching the burning ember of an herb to acupuncture points along the affected part of the body. The process is very painful and leaves permanent cigarettelike burns. Child abuse workers operating from a cultural deviance perspective view both practices as bad because they do not conform with western medical views, leave marks, and may be painful. Those workers operating from a cultural relativism perspective view both practices as equally acceptable because both derive from traditional Southeast Asian culture. It appears that a more reasonable stance is to evaluate the degree to which any given culture and any given aspect of that culture allows its members to function while having a minimum negative impact on others. This perspective would differentially evaluate the two practices and would differentiate between using burning on a child versus an adult. This perspective is entirely consistent with the fundamental philosophy and primary treatment goal of Ecosystemic Play Therapy.

Before proceeding further with the discussion of the value of living in and maintaining a pluralistic society, we need to expand on the theory of phenomenology as it was introduced in the first chapter. Phenomenology is a philosophy that posits that every individual perceives and, therefore, understands the world in a unique way. The purist phenomenologic view states that although we may come to some consensus about what comprises external reality, we can never actually know whether that reality exists or even whether those with whom we have reached a consensus really view the world in the same way we do. As it is incorporated in Ecosystemic Play Therapy, phenomenology is the basis for emphasizing the importance of having the play therapist attempt to view and understand the world the way the client views and understands it.

The idea of phenomenology can be made more concrete by thinking of every individual wearing a pair of glasses, the lenses of which have a unique prescription. These "lenses" are made up, over time, from the residue of everything the individual experiences. The range of contributing factors is as broad as the range of human experience, from the most minute neuropsychological variations, to mass trauma resulting from natural disasters, to the passage of time. Although individual experience is a major contributor to the make-up of the lenses, the groups in which one is a member also make enormous contributions. And although no one experiences group membership in exactly the same way, the lenses through which members of the same group view the world may share certain commonalties.

To recognize and value cultural diversity, it is critical that one develop an understanding of the types of lenses that membership in different groups creates for the group's members. To do this, it is important first to dispense with the idea that some lenses are more accurate than others and the accompanying assumption that they are, therefore, better. We have talked about the notion that there is no absolute reality in any given situation and that each of us interprets that reality slightly differently given the lenses created by our culture and experience. Is the accuracy of these lenses important? Probably only to a limited extent. Different lenses create different perspectives and each may lead to a slightly different problem-solving approach. Although in any one situation one lens may prove better, or at least more efficient, than another, it is extremely unlikely that any one lens would prove superior in all situations. Limiting ourselves to any one perspective would probably greatly reduce our ability to problem solve and, consequently, limit our ability as a species to get our needs met effectively and appropriately. In other words, it appears that diversity is critical for the long-term survival of the species and works to the betterment of individuals on a day-to-day basis. Much as ecologists have come to see the value of every organism to the overall health of the planet, Ecosystemic Play therapists must come to see the value of diversity to the overall health of humankind. When a culture disappears, an entire way of viewing the world goes with it, and it is the existence of alternative world views that enables optimal problem solving and ultimately benefits us all.

BECOMING DIVERSITY COMPETENT

Because of the increasing diversity within most countries and because maintaining diversity is critical to the welfare of the world population as a whole, play therapists must struggle to become competent with respect to all aspects of human culture and diversity. This is complicated by the present lack of diversity among mental health professionals, which may often mean that client and play therapist will be of different groups, making cultural or diversity competence even more important in the conduct of good treatment. Failure to become competent with respect to diversity increases the chances that the play therapist will not succeed in helping a client find ways to get his or her needs met effectively in ways that do not substantially interfere with the ability of others to get their needs met. That is, the client may become more like the play therapist in an attempt to get his or her needs met only to ignore or override the needs of the cultural group of which he or she is a member. Who is best served when a girl from a traditionally organized family is able to override the expectation that she live at home until married and instead goes away to college (the way her therapist did) only to lose the love and support of the large extended family network she has always relied on? Obviously, the needs of the client and those of the system in which he or she is embedded need to be balanced.

As of this writing, most play therapists have an Anglo-American or Euro-American background and are of the middle class. As followers of Western traditions, they tend to focus on the individual, to stress the importance of cause and effect, and to value insight, openness, and verbal expressiveness, and the nuclear family. Many of these values are in direct conflict with those of persons of Native American or Eastern backgrounds. Some are even in conflict with the values of more traditional European cultures, such as those that value the extended family. As members of the middle class, play therapists tend to value long-range planning, adherence to schedules, and to have a high tolerance for ambiguity. Whether or not one believes these values to have any inherent importance, it is clear that these cannot even come into play until one is living at a relatively high level on Maslow's (1970) hierarchy of needs. When one is concerned about where his or her next meal will come from, long-range planning is a luxury that simply cannot be afforded.

As we enumerate these potential client–play therapist differences, it becomes apparent that it may not be easy for the average play therapist to see the world through the highly variable lenses of his or her clients. However, the more the client and play therapist differ, the higher the risk of serious problems with respect to both transference and countertransference problems. Therefore, the play therapist must strive to become culture/diversity competent in order to practice effective Ecosystemic Play Therapy. To become culture/diversity competent, Abney (1996) suggests that play therapists must develop appropriate values, a broad knowledge base, and a range of methods suitable for working with a variety of clients.

The values base of the culture/diversity competent play therapist includes three things. First, the ability to recognize diversity in others requires that the play therapist has first developed a sound sense of his or her own identity with respect to membership in a wide variety of groups. Second, the play therapist must be able to accept the "dynamics of difference." That is, the play therapist understands that humans seem prone to perceive difference as threatening and must actively work to overcome such perceptions. And, third, the play therapist must accept the existence of biases, myths, and stereotypes. Color (diversity)-blindness is not a virtue. Such blindness ignores essential elements of individuals and their experience, and it diminishes them in very direct ways. Difficult as it may be to believe, there are still people whose ultimate position with respect to issues of diversity is that these issues do not exist. This belief manifests itself in statements such as, "children are all the same," or "underneath, all children basically need the same things." Although such statements are generally well meaning, they not only deny

the existence of diversity but devalue it as well. The same is true of people who claim to be blind to diversity with such statements as "A child's color isn't important to me. I usually don't even think about it." Or "I don't focus on a child's physical handicap. I only focus on the capacities he or she does have." Again, the sentiments behind these statements are well intentioned, but they deny a fundamental characteristic of the client and thereby devalue it. The implication is that children are all right and acceptable only when the play therapist pretends that they are the same as him or her.

In addition to operating from a values base that fosters effective work with diverse populations, the play therapist also needs to have a solid base of knowledge about the group(s) to which the client belongs. The play therapist needs to be wary of accepting myths and stereotypes as actual knowledge and should seek out instead accurate and timely information. The play therapist should also be wary of relying on the client as a cultural guide. When the client must serve as his or her own interpreter and convey substantive knowledge about his or her group to the play therapist, he or she leaves the client role and becomes the professional who is training the play therapist-cum-student. Although this may meet the play therapist's needs, it is rarely in the best interests of the client, especially if it goes on for any length of time. The therapeutic hour is there to be used by the client to gain the knowledge and skills he or she needs to gain an optimal level of functioning. It is not structured to meet that need for the play therapist.

There are four areas of focus that will assist the play therapist in developing the skills necessary to work with different cultural groups. First, the play therapist needs to understand and apply the concept of culturally and individually derived lenses, as previously discussed. Although it is impossible to set aside one's lenses to see the world exactly the way someone else sees it, it is possible to come close. This ability seems most readily developed when the play therapist begins by having a very solid sense of the way in which he or she views the world. The ability to see through another's lenses is enhanced by comparing the way in which one views the world with the way in which others more or less similar to oneself view the world. The greater the number and variety of comparisons one makes, the more one is able to predict how other's views will vary from one's own. Therefore, one's own world view serves as the reference point from which to understand others. Because we cannot know absolute reality, free from the distortions of our own lenses, we can only use our own perspective as a stable base from which to explore other perspectives. Toddlers can actively and confidently explore the world if they have sure knowledge of their caretakers as safe bases. Similarly, those who are sure of their own cultural identities are able to explore the cultural world of others using self-knowledge as a secure base. Cross-cultural exploration tends to produce understanding at an exponential rate. That is, the first explorations go slowly and often lead to limited understanding and clumsy interactions. But once one masters understanding and interacting with one group that is different from one's own, then understanding and interacting with another group comes much faster and it comes still faster with the next group.

Second, the diversity-competent play therapist should use any or all methods that have been found to be effective with a particular group. This also means that the play therapist accesses resources that may be an inherent part of that group, such as social networks, clergy, or indigenous healers.

Third, the play therapist must not only be committed to understanding and working within different cultural perspectives, he or she must also be committed to fostering change in ways that maintain rather than minimize diversity. One important way this can be accomplished is by helping clients value their own group membership. Many play interventions are designed to develop children's identities and to strengthen their self-esteem. These can easily incorporate a focus on the child's membership in a variety of groups. Family sessions that encourage the family as a whole to develop its culture, rituals, and identity can have an incredible stabilizing effect, especially if other aspects of the environment tend to be chaotic. This can be an especially difficult but important task when the family members do not all share a similar cultural identity.

A clinical example of this issue can be seen in an African-American family that sought treatment for behavior problems their child was manifesting in a number of different settings. As treatment got underway, it became apparent that there was also substantial intrafamilial conflict as to the child's identity. Because the child was very light-skinned and had straight hair, the parents had encouraged him to pass for Caucasian in order to avoid racism. Although they believed they were acting in their child's best interests, their child experienced their behavior as rejection, feeling that they did not want him to be like they were and, therefore, that they did not want him to be a part of the family. Again, the needs of the various individuals, the family, and the cultural systems must be balanced to obtain the best outcome.

Not only does cultural group identification enhance children's self-image and self-esteem, it also provides them with cues as to additional sources of interpersonal resources. That is, we tend to see others like ourselves as more readily accessible than persons who are substantially different. We once conducted a play therapy group in which children at very different developmental levels and from vastly different racial, ethnic, and socioeconomic backgrounds interacted easily and positively, partly because they all had severe asthma in common. These children would not normally have sought each other out; however, the shared illness experience made them excellent resources for one another as they attempted to cope with long-term hospitalization.

Lastly, although empowerment is a common and useful goal in play therapy, the play therapist must understand that members of traditionally victimized groups find it contrary to their experience. Empowerment implies an internal locus of control, and yet those who have been victimized tend to see control as external to themselves. The play therapist may have to assume a fairly active advocacy role early in play therapy to help such clients develop a sense of their own power to effect change.

CELEBRATING DIVERSITY IN PLAY THERAPY

Clearly, to be an effective play therapist, it is important to have the capacity to recognize culture and its impact on clients. It is also important that the play therapist develop knowledge and skills specific to addressing and working within the cultural frame of the client. Even though these are certainly necessary conditions for effective play therapy, these still do not seem sufficient. Beyond striving to be effective, we also think it is important for the play therapist to use every opportunity to join the client in celebrating his or her culture. For example, for a play therapist working with a Mexican-American child, recognizing, addressing, and celebrating culture would each make a unique and important contribution to the play therapy.

The play therapist must, of course, recognize the fact of the child's and family's Mexican-American identification and the ways in which they have made this identification uniquely theirs. The play therapist must be able to understand the day-to-day implications of this identification. What positive and negative contributions does membership in this cultural group make with respect to the child's ability to get his or her needs met effectively and appropriately? What sort of life context does being Mexican-American create for the child?

Having recognized the child's culture and its impact, the play therapist must then be able to address in the play therapy those issues that affect the problems the child is experiencing. The play therapist must also have knowledge of any specialized techniques or interventions that have been found to be particularly effective with children whose cultural identification and experience is similar to that of the child client. And, finally, the play therapist must be able to implement that knowledge in the play therapy process.

It is at the level of celebrating the child's culture that the play therapist really moves beyond the level of simple competence. Celebration of the child's culture can rightfully be incorporated into the play therapy even when cultural issues have no direct bearing on the presenting problems. For example, it not uncommon for a play therapist to acknowledge a child client's birthday in session. This creates at least one potential culturally related problem and multiple opportunities for incorporating culturally derived celebratory activities. The problem arises with children whose religious affiliation does not allow for birthday celebrations of any type. For those children who do celebrate birthdays, it is easy for the play therapist to incorporate discussions about, preparations for, or actual implementation of culture-specific activities. Making a simple paper piñata by stapling two drawings together to form a pouch and filling it with written birthday wishes could easily reinforce a child's positive identification with the Mexican culture while addressing treatment content through the messages placed into the piñata. Even if self-esteem is not a problem area, children can only benefit from the inclusion of activities that reinforce it. It is this type of active valuing of culture that differentiates the culturally competent play therapist from the culturally gifted play therapist.

In summary, recognizing, addressing, and celebrating diversity should be considered essential elements of all children's play therapy regardless of the reason for the referral. Therapy cannot be optimally effective unless the needs of the individual and of the various systems in which he or she is embedded can be balanced to the betterment of all concerned. Cultural differences are a reality of the world with which the child must learn to cope. Ignoring differences will result in poor problem solving that will, in turn, result in the child not getting his or her needs met effectively and appropriately. At best, attempting to eliminate cultural differences minimizes the value of both the culture in question and the individual child. At its worst, attempts to override cultural differences result in a diminution of the complexities of human thought and behavior that have made us such a rapidly developing species. If we as a group are to survive, we must be able to continue to problem solve effectively. To problem solve effectively, we must be able to approach problems from a wide variety of perspectives. To ensure a continuous supply of rich and varied perspectives, we must strive to maintain and value the cultural differences among us.

· 3 ·

LOGISTICS

OVERVIEW

The purpose of this chapter is to provide some guidelines for structuring the data-gathering process. These are only guidelines; they do not represent the only or necessarily the best way to structure this process. There are many approaches to gathering intake and assessment data that could be consistent with Ecosystemic Play Therapy. The process used should meet the needs of the client, the therapist, and the system in which treatment is to be implemented.

Key components of an Ecosystemic Play Therapy intake process include:

1. defining the presenting problem from the perspective of the child and from the perspectives of the child's caregivers and other relevant systems;
2. obtaining a developmental history focusing on the child's and family's experience at different points in the child's development;
3. reviewing the child's current and past functioning within all relevant systems, including, at a minimum, dyadic relationships, family, and peers, and any other systems that have directly or indirectly had an effect on the child's experience or functioning; and
4. exploring the influence of sociocultural and other metasystemic variables on the child's experience and functioning.

Each of these is discussed in detail in Chapter 4, "Data Collection: Intake and Mental Status."

The point of entry into the systems review is the individual child. That is, the systems are not reviewed out of context. Rather, each system is reviewed in terms of the identified child client's interactions with it. Even when information is gathered about other family members, such as a sibling's medical history or a parent's legal history, it should be recorded only if it is related specifically to the child's issues. This is critical. It is impossible to evaluate a child's functioning from an ecosystemic perspective without considering the influence of the functioning of other people in that child's ecosystem. At the same time, the intake becomes a legal document about that child that can be requested by courts or other professionals. When this occurs, the caregiver or agency who holds the privilege to release this information has some decision-making power about the information being released. Often, however, information about other people in the document becomes included in this dissemination process without those persons having given direct permission. This is both ethically and legally acceptable only if the information is directly relevant to understanding the child's functioning and experience.

It may seem contradictory that we retain the concept of an "identified client" in a systems theory. As discussed in Chapter 1, we consider the child to be the basic systemic unit because the very nature of both systems and the individuals that make them up is determined by each individual's experience. In the case of play therapy, the experience of the referred child is the focus of the treatment. The other reason we include an identified child client has to do with our view of the role of children in most of the systems in which they are embedded. That is, children are unique in that they are almost entirely dependent on others and are either unable or not allowed to alter substantially the systems with which they interact. Children cannot choose a different family if they decide the one they have is defective. They cannot change to a different classroom because of a fundamental personality conflict with a teacher. And they cannot choose to ride a different bus to school because they are afraid of some of the children who ride their current bus. By allowing a child to be the identified client in any intervention, we allow for the possibility, if not the probability, that we may have to take an advocacy role at some point in the intervention process. Children may need us to provide fairly direct assistance in changing a system or systems to better meet their needs. To make this possibility clear to all, the play therapist establishes himself or herself as being on the child's side from the outset. Most caregivers do not have trouble with this, especially if they are assured that the play therapist has no intention of riding roughshod over their needs and feelings. They can accept that their child is more likely to need the therapist as an advocate than they are.

Given the previous statements, we structure the intake interview in such a way as to gather information about a number of systems as they affect the life of the identified child client. At a minimum, we like to meet with the caregivers alone to gather a thorough history, meet with the child alone to understand the child's perspective, and meet with the child in the context of the family. Additional information sources include but are not limited to dyadic interviews with individual caregivers, interviews with teachers, counselors, and so on, observation of the child in different settings, records from other systems, and additional assessments conducted by the therapist or referred to another examiner. In the following discussion, we address the initial contact, the interview with caregivers, the interview/play observations with the child, and the family interview.

The majority of the information contained in the workbook will be obtained through intake interviews with the child and his or her caregivers. However, the workbook does not work particularly well as a format for conducting intake interviews. Because of the amount of detail included, the format tends to make for a stilted and lengthy interview. Furthermore, the organization does not follow the usual flow of the intake in

that a child or caregiver is not likely to discuss any one system in isolation. Therefore, we recommend using a much less structured interview format and following up with specific questions only as needed to complete the workbook.

The focus of this chapter is the unique issues involved in completing an Ecosystemic Play Therapy intake. There are several other references that go into detail about the general issues involved in the intake process, including O'Connor (1991). Thus, these issues are addressed only briefly here.

INITIAL CONTACT

The initial contact is critical because it sets the stage for the rest of the intake, assessment and ultimately the treatment. Establishing some degree of rapport at this point goes a long way in ensuring that the family follows through with seeking treatment. A key aspect of establishing rapport is recognizing and acknowledging the difficulty of the situation or problem from the perspective of the caregiver seeking treatment. Children seldom make the decision to come to treatment. Caregivers frequently have control over whether or not the children receive the help they may need, so connecting with the caregiver's experience is critical to helping the child access clinical services.

During the initial contact, gather basic demographic information, determine who is involved with the child and who should participate in the intake process, explain the structure of the intake process, and convey information about policies, fees, and so forth. Address any crisis issues that become apparent during this initial contact.

The specific structure of the intake process depends on the developmental level of the child, the structure of the child's ecosystemic context including culture, and the therapist's approach and work setting. It is critical that the therapist convey the importance of individual meetings both with the child and with the caregivers and the importance of the family meeting(s). Some caregivers expect that the child will be seen alone and expect the problem to be "fixed" with minimal involvement on their part. Other caregivers expect to receive family therapy and to be included completely in the process. The therapist needs to convey to the caregiver that the treatment plan develops out of the initial data-gathering interviews, which will include at a minimum both individual and family meetings. Furthermore, the actual treatment modalities selected are variable and may include individual play therapy, family play therapy, dyadic attachment work, consultation with the school, and so forth, depending on the needs of the child and the particular ecosystem in which the child is embedded. It is useful to expand the caregiver's expectations of the potential options for carrying out the treatment.

Typically with children under 10 years old, we conduct the initial intake session with the caregivers only. In cases in which the child is living in foster care or some other alternative arrangement, it is useful to have a social worker or someone familiar with the child's early history participate in this part of the intake. This interview usually takes 1.0 to 1.5 hours to complete and none of the children in the family should be present while it is being conducted. This format allows the caregivers to be as open as possible in discussing all aspects of both the child's individual functioning and the family's functioning. An interview with the family and a play interview with the child is arranged for the second session.

With preadolescent and older children, the therapist should consider whether or not the working alliance may suffer if the caregivers are interviewed first. For children at this age, seeing the caregivers first may be interpreted as proof that the therapist is in league with the caregivers against the child. This is more likely in cases in which the presenting problem involves acting out. The child knows that the caregivers think his or her behavior is "bad" and assumes that they have convinced the therapist of the same. In these situations it may be helpful to give the child the option of coming into the office first. The child should be made aware of the fact that the intake with the caregivers will take place regardless and that he or she will not be allowed to be present when it does. The child can be reminded that the caregivers will also not be allowed to be present during his or her interview. Caregivers and children can be assured that when both intakes have been completed they will be made aware of any discrepancies in the information provided and will be allowed the opportunity to provide additional input or explanation. Given these rules, most children will want their caregivers interviewed first, if only to put off having to come to a session at all.

Regardless of whether the older child is seen alone in the first or the second session, arrangements should be made to meet with the family system (including nonrelated people living in the home or family members out of the home who are involved in the child's current functioning). This family contact provides an opportunity to observe the child within the child's most influential ecosystemic context and to determine the resources and problems which that system presents for the therapeutic process. In complex family arrangements, such as divorce situations or when children have been placed in foster care, it may be necessary to meet with more than one family system to complete the intake process.

This leads to another aspect of the initial contact with families of preadolescents and adolescents. Although it is most often a caregiver who makes the initial telephone contact with the therapist, it can be very useful for the therapist to have telephone contact with the client as well, before any interviews are conducted. This gives the older child more of a sense that he or she will be an equal partner in the interview and therapy process and is positively empowering. It allows the therapist the opportunity to offer the choices just described and to include the child in determining the appointment times. Caregivers can be made aware, for example, that it is often worth having the child miss some disliked class at school to come to the intake rather than trying to meet after school. After all, a little indirect reinforcement goes a long way.

INTERVIEWING CAREGIVERS

As was mentioned earlier, the actual process of gathering the intake information differs from the organization of the data in the workbook, even though the workbook is organized to create an intake document when it is completed. What follows is a useful structure for actually gathering the information. Before gathering this information, pragmatic concerns such as fees, scheduling, confidentiality and limits of confidentiality, and consent to treat a minor should have been addressed.

The intake process starts by gathering basic information from the caregivers about the family members and the current context for their family, such as ages, grades, employment, who is in the home, and so forth. This is relatively nonthreatening as an initial warm-up process and provides a sense of the current ecosystemic context for the child. It is helpful at this point to get some sense of the ethnocultural context of this family, although this should be addressed throughout the interview as well.

Address the presenting problem next, as this is the reason why they are seeking treatment. Gather specific information about the problem or problems, including what it looks like behaviorally, how often it occurs, where and when it occurs, what sets it off, how have they tried to deal with it, how has it changed over time, how does it affect the child, how does it affect other people, how would they like to see it changed. It is important to address the problem as perceived by as many caregivers and reports as are available at this initial interview.

The next step is to gather a developmental ecosystemic history focusing on the child's and family's experience at different points in the child's development. The overall structure we use for interviewing caregivers is to ask them to answer the same unstructured question with respect to each stage of their child's development. That is, we instruct them to "Tell me about life in your family when. . . ." We start by having them describe family life before conception of this child, and here we focus on the nature of the couple's relationship. Next, we ask about each caregiver's reaction to discovering that the mother was pregnant with this child. The interview proceeds in this format as each developmental stage is covered. At each stage the following questions may be posed either directly or indirectly: How did they feel about the child at this age? Was it a difficult time or an easy time? What did they enjoy about the child? What did they worry about? What critical environmental events occurred during this stage? The following is a brief outline of the specific issues that may be addressed at each developmental stage.

The preceding instructions assume that both of the child's biological parents raised the child and are available to provide the developmental history. When this is not the case, for whatever reason, the developmental history should be obtained from those best able to provide it. If the child was adopted as an infant this will be the adoptive parent or parents. If the child was adopted later or is currently in foster care the best source of developmental data may be the child's case file. The play therapist needs to be resourceful in obtaining this information as it may prove critical to the development of an optimally effective treatment plan.

A. Prepregnancy
   1. Couple/marital history
   2. Other children prior to this child
B. Pregnancy
   1. Wanted or unwanted, planned or surprise. Note that not wanting to be pregnant and not wanting the baby are two different experiences and should be differentiated.
   2. Feelings/hopes/fears and images of baby during pregnancy
   3. Physical problems during the pregnancy and caregivers' understanding of and emotional reactions to those problems
   4. Drug or alcohol use, including cigarettes and prescription drugs
   5. Stressors during pregnancy
   6. Support system during pregnancy
C. Birth
   1. Weight, height, first memory of child
   2. Who was present at the delivery and what were the reactions of those present? If spouse or partner was not present, why not?
   3. How long was the delivery? How difficult? Were there any problems during delivery for the child or the mother? In particular, were mother and child separated during this time and what was the role of other caregiver if available?
D. Birth to 12 months (attachment/basic trust)
   1. Who was (were) the primary caregiver(s)?
   2. Were there any disruptions in caregiver–infant relationship?
   3. Type of baby
      a. Affective responsiveness to caregivers
      b. Ability to calm down and to attend to and explore world
   4. Caregiver experience of and reaction to baby
      a. Process by which parents and baby began to know each other
      b. Affective experience and feeling of connectedness
      c. Experience of caregiving (e.g., competent, overwhelmed, etc.)
   5. Day care arrangements and reactions to day care and other separations and reunions
E. 1 year to 3 years (security/autonomy/exploration/limits)
   1. Developmental milestones, such as sitting, walking, talking, toilet training—bowel and bladder (note if parent cannot remember)
   2. Developmental delays may become apparent at this stage. Were any noted?
   3. How did caregiver handle toilet training and limit setting during this stage?
   4. How did child respond to toilet training and limit setting during this stage?
   5. Type of toddler
      a. Ability to calm
      b. Willingness to seek and receive affection
      c. Comfort with exploring environment
   6. Caregiver experience of relationship
   7. Day care arrangements and reactions to separations and reunions
   8. Relationships with siblings
   9. Relationships with extended family
F. 3 years to 5 years (sense of initiative/family relationships)
   1. Relationship with caregivers—how child handled triadic relations and family relationships
   2. Relationships with siblings
   3. Preschool arrangements and reactions to separations and reunions
   4. Relationships with peers

G. 5 years to 11 years (academic and social competence)
    1. School history with emphasis on adjustment to kindergarten, first, third, and sixth grade. Look at both academic and conduct adjustment.
    2. Social history—close friends, problems getting along with peers
    3. Family relationships
H. 12 years to 18 years (self-identity)
    1. Relationships with peers
    2. Relationships with authority figures, including legal system
    3. Family relationships
    4. Drug and alcohol use or abuse
    5. Antisocial behaviors (e.g., lying, stealing, sexual misconduct)
    6. Beginning intimate relationships
    7. Future goals

When this portion of the interview is complete, go back and ask more detailed questions about any specific points or events that were not covered in response to the open-ended probes. The emphasis here is on gathering a complete understanding of the ecosystemic context both past and present. Refer to Chapter 4, "Data Collection: Intake and Mental Status," for a thorough discussion of the information that can be targeted relative to each of the systems.

Occasionally, caregivers will disclose a family secret during the intake and will ask that the therapist participate in keeping this secret from the child. Such secrets might be as significant as the fact that the child was adopted to something as seemingly trivial as the fact that the mother obtained a Graduation Equivalency Diploma rather than having actually graduated from high school. Therapists need to be cautious in these situations lest they agree to a contract that later hobbles the therapy process. It is usually best not to make blanket agreements of any kind early in the intake or therapy process. Therapists should be direct and state that they are unwilling to make such a commitment without knowing its potential impact on the therapy. The caregivers can then be reassured that disclosure would never take place without their prior knowledge and consent. Caregivers should understand that although they remain holders of the privilege with respect to the secret, the therapist retains control over the therapy and may choose to terminate the treatment if keeping the secret makes progress impossible. The caregivers should also be made aware that, given communication patterns in most families, the child probably already has some idea that a secret exists and may have some, albeit distorted, notions of its nature. It is these very distortions that often make disclosure so important.

For example, one child began regularly engaging in pretend play in which the children were living with adults who were not their "real" caregivers. Upon investigation, the therapist discovered that there had recently been an incident in which the caregivers had to bring the child's birth certificate to register the child for an after school sports program. When the child asked to see the document, the mother became distressed and refused to show it to him. The child became convinced he was adopted. The reality was that the child had simply been born before his caregivers were married. For this child, the real secret was far less distressing than the fantasized one.

Because the social–emotional developmental level of the child is so critical to treatment planning, we usually try to assess the child's level by completing with the caregivers a brief development tool called the Developmental Therapy Objectives Rating Form—Revised (DTORF-R) (Developmental Therapy Institute, 1992). Once the therapist becomes comfortable using the DTORF-R, it can be completed in 10 to 15 minutes. This tool provides an overall sense of the social–emotional level at which the child is functioning with respect to behavior, communication, and socialization, and it provides specific tasks or goals that can become a focus of the treatment plan. The DTORF-R is discussed in more detail in the Chapter 5, "Assessment."

INTERVIEWING CHILDREN

The intake interviews with children usually focus more on the presenting problem and their perception of it than on the complete history. It may be useful, however, to verify their perceptions of any major life events that were reported by the caregivers. During the intake the therapist will also be completing a mental status exam. One format for doing so is presented in Chapter 4. Besides these tasks, the intake is the time when the therapist is providing the child with his or her first therapeutic experience by focusing on the child's needs. For many children, this will be one of the first times they have interacted with an adult who remains consistently interested in how they feel and the outcomes they desire. By helping the child identify areas of distress that might be reduced or remediated in therapy, the therapist will provide a crucial base for subsequent treatment contracting and for the beginning of a positive working relationship.

When interviewing children, there are three verbal strategies that tend to induce greater responsiveness (adapted from Goodman & Sours, 1967/1994, p. 29).

- With younger children, the therapist should attempt to speak slowly and deliberately, and yet he or she must avoid sounding condescending. Children have trouble following complex or abstract language and yet even very young children resent being babied. Children tend to tolerate and actually appreciate when adults are direct or even blunt.

• Use of the subjunctive tense tends to increase children's tendency to talk about themselves. "Suppose you were listening to your parents talking in the next room even though you knew you shouldn't. What do you suppose you might hear them saying?" What if you had a secret listening device and you could hear what your friends were saying about you when you weren't there, what might they say?" These questions allow children some distance and invites them to engage in fantasy.

• The use of exaggerated statements and somewhat theatrical gestures will often capture a child's attention and elicit a response. Exaggerated negative statements often cause the child to correct and elaborate spontaneously on the content.

Although we strongly encourage therapists to ask children directly about specific experiences, one must recognize that children are somewhat prone to suggestion. This poses a dilemma. If the therapist does not ask, there is a good chance that the child may leave out necessary details. If the therapist leads the child even slightly, then the child may attest to details that are inaccurate or even false (Saywitz & Goodman, 1996). The best compromise seems to have the therapist ask open-ended questions first, followed by specific questions that do not introduce new material, and then, only if absolutely necessary, to ask questions in which assumed material is presented. If the child does not provide information about the event until the final level of questioning, the therapist should be cautious in accepting the veracity of the statements. This is especially true of very young children. The three types of questions are illustrated in the following:

• **General:** Has anyone ever done something that hurt you?
• **Specific:** Has your father ever hurt you?
• **Specific/Leading:** When your father hurt you, did he use his hand or something else?

It may also be helpful to ask the child some questions that pull for socially desirable and yet unlikely responses over the course of the interview. Such questions include: Do you ever get angry? When you play a game would you rather win or lose? Do you always tell the truth? If the child answers all of these in the socially desirable way, there is a good chance he or she is seeking to please the therapist and that the veracity of other responses may be in question.

One other issue to be considered is young children's attitudes toward confidentiality. Young children tend to be very careful to protect their feelings and their relationship with their parents and yet will often volunteer a great deal of detail about their home life (Goodman & Sours, 1967/1994). They are also likely to disclose volatile material about others, such as the content of arguments between the parents or between the parents and the other siblings. If they do not see the disclosure as somehow threatening to their security, then they tend not to censor the material. Alternatively, they are not as likely to disclose details of their own thoughts and feelings as easily.

When conducting the interview, it is not necessary to cover every item in detail. However, some portions of the workbook should be specifically covered with every child. For example, all children should be asked about their experience of hallucinations, suicidal and homicidal ideation. In our experience, children are not likely to report these phenomena spontaneously, and yet, if they are experiencing them, will acknowledge these readily if asked directly. Given the significance of these symptoms, it is imperative that the therapist uncover them as early as possible. Specific strategies for assessing these areas will be discussed in Chapter 4: Data Collection: Intake and Mental Status. *Clinical Interviews with Children and Adolescents* (Barker, 1990) is also a useful resource.

Finally, a comment about the physical setup when interviewing children. It is often easier for children to talk in a setting they do not perceive to be too formal or too much like school. It is also helpful for many to have something to do while they talk. However, the toy or activity should not require too much concentration or skill or it will distract them from the interview. A simple coloring book picture or even a lump of clay will often suffice. Also, children tend to disclose more to someone who is at or below their eye level. The therapist should not carry this to the point of appearing silly, but I have had some wonderful sessions with children where I lay on the floor with my chin on my hands and watch them play while we talk.

As was noted, having play materials available can facilitate the child's comfort with the interview situation. Beyond this, however, it is important to develop a sense of the child's ability to engage in interactional play with the therapist and in symbolic play with the toys, as these observations will affect the treatment planning process as well. Specific observations and assessment of a child's play are discussed in Chapters 4 and 5. For now, the concern is on how to structure the interview. Too many toys can detract from the gathering and communicating of information that needs to occur in the first part of the interview. Therefore, play materials should be limited as described previously until the child and therapist have addressed the important content issues. At that point, the child may be encouraged to engage in some exploration of play materials and activities with the therapist which the therapist makes available to the child. These may include doll house items, toy animals in a sandbox, puppets, and so forth.

INTERVIEWING FAMILIES

There are three primary goals in completing a family interview:

1. To observe the interactions between the family members, particularly as they relate to the child client.
2. To gather information about the different family members' individual perceptions of the problem and possible solutions.
3. To gather information about the strengths and support the family may provide, as well as the weaknesses and interference the family may create for the treatment process.

With respect to conducting the family interview, there are many approaches. It is up to the therapist to find the approach that best enables him or her to engage and work with families. There are many books that talk about family treatment theory and strategies, but very few actually define how to structure an initial assessment interview. Two helpful books are Karpel and Strauss (1983), *Family Evaluation,* and Worden (1996), *Family Therapy Basics.* What follows is a brief structure for completing a family interview. However, meeting with groups of people, especially related groups of people, is less predictable and often more fast-paced than individual interviews or interviews with caregivers focused on gathering a history. Thus, family interviewing requires skills in managing this systemic process so that it is, at a minimum, not destructive and, it is hoped, a constructive experience for those attending.

The phases of a family interview can be separated into the following stages (adapted from Worden, 1996): (a) greeting/engaging, (b) defining the problem, (c) moving in a systems direction, and (d) establishing goals/closure.

Greeting/Engaging

The purpose of this stage is to acknowledge the family members and to establish some level of comfort before moving on to the task. At this point the therapist

has already met with some of the family members, so it is important to establish connections with those who have not yet met the therapist. Gathering general information about names, ages, interests, and so forth, helps establish a beginning relationship with the family. At the same time, the therapist should be observing how the members of the family have arranged themselves in the room and how they interact with each other and with the therapist.

At this point, one of the BIG questions in a family interview comes up. Who does the therapist address first? According to Worden (1996), the therapist starts with the youngest child and moves up to the caregivers, speaking first to the caregiver who made the initial contact. According to Karpel and Strauss (1983), addressing the adults first is most appropriate because it reinforces the therapist's expectations about the parent subsystem as having leadership and responsibility roles within the family; then the therapist moves to the youngest child. One also has to consider cultural issues. If the culture is patriarchal, does one address the first question to the male head of the family? If the culture places a high value on age, should the grandparent be addressed first? There are no easy answers to this question. The therapist must be aware of the cultural and relationship issues involved. Because we have already established contact with the caregivers, unless cultural issues dictated otherwise, it would be our tendency to start with the youngest child and move logically through the family. Regardless, it is best to start with someone other than the identified client because this takes the spotlight off the child and emphasizes the importance of understanding the problem within the family context.

The therapist also provides structure for the meeting by defining the purpose. This reduces the family's anxiety to some degree. This also provides an opportunity for the therapist to place the child's problem and treatment in an ecosystemic context. Specifically, the therapist indicates an awareness that the problems have been affecting everyone in the family to some degree or another. In addition, because they are all members of the child's family, they are a part of his or her life and they may have ideas about how the problem can be changed. Meeting with everyone provides an opportunity for the therapist to meet the people important to the client and to understand everyone's point of view.

Defining the Problem

The focus here is on understanding each family member's perspective on the problem. Because the problem is a source of pain for many people in the family, it is important that the therapist provide a high level of structure during this part of the interview. Research has shown that a lack of structuring early in family treatment is associated with a deterioration in clients' conditions during family therapy (Gurman, Kniskern, & Pinsof, 1986). This is a good time for straightforward questions and answers directed at individual members one at a time. In addition to addressing the problem, members should address how the problem affects them directly and how they would like it to be changed.

Although gathering specific information is important in itself, it is even more important to help the family experience the possibility of other perspectives as legitimate understandings of the problem. The therapist needs to assess the degree to which the family can engage in this flexible understanding of the problems. Often, members of dysfunctional families see things in black and white terms and have a difficult time seeing any other perspective as being valid. The therapist promotes this process by modeling an empathic understanding of each individual's perception and experience in one-on-one interactions as he or she directs questions to the different members of the family.

Moving to a Systems Definition of the Problem

Because the therapist has already spent considerable time gathering information from the caregivers and the child, it is useful to use the family interview as a time to highlight ways in which the problem is perceived differently or similarly by different members of the family. This link between family members' experiences begins to shift the interview in a systemic direction. The family may resist this shift to a more interactive and systemic understanding of the problem because it challenges their individual perceptions and the shared family perception. The therapist can then move to a more general understanding of the family as a system by having the family describe a typical day.

At the same time that the therapist is gathering information and interacting with the family, he or she should be observing several relevant systemic dimen-

sions in the family's style of relating to each other. Specific systemic dimensions include:

- *The enmeshment–disengagement continuum.* How does this family handle closeness and distance? Healthy families tend to have a healthy balance between closeness and distance.
- *Power hierarchies.* How is power distributed in the family? How is it maintained? Are there alignments between parents and children that affect the parental subsystem's functioning as a unit?
- *Emotional atmosphere.* Is the atmosphere one that is supportive or one that is cold and critical? Who takes care of whom? How is anger handled? Sadness? Playfulness?

Other systemic concerns include family rules and roles and communication patterns. Karpel and Strauss (1983) and Satir (1972) present different strategies and probe questions for exploring systemic concerns with families.

Establishing Goals/Closure

Toward the end of the interview, the therapist should summarize the interview for the family, being particularly careful to represent each individual member's experience. At this point, the therapist should have some idea about whether or not direct family work, such as family play therapy, may be part of the treatment plan. If so, the therapist should present this as a possibility and explore the level of motivation present in the family to be involved in the treatment process.

SUMMARY

This chapter addresses some of the logistics involved in gathering the intake information needed for successful Ecosystemic Play Therapy treatment planning. The next two chapters on intake and assessment address in more detail strategies and tools for completing this intake process.

· 4 ·

DATA COLLECTION: INTAKE AND MENTAL STATUS

OVERVIEW

As mentioned in the introduction to this book, the Workbook itself was designed to meet several needs experienced by play therapists. First, it provides a straightforward and yet comprehensive way to organize and present intake data in case files. Second, it organizes the material in a manner consistent with Ecosystemic Theory so as to facilitate movement from the data to the theoretical model and back again. This allows for more efficient and consistent development of case formulations and treatment plans. Last, and most important, the Workbook and its Appendix are designed to facilitate the development of a comprehensive set of ecosystemic treatment goals and a complete intervention plan.

The Workbook is physically divided into two major components. The first component is the Workbook proper and contains the intake and treatment plans. This includes identifying information, presenting problem, relevant history, mental status, assessment data, diagnosis, initial treatment contract, and plan. There is a place for signatures at the end of this part of the Workbook and it may be directly incorporated into a clinical chart. The second component is an Appendix that structures the intake information to facilitate development of the case formulation and treatment plan. Logistically, the Workbook should be completed in three stages. First, the relevant information is gathered and

entered into Workbook Parts I, II, and possibly III. Second, the Appendix is completed, generating hypotheses and treatment goals. Finally, Workbook Parts IV through VII are completed.

This chapter provides the reader with instructions for completing Workbook Parts I and II. The rationale or function underlying each of the sections is also discussed. Where relevant, specific strategies and questions are presented for obtaining the information for that section of the Workbook. For those readers who are old hands at conducting intake interviews, please bear with us if some of the material seems basic or obvious. Hopefully, we have included a few tips everyone will find useful. For those readers who are not used to this level of detailed intake inquiry, we hope you find the following discussions comprehensive and useful.

To illustrate the completion and use of the Workbook as fully as possible, we have included the relevant sections of the Workbook for the case of Steven Johnson, a 12-year-old preadolescent male, who was seen initially in the context of being admitted to a comprehensive day treatment program for children with significant emotional and learning problems. Several details have been changed to protect the identity and confidentiality of the client. For those readers who find it difficult to track this case because it is fragmented by the inclusion of substantial explanatory materials, a second completed Workbook containing another case is presented in its entirety in Chapter 10.

All of the information to be gathered is organized in a manner consistent with the ecosystemic perspective, generally working from the smallest system, the child client, progressively to the larger systems in which the child may be embedded. The data collection process gathers information about the child and the problem from many different perspectives. The subjective perceptions of the child and of the relevant people involved with the child, the current and past functioning of each of the relevant systems, and observational information is all gathered as relevant. The gathering of more objective assessment data is discussed in the next chapter. The overarching purpose of this data collection is to answer the following questions:

- How do the child's problems interfere with getting his or her own needs met?
- How do the child's problems interfere with others getting their needs met?
- What is the etiology of the problems? What maintains the problems?
- What is the child's functioning across the many systems in which he or she is involved? What is the history of that functioning?
- How do those systems interact with the child and problem? Are these sources of support or do they contribute to the problem?
- How does the historical and political/cultural context contribute to the problem or to its resolution?

It may be helpful to keep these questions in mind as you complete the Workbook.

WORKBOOK, PART I: IDENTIFYING INFORMATION

The first part of the Workbook covers material generally required for business purposes and by most third party payers.

Intake, Assessment, and Contracting Contact Record

This table allows one to keep track of the person or persons who were contacted in order to obtain the information contained in the intake. If more than one person was responsible for gathering the information, it can be noted in the column Person(s) Completing the task. A quick glance at this chart gives one a good sense of the degree to which a comprehensive ecosystemic view of the child's problems has been obtained.

Case Example

I. **IDENTIFYING INFORMATION**	**CASE NAME:**

INTAKE, ASSESSMENT & CONTRACTING CONTACT RECORD

DATE	PERSON(S) ATTENDING	TASK COMPLETED	PERSON(S) COMPLETING
9/20/93	(Physician Report)	Reviewed records of medical examination completed 6/93	Ammen
	(Language Report)	Reviewed records of language, speech and hearing evaluation completed 6/93	Ammen
	(Educational Psychologist's Report)	Reviewed records of cognitive and educational evaluation completed 6/93	Ammen
9/28/93	Mother	Intake, History, DTORF and PIC	Ammen
	Client	Play Interview	Ammen
10/5/93	Client	Psychological Testing	Ammen
10/6/93	Client's Teacher	Telephone Interview	Ammen
10/12/93	Mother, Client, Sister, Step-Father	Family Interview	Ammen

Steven's referral to a comprehensive treatment program was preceded by a fairly extensive medical, language, and educational evaluation. These records were obtained and reviewed before meeting with Steven's mother to complete the intake. As part of the intake in- terview, the DTORF (Developmental Therapy Institute, 1992) was used to evaluate Steven's level of social–emotional functioning. This instrument is rated using information gathered from primary caretakers and teachers who have direct contact with the child. While Steven participated in a play interview, his mother was asked to complete the Personality Inventory for Children (PIC) (Wirt, Lachar, Klinedist, Seat and Broen, 1977), which creates a profile of a child's problems similar to the Minnesota Multiphasic Personality Inventory (MMPI) (Hathaway & McKinley, 1991). These instruments, along with other instruments and assessment methods we have found useful in our work, are discussed in more detail in Chapter 5.

Because Steven's problems were affecting both his family and his educational setting, a family interview was arranged and a phone interview was conducted with his teacher. Even though his mother and stepfather had separated a few months earlier, his stepfather still maintained contact with the family and was, therefore, included in the family interview.

Responsible Adult(s) Information

This part of the Workbook simply establishes who will be responsible for payment.

Case Example

RESPONSIBLE ADULT(S) INFORMATION

Adult 1 Name: Jane Gilbert **Relationship:** Mother

Home Address: Same as above.

City: _____ **State:** _____ **Zip:** _____ **Phone:** _____

Employer: Minimart **Position:** Manager

Work Address: 555 Wilsonia Ave.

City: Fresno **State:** CA **Zip:** 99999 **Phone:** (999) 555-6666

Insurance Carrier & Number: None. State of Arizona, Department of Education will fund assessment and therapy.

Adult 2: Name: None **Relationship:** _____

Home Address: _____

City: _____ **State:** _____ **Zip:** _____ **Phone:** _____

Employer: _____ **Position:** _____

Work Address: _____

City: _____ **State:** _____ **Zip:** _____ **Phone:** _____

Insurance Carrier & Number: _____

In this case, because the problems are significantly impairing Steven's functioning in an educational setting, he was referred to a program jointly funded by the local and state educational systems.

Family Constellation

This chart details the persons directly involved in the child's family life. The HH column identifies the person or persons who are the heads of the household or households in which the child lives. The head or heads of the household in which the child spends the majority of his or her time is indicated by a 1 in this column. If the child spends time in another household the head or heads of that household is indicated by a 2 in the HH column, and so forth. In the %H1 and the %H2 columns, the amount of time each of the members of the family spends in each of the households is recorded. The total of the entries across the two columns should always equal 100.

C a s e   E x a m p l e

FAMILY CONSTELLATION (Include all persons named above. For all persons mentioned here and throughout the workbook be as specific as possible about their relationship(s) to the child, e.g., maternal grandmother, half-sibling through mother, step-parent, etc.)

Name	Relationship	HH	%H1	%H2	BD	Age	Ethnicity	Grade/Work
Client	**Self**		100		6/25/81	12	Anglo American	starting 7th
Jane Gilbert	Mother	1	100	0		35	Anglo-American	Manager
Sara Johnson	Sister		100	0		15	Anglo-American	10
Henry Gilbert	Step-Father	2	0	100		41	Anglo-American	self-employed
George Johnson	Father	3	0	0		40	Anglo-American	Unknown

[In column HH put a 1 for the Head of Household 1, a 2 for the Head of Household 2, etc. Put 0 if not Head of Household. In column %H1 put the % of time each individual spends in Household 1, repeat for time spent in Household 2.]

A quick glance at this table reveals that Steven lives in one home all of the time with his mother and his sister, and that a biological father and a step-father are also part of his family constellation. In Steven's case, his biological father has not had contact with him since he was very young. His step-father joined the family when Steven was 5 but separated from Steven's mother approximately 6 months ago. However, because the earlier Intake, Assessment & Contracting Record revealed that the step-father was willing to come in for a family meeting, there are indications that he still has some investment in Steven.

Presenting Problem

Although the contents of this section will seem obvious, the focus used by Ecosystemic Play therapists differs in two ways from that of the more traditional approach to defining the presenting problem. One has to do with defining the problem from multiple perspectives. The other has to do with defining the problem in terms of unmet needs; that is, how it affects the client and how it affects others. Although these two aspects of problem definition are often taken into account at some level in traditional treatment planning, in Ecosystemic Play Therapy they become a guiding focus for defining the presenting problem. It is important to address the problem both as it is acted out in the world (behavior) and as it is experienced and conceptualized by those directly affected by it (feelings and beliefs).

Multiple Perspectives

Ecosystemic Play Therapy recognizes multiple realities with respect to defining the presenting problem; that is, the problem as experienced and understood by the parents may be very different from the problem as experienced and understood by the child. Consistent with our subject-dependent theoretical perspective, we see each participant's view of the problem as critical, because each is making decisions and acting based on his or her own perception and not on some "objective" view of the problem.

Traditionally, the goal of the intake has been to define the problem as an objective event that is manifested by observable behaviors and symptoms. This "objective" approach is consistent with the Diagnostic and Statistical Manual-IV (DSM-IV) (American Psychiatric Association, 1994) diagnostic system and assumes that the problem is an entity in itself that can be captured by accurate description. However, this definition of the problem does not allow for multiple perceptions and experiences of the problem. This often means that the child's view of the problem is taken into consideration only when it conforms with the perceptions of key adults in the child's life. Caretakers' and children's definitions of the presenting problem most often agree when the child is experiencing an internalized, anxiety-based problem that does not involve much, if any, acting out. In our experience, these are not the majority of children brought to treatment. Rather, most of the clients we see are brought to treatment because their behavior has become intolerable to someone else. In these cases, caretakers and children rarely agree on the presenting problem.

To give an example: Johnny does not typically see beating up his younger sister as a problem. He is much more likely to see the fact that he experiences her as unbelievably and perpetually annoying as the primary problem. If the play therapist chooses to base the treatment on the caretaker's view of the problem, it is likely that he or she will have a difficult time engaging Johnny in the treatment process. After all, Johnny sees his current behavior as addressing his most pressing problem, and may see pleasing his caretakers and the play therapist as relatively unnecessary.

It is critical, therefore, that the play therapist identifies a problem that is currently and genuinely distressing to the child to ensure that the child will, at least initially, want to be involved in the treatment. This may mean that the play therapist is faced with what appear to be opposing problems, one identified by the caretaker(s) and one by the child. This difficulty can be addressed through effective treatment contracting as it is described in Chapter 7, "Treatment Planning."

Unmet Needs

Consistent with our definition of pathology as discussed in Chapter 1, a child's atypical behaviors, feelings, or cognitions are not problems in and of themselves. Problems occur when these behaviors, feelings, or cognitions interfere with the child's ability to get his or her needs met effectively and appropriately. This means that when gathering information about the problem it is important to gather information about how it adversely affects the child (from the child's, parent's, and other's perspectives) and how it adversely affects others.

The presenting problem or problems becomes the hub around which the other treatment goals are organized. The strategies and tasks of play therapy can be viewed as the spokes emanating from the hub that are used to reach the overall goal of optimizing children's developmental functioning and enhancing their ability to get their needs met efficiently and without interfering with others getting their needs met.

Potential Interview Format: Caretaker(s) To obtain relevant information about the presenting problem or problems the following questions may prove useful.

- **What?** *Please tell me, as specifically as possible, the types of problems your child is having.* (The overall goal is to obtain an operational definition of the problem(s), e.g., specific behaviors, how often do they occur, how severe. Encourage them to be specific, e.g., "twice a day," "disrupts dinner to the point that I have to leave the table.")
- **Why now?** *Given that the problem has been going on for some time, tell me what happened to trigger your calling to make this appointment.*
- **Systemic impact.** *What effect does this problem have on you, your child, your spouse or domestic partner, your other children, others?*
- **Caretaker attunement to child's perceptions.** *In what ways do you think your child's description of the problem will differ from yours?*
- **Child preparation for interview.** *What did you tell your child about why you were consulting a play therapist?*

Potential Interview Format: Child The following interview format and specific questions may prove useful in helping the child to identify a suitable presenting problem.

- *Tell me about the problem that brought you here today.*

Ideally, the child will relate something that he or she finds truly distressing and that could be addressed in treatment. If so, then you are both very lucky and ready to proceed with the intake. If the child says I don't know in response to the question, press the child a little before describing the problem the caretakers related. If you resort to their description of the problem too soon it tends to show the child that you were not really interested in his or her view and that you had, in fact, already accepted the caretaker's perspective.

"You don't know?"
Child shakes head, "No."
"Do you always agree to go talk to a total stranger for no reason?"
Child does not respond but smiles.
"Boy, you sure are trusting. It's sort of like agreeing to go to the doctor when you aren't even sick. Do you do everything your parents tell you without ever asking why?"
Child nods, "Yes," but smiles and avoids eye contact.
"Well, your parents gave me one reason they brought you, but I am more interested in what made you agree to come. If you're sure that you have no idea why you are here I'll get them back in here to tell you what they think. If you have a guess or a reason of your own we won't bother with them. Either way, what I'm most interested in is the problem you are having and why you agreed to come."

Again, if the child relates a problem he or she finds genuinely distressing then you are ready to proceed. If, however, the child relates a problem that mimics the one described by the caretakers but does not seem to distress him or her, this discrepancy should be probed.

"Well, you told me just about the same thing your parents told me. But I don't really see why that bothers you. I mean I can see where hitting your sister bothers them and why it would bother her, but I'm not sure why it bothers you. I mean it must stop her from doing something you don't like."
"Yeah, but every time I hit her I get in trouble."
"Oh, so the problem is that you don't like what your sister does and you don't like getting in trouble."

Having now defined a problem that the child finds distressing, you are ready to proceed. The worst case scenario involves the child who adamantly denies any difficulties in the face of substantial probing. In such cases you may have to frame the very fact of being brought to treatment as the presenting problem.

"Well, if there you are not having any problems in your life and you don't agree with the reasons your parents gave for bringing you here, you must be pretty angry about being here."

"Yeah, my parents think there is something wrong. Well, there is. They're what's wrong. They have some kind of problem."

"Well then it seems like the problem you are having is not being able to find a way to convince them you don't need to be here."

"Yeah, I don't want to be here."

"OK, then our plan will be to spend some time trying to figure our why your parents think you need to be here and what you can do to convince them they are wrong."

Case Example

PRESENTING PROBLEM (Define in behavioral terms, including onset, frequency and severity. Be sure to include reporters affect regarding the problem.)

Child's View: Steven states that he gets uncomfortable around other kids and sometimes they make fun of him. Sometimes people get mad at him even though he is not sure what he did and then he cries a lot. He does not like to have people mad at him and he does not want to cry so much.

Parent's View: Mother states that Steven seems unhappy (cries 2-3 times/day for no apparent reason). He does not get along with other children because he is immature or inappropriate and they avoid him or tease him. When he is anxious he has problems with enuresis and encopresis (2-3 times/week). He gets frustrated easily, then blows up, yelling and crying and stomping his feet (at least 1 time/day). Most of the problems occur at school rather than at home. She feels scared about his unhappiness and his future.

Other's View: Steven's teacher describes Steven as extremely hypersensitive such that he becomes rigid, noncompliant and overly emotional in new situations or when he feels unable to meet the demands of school. He usually cries but more recently has begun throwing temper tantrums (throws papers, stomps feet, yells and cries). Problems are occurring several times/day. Other children tease him about his enuresis and encopresis. Steven acts like it does not bother him and ignores them.

In this case, the child, mother, and teacher all have similar, though unique, views of the problem, that is, he cries and gets frustrated. From Steven's perspective, he has minimal awareness of his feelings or how his behavior causes problems for others. He is aware that he is uncomfortable and that he does not want to have others angry at him, which provides a hook for getting him involved in treatment. His mother is most concerned about his sadness and how his problems affect his ability to function effectively in his world. She does not directly identify discomfort with how his behavior affects her or the rest of the family, which is somewhat unusual. His teacher is most concerned about the disruptive effect of his behavior on his functioning in the classroom and with his peers.

History of Presenting Problem

In this section of the Workbook, the play therapist should try to expand the operational description of the presenting problem. The goal here is to discover the historical origins of the problem, the current stimuli that trigger its appearance, and any variables that contribute to or change the problem. From a behavioral standpoint, this means identifying the stimulus and the contingencies connected to the problem. From a psychodynamic point of view, it means identifying the internal conflict that remains unresolved. And from an ecosystemic perspective, it means identifying each of the systems that play or played a part in creating and maintaining the problem.

This information will be used to derive hypotheses about the etiology of the problem and the factors contributing to its continuation. The derivation of these hypotheses and their use in treatment planning are discussed at length in Chapter 6.

Potential Interview Format: Caretaker(s) & Child

Any of the following questions could be pursued with either the caretakers, the child, or both.

Historical Information

- *When did the problem start?*
- *What was the initial stimulus?*
- *Has the problem changed over time?*
- *Has the problem generalized to new stimuli or situations?*

Systemic Factors

- *What effect has the problem had on each of the systems?*
- *How did/do the various systems react to the problem?*

- *Does the problem change in nature, frequency, or intensity when the child is operating in different systems?*

Response to Interventions

- *What attempts have been made to address the problem?*
- *What type of results have these attempts produced?*

Affective Impact

- *How does the child feel about the problem?*
- *How do others in the child's environment feel about the problem?*

Case Example

HISTORY OF PRESENTING PROBLEM (Define precipitants, impact on/reaction from environment, situations variations, attempts to resolve problem and results, and changes in problem over time.)

While these problems have been present for some time because of Steven's developmental delays, they have become more pronounced over the past year. Approximately 6 months ago, his mother and stepfather separated and this was difficult for him. He also seemed to have more difficulty adjusting to the 6th grade than he has had making previous transitions perhaps because it is located in a Junior High School and required a move from his familiar school site. The problems at school have become pronounced enough that it is disruptive to the other students in his classroom and Resource program and the school has initiated this referral for a comprehensive educational and mental health evaluation and intervention program.

WORKBOOK, PART II: SYSTEMS REVIEW

This section of the Workbook includes a complete review of the various systems in which the child may be embedded. The major systems are individual, familial, social, educational, legal, medical, and mental health. Although the cultural, religious, and community contexts have an impact on all of these systems, we specifically target the impact of these relative to the family context. At the end of the systems review, the broader metasystemic context is examined with respect to the regional cultural system, dominant cultural/political system, world community, and historical time as they relate to a particular case.

Individual System: Developmental History

Most of the information to be gathered in this section of the Workbook is quite standard. The focus is on constitutional (biologic, neurologic) and maturational (developmental) factors. In early childhood, these two factors are closely linked. The data will be used primarily to answer the question: Is there any reason to suspect

that this child has fundamental biologic, neurologic, or developmental problems that may be contributing to the present problems? Relevant information includes details of the pregnancy and birth experiences, because these may have had an adverse effect on the child's neurologic development. This information is listed in the sections on pregnancy and labor and delivery.

The APGAR score is a 10-point rating of a newborn infant's heart rate, respiration, muscle tone, reflexes, and color at one minute and five minutes after birth (Apgar, 1953). Any score below 7 means the newborn needs help breathing or is in immediate danger. Parents who have attended prepared childbirth classes are often aware of the APGAR scores of their children. If the parent reports that the child had a low APGAR at birth, this is a red flag from two perspectives. First, the child may have subtle or apparent neurological problems. Second, the parent may react to this low score and perceive this child as especially vulnerable, whether or not the child has problems. This discussion of the APGAR score points out the importance of considering any information gathered during the history both in terms of what it reveals about the child's functioning and in terms of the meaning attributed to that information by the child and other people in the child's ecosystem.

Delays in reaching developmental milestones can be a useful indicator of underlying neurologic problems that are interfering with the child's development. The source of these problems may be inherent to the child (e.g., autism and genetic difficulties), related to events during the pregnancy, such as prenatal exposure to alcohol or drugs, or related to medical problems that occurred at, or soon after, birth. Delays may also be related to a severely neglectful environment in which the child does not experience emotional engagement and sensory stimulation from the caretakers. Recent research found that children from neglectful environments demonstrated significant delays, particularly in their language and social development (Crittenden & Ainsworth, 1989; Erickson & Egeland, 1996; Katz, 1992). Children with early childhood abuse histories may also demonstrate delays, but these tend not to be as severe as those seen in children from neglectful environments.

Although there is considerable variability in when children achieve various developmental milestones, the following list provides useful reference points:

- Walking: 15 to 17 months
- Talking: words, 12 to 14 months; sentences, 23 to 25 months
- Bladder control: daytime, 28 months; nighttime, 3 years (with girls generally training 2 to 3 months earlier than boys)
- Bowel control: 18 to 24 months

(Caplan, 1973; Caplan, F. & Caplan, T., 1977; Caplan, T. & Caplan, F., 1983). For additional information on the assessment of developmental difficulties the reader is referred to Chapter 5, Assessment, of this text.

Early developmental data also provides the play therapist with a sense of the context into which the child was born. Was the pregnancy planned or not, and how did that affect parental experiences? What were the parental perceptions and expectations of the infant during the prenatal period? (See Ammaniti, 1991.) What was the experience of support and stress in the child's caregivers during this time? Stressful life events during this time can affect the caretakers' emotional availability to the child at birth and there is even evidence to suggest before birth (Verny, 1981). The emphasis in this section is on the child's early development and the caregiver's individual experience. The caretaker–child relationship is addressed in a later section. The section on gender identity development, gender role behavior, and sexual orientation is included for those situations where these are related to the presenting problem. While this is not often the case and such situations warrant that the play therapist take particular care not to assume a heterosexist stance, the following examples illustrate how these issues may come into play.

In one case, the play therapist was called by the caregiver of an 8-year-old boy, who, they feared, had a Gender Identity Disorder. A few questions established that the boy was clear that he was a boy, seemed satisfied with that fact, and had never expressed the desire to be a girl, thereby, ruling out a gender identity problem. The mother then conceded that they were uncomfortable with the amount of traditionally feminine behavior their son exhibited. Again, a few questions established that the only aspect of the feminine behavior that really worried the mother was the fact that her son was often rejected by his peers and had no friends. A few more questions established that her underlying concern was that her son was, or would be, gay. At this point the play therapist stated that there was no psychological data to support the identification of same-gender sexual orientation as a problem per se, and furthermore there was no evidence that it could be altered with play therapy. He stated that there were play therapists who believed otherwise and offered to refer the mother elsewhere. Interestingly, the mother chose not to accept a referral and instead to bring her son to this play therapist. The treatment goal that was agreed on by both mother and son was to work on improving and increasing the son's peer and sibling relationships. In this case, gender identification, gender role behavior, and sexual orientation were all potential issues that were ruled out as a focus of the treatment once they had been fully explored.

The other case is substantially more complicated. In this one, the play therapist was referred a 2-year-old child in order to prepare her and her family for gender reassignment surgery. This child was born male with numerous congenital deformities of the lower abdomen and pelvis. At birth, the physician determined that there was no penile tissue present and advised the mother to have the child's gender reassigned. The mother did this and for 2 years raised the child as a girl. Both she and the child completely accepted this reassignment and the child clearly and solidly identified herself as a girl. During an examination before a fifth corrective surgery, a urologist discovered that both a penis and testicle were present in this child but that they were inside the abdominal cavity. After multiple consultations, the mother was advised that the best medical outcome for this child could be achieved by reassigning her gender for a second time. Although emotionally devastated, the mother agreed on the basis of the possibility that her child would grow up to be a functional and fertile male rather than a hormone-dependent, infertile female. In this case, the entire focus of play therapy was on surgical preparation and initiating the shift in the child's gender identification as well as in the family's view of the child.

Interview with Caretaker(s)

The following questions may be useful in gathering data regarding the child's early developmental history.

- Please describe life in your family before the time (client) was conceived.
- How did you and other family members react to finding out you were pregnant?
- Please describe life in your family during your pregnancy with (client).
- Tell me about (client's) birth?
- Tell me about life in your family once (client) was born.
- Describe what (client) was like as a baby.
- Describe what (client) was like as a toddler.
- Please tell me about life in your family once (client) became a toddler.

The interview proceeds in this format, covering each of the developmental or life stages the child has reached to date. Specific probes are added only when the information needed is not reported in response to the more open-ended items.

Interview with Child

The developmental history taken from the child does not need to duplicate everything covered in the interview with the caretakers. The format and open-ended questions used with the caretakers can be reworded for use with the child after establishing a reasonable beginning point.

- Tell me about the earliest (first) thing you remember in your life.
- What do you remember next after that?

The play therapist should also inquire as to the child's experience of any major events that were noted in the interview with the caretakers. The play therapist can verify the child's recall of the event as well as his or her understanding of the event and emotional reaction to it.

Case Example

II. INTAKE: SYSTEMS REVIEW

INDIVIDUAL SYSTEM: DEVELOPMENTAL HISTORY

Pregnancy

Planned: ☒ **No**   ☐ **Yes, Describe:** <u>Mother was using oral contraceptives but thinking about getting pregnant. Husband initially wanted another baby, but after she became pregnant, he did not want to be involved and began to distance himself from the family.</u>

Discomfort/Problems: ☒ **No**   ☐ **Yes, Describe:** _____

Drugs/Alcohol during pregnancy: ☐ **No**   ☐ **Yes, Describe:** <u>Continued on birth control pills until she realized she was pregnant.</u>

Stressors/Complications with the pregnancy: <u>Marital problems developed during the pregnancy. Mother developed Gestational Diabetes during the 8th month of the pregnancy which was managed solely with dietary changes.</u>

Support System: <u>Mother's mother served as her primay support system.</u>

Labor & Delivery: WT: <u>7 lbs.</u>   **APGAR:** <u>UK</u>   **Who present at delivery:** <u>Mother's mother.</u>

How long/how difficult/problems: <u>Normal labor and delivery. No problems noted.</u>

If problems - what happened: <u>Although the birth was normal, client developed viral encephalitis at 17 days of age and was hospitalized in Neonatal Intensive Care Unit for 10 days during which the mother was informed that he would probably die. She stayed at his bedside most of that time. The father was essentially absent.</u>

Developmental Milestones: Walk: <u>13 months</u>   **Talk:** <u>   </u>   **Words:** <u>12 months</u>

    Age Toilet Trained: Bladder: <u>4 yrs</u>   **Bowel:** <u>4 yrs</u>

        Problems: ☐ **No**   ☒ **Yes, Describe:** <u>continues to have frequent daytime enuresis and occasional daytime</u> <u>encopresis</u>

Developmental Delays:

        Language: ☐ **No** ☒ **Yes,** ☒ **Expressive**   ☒ **Receptive**   ☐ **Articulation** ☒ **Auditory Processing**

            Describe: <u>Areas noted above were and continue to be significantly delayed.</u>

        Motor: ☐ **No** ☒ **Yes, Describe:** <u>Steven displayed mild delays in his fine motor coordination.</u>

        Adaptive Behavior: ☐ **No**   ☒ **Yes, Describe:** <u>Steven's adaptive behavior was and continues to be</u> <u>significantly delayed.</u>

        Other: ☒ **No** ☐ **Yes, Describe:** <u>   </u>

Gender Identity, Gender Role Behavior and Sexual Orientation

    Gender Identity Divergent From Biologic Gender: ☒ **No** ☐ **Yes, Describe:** <u>   </u>

    Gender Role Behavior Divergent From Socio-Cultural Norms: ☒ **No** ☐ **Yes, Describe:** <u>   </u>

    Sexual Orientation Development

Steven's early developmental history reveals the significant influence of neurological and developmental factors on this case. Logistically, Steven's history of encephalitis could have been presented later in the Medical System section rather than here because it was not directly related to his birth, but because of its early timing and probable contribution to Steven's developmental delays, it was also included here.

Individual System: Mental Status Examination

The Mental Status Examination (MSE) is one way of gathering much of the information needed to make a traditional psychiatric diagnosis within the structure of the Diagnostic and Statistical Manual of Mental Disorders, 4th Edition, DSM-IV (American Psychiatric Association, 1994). Its aim is to sample a wide array of mental functions known to affect or be affected by various mental disorders. Although widely used by psychiatrists, it tends to get mixed reviews from other mental health professionals. There seem to be three bases on which the mental status exam is negatively evaluated. First, it is too small a sample of behavior on which to base something as critical as a psychiatric diagnosis. Second, children are not reliable reporters of their own experiences and may, therefore, inadvertently distort the exam results. Finally, because children are susceptible to suggestion, the very direct format of the

exam questions may elicit positive responses in the absence of the children having actually experienced that to which they are attesting. All of these criticisms have a certain validity. However, rather than overreact and throw out the baby with the bath water, these should be taken as reasons to embed the exam within the context of a more comprehensive intake evaluation, to interpret the data the exam produces with caution and within a developmental framework, and to cross-validate areas of significant concern with information gathered from other sources or from formalized assessment. Goodman and Sours' (1967/1994) book, *The Child Mental Status Examination,* remains a useful guide for conducting mental status examinations with children.

Each area of the MSE is assessed in the context of the child's chronological age and actual developmental level. The majority of this information is obtained through observation during the intake interview with the child. Direct questioning should be used only when the information has not come up spontaneously in the course of the interview. Even then, the play therapist should be careful not to ask more questions than are absolutely necessary to evaluate the child's functioning in a given area. The therapist should try to use the child's words to illustrate observations wherever possible.

The MSE is useful in two ways. First, it helps us gather information by delimiting some very specific areas that need to be questioned, by asking a caretaker, the child, or both. Second, it provides a structure for organizing the content of observations and impressions of the client. It is critical, however, that "the mental status examination be as devoid of inference as possible and that we record what we see and hear, rather than what we think it means" (Bird & Kestenbaum, 1988, p. 27). It is almost impossible not to make some inferences. But the degree to which we can support these inferences with the behavior and verbalizations of the client provides a more objective baseline for other professionals who might work with this child.

We have organized the Mental Status Examination section to be consistent with our conceptual model that posits that the child's behavior (as we experience it), cognitive processes, and subjective experiences are all critical to understanding his or her individual functioning. Because of the immediate implications of dangerous behaviors and cognitions for treatment planning, these are also addressed in the MSE.

Individual System: Mental Status Examination—Behavioral Observations

Appearance

This area is assessed for three reasons. First, the play therapist should consider the first impression the child makes. We are all aware that people's initial reactions can be powerfully affected by the way a person looks. The play therapist should particularly note the degree to which the child's appearance deviates from what was expected given the child's age, gender, parentage, and so forth. Second, the child's appearance can give useful clues about how well the child is cared for. It may be the first clue that there is abuse or neglect taking place. Finally, appearance can be an indicator of mental health when it is affected by the child's mood or overall functioning. At a minimum, the play therapist should provide a general description of the child, quality of grooming, whether or not the child appears his or her stated age, and any unusual characteristics.

Motor Activity

At the high and low extremes, children's motor activity is usually associated with Attention Deficit Disorders (ADD) and depression, respectively. The play therapist should evaluate the child's motor activity to determine whether there is an impulsive quality, that is, a recklessness and reactivity to stimuli in the environment, rather than just high energy. High activity or constricted behavior may be signs of anxiety. It should be noted how the child's activity level changes as he or she becomes more comfortable with the play ther-

apist or in response to the presence of different persons. The child's activity level can also provide a rough measure of the child's overall developmental level. Often, play therapists unfamiliar with young children come out of their first session with a 2- or 3-year-old positive that the child is hyperactive. Figure 4.1, from the Gesell Institute of Child Development (Ames & Ilg, 1976), illustrates typical behavior patterns in young children. Although the 2-year-old may spend less than a minute at any one activity, the typical 3-year-old still goes to three different activities in a 7-minute period.

Speech

Because we relate largely through the medium of language, the child's ability to use language is critical to his or her competent functioning. Problems in this area have implications for both academic and social functioning that, in turn, have the potential to affect emotional functioning. There are many aspects of speech that may be evaluated (see Othmer & Othmer, 1989, for an extensive discussion of the assessment of mental status functions, including speech), however, three warrant specific observation: (a) How well is the child able to communicate? (b) Is the child's language age-appropriate? (c) Are there indications of neurologic or psychiatric problems?

Emotions (Mood and Affective Range, Appropriateness, and Control)

Mood is the subjective emotional state of the child, whereas affect refers to the external manifestations of emotion observed by the play therapist (Othmer & Othmer, 1989). Mood may be reported spontaneously or may require direct inquiry about how the child is feeling. There are three aspects of affective expression that can be assessed by observing the child's emotional responses over the course of the interview: range, appropriateness, and control. Range refers both to the child's capacity for experiencing and expressing a variety of affects as well as a variety of intensities of affect. Appropriateness refers to the degree to which the child's affects and the intensity of those affects are appropriate given the event to which they are attached. For example, does the child display sadness when talking about a death in the family and is that sadness more intense when talking about a close relative than it is when talking about the demise of the family's goldfish? Control refers to the child's ability to manage his or her affects. This is not to imply that the child's affect must be restrained and never acted on. Rather, control is meant to refer to children's abilities to channel their affects in a manner that allows them to get their needs met in ways

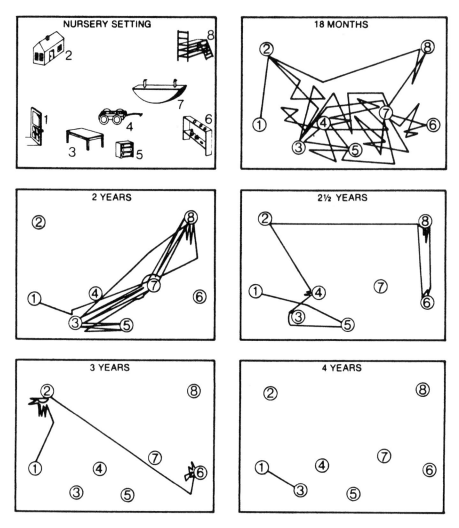

FIGURE 4.1 Seven clocked minutes of nursery school behavior at different ages. From *Your Three Year Old* by Louise Bates Ames and Frances L. Ilg. Copyright © 1976 by the Gesell Institute of Child Development, Frances L. Ilg and Louise Bates Ames. Used by permission of Delacorte Press, a division of Bantam, Doubleday Dell Publishing Group, Inc.

that do not substantially interfere with others getting their needs met. When faced with a trauma, a child may sob uncontrollably and still allow himself or herself to be held and nurtured. This would be an appropriate level of control for the situation. Of these three aspects of affective functioning, control is most affected by developmental level, with younger children having less control.

Attitude

Attitude refers to what the child communicates about being in the interview: level of motivation, defensiveness, cooperation, and so forth. Does the child's attitude seem to be situation-specific, that is, is he or she anxious about talking to a play therapist, or is the child's attitude reflective of a more pervasive way of approaching the world?

Relatedness

This refers to the child's capacity to form relationships in a new setting, specifically, when interacting with an adult. It is a very rough measure, as the context of the intake interview is unusual and children are generally aware that they are being evaluated on some level. Both intense, immediate attachment and persistent inability or refusal to interact are generally seen as indicators of potential attachment problems and/or social skills deficits. It is useful to evaluate eye contact and the child's use of physical space, while keeping in mind the cultural implications of these two variables.

Case Example

INDIVIDUAL SYSTEM: MENTAL STATUS EXAMINATION

Behavioral Observations

Appearance: Steven is moderately overweight. He was casually dressed and appeared younger than 12 years old.

Motor Activity: He was somewhat restless and fidgety at times and at other times well controlled.

Speech: (Content and Productivity) Steven's use of language was immature in both content and structure. He struggled to find words at times and either changed the topic or used an incorrect word which made it difficult to follow his conversation.

Emotions

Mood: Steven's mood was generally positive.

Affect: (Range, Reality Base, Control) His range of affect included anger and frustration with others as well as sadness when talking about how he feels about himself. His affective control was appropriate in the structured setting of the interview. His affects seem appropriate to the situations that trigger them.

Attitude: He was cooperative and seemed to enjoy being the center of an adult's attention. His limited awareness of his feelings and the effect of his behavior on others seemed genuine rather than resistant.

Relatedness: Steven made variable eye contact. He looked to the therapist for approval and avoided eye contact when discussing uncomfortable topics.

Individual System: Mental Status Examination—Cognitive Processes

Estimated Developmental Level

It is critical to have some sense of the child's cognitive development because it affects how that child organizes and processes information in his or her world. There are two aspects of this assessment to take into account: the child's actual developmental level and whether that developmental level is consistent with the child's age. The child's level of cognitive development has significant implications for interpreting the child's functioning with respect to the other cognitive processes. For example, compare two 9-year-olds who demonstrate significant impairment in insight and judgment for their age. One is functioning at the Preoperational stage of development, and the other is functioning, as expected, at the Concrete Operations stage. In the first case, the child is not cognitively capable of age-appropriate insight and judgment. In the second case, the child is cognitively capable, but is experiencing interference from some other source.

Orientation

Orientation simply refers to the child's understanding of who, what, when, and where relative to his or her present life situation. It is a gross measure of the child's reality testing and intellectual functioning, as well as a strong indicator of neurological problems if disorientation is present. Children should know who they are and generally where they are. Evaluating time depends on developmental level. For younger children, do they know what time of day it is, whether or not it is a work/school day or a weekend, or what day of the week it is? A full understanding of time is usually not appreciated by children until around 7 or 8 years of age (Friedman, 1982). Usually it becomes apparent almost immediately that the child is oriented to time, place, and self. Orientation to purpose, that is, being aware of the reason for meeting with the play therapist, is more difficult to assess in children, as they may not know why they are there because they were told nothing or given erroneous information. In these cases, the child's confusion is not related to disorientation due to problems with neurological functioning. Some useful questions include:

- What is your whole name?
- Where do you live?
- Do you know what day (date, month, year) it is today? Day of the week? Time of day?
- Have you ever lost track of time?
- Have you ever found yourself somewhere and had no idea how you got there?

Memory

Moderate-term and short-term memory can be assessed directly. At the beginning of the interview tell the child to pay attention because you are going to say some words and that you will check to see if the child can remember them just before he or she leaves the office. Then say about five unrelated words suited to the child's developmental level. At the end of the interview ask the child to repeat all of the ones he or she can remember. Short-term memory is most often assessed by having the child repeat progressively longer strings of single digits that the play therapist has just presented out loud. In addition, some of the following questions may be useful to assess longer term memory.

- How old are you?
- How old were you when you started school?
- What did you have to eat yesterday?
- What were you doing just before you came to talk to me today?

Concentration

This area is self-explanatory. It refers to the child's ability to remain focused in a variety of settings. Note that many children with ADD are much more focused in one-on-one situations such as the intake interview in which the external distractions are minimal. These children typically fare much worse in group situations in which several things are occurring at once, such as in a classroom. A task sometimes used to assess both concentration and memory is to give the child a sequence of directions to follow. The interviewer says, "Please bring me the book from the table over there, then slide the other chair over here next to yours, and then sit back down." The task should require that the child move about the room as this increases the degree of focus required to stay on task. The task generally should not include more than three steps and its complexity can be adjusted up or down depending on the age of the child. Additional questions can be used to clarify the child's experience.

- Do you get confused sometimes?
- Is it hard for you to remember the directions the teacher gives at school?

Children with trauma-related problems may demonstrate the onset of concentration problems at school after the trauma or after events that remind them of the trauma, such as a temporally associated holiday. For these children, concentration problems are usually related to the intrusion of thoughts and feelings related to their traumatic experience.

Abstraction

This is a difficult area to assess because, by definition, children under the age of about 11 should be minimally able to engage in abstract thinking (Flavell, 1963). We generally, consider children's ability to include affects or motives in their discussions of behavior and their ability to offer more than one explanation for the same event to be excellent signs of early abstract reasoning as it relates to mental health.

- Tell me about how you were feeling just after your brother took the toy you were playing with?
- Besides just wanting the toy, can you think of another reason your brother might have decided to take the toy you were using?

Intellect

This area is usually evaluated through children's responses to other portions of the interview. Unfortunately, mental health professionals are known to be notoriously poor judges of intellectual functioning when using interviews alone. The play therapist should be careful to do no more than make a very rough estimate of the child's functioning. What is useful, however, is to make note of one's reaction to the child. If the play therapist ends the session with a sense that the child is either very intelligent or very slow, then chances are that others who interact with the child will have the same reaction. Whether or not the reaction is accurate, it likely colors the way people react to and treat the child, and this, in turn, will affect the child's self-concept and behavior.

Judgment

This is usually evaluated relative to descriptions of the child's behavior over time. The most obvious evidence of poor judgment are those times the child engages in behavior that is self-endangering or that results in negative consequences that should have been readily anticipated. Impulsive behavior is, by definition, an example of poor judgment. At the higher levels of development, good judgment is difficult to differentiate from high-level moral development. In addition, the play therapist can assess the child's capacity to make good intellectual judgments even in the absence of reasonably thought-out behavior.

- Can you tell me the difference between the truth and a lie?

- What kinds of things do you like to buy with your money?
- What would you like to be when you grow up?
- Is it all right for a child to steal something if he or she is absolutely sure that he or she will not get caught?

Insight

Although the concept of insight is widely used by mental health professionals, it is not always easy to assess, especially in children. Insight can be thought of as occurring at four levels, all of which must be evaluated in light of the child's overall development and age.

Functional Insight The child is aware of the thoughts, feelings, and motives underlying his or her behavior and is able to use that knowledge to adjust to internal and external demands as needed.

Above-Average Insight When evaluated against most children of the same age, the child has greater awareness and is able to use that knowledge effectively.

Limited Insight The child is at least partially aware of the thoughts, feelings, and motives underlying his or her behavior but is *not* able to use that knowledge to adjust his or her behavior.

No Insight The child is unable to describe at all the thoughts, feelings, or motives underlying his or her behavior.

Insight is best evaluated by asking children to explain their own or others' behavior at several points during the intake.

- Child reports seeing another child cheat on a test. Play therapist then asks, "Why, do you think he/she would do that? How do you think he/she felt while he/she was cheating?"
- Child reports feeling a "weird feeling in his/her stomach" just before taking his/her turn to read in front of the class. Play therapist, "What feeling—like happy, mad, sad, and so on—goes with weirdness in your stomach?" (Here the play therapist specifically avoids using the word *feeling* in reference to a physical sensation). "What usually happens if a child in your class does a good (or bad) job when reading in front of the class?"

Organization of Thought Processes

This relates to the organization of the child's cognitions. Are there any abnormalities in the organization such as loose associations and tangential thinking? Are the child's thoughts so disorganized as to be chaotic, as in a psychotic state? Is the organization rigid, either because of organic problems such as perseveration in which the child is unable to change set, or because of anxiety leading to obsessional thinking?

Hallucinations

The child should be directly asked about hallucinatory experiences, even if there is no overt evidence that these are occurring. When interviewing the child regarding potential hallucinatory experiences, it may be useful to start with general questions such as

- *Do you often imagine things?*
- *Have you ever had a dream while you were awake?*

These can be followed by this series of more specific questions:

- *Have you ever been walking alone, or sitting watching TV, or maybe doing your homework and you hear somebody call your name? Then when you check there either isn't anybody around or they say they didn't call you?*

Most children will answer yes to this question, at which time you should ask them to explain the phenomenon. The child should be able to give a reasonable explanation within the limits of his or her developmental level. A response that suggests the child recognizes the experience as imaginary is obviously most healthy. However, regardless of the child's response you should go on to ask

- *Have you ever heard more than your name when there was no one else around?*

Again, if the child says yes, it is important to ask him or her to explain the phenomenon. The final question in the series is

- *Since sometimes people hear things that no one else hears, like someone calling their name, I wondered if you have ever seen anything no one else could see?*

As with each of the previous questions it is important to understand what the child makes of a positive response to this question. Seeing Santa Claus on Christmas Eve when everyone else is in bed is one thing, whereas seeing your dead brother's face in the mirror is quite another. The goal with this group of questions is to rule out both psychosis and organicity.

Delusions

Delusions can be seen as a form of distorted insight in which the child's explanations for his or her behavior are unrealistic or bizarre. The level of distortion may range from illogical to psychotic. The most common delusions are those in which the individual feels persecuted or in which the individual has grandiose beliefs about himself or herself.

Trauma Symptoms

Traumatic experiences are processed and stored in the brain differently from other events (James, 1994). Memories of these experiences are stored separately and may be partly or fully out of conscious awareness. Intense recollections of the traumatic event may intrude into consciousness through vivid nightmares or be triggered by some cue in the environment that reminds the person of this event. At those times, the person will feel as if he or she is reexperiencing the event with all of its previous intensity, associated affect, and physiological sensations. These flashbacks tend to feel out of the person's control and are experienced as extreme reactions or out-of-context behavior by others. Often, children who have witnessed or experienced trauma will engage in reenactment behaviors, either directed toward others in their environment, such as abuse-reactive behaviors, or repetitive reenactments of the events in their play. Alexithymia, although not directly a cognitive process, refers to the inability to name or use symbolic language to communicate an emotional experience even when one is aware of the physiological reactions, such as increased heart rate and dry mouth (James, 1994; Krystal, 1988). This is thought to be the result of traumatizing experiences being encoded in the primitive, nonverbal part of the brain. "Dissociation is a sudden, temporary alteration in the integrative functions of consciousness and/or identity, whereby one's experience is separated from one's conscious awareness" (James, 1989, p. 101). Defensive dissociation can be seen as a natural mechanism to protect trauma survivors from experiencing thoughts, feeling, and sensations that would otherwise overwhelm them and keep them from being able to function (James, 1989, 1994). Dissociation can be conceptualized as a continuum of increasing loss of awareness, starting with daydreaming, momentary loss of awareness when

in a stressful situation, depersonalization experiences, all the way to fully developed Multiple Personality Disorder or MPD (Braun, 1984). Severe childhood abuse has been identified as a predisposing factor in more than 95% of patients identified with MPD. Thus, one should be particularly aware of the potential for disassociative phenomena when working with children with abuse or trauma histories.

Identifying disassociative phenomena in children can be difficult because children may be less organized and clear in their use of language to describe their experiences and are still in the process of identity formation. James (1989) includes a checklist in the appendix of her book called the "Dean Behavioral Checklist for Child and Adolescent MPD" to assist in this identification process. James (1989, pp. 104–105) also identifies the following symptoms as potential red flags for disassociative problems, though they may be related to other problems.

1. Spontaneous trance states, when the child "spaces out" or stares off into space
2. Use of another name
3. A claim not to be himself or a claim of dual identity
4. Referring to self as "we"
5. Change in ability to perform tasks
6. Denial of behavior that has been observed by others
7. Changes in vision, handwriting, style of dress
8. Drastic changes in behavior, unexplained outbursts, disorientation
9. Hearing voices
10. Loss of time
11. Drawing self as multiple persons
12. Describing self as "unreal at times, feels like an alien" (a mild form of this is not uncommon in typical adolescent experience)
13. Describing surroundings as becoming altered, feels remote from his environment
14. Getting lost coming home from school or from a friend's house

---

Case Example

Cognitive Processes (*WNL = Within Normal Limits for Age)

Estimated Developmental Level: WNL: ☐ **Yes**   ☒ **No, Describe:** <u>Should be moving toward more</u>
<u>abstraction, but thinking is very concrete and dependent on direct cues from the environment</u>

☐ **Sensorimotor**   ☐ **Pre-operational**   ☒ **Concrete Operations**   ☐ **Formal Operations**

Orientation:... WNL: ☒ Yes ☐ No, Disoriented: ☐ Time ☐ Place ☐ Person ☐ Purpose

Memory:....... WNL: ☒ Yes ☐ No, Impaired: ☐ Immediate ☐ Intermediate ☐ Long Term

Concentration: WNL: ☐ Yes ☒ No, Difficulty is: ☐ Severe ☐ Moderate ☒ Minimal

Abstraction: .. WNL: ☐ Yes ☒ No, Thinking is: ☒ Overly Concrete ☐ Overly Abstract

Intellect:....... WNL: ☐ Yes ☒ No, Intelligence is: ☒ Below Average ☐ Above Average

Judgment: ..... WNL: ☐ Yes ☒ No, Impaired: ☐ Severe ☒ Moderate ☐ Minimal

Insight:......... WNL: ☐ Yes ☒ No, Insight is: ☐ Absent ☒ Limited ☐ Above Average

Organization:. WNL: ☒ Yes ☐ No, Thinking is: ☐ Chaotic ☐ Loose ☐ Rigid

If No, Describe: _____

Hallucinations:....... ☒ No ☐ Yes, Type: ☐ Visual ☐ Auditory ☐ Other: _____

If Yes, Describe: _____

Delusions:............. ☒ No ☐ Yes, Type: ☐ Persecutory ☐ Grandiosity ☐ Other: _____

If Yes, Describe: _____

Trauma Symptoms:. ☒ No ☐ Yes, Type: ☐ Nightmares ☐ Flashbacks ☐ Alexithymia

☐ Reenactment Behaviors ☐ Disassociative Phenomena ☐ Other: _____

If Yes, Describe: _____

In Steven's case, he presents with below average intelligence, limited insight, mild concentration problems, is overly concrete for a 12-year-old, and demonstrates moderate impairment in his judgment, particularly relative to social situations. There is no evidence of psychotic processes or trauma symptoms.

Individual System: Mental Status Examination—Subjective Experience

Self-Concept

This term is often used to refer globally to several different but related aspects of the child's functioning. In the broadest and most abstract sense, self-concept refers to the child's identity. This includes everything from the sense of one's self as a separate and autonomous being to such concrete areas as gender or ethnic identity. The second aspect, often incorporated under the term self-concept, is the child's ability to describe accurately his or her characteristics and attributes. This area includes two subareas. One is the child's ability to describe his or her own likes, thoughts, characteristics, and so forth. The other is the child's ability to see himself or herself as others see him or her. The last aspect usually considered to be a part of self-concept is self-esteem. This is the appraisal one makes

of the characteristics noted in the other two areas. It is the positive or negative valuing of the self. Any or all of these aspects may be reviewed and presented in this section of the Workbook.

View of World

Whereas self-concept addresses the child's view of himself or herself, the view of the world addresses the child's perception of his or her context. In particular, this addresses the child's view of others and the degree to which others can make life satisfying or more difficult. Generally, does the child view the world as a safe place where needs get met, or as a place that is demanding or dangerous?

Three Wishes

The three wishes task is a simple projective tool. For this portion of the exam, children may be simply asked what three wishes they would make if they were given the opportunity. For younger children, a fantasy context can be created by having them imagine finding a magic lamp or encountering a good fairy. The responses give a glimpse into the child's fantasy life and often a clue to the child's unmet needs. This latter information is critical in setting treatment goals. Another approach is to ask children what they want to be when they grow up—again getting relevant information about the child's perception of his or her needs and desires.

Reality Testing

This is a somewhat confusing concept in that we tend to think of it as the degree to which the child is able to be logical and to think like an adult. But our reality testing and that of a 3-year-old are very different. Young children have a relatively hard time differentiating fact from fantasy. They believe in monsters, most things they see on television, and most things they are told by adults. They are in a word, concrete, and believe in things they can sense and in many things they can only imagine. This does not mean their reality testing is poor. It does mean that it will be much more difficult to assess deviations from the norm, as subtle distortions will be harder to detect.

In addition to assessing whether those things the child believes to be real are appropriate for his or her developmental level, it is also useful to assess the content of the child's fantasy material. Although it is common for young children to believe in Santa Claus and superheros, it is not common for them to believe that there are monsters living in the walls of their house that are able to read their thoughts and seduce them into misbehaving. With younger children, it is often such bizarre, frightening, or morbid content that signals the presence of poor reality testing.

One other issue to consider here is children's perception of their own and others' ability to control events in their lives. This is similar to the notion of locus of control, but we are conceptualizing it in a much broader and flexible manner. Does the child have a realistic sense of his or her ability to effect change in his or her environment? If not, is the child prone toward feelings of omnipotence or helplessness. Again, there will be considerable developmental variability on this dimension. Toddlers and preschoolers tend to see themselves as invincible and the absence of such feelings usually indicates significant problems. Similarly, adolescents tend toward feelings of omnipotence, although they are more likely to alternate these with episodes of helplessness. In any case, the degree to which the child's sense of control is realistic for a given situation should be assessed. A child who believes he or she has the power to make the caregiver stop drinking is going to be repeatedly frustrated. Alternatively, the child who believes he or she is helpless to stop peer teasing is likely to continue being a victim.

It is also important to assess the child's perception of others' power and control. Children who believe their parents have the power to cure their cancer but choose to let them suffer through chemotherapy instead will feel rejected and abused. Alternatively, children who believe their parents are totally unable to protect them from being abused by a relative will tend to feel completely helpless to the point of questioning the utility of maintaining a relationship with their caretakers. Such children are likely to withdraw into themselves believing that if their own parents are helpless then no other adult has a chance of being effective. Or they may desperately seek out those they feel may be able to protect them, including the abuser.

The child's ability to engage in developmentally appropriate reality testing will be one factor in determining how structured the play therapy sessions will have to be. The weaker the child's reality testing, the more likely a structured and organized play session will have a therapeutic effect. Additionally, children's ability to appropriately assign or assume control will determine how willingly and effectively they will be able to engage in the process of problem solving over the course of the treatment.

Case Example

Subjective Experience

Self Concept: Sees himself as "stupid and ugly"

View of World: Demanding, wanting more performance from him than he feels able to give, doesn't understand him. He wants to withdraw to avoid these demands.

3 Wishes: Wants to be a policeman when he grows up so he can be powerful and in control. Wishes he had lots of money.

Reality Testing: Thought content immature, appears to think of world in naive, wish fulfillment terms more derived from fantasy than a realistic appreciation of his social circumstances

Individual System: Mental Status Examination—Dangerous Behaviors

In addition to the areas just covered, all children should be interviewed with respect to the following critical areas: self-injury, suicidal ideation, aggression, homicidal ideation, sexually inappropriate behavior, and fire setting. Because of the significance of these, both the caretaker and the child should be asked directly about each, even if these seem unconnected to the presenting problem.

Self-Injurious/Destructive Behavior and Suicidality

When interviewing for suicidal ideation, it helps to have first identified one or more strong negative feelings that the child will admit to having experienced. The specific affect is not important. That is, it is not necessary for a child to report feeling depressed or sad to segue into a discussion of suicide. Many children report suicidal ideation in response to frustration or anger. In any case, the play therapist may begin by asking the child:

- Have you ever felt so (strong negative affect) that you felt like hurting yourself?
- Have you ever felt so (strong negative affect) that you wished you were dead?
- Have you ever felt so (strong negative affect) that you thought about making yourself dead, or killing yourself?

If the child gives a positive response to any of the above questions you should ask follow-up questions to probe for details.

- Have you ever actually hurt yourself? If so, what happened that made you do it? How did you do it? Do you think you would ever do it again?
- What kinds of things make you wish you were dead? What do you imagine other people doing or thinking if you were dead?
- What happened to make you think about killing yourself?
- Have you ever tried to kill yourself? Would you ever try it? (or Would you try again?)
- What would make you decide to kill yourself?
- How would you kill yourself?

A positive response to any of the questions regarding suicidal ideation should be taken seriously. Many adults tend to dismiss suicidal ideation in children saying that children do not fully understand death and so cannot formulate the intent to die. Our own clinical experience suggests the reverse. Because children do not fully understand the implications of dying, they are much less averse to the idea than are adults and often formulate the intent to die in response to relatively low-level stresses. In addition, their lack of understanding makes them prone to impulsive acting out and to selecting methods that are easily available and unpredictable in their lethality. A 5-year-old who threatens to run out in front of a car is in grave danger. His or her impulse control is very limited and the means selected is both available and potentially lethal. Adults also dismiss suicidal ideation in children as manipulative. Again, the lack of impulse control and judgment make for a dangerous combination that should be thoroughly evaluated so that adequate precautions can be taken. A subsequent discussion in this chapter on play interviewing describes features of play associated with suicidal risk.

Aggressive Behavior and Homicidality

The interview for homicidal intent follows the same format as the interview for suicidal intent. The questions are the same except that "hurting/killing someone" is substituted for "hurting/killing yourself." As with suicidal ideation, homicidal ideation should be taken seriously and treated immediately. Children's judgment and impulse control is not good, especially when in the midst of experiencing a strong emotion, and the risk to others can be very real.

When either suicidal or homicidal ideation is disclosed, the caretakers should be immediately informed and appropriate action taken to ensure the safety of those involved. The ability of the caretakers and the environment to keep the child and others safe must be evaluated and an immediate intervention plan designed. This response plan should be documented in the appropriate place in the Workbook. The use of behavior contracting as an intervention for suicidal and homicidal children is discussed in Chapter 8.

History of Sexually Inappropriate Behavior

This category includes both self- and other-directed sexual behavior that is not appropriate given the child's developmental level. Masturbation that is either excessive or situation-inappropriate would be included here, as would age-inappropriate sexual play. Sexual aggression toward others would also be included. If the child has been the victim of sexual abuse but is not acting out sexually, it is not included here, but rather should be noted under the review of the Legal Systems later in the Workbook. However, if the behavior is abuse-reactive secondary to a history of sexual abuse, then the behavior should be addressed here as well as in the Trauma Symptoms section.

History of Fire Setting

This section can be used to record anything from an unusual interest in fires to actual arson. Fire-setting incidents need not be serious to warrant concern. Setting the contents of a trash can on fire may reflect a potentially serious problem. This area is explored for two reasons. The main reason has to do with the suspected clinical association between fire setting and the more serious forms of psychopathology. This, especially when accompanied by bed-wetting and aggression toward animals, is seen as an indicator of the need for treatment. The other reason fire setting is important has to do with dangerousness. As with suicidal or homicidal ideation, the child who is setting fires may be a very poor judge of the potential dangerousness of his or her behavior. One child who started by setting some garbage on fire later set a small grass fire. The grass fire quickly burned out of control and a home was damaged. The child was truly distraught as he had no intention of doing any real property damage but had instead underestimated how dry the grass was and the direction of the wind.

C a s e   E x a m p l e

Dangerous Behavior

Self-Injurious Behavior or Ideation: ☒ **No**   ☐ **Yes, Describe:** _____

   Prior Acts or Ideation: ☒ **No**   ☐ **Yes, Describe:** _____

Suicidal Behavior or Ideation: ☒ **No**   ☐ **Yes, Describe:** (Include: imminence, plan, means, reality base,

dangerousness, etc.)**:** _____

   Prior Attempts or Ideation: ☐ **No**   ☒ **Yes, Describe:** <u>Although Steven denies currently wanting to</u>

<u>hurt or kill himself he has, in the past, made comments about killing himself to his teacher and his mother when</u>

<u>he was frustrated. He has never formulated a specific plan.</u>_____

   Family History of Suicide: ☒ **No**   ☐ **Yes, Describe:** _____

   Support/Response Plan: <u>None.</u>_____

Aggressive Behavior or Ideation: ☒ **No**   ☐ **Yes, Describe:** _____

   Target(s): ☐ **Property**   ☐ **Animals**   ☐ **Children**   ☐ **Adults. Describe:** _____

   Prior Acts or Ideation: ☒ **No**   ☐ **Yes, Describe:** _____

Homicidal Behavior or Ideation: ☒ **No**   ☐ **Yes, Describe:** (Include: imminence, plan, means, reality base,

dangerousness, etc.)**:** _____

   Target(s): _____

   Prior Attempts or Ideation: ☒ **No**   ☐ **Yes, Describe:** _____

   Family History of Violence: ☒ **No**   ☐ **Yes, Describe:** _____

   Support/Response Plan: _____

History of Sexually Inappropriate Behavior: ☒ **No**   ☐ **Yes, Describe:** _____

History of Fire Setting: ☒ **No**   ☐ **Yes, Describe:** _____

Individual System: Mental Status Examination—Observations of Play Behavior

The final piece of the Individual Systems Review is observations from the play session. There are several uses of play in the intake process. First, play is familiar to children and may help them feel more comfortable with the process. Second, play materials, such as drawing paper and crayons or puppets are media through which children may communicate what they are thinking or feeling. Third, the child's play in itself provides considerable information about the child's developmental functioning. And, last, clinically relevant information may be obtained both from the structure and the content of the child's play. How to structure and incorporate a play interview into the intake process is discussed in Chapter 3. Here, we address how to organize the developmental and clinical information obtained from the play interview. The amount of information that can be obtained from a play interview is large, and we will not attempt an exhaustive review here. The following discussion only addresses a few areas that we have found to be useful in our treatment planning.

Structure of Play

In their discussion of the use of a play interview in the Mental Status Examination, Goodman and Sours (1967/1994, pp. 80–86) identify several questions that the play therapist can ask about the child's play. The focus here is more on how the child plays than on what the content of the play symbolizes.

• **Initiation of play.** How does the child initiate play activities? Can the child maintain the play without steady reinforcement from the play therapist?

• **Integration of play.** Is the play goal-directed or fragmentary? Are there bizarre or idiosyncratic elements to the play?

• **Gender (culture) appropriateness.** Is the play consistent with what is expected for the gender of the child? Here, the play therapist must take precautions not to apply heterosexist or culturally biased standards to the evaluation of the child's play.

• **Creativity.** Is play imaginative or stereotyped? Is it amenable to improvisation?

• **Maturity.** Is form or content of play immature, age-appropriate, or precocious? Does the maturity of play shift depending on content of interview?

• **Mode and Intensity of Aggression.** Does the child throw, tear, or destroy toys? Is aggression random or does it have a purpose? Does child appear angry or impatient with play productions? Is the aggression projected into the play? Is child reluctant or unable to engage in aggressive themes? Is child a danger to others or playroom?

Representational Play

When developing an Ecosystemic Play Therapy treatment plan, it is important to assess the child's developmental level with respect to representational play. Westby (1991) gives an excellent discussion of the development of representational play in children. Three dimensions of the development of symbolic play are (a) decontextualization, or the ability to move play from life-size realistic props to miniature toys or the absence of props; (b) play themes, from everyday activities to totally invented situations; and (c) organization of play themes, from limited symbolic actions to sequentially organized play. For example, at 2 years old, a child would be expected to use lifelike props such as toy dishes, themes about everyday activities such as cooking, with short schema such as pretending to cook something and feeding it to himself or herself or to someone else. At 5 years old, children should be able to use small representational toys or create pretend sequences that may not even involve any toys and plan a complex sequence of pretend events that may be about events that the child has never experienced, such as flying to the moon in a spaceship.

Because we view play as an important medium for helping children to communicate with others and to reflect on their own experiences, it is important to know whether or not the child is capable of using play symbolically. Whereas most children have well-developed symbolic play skills by the age of 5, many children in play therapy may have experienced factors that interfered with the development of these play skills. The most insidious factors are developmental delays or learning disabilities that affect the child's use of internal language. These deficits may have resulted from neurologic problems, environmental neglect, or some combination thereof. These children may require direct modeling and structuring from the play therapist in order to develop symbolic play.

Trauma also interferes with symbolic play because the child becomes caught up in compulsively reenacting the trauma. Then, because the experience is isolated in memory from the parts of the brain involved in language processing, the trauma is never resolved and the child is unable to move on. Alternatively, the play materials make the child so anxious that he or she resists any kind of representational play at all. When this is the case, the play therapist will need to focus on establishing a secure relationship with the child before attempting to have the child work, even symbolically, with the traumatic material.

Mastery Motivation

The term, mastery motivation, has been used to refer to the inherent motivation in normal children to explore and attempt to master both the physical (e.g., toys) and social (e.g., other people) environments (Morgan, Maslin-Cole, Biringen, & Harmon, 1991). There are four aspects of mastery motivation that can be observed. The first is interest and curiosity. The second is the desire to engage in tasks that present some challenge. The third is persistence in attempting to master a given task. And the fourth is the experience of pleasure when the task is completed.

Children should demonstrate an interest in exploring their environment through play once they feel comfortable with the situation. A child who moves too quickly to the toys with little reaction to being in a new room with a new person may have attachment problems or impulsive behavior problems. A child who remains cautious and reluctant to explore may be anxious, depressed, traumatized, or disengaged from the environment because of limited stimulation and interaction with caregivers.

By the age of 4, children should indicate a preference for challenging tasks (Morgan, Maslin-Cole, Biringen, & Harmon, 1991). Children with learning problems are frequently uncomfortable with any type of challenge. They have experienced so much failure as a result of their disabilities that they often develop a strategy of avoiding challenging tasks as a way of coping. Overanxious children may have similar reactions but for different reasons. They usually have the cognitive ability to accomplish the task but are paralyzed by their fear of failure. This has significant adverse developmental implications because it will interfere with the acquisition of new skills. Children who have problems with task persistence may have attention deficit or impulse control problems. Depression has also been associated with children who show little pleasure when they master a task (Morgan, Maslin-Cole, Biringen, & Harmon, 1991).

Assessment of Suicide Risk

Pfeffer (1979) identifies four features of play that are associated with suicidal behavior in children: (a) reacting to separation from the caretaker by engaging in aggressive or risky play such as throwing objects or jumping off of high places, or, in older children, representational play in which the characters engage in dangerous behaviors; (b) using play objects in an abusive or violent way, themes of punishment, or throwing toys away; (c) engaging in play behaviors outside of the playroom that are reckless and place the child in a dangerous situation, such as jumping off of fire escapes; and (d) identifying with superheros such as Superman or Power Rangers when the characters actually get hurt or are in more dangerous, violent situations before getting rescued than is typical for most children. Although this content may be present in the play of nonsuicidal children, the play of suicidal children tends to be qualitatively more out-of-control, has less protection from realistic dangerous situations, and has a repetitive, compulsive quality to it that is resistant to play therapist's attempts at modification or interpretation.

Case Example

Observations of Play Behavior

During the play interview Steven engaged in some dollhouse play with the theme of being criticized by his stepfather. He was not able to develop the theme much and the organization of the play was very limited.

Dyadic System: The First 3 Years

The data gathered in this section will be used to answer the question What was the nature of the relationship between the child and his or her primary caretaker during the first 3 years of the child's life? This section reflects our own emphasis on early attachment and object relations. Our experience suggests that problems in the early caretaker–child relationship often underlie a large percentage of the problems children present later in life. This is an area that the play therapist may also specifically want to assess, and strategies for doing so are discussed in Chapter 5, Assessment.

Primary Caretaker(s)

It is important to identify the primary caretaker(s) in the child's life. This can be challenging if there have been nonparental caretakers involved in the child's life, such as a nanny or other relative. What is critical is to identify who spent most of the time meeting the child's basic needs, from whom did the child seek comfort when hurt or tired, and is there a difference between who the child might identify and who the caretaker might identify as the primary caretaker. It should be noted that quantity of contact does not guarantee that a relationship will become the primary caretaking rela tionship for the child. The child's choice of caretaker when distressed is the strongest indicator of who the child experiences as the primary attachment figure. It is also possible for a child to identify more than one person in his or her support network as primary attachment figures.

Significant Disruptions in the Primary Relationship

A second critical issue is whether or not there has been any disruption in the primary caretaking relationship. Although the focus of this section is the first 3 years, it should be noted that any major disruption or loss of a primary attachment in the first 7 years usually has far-reaching effects on the mental health of that child (Bowlby, 1980). Look not only for actual disruptions that led to separation, such as death, divorce, parental military service, or hospitalization of child or caretaker, but also for emotional disruptions. One of the most common is when the caregiver becomes less emotionally available to the child because of the death of the primary caregiver's caregiver (e.g., maternal grand-mother).

If the therapist has not asked earlier, this is a good time to ask whether the mother had any pregnancies that did not go to term during this period. Many women will not spontaneously report miscarriages or even the death of an infant. This may be either the result of a defensive psychic operation or the fact that most interviews about family structure are conducted in the present tense so that there is a tendency to omit important persons who were a part of the family system for only a short while at some point in the past. Whatever the reason, the occurrence of failed pregnancies often results in a period of time when the mother was physically and/or emotionally unavailable to the other children. Like any other type of disruption, this can have negative effects on the primary relationship. Aside from the reasons that the pregnancy may not have been mentioned, this type of disruption may not be reported because of the caretaker(s) feelings of guilt regarding the time they were unavailable to the client.

First Year

The critical task in the first year is to establish secure attachment or basic trust. We have assessed this by examining what the child brings to the relationship and what the caretaker brings. The child component is assessed by asking the caretaker to describe the baby. The caretaker component is assessed by asking for the parental subjective experience of the relationship (caretaker's internal model). Finally, one of the key ways to assess the quality of the attachment relationship during the first year is the affective reciprocity between caretaker and child. Could the baby accept and receive affection? Did the baby spontaneously seek affection? How comfortable was the caretaker with responding to these affective needs? We recognize that this assessment may not reflect the actual relationship at the time the child was a baby, as it is based on the caretaker's current perception of that early relationship, but it does provide us with some clues.

Case Example

DYADIC SYSTEM: FIRST 3 YEARS

Primary Caretaker(s): <u>Mother</u>

Significant Disruptions in the Primary Relationship: ☐ **No** ☒ **Yes, Describe:** <u>When Steven was 1 year old his maternal grandmother died and his parent's marriage broke up. Mother identifies this as a period of time when she was depressed but she felt that she remained emotionally invested in Steven because she believed he needed her.</u>

First Year

   Type of Baby: <u>Mother described Steven as happy but not as responsive to his environment and others as she expected him to be. She began to question her pediatrician about these observations but was repeatedly told that Steven was fine.</u>

   Description of Bonding (Parental experience of relationship to the child)**:** <u>Mother reports feeling very "bonded" to Steven from the time of his birth. Her feelings intensified by his hospitalization at 17 days of age when she feared he would die and was very grateful when he did not.</u>

   Affective Responsiveness of Child to Parent: <u>Mother describes him as a loving child who sought and accepted affection easily from both her and the other significant people in his life.</u>

Second and Third Years

The attachment relationship during the second and third years becomes more complicated, adding autonomy issues to the basic trust issues. Again, we ask for a description of the child and the caretaker's subjective experience of the relationship during this stage. Strivings for autonomy are represented in the child's desire to explore his or her physical and social world. The attachment relationship contributes to the child's willingness to explore and comfort with exploring his or her world. As the child strives for autonomy, the issues of limits and control become more pronounced and can be reflected in how potty training and discipline are handled during this stage. It is also useful to gather information about how the child reacted to these new limits and how the caretakers felt or feel about their own ability to manage the child.

Finally, separation and reunion experiences are windows to the quality of the attachment relationship. Day care and preschool provide typical experiences in which the child and caretaker have to cope with separations and reunions. Again, it is useful to gather information about what the child did, what the caretaker did, and how the caretaker felt about it. In particular, did the child protest separations? Did the protest lessen when the child felt more comfortable in the new situation? Did the child seek and accept comfort upon reunion?

Case Example

Second & Third Years:

Type of Toddler: Mother reports that Steven was hyperactive and rocked excessively from the ages of 2 to 6.

Description of Relationship to Caretaker: Steven is reported to have been very dependent on his mother, wanting to have her close at all times. She experienced this as his needing her and primarily responded by being protective and loving though she felt a little tied down.

Description of Relationship to Other Family Members: Older sister reported to be tolerant with him and he followed her around at times

Description of Child's Exploratory Behavior: Steven was never an active explorer of his environment. He preferred to stay close to his mother and to have her help him explore and learn. He quickly became frustrated when trying to learn new things.

How was Toilet Training Implemented? Mother tried to use encouragement and accepted his mistakes.

    What was Child's Response? Steven has not yet fully accomplished toileting and seems to find the process a very difficult one.

What Type of Discipline was Used? Even though Steven's developmental delays were not diagnosed until he was 6 years old his mother indicates that she sensed something was wrong long before this and geared her management of him toward tolerance and acceptance of his behavior. At the same time she tried to establish a protective environment where the routine was consistent and he was not placed in difficult situations such as daycare or with a baby sitter. She did not use physical punishment. Although she reports that Steven's stepfather is much more critical he has not resorted to corporal punishment either.

    What was Child's Response? By temperament, he was easy going as long as he experienced no demands. He responded to demands with tantrums and confusion which often led to a reduction in the demands, particulary on his mother's part.

Separations/Reunions

    Attended Daycare/Preschool: ☒ **No**   ☐ **Yes, Describe:** Although his older sister attended preschool when she was 4 years old Steven's mother chose not to send him because he had such difficulty being separated from her.

Child's Reaction to Separation & Reunion: Steven became very upset if his mother was not available or left him for even a short time. He cried and tantrumed. He immediately sought comfort from his mother upon her return but took a long time to settle down.

Parent's Response to Child's Reaction: Steven's mother responded to his distress by avoiding being away from him as much as possible.

Observations of Child–Caretaker Interactions

The current dyadic relationship contains the seeds of the early relationship and illustrates the degree to which that relationship has evolved as the caretaker and child have developed. The following section suggests observations of the current dyadic relationships that can be made while keeping in mind the earlier developmental context of those relationships. Carson and Goodfield (1988, p. 118–119) identified 13 clusters of questions for the clinician to ask himself or herself when observing a child and caretaker to develop a profile of the attachment relationship between them:

• Does the child show protest behavior at separation from the primary caregiver? Does he show any response at being separated from a person who has provided him with nurturance and security?

• Does the child have difficulty tolerating emotional intimacy, instead seeking objects as an expression of caretaking? Is it more important to this child that she have an object given to her than an emotional response from the person taking care of her?

• Does the child engage in molding with the primary caretakers? (Molding refers to what an infant will do when he relaxes while being held by an adult.)

• Does the child show affection spontaneously? Will the child initiate a hug, a kiss, or a touch?

• Does the child seek affection in an indiscriminate manner? Does the child show selective preference toward adults?

• Does the child respond with satisfaction to adult intervention? Does he look for others to help him when he needs help? Does he show pleasure in the attention given him?

• Is the child clingy? Does the child allow the adult to have any body space? Does she seem to get enough gratification from the adult to permit her to separate even briefly?

• Is the child able to engage, unsupervised, in age-appropriate play? Can he get along with peers? Does he wish to have peer interaction or does an adult have to be present to intervene and set limits?

• Is the child free to explore the environment? Is she curious about the world around her? Is she free to learn in school? Does she take pleasure in new challenges and tasks?

• Can the child assimilate and utilize new information? Does he learn from experience? Does he retain information?

• Does the child show empathy? Is she responsive to the emotions of others?

• Can the child enjoy successful or pleasurable experiences without engaging in negative behavior afterward? Can he allow himself to have a good time? Does he seek to destroy pleasurable interchange?

• Does the child imitate other children's behaviors that she sees reinforced by adult approval? Can she spontaneously initiate behaviors based on a sense of herself? Can she use her behavior as a means toward achieving positive recognition?

Case Example

Observations of Child–Caretaker Interactions

Steven's interactions with his mother are noted to be similar to that of a preschool child rather than a 13 -year- old. He sat close to her, made physical contact by touching her arm, and looked to her to help him answer questions. He became restless, avoided eye contact with her and tried to change the subject when she talked about some of his difficulties. She responded to his discomfort by going along with the change in topic in order to reduce his distress.

Family System

From an ecosystemic perspective, full understanding of the problems that bring a child to play therapy requires an understanding of the historical, developmental, and ecosystemic context. For children in particular, the most influential system is the family. The developmental and historical contexts influence the child at both the individual and the familial level. Here, the play therapist attempts to get a sense of the family's current structure, past experiences, specific subsystem functioning and effect, developmental status, social context, and identification. During the interview and observation of the family system, the play therapist gathers information about the family's understandings of and reactions to the child's problem, as well as the dynamics of the family system that are revealed in the interactions. Each of these areas is addressed in detail in the following sections.

Family System: Genogram

The genogram gives the play therapist a visual representation of the family structure and history. A sample of the formats and symbols used to represent various familial relationships is included in the Workbook. For additional information on creating genograms, see McGoldrick & Gerson, *Genograms in Family Assessment* (1985). The genogram should go back at least two generations and include all first-order relatives to provide as clear a picture of the family as possible. There are several items that should be specifically noted on the genogram.

1. All family members should be included. This means that you may have to ask directly about miscarriages, stillborn infants, and children who died in infancy. Often, families do not mention these members as they are not currently a part of the family.

2. It may be useful to include unrelated persons who live in the same household as part of the genogram. Again, this will give a more complete picture of the family and the nature of their relationships.

3. Any hereditary or recurring illness, both medical and mental, should be noted. If necessary, the genogram should be expanded to show how these individuals fit into the family tree.

4. Intergenerational child abuse and/or substance abuse and/or mental illness should also be noted.

Case Example

FAMILY SYSTEM

Genogram [Complete by Hand]

Family System: Family Functioning and History

Current Family Relationships and Dynamics

To begin, we need a clear picture of the current family context for the child client. This means knowing with whom the child is living, who else is living there, if this is not the child's family of origin, where is that family and how did the child come to be with this family, and so forth. It is important that family relationships be clearly defined especially with respect to maternal and paternal relationships. For example, if it is noted that the children are living with their grandparents, does this refer to mother's parents or to father's parents?

Family History

We need to gather information about the family history, particularly with respect to major events, losses, and changes, such as relocations or the addition of a grandparent to the family home. Because children respond to these events and changes differently depending on their developmental stage at the time the event occurred, it is important to anchor these events in time relative to the child's age. This section refers specifically to the child's family situation and not to the caretaker's family history, which is addressed in the next section on extended family.

Extended Family History

Information about the extended families is useful for several reasons. One, it is important to understand how the extended family is currently involved with the child client and his or her family. Also, because many caretakers bring their own histories of being parented into parenting relationships with their children, information about their family-of-origin experiences may be helpful. How much you decide to focus on this area when gathering the initial intake information depends on how much the presenting problem seems to be related to family-of-origin issues. It is always possible to explore this area later if it becomes apparent that it has a significant effect on the problems.

For example, I had a case in which the presenting problem was a drop in grades for a 12-year-old child over the previous 6 months. I met with the child and the family and gathered information from the school but something seemed to be missing. As it turned out, the maternal grandmother had moved into the home approximately 8 months earlier and was providing after school care for the child. She was an alcoholic and extremely critical of the child. One family session that included the grandmother provided a clear picture of the destructive interaction between this grandparent and the child for both the play therapist and the caretakers. The caretakers immediately made changes in the environment to limit the contact this grandparent had with the child and provided the child with messages to counteract the critical negative messages she had been getting from the grandmother. The parents were referred to Al-Anon resources in the community. Within a month, the child was doing better in school and play therapy was discontinued.

Case Example

Family Functioning & History

Current Family Relationships & Dynamics: Steven lives with his mother and sister. Both of them are protective toward him and tolerant of his behavior because of his cognitive limitations. Recently, his socially inappropriate behaviors have reached a point where both are becoming frustrated with him. Steven identifies his stepfather as his "new" dad and continues to do so although Mr. and Mrs. G separated about 6 months ago. Besides the nuclear family Steven has some contact with his paternal grandparents and frequent contact with his maternal aunts and uncles who serve as a source of emotional support for the family.

Family History: (Include changes in family membership &/or home location, major events, significant losses, and support system) Steven's mother and father began having problems during the mother's pregnancy with Steven because the father was ambivalent about having another child. Although they did not divorce until Steven was about a year old Steven's father was never more than minimally emotionally involved with him. Mr. J has had no contact with Steven or his sister for several years. In addition to the marital problems the first 2 years of Steven's life were chaotic. There were frequent moves and the death of his maternal grandmother. His mother remarried when Steven was 5 years old. Mr. and Mrs. G separated about 6 months ago but maintain frequent contact due to some mutual business interests. When he was living at home Mr. G was not very tolerant of Steven's behavior and was verbally critical. Steven expresses a combination of loss and relief (due to reduced criticism) since Mr. G moved out of the home.

Extended Family History: No information was available regarding the paternal extended family. Mrs. G's parents divorced when she was 8 years old due to her father's alcoholism. Mrs. G is the youngest of 2 brothers and 2 sisters. She maintained close contact with her mother until her death due to cardiac problems when Steven was 1-1/2 years old. The family maintains regular contact with mother's siblings but they do not live in the local area.

Sibling, Spousal, and Occupational Subsystems

Healthy families include at least four systems or roles even when they consist of only one child and one adult. These systems or roles govern the nature of the interactions between family members and are critical for healthy functioning of the family as well as the growth and development of the child. The four essential systems or roles are individual, sibling, parental, and spousal. Possible additional systems include grandparental, biologically unrelated household member, and so forth.

The individual system or role includes those rules that govern the functioning of the individual within the family system. These include everything from how actual personal space is allocated to how the family responds to the thoughts and feelings of its members. Each person must be able to have his or her own space, thoughts, and feelings without suffering sanctions imposed by other family members. A child must be allowed to be angry with a peer without bringing down the wrath of his or her caretakers. Similarly, a caretaker must be allowed time to recover from a bad day at work before being subjected to the full force of the emotional and physical demands of his or her children. The degree to which such physical and emotional space is given varies enormously from one family to another and from one culture to another, but it is always present in some form when the family is functioning well.

The spousal system includes the rules governing the interaction between adult members of the household. The rules specify the conditions for emotional and sexual intimacy. These rules should remain operational even if there is only one adult in the household. The rules governing the spousal role protect children from becoming the emotional and sexual intimates of their caretakers. They are protected from having to meet the adult needs of their caretakers and are allowed to maintain their dependent status. Ideally, the single adult caretaker will find ways to meet his or her adult needs for emotional and physical intimacy with other adults rather than with the child.

The parental system or role includes those rules that structure the interaction between adult caretakers and children. The adult assumes responsibility for the welfare of the children. The children are allowed to be dependent on their caretaker. The caregiver makes the rules, the children follow the rules. At the core of the caretaker role is the ability to act effectively and consistently in the best interests of the child. This role defines the boundaries that exist between the adults and the children from the adults' perspective.

As with the spousal role, a sibling role exists even if the child is an only child, for the sibling role governs the interactions between children in the family. Much like the spousal role, the sibling role specifies the level of emotional intimacy and caretaking that occurs between the children. Issues and behaviors associated with the effects of birth order are a subset of the sibling system or role. The role defines the boundaries that exist between the children, as a group, and the caretakers from the children's perspective. For example, from an only child's perspective the sibling role includes those emotional and behavioral interactions that would never be engaged in with an adult caretaker even if no other children are readily available. An only child may bring a friend or relative in to meet the essential elements of the sibling role.

In addition to the parental and spousal subsystem roles, the adults in the family have occupational roles and responsibilities. Whether the work is done in or outside of the home. Satisfactory functioning in this role, both in terms of concretely meeting the family's basic physical needs and in terms of experienced satisfaction with one's occupational role has an effect on the child's experience of stress and support within the family.

When assessing the existence and nature of any of these roles, the play therapist must keep in mind that all of these are subject to significant variability. The roles are defined by the nature of the individuals that fill them and by the community, cultural, and historical context in which they exist. There is no one right or best structure or set of rules for the operation of any of these systems. Families are endlessly creative in developing effective structures and ways of functioning. The play therapist should ascertain the nature of those structures but not impose a value judgment based on the degree to which they meet a predetermined model. Rather, the play therapist needs to assess the degree to which the structure allows each member of the family to get his or her needs met consistently in ways that do not sub-stantially interfere with the ability of others to get their needs met.

In keeping with the ecosystemic perspective of the interdependency between the child's functioning (presenting problems) and the functioning of the systems in which the child is embedded, the following information is gathered with respect to each of these subsystems: What is the role of the subsystem in the presenting problem? What is the effect of the presenting problem on that subsystem? Although these questions are specifically directed at the subsystems of the family, they represent the overarching goals of the ecosystemic review of all systems.

Case Example

Sibling Subsystem

Relationships with Siblings: <u>Steven's older sister is protective of him. He admires her and wants to spend time with her.</u>

Role of Siblings in the Presenting Problem: <u>To some degree Steven's sister may be overprotecting him and not giving him enough feedback about the social inappropriateness of his behavior.</u>

Impact of the Presenting Problem on Siblings: <u>Steven's sister is sometimes distressed when he exhibits enuresis, encopresis or tantrums in front of her friends when they visit.</u>

Spousal Subsystem

Persons in Spousal System: <u>Mr. and Mrs. G.</u>

Current Problems: ☐ **No** ☒ **Yes, Describe:** <u>Although separated Mr. and Mrs. G are currently getting along fairly well.</u>

History of Problems: ☐ **No** ☒ **Yes, Describe:** <u>Mr. and Mrs. G separated about 6 months ago due to problems in their emotional communication and differences in their discipline styles.</u>

Role of Spousal Difficulties in the Presenting Problem: <u>The conflict between Mr. and Mrs. G with regard to discipline has created increased stress for Steven.</u>

Impact of the Presenting Problem on Spousal Relationship: <u>Steven's difficulties contributed to marital stress and is named as one of the factors leading to the separation.</u>

Significant Adults' Current Occupational Functioning

Adult 1: <u>Mrs. G</u>   **Employed:** ☐ **No** ☒ **Yes, Describe:** <u>Manager of a mini-market.</u>

Occupational History/Problems: <u>None. Has been promoted regularly over the years.</u>

Role of Occupational Difficulties in the Presenting Problem: <u>None.</u>

Impact of the Presenting Problem on Occupational Functioning: <u>None.</u>

Social Network

Family social functioning addresses the degree to which the family is "open" or "closed" with respect to being able to use others in their support network. This is a critical factor when assessing the ecosystemic resources that a family brings to treatment. In particular, to what degree is the family able to use others as sources of information, support, and play? Sources of support may include the family's extended family, church community, ethnic community, and friendships. Identification of the family's social support system provides the play therapist with information about the vulnerability of the family and about potential re-sources that may be used in assisting the family. A family system that is relatively isolated from social support, that is, "closed," is at greater risk of having problems when attempting to negotiate both normal developmental tasks, such as a child entering adolescence, and external crises, such as job loss. They have fewer resources for coping with stress and are at greater risk for abusive behavior.

Sometimes families are not only isolated from social support networks but when they do engage, the interactions are problematic. A family who reports that they have conflicts with their neighbors and with people at church provide evidence that they may have problems relating in a nonconflictual way with people in general.

Case Example

Social Network

Social Support: The maternal relatives serve as the primary support system for the family. Mrs. G also has a network of friends from work.

Problems in Social Network: None.

Family System: Family Development

Understanding the particular stage or stages of family development that a family is negotiating at this time is important because families are at greater risk of developing problems during transitions between stages (Kilpatrick and Hollard, 1995; Zilbach and Gordetsky, 1994). Stages of development refer not only to the family as a whole, but also to transitions within the subsystems and to individual members of the family. For example, a family with caretakers in their early forties, a child entering adolescence, and a young child preparing to enter school are coping with three fairly divergent developmental transitions. The caretakers may be coping with the physiological changes of getting older and reviewing their career goals. At the same time, they are coping with developmental tasks traditionally experienced by younger caretakers as their child transitions into school. Finally, they are faced with the developmental task of assisting their adolescent child toward developing an integrated sense of himself or herself as an individual moving toward adulthood. Questions that the play therapist might explore are What stage or stages of family development is this family currently negotiating? Are they in a transition stage?

Case Example

Family Development

The major transition this family is facing is Steven's adjustment to middle school and his physical development as his body matures. His sister has already made a successful transition into high school.

Family System: Familial Identification

With respect to familial identification, it is important that the play therapist understands the way in which the family views and labels itself as opposed to the ways others might categorize or label it. Families may have a distinctive feature such as physical appearance or a family name that subjects them to labeling by others. They themselves may not embrace such an identification and may even find the discrepancy between other's attributions and their own experience to be a source of conflict. Two areas receive special attention in the Workbook, familial ethnocultural identification and religious affiliation.

Race is not treated separately but is incorporated under the concept of ethnocultural identity. This is because race is neither a scientifically accurate nor a socially valid basis for grouping people in the majority of situations. Even on a genetic basis there is more variability within racial groups than between them. Most individuals, professionals included, are unaware that there are only three racial groups: Caucasoid, Negroid, and Mongoloid. People frequently confuse race and ethnicity. For example, they will label Anglo or Euro-Americans as Caucasians, and Hispanic Americans as Hispanics or Latinos when both are, in fact, Caucasian. Furthermore, in most cases, it is one's ethnic or cultural identity that is the most powerful lens through which one views the world. A Black man raised in an African village may no more share the world view of a Black man raised in the United States than does any particular White man. For this reason, we have chosen to focus on the ethnocultural identification of families rather than on their racial identity.

We also allow for a very broad definition of ethnicity or culture, viewing them as roughly equivalent. "Culture is a set of beliefs, attitudes, values and standards of behavior that are passed from one generation to the next" (Abney, 1996, p. 409). Culture organizes our experience. It is the lens through which we view the world. To some extent every identifiable group has a culture if it continues to exist across generations. This implies that gays and lesbians have a culture because they have a set of beliefs, attitudes, values, and standards of behavior that are passed across generations and that only slowly yield to the changes brought on by the passage of historical time. Similarly, it can be said that there is a culture, of sorts, associated with having a particular physical deformity or problem in the United States. There are specific social groups and networks that exist to support persons with various illnesses and disabilities, and there exists within these groups expectations as to the "right" way to think and behave as a member of that group. In any case, the existence of a cultural group with which the individual or family can

be linked makes no difference if they do not see themselves as members of that group.

The need to assess and understand a family's ethnocultural and religious identification cannot be overestimated. This includes not only their current identification and level of involvement, but also the caretakers' religious involvement within their families of origin. Religion can have a powerful influence on behavior and feelings about one's behavior because of its strong link with values and expectations. Many holidays and family rituals have religious meanings. Changing religions, abandoning one's religion, or entering into a religiously mixed relationship all have implications concerning the degree of support and stress the family may experience.

Useful questions for gathering information from the caretakers about the cultural and religious identifications of their family include

- Of what ethnic, religious, cultural, or social groups are you or your family members?
- Do you or your family ascribe to a particular cultural or ethnic identification?
- How do you think membership in that group affects the operation of your family and the way in which you raise your children?
- As you have identified several groups, which do you think is most influential on a day-to-day basis?
- What holidays or rituals commonly associated with that group do you or your family celebrate or observe?
- Do you see a difference in the ethnic identities of your family of origin, your present family, and the identities of your children?

With children, it may be useful to follow up on the questions about family holidays and rituals and the differences the children perceive between their own identity and that of their caretakers or family. In any case, it is important to remember that the purpose of this section of the Workbook is to establish the family's subjective ethnocultural identification as opposed to an objective classification. We are most interested in the way in which the child and the family view themselves, because this identification will form one of the most powerful lenses through which they view the world and understand their experiences.

Case Example

Familial Identification

Familial Ethnocultural Identification: <u>Family self-identifies as Anglo-American with no strong ties to any</u> <u>specific cultural heritage. They identify more with being of the "working class."</u>

Familial Religious Affiliation (Identification and degree of involvement)**:** <u>Protestant. The family is not and has</u> <u>never been actively involved in the church.</u>

Family System: Observations of the Family System

Assessment of the child's problem in the context of the family is critical both to understanding the problem and to developing a treatment plan that addresses the family system's role in contributing to the problem as well as the family's potential for serving as a resource. A family interview is the most efficient and effective way to gather this information even if the plan for future treatment does not involve family play therapy. Strategies for initiating and structuring a family interview as a part of the intake process were discussed in Chapter 3. Here, we address how to organize the content and interactional information obtained from the family interview. It is important to consider this information in the context of the child's problems and needs.

Content

One purpose of the family interview is to obtain information about the familial view of the problem as perceived by each of its members. Specifically, how does the problem affect each member of the family and how do they think the problem can or should be solved? In addition to problem exploration, it is useful to explore the strengths of the family as perceived by the different members. Additional content might include how the family handles discipline, how they play, what a typical day is like, and how they handle feelings.

Interactions

While the family is responding to the content of the interview, the play therapist can observe the process through which they accomplish this task. Who talks first? Who interrupts? Who allies themselves with whom? Do their interactions match their perceptions of the ways in which their family functions? What is the emotional atmosphere of the family? What is the child's experience of the family? What is the family's experience of the child? Would the play therapist want to live in this family?

Case Example

Observations of the Family System

During the family interview Steven sat between his mother and sister. Their stepfather sat some distance away. Mr. G expressed some frustration with Steven's problems but, for the most part, did not seem emotionally involved with any of the family members. When problems were discussed Steven tried to change the subject and/or moved closer to his mother. Both his mother and sister supported his attempts to change the subject but returned to the task at hand when redirected by the therapist. Both Steven's mother and sister had difficulty identifying the effect of Steven's problems on their lives, instead, they focused on their concerns for Steven. At the same time both indicated that they were involved with their own pursuits (friends, school/work) independent of the problems in the family.

In the remaining system reviews, the current functioning of the child within each system is addressed, followed by the history of the child's functioning within that system. Most of the sections are structured to allow for the inclusion of information about the functioning of family or non-family members other than the child in the system. Although the introduction of family material is useful and at times critical to understanding the dynamics of a case, it should be recognized that when the Workbook is included in a case file it becomes a legal document. If it is subpoenaed, it may be inappropriate or even illegal for explicit information about another person to be present in the record. For example, a play therapist might include information about a parent's medical history that was obtained from confidential medical records in the Workbook. If the caregiver later releases the play therapist's records to another party, he or she has inadvertently released his or her medical records as well. This type of secondary disclosure of information has been challenged in court and the professionals involved have been held liable. Therefore, the play therapist should follow two basic guidelines when including information about family members in the child's record. One is to include only information that is directly relevant to the child's presenting problem and treatment. Although much of the family history may be interesting, it does not necessarily belong in a mental health record. When information about another family member is included, specific reference should be made as to why that material is important in terms of understanding and treating the child. The other guideline is to include the information with reference to how the individual is related to the child rather than using the individual's name, such as "maternal uncle in jail for drug dealing."

Social System

For the most part, this section is self-explanatory. Problems with peers should include both acting-out problems and problems in which the child is socially withdrawn. If possible, gather information about the motivations behind the child's peer interactions. Is the child trying to engage but being impulsive or immature and therefore unsuccessful? Is the child interested in relationships but fearful of rejection? Or is the child avoidant and disinterested in social engagement?

When addressing the child's history of social functioning, it is important to identify any significant changes over time. This may be particularly relevant if the possibility of abuse is being considered or if there has been a significant trauma or loss in the child's life. It also provides information that is useful from a prognostic standpoint, because the child who has relatively intact functioning at some time in his or her life has a greater potential for returning to that level of functioning with less intensive intervention. On the other hand, the child who has limited social skills in general may require specific interventions to address the social skill deficits in addition to addressing any trauma-related issues.

The items covering sexual history are included in recognition of the fact that children are engaging in sexual relations at ever younger ages. This section is not meant to include sexually abusive relationships; those should be included in the review of the legal systems. As with inquiries about hallucinations, suicidal ideation, and homicidal ideation, play therapists should routinely ask about the sexual behavior of at least most preadolescent and older children. Such questions usually follow fairly smoothly if the child reports an ongoing and emotionally significant relationship with a peer. Several cautions are warranted here:

1. You must present questions regarding sexual behavior in a tone that is no different from that used to ask about other behaviors. Most of us, including children, are so sensitized to sexually related content that we shut down at the slightest hint of discomfort.

2. Do not assume a heterosexual orientation on the part of all your clients. Many gay and lesbian adults report knowing as early as age 7 or 8 that they were physically attracted to members of the same sex. Inquire about same-sex sexual contacts in the same direct way you ask about heterosexual contacts.

3. Be sure to ask about involuntary sexual contact with peers when and if you inquire about other sexually abusive interactions. Many play therapists see the signs of sexual abuse in their clients but dismiss the possibility if they fail to uncover an adult perpetrator. I have worked with several young adolescents who were raped by peers and recent research shows a preponderance of adolescent offenders (Barbaree, Marshall and Hudson, 1993). Sibling sexual abuse is also becoming more recognized (Wiehe, 1990).

Potential Interview Format: Caretaker

The following questions may be useful for obtaining information about the child's sexual behavior.

- *Does your child have one peer to whom he or she seems particularly attached?*
- *What sorts of information regarding sex and sexual behavior have you provided your child?*
- *Have you noticed any signs that your child may be sexually active?*
- *If your child were sexually active would he or she tell you about it? Would you want him or her to do so?*

Potential Interview Format: Child

The use of what is sometimes referred to as a stress interview is discussed at some length later in this chapter with respect to gathering data about substance abuse. Stress interview techniques also tend to work well when asking about sexual behavior. The basic technique involves phrasing questions so that they convey the assumption that the behavior occurs, requiring the client to respond to undo the question if the assumption is incorrect. In this context, the play therapist would not ask, "Do you masturbate?" but rather, would ask, "How often do you masturbate?" or, "Do you masturbate more than twice a day?" A series of such questions can be used to pursue the amount and type of sexual behavior in which the child has engaged. This level of inquiry need not be pursued with every client, but our experience is that it is too often excluded because of the play therapist's discomfort rather than because it is not relevant to the client's presenting problems.

- *Tell me what your parents have told you about sex.*
- *Besides what they have told you, what else do you know about sex?*
- *When you are with your friend, X, how often do the two of you: kiss, touch each others bodies, have sex, and so forth?*

Observations of Peer Interactions

Observation of the child with peers is most likely if a visit to the school has been built into the initial assessment. If peer relationships are a significant problem area actual observation of the child with his or her peers can be an invaluable part of the treatment planning process.

Case Example

SOCIAL SYSTEM

Current Social Functioning

Close Friends: ☒ **No**   ☐ **Yes, Describe** (Number/Duration): _____

Problems with Peers: <u>Peers tend to see Steven as immature and to avoid him or make fun of him. He is interested in interacting but has few expectations for success with his peers so he focuses his energies on adults who are more tolerant of his behavior.</u>

Problems with Adults: <u>When Steven feels that authority figures are being critical or making unreasonable demands he withdraws, cries, tantrums or becomes enuretic or encopretic.</u>

Past Social Functioning

Problems with Peers: <u>Steven has never had any close friends.</u>

Problems with Adults: <u>Steven gets along with most adults unless they demand that he perform which is the case with most of his teachers. Steven's problems with teachers have become more pronounced over the past year since his transition to a larger middle school.</u>

Interpersonal/Sexual History

Involved in Significant Intimate Relationship: ☒ **No**   ☐ **Yes, Describe:** _____

Problems in Sexual Relationship: _____

Problems in Previous Relationships: _____

Observations of Peer Interactions

<u>Steven was not observed in direct interaction with his peers at the time of the intake interview.</u>

Educational System

The review of the educational system is fairly self-explanatory. It is useful to take the time during the initial interview to get the names and phone numbers of relevant people from the school, such as the child's teacher and counselor, to be able to contact these people should the play therapist decide that it is appropriate to the treatment plan. One of the strengths of the Workbook is that it provides easy access to this type of important information. It should go without saying that whenever the play therapist makes contact with any part of the ecosystem outside of the child and nuclear family, he or she must obtain the proper releases of information from the individuals with the legal right to give that permission. It is useful to obtain some degree of assent or agreement from the child as well.

Many children who come for mental health treatment are already involved in the special education system at their school. Often, children with learning problems tend to have problems getting along with others and have self-esteem problems that put them at risk for emotional problems. Furthermore, children with abusive histories often have learning problems because of a neglectful environment and/or emotional interference with their learning. One advantage relative to the intake process with a child who is already involved in the special education system is that there should be readily accessible assessment data that can be obtained with a release from the school and can then be included in the Workbook in Part III, "Assessment Data."

If the child is not involved in special education services, it is important to identify whether he or she is experiencing any interference with academic functioning that has not been recognized by the school. Sometimes it may be that the child's emotional problems are directly related to problems at school. At other times, the traumatic events in a child's life may be affecting his or her ability to be available for learning (e.g., concentration problems, low frustration tolerance, disassociative experiences) and the school may be unaware or may not recognize a relationship between the outside events and the child's performance in school. Regardless, it is important to recognize the interdependent effect of school on the child's emotional functioning and the effect of the child's emotional functioning on academic functioning, and, where appropriate, to build interventions into the treatment plan that address these problems. Beyond being a source of problems for the child, the school may also be a resource and a source of support.

School Placement History

The school placement history provides information about the stability of the child's academic experience. It is important to determine whether changes are due to the child's behaviors and needs, to family changes in residence, and/or to school district routines. The play therapist should ask about changes in schools directly, as many caretakers fail to mention those changes that are local or that are part of the routine. For example, one child attended a school where the district boundaries were changed, requiring mid-year school changes for many children. The caretakers did not report this during the intake because it was not something related to specific events in the family's history so its importance was overlooked.

The play therapist should also gather information about other transition points common in the client's school:

• Do the children move to a different building or catchment area at specific grades?
• Is this a district with an elementary school, junior and senior high school arrangement, one in which children move directly from elementary to high school, or one with a middle school arrangement?
• Does the client's school follow the district sequence of changes or is it somehow idiosyncratic?

For example, one child I saw moved to another building on a different campus for just the fifth and sixth grades simply because of space limitations at that particular school as opposed to the organization of the district as a whole. Although most of these transitions are experienced by all of the children in a given school, making them less traumatic for any one child, they are still worth noting for their potential disruption of the client's academic and social progress.

In taking the school history, it is also important to be aware of transitions that occur within the client's specific school program, even if the child stays in the same school system for his or her entire education. In the Workbook, grades K, 1, 3, and 6 are given special attention because they mark common shifts in children's school experiences across American school districts.

Kindergarten used to mark children's entry into the school system, and for many it was their first experience with a structured program that required they interact with peers for a sustained period of time. With more and more children attending day care and preschool, kindergarten now tends to reflect a different type of adjustment. Instead of going to the same preschool all day while the caretaker is at work, many children must now adjust to going to preschool for several hours and kindergarten for several hours. These children must often cope with not only significant programmatic changes but changes in peer groups as well. For these children, kindergarten is difficult not because it is more structure than they are used to but because it is more chaotic.

The changes involved in making the transition from kindergarten to first grade vary substantially from one school to another. In some schools, kindergarten is quite academically oriented and first grade is just more of the same. Other schools focus on establishing peer social skills in kindergarten and leave academics for first grade, thereby creating a much more significant transition. Similarly, the variability in what is required of third graders is substantial across schools. In most, however, third grade marks the introduction of more abstract learning, such as multiplication, into the curriculum at a point when only a few children are prepared for it. This tends to make the differences between the high and low academic achievers more pronounced and to trigger shifts in children's attitudes toward school. By sixth grade most academic programs have shifted to a curriculum that is heavily dependent on reading and writing. Children who have difficulties in these areas will begin to fall behind in spite of having done well up to this point.

Another critical aspect is the caretakers' and child's subjective experiences of safety and cultural comfortableness within the school environment. An 8-year-old African-American boy placed in a predominantly Anglo-American school because of his foster home placement came to play therapy reporting anxiety and the feeling he did not belong. A transfer to a more culturally diverse school setting resulted in a decrease in anxious symptoms and an improvement in his academic performance. Another 10-year-old child was doing poorly in the public school system because of pressure to be involved in ganglike activities, making it difficult for him to concentrate. A transfer to a smaller private school program resulted in significant emotional, social, and academic gains for this child.

When there have been problems, it is useful to know what interventions have already been tried, how effective they were, and the family reaction to these interventions. One family was given an intensive behavioral intervention program for their child's impulsive behaviors, attention problems, and obsession with guns in play. They experienced the program as intrusive and inconsistent with their parenting style. Although they attempted to use it for more than a year, their child's behavior did not improve. When a combination of dyadic and play therapy interventions was implemented, the caretakers became more responsive and the child's problem behaviors improved.

Family History of Learning Problems

The family history of learning problems is important for several reasons. Because learning problems may be either emotionally or organically based or a combination, it is helpful to know whether there is a genetic vulnerability to learning problems or Attention Deficit Disorder. Medications are likely to be most useful as an adjunct when there are biological factors involved. In addition, if a caretaker has a history of learning problems, this may affect the caretaker's response to the child's problems. The caretaker may feel guilty, may try to deny the problems because he or she does not want the child to go through a negative experience, or he or she may be able to be particularly supportive and empathic because of his or her own personal experience.

Site Visit Information/Observations

If the child's problems appear to be related to the school environment or if the child's problems are affecting his or her functioning in that environment, it may be useful to set up a site visit. This allows the play therapist to establish contact with critical people involved with this child and allows first-hand observations of the child's functioning and interactions in this environment.

Case Example

EDUCATIONAL SYSTEM

Current School Circumstances

Grade: 6th **School/District:** Fresno Middle School/Fresno Unified   **Telephone:** 222-2222

Teacher(s): Ms. Brown   **Counselor:** Ms. Green

Special Education or Support Services: ☐ No ☒ **Yes, Describe:** Steven attends regular classes and is pulled out to a special resource program on a daily basis.

Specific Problems: Steven exhibits significant delays in all academic areas: 2.5 year delay in math, 2 year in spelling and 1 year in reading comprehension. Emotional and behavioral interference in the learning process is increasing as he is now exhibiting daily tantrums.

School History

School Placement History: Steven attended the same grade school throughout. He moved to a new middle school this past year.

Problems (Especially note adjustment to K, 1st, 3rd and 6th grades)**:** Steven's learning difficulties were first identified when he entered kindergarten.

Interventions/Outcomes: Steven has received Special Education services since he was in kindergarten.

Family History of Learning Problems

One of Steven's cousins has Down's Syndrome. No other history of learning problems was reported.

Site Visit Information/Observations

Steven was not observed at his school site at the time of the intake.

Legal Systems

Overview

This is one of the more detailed parts of the Workbook, reflecting the complexity of the interactions clients may have with the various components of the legal system. This format is also an attempt to reflect the complexity of interactions within and between the legal systems. Many clients and play therapists become frustrated in their interactions with these systems because they do not understand the way in which these systems are structured or the way in which they interact. The information in this section is used to answer the question: In what ways has the legal system or systems contributed to, responded to, or played a part in maintaining any aspect of the presenting problem?

Part of the difficulty in preparing this section is the variability that exists from state to state, because the structures of the legal systems and the interpretations of the laws are largely defined by state statutes. In addition, specific names of the different court systems or agencies involved may vary depending on locale. Play therapists should make every effort to know the structure (both actual and political) of the legal systems in their area. We have tried to make the following discussions generic so that they meet the needs of most practitioners in the United States.

There are four major legal systems that often come into the lives of children in play therapy: Law Enforcement, Juvenile Court, Domestic (or Family) Court, and Criminal Court. A play therapist may become involved in any of these court systems either by choice (as an expert witness) or by subpoena as a result of involvement in a case. The Workbook is organized in terms of the legal involvement that most directly relates to caregiver–child relationships versus legal involvement relating to activities that interfere with the rights of others. The degree to which any of the four legal systems plays a role in either of these areas is variable and may overlap. Before proceeding with an explanation of this section of the Workbook, the three court systems are described to clarify the different responsibilities of each and their interrelationships.

Juvenile Court System   The juvenile justice system was founded largely on the belief that children warranted a separate legal system from adults because of their unique developmental and psychosocial needs (Workgroup on Psychiatric Practice in the Juvenile Court of the American Psychiatric Association, 1992). The Juvenile Court has jurisdiction over children in need of protection (child abuse and neglect) and over children who are engaging in behaviors prohibited by

law. If the youth commits an act that would be a crime if committed by an adult, he or she is referred to by the court as a delinquent. If the youth commits an act that is prohibited by statutes governing the behavior of children, such as running away or being truant, he or she is referred to by the court as a status offender. Bulkley, Feller, Stern, and Roe (1996) provide an excellent discussion of the legal proceedings involved in child abuse and neglect cases. The Workgroup on Psychiatric Practice in the Juvenile Court of the American Psychiatric Association (1992) gives the juvenile court procedures for delinquent youth and status offenders.

Even though the Juvenile Court is responsible for both children in need of protection and children in need of control, we have separated these two content areas in the Workbook. Child abuse is addressed in its own section because of its overwhelming significance in the lives of children and their families. Child abuse is also treated separately because it involves situations in which the child is a victim rather than a perpetrator. Status offenders and delinquency are addressed in the section, "Juvenile Offender System and Legal System (Criminal)."

Domestic Relations (Family) Court   Domestic relations include separation, divorce, custody, child support, and adoption issues. In some states, these issues are managed by the Juvenile Court. In other states, they are managed by the State Supreme Court. In some states, such as California, the court that manages domestic relations is called the Family Court and is separated from the Juvenile Court. In other states, the Juvenile Court is called the Family Court. In the Workbook we refer to this cluster of functions as the Legal System (Noncriminal). Note that we are referring to legal decisions that have a significant effect on caregiver–child relationships.

Criminal Court   This court addresses questions of guilt and punishment relative to the commission of crimes by adults. By definition, children are not involved in the Criminal Court system unless they are adjudicated as adults. However, adult involvement in this system may have a significant effect on the lives of child clients.

Differentiation of the Legal Systems   One of the confusing aspects of the legal system is the occurrence of what appear to be conflicting decisions with respect to the same case across the different systems. These are often most obvious in child abuse cases. The Juvenile Court may determine that the children should be removed from the home and the parental rights terminated. While, at the same time, a Criminal Court may fail to convict the parents of criminal child abuse. The reason for this is that the two systems operate according to different standards of evidence. In Juvenile Court, decisions may be based on clear and convincing evidence because the goal of the court is protection and rehabilitation rather than punishment. A similar rationale applied to Juvenile Court proceedings against delinquents until 1970 when the evidentiary standard was changed to "beyond a reasonable doubt" as it is in Criminal Court (Sacks & Reader, 1992). In Criminal Court, individuals are assumed innocent until proven guilty and a much higher standard of evidence applies. In many situations there are also statutes that maintain the separation of decisions in each of the courts. For example, in California, conviction of a felony is not considered sufficient evidence for the termination of an adult's parental rights. A good understanding of the various legal systems that operate in the play therapist's locale can guide him or her in the development of an effective treatment plan for cases in which the child is, in any way, involved with the legal system.

Child Abuse/Domestic Violence

The first legal systems addressed in the Workbook are those that respond to child abuse. We have included domestic violence in this section because of the common connection between the two. In most states, exposing a child to domestic violence is considered to be a reportable form of child abuse. Furthermore, it is not uncommon to find child abuse in homes where domestic violence is a problem. All 50 states mandate the reporting of suspected child abuse by mental health professionals. Failure to do so may result in the play therapist being held professionally, civilly, or criminally liable (Kalichman, 1993). Consequently, we have provided a section for explicating the fact that a report was made, when and by whom, if the abuse is identified as part of the history.

We have separated these issues from a discussion of specific legal systems because so many systems may be involved in a given case, and the names and organization of these systems is not always consistent from one region to another. We repeatedly refer to Child Protective Services (CPS), which is generally the primary social and legal agency mandated responsibility for child abuse assessment and intervention. However, not all regions call this agency the same thing and not all areas even have an equivalent agency. Again, it is incumbent on play therapists to know the systems in their area so that they can manage abuse cases appropriately.

This section should be completed even if the child is currently safe in foster care but was placed there in response to an abuse incident. This part of the Workbook provides easy access to information that is frequently needed, such as the CPS worker's name and phone number. Because violent homes may have more than one perpetrator or victim involved in the abuse, or the client may have been a witness rather than a victim, the categories "perpetrator" and "victim" have been left open. This is a situation in which having at least the first names and the specific relationships of the people involved is critical to treatment. "Relationships" refers to the relationship to the client, such as step-caregiver, maternal aunt, and so forth. Criminal charges against a perpetrator of abuse or domestic violence should be noted in the later section, Legal System (Criminal).

Emotional abuse is seldom reported by itself. However, emotional abuse is usually a component of other types of abuse. Recent research indicates that the degree of emotional abuse involved in sexual or physical abuse cases is more predictive of a negative outcome for the child than the actual severity of the abuse. Therefore, the play therapist should try to get information about independent or concurrent emotional abuse. "Psychological maltreatment is the core construct and key to understanding the dynamics of all child maltreatment. It not only exists in its own discrete forms, but it also is embedded in or associated with all other forms of maltreatment and appears to be the strongest influencer and best predictor of their developmental consequences" (Hart, Brassard, & Karlson, 1996, p. 85).

With respect to neglect, the specific type or types of neglect should be clarified, such as physical, medical, or emotional neglect. The last is the most damaging and has the potential for the most negative long-term effects, even more than emotional abuse, because it refers to a failure on the part of caretakers to engage with and be available to the child. Emotional neglect is defined by the American Humane Association as "passive or passive-aggressive inattention to the child's emotional needs, nurturing or emotional well being" (Brassard, Germain, & Hart, 1987, p. 267). Even abusive engagement is better than an absence of involvement (Erickson & Egeland, 1996). The Description section allows the play therapist to elaborate these details as they manifest in a particular abuse case.

If the child is involved in the CPS system, there is specific information the play therapist will need in order to develop a relevant treatment plan. To use an analogy, when a play therapist sees a child who is not involved with CPS, he or she must also confer with that child's legal guardian. They have the authority to allow the play therapist to provide treatment for their child. Furthermore, the child lives with them and is greatly influenced by interactions with them. Thus it is crucial to know what their perceptions of the problem are and to engage them in the treatment process. Even when the child wants treatment, if the caretaker is unwilling to bring the child, treatment is unlikely. When a child is involved with CPS, the system assumes certain guardianship functions. The caseworker can determine whether or not a child is seen in treatment and for what purpose. The caseworker can sign the consent for treatment, transport the child, and make decisions about the child's life that can have a dramatic effect on play therapy, such as changing the child's home placement. Successful treatment of a child in the CPS system requires the play therapist to be actively involved with that system for many reasons. First, so that the play therapist has information about CPS decisions that can be addressed in treatment. This might include preparing the child for a court appearance, visits, or reunification. Second, the play therapist needs to be able to work with the many other systems that may be involved in a CPS case, including the biologic and foster families, to assist them in achieving the least intrusive and most constructive resolution of the problem for the child. Finally, active involvement with the caseworker provides the play therapist with the opportunity to affect the decision-making process at the level of the legal system. Play therapists who work with abused children recognize that in spite of the best intentions of the many systems that respond to child abuse situations much of the trauma many of these children experience is the result of the intervention itself, such as multiple out-of-home placements and court appearances. A play therapist who is attuned to the child's experience can do a great deal to advocate for the child within the CPS and court system.

The CPS process illustrated in Figure 4.2 may vary in other locales, but it captures its essence. The involvement of CPS starts with a complaint that child abuse may have been or be occurring. A caseworker investigates and makes one of three decisions: (a) that no response is required, (b) that the child can be left in the home but the family needs support services (family maintenance), or (c) that the child is to be removed from the home (emergency response).

If the child is removed from the home and placed in foster care or with a relative, a hearing must be held within 72 hours to determine whether the child needs to be detained further because of a lack of safety in the home. If the child is detained, then the child is made a dependent of the court and the court assumes the care, custody, and control over the child's life for the present (dependency). If the child is made a dependent of the court, a plan is developed regarding reunification of the child with his or her parents. This plan is usually to work toward family reunification for at least 6 to 12

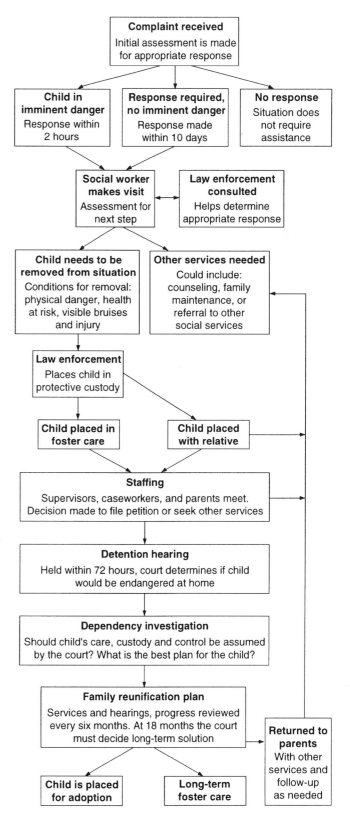

FIGURE 4.2 How CPS handles complaints. Source: Fresno County Department of Social Services. Reprinted with permission of the Fresno Bee.

months. If, after 12 to 18 months, the family has not made adequate progress and the prognosis is poor, or if the abuse is so severe that the court does not even consider family maintenance as an option, then termination of parental rights may be considered so that a permanent plan can be developed for the child. This plan may include long-term foster care, plans for adoption, or placement with another relative. What is important here is to identify where the case is in the process when the child is brought in for treatment. It is helpful to identify the next court date and the purpose of that hearing.

As mentioned, domestic violence is included here because evidence suggests that children in violent homes may be traumatized as much or more by witnessing parents or siblings being abused as they are by experiencing the abuse themselves. The CPS may or may not become involved in domestic violence situations. If the family is in an emergency shelter to protect them from domestic violence, this should be noted along with the name of the shelter manager. An Order of Protection (restraining order) may be issued by the court to protect the family or a family member from someone who is threatening them. These are often issued at some point in a domestic violence situation. If such an order was issued, it should be noted here because it is a good indicator of the intensity of the problems and the degree to which those involved are accessing the legal system.

Previous incidents of child abuse and domestic violence should be noted in the next section and relevant details entered into the Description section. When intergenerational patterns of abuse exist they should be documented where indicated. For example, does the abusing mother also come from a family in which her parents were abusive to her and her siblings, and was her father's father abusive to her father? If such an intergenerational pattern exists it should also be noted on the genogram.

Legal System (Noncriminal)

Following the collection of data regarding abuse and domestic violence, the child's and family's involvement in the legal system for noncriminal reasons is noted. Divorce and custody proceedings are addressed first. If the child is from a divorced family, it is important to know whether the custody arrangements have already been determined, because this has implications for who can give permission for the child to receive treatment and who can receive confidential information about the treatment. It is also important to note how this custody situation fits into the request for mental health treatment. Is there an expectation that the play therapist will be gathering information to present

at a hearing? Does the caretaker see play therapy as an evaluation rather than treatment? Is this a formal referral by the court? Are both parties to be involved with the treatment? Are there hidden agendas? If testimony or evaluation are part of the expectations, the play therapist will need to decide whether or not this is within his or her competence and interest. In addition, it is important to be clear about the limits of what can be communicated to the court if both parties are not involved. If necessary, the names and phone numbers of the mediator and lawyers should be noted.

The remaining two categories are about a child's placement outside of the biologic parents' home. Foster placement is usually imposed on families as the result of abuse or neglect, but it can also be effected voluntarily. This sometimes occurs in cases in which the caretaker is seriously or terminally ill. Foster placements can be noted in this section. Adoptions happen for all types of reasons and the motives of both the birth parents and the adoptive parents, the circumstances of the adoption, and the child's understanding of and response to his or her adoptive status may need to be explored.

The remaining sections of the Legal Systems review have to do with behavior that is specifically prohibited by law. The reader should note that we do not intend to imply that child abuse, which was included in an earlier section, is not criminal. The decision to relegate it to its own section is a reflection of the importance we place on the problem rather than an attempt to minimize its criminality. All other status and criminal behavior is recorded in the remaining three sections: Law Enforcement, Juvenile Offender System, and Legal System (Criminal). When necessary for a complete understanding of the case, the criminal behavior of other family members can be documented where indicated in any of these sections.

Law Enforcement System

This system refers exclusively to contacts with the police or officers of the court such as truant officers. It is included here to make sure that those children who are getting into trouble with the law, but who are managing not to end up in court, are identified.

Juvenile Offender System

Statutory violations refer to activities that would not be considered a crime if the individual was an adult, such as running away or curfew violations. If the client has been arrested for a statutory violation, misdemeanor, or felony, the specific illegal activity and the consequence should be described. If the client is currently in Juvenile Hall, the length of time he or she is scheduled to be there should be noted. If the client is on probation, the terms of the probation (e.g., house arrest), length of time, and name and phone number of probation officer should be indicated. Other family involvement typically refers to siblings who are older and who are involved in illegal activities. The age, gender, and first name of the sibling could be used. If possible, describe the quality of the relationship between the client and this sibling and the potential for negative influence. Gang involvement is a particular concern these days.

Legal System (Criminal)

Because, by definition, the child cannot be involved in the criminal court system except as a victim, this section addresses the impact of family members who may be involved in this system. Because this is the client's chart, the full name of the adult should not be used un-

less the treatment directly involves them as well. Instead, reference should be made to the relationship with the child, such as maternal uncle. If an adult family member has been arrested for a misdemeanor or a felony, what the crime was, when it occurred, and the consequences should be noted. If the person is currently incarcerated, it should be noted where indicated, with reference to the specific institution and the anticipated length of time of incarceration. This becomes important as an increasing number of child clients come into treatment, having been separated from caretakers, because the caretakers are in prison, often for drug abuse-related charges. If the adult is on probation or parole because of a crime against the child client and the circumstances of that crime are part of the treatment plan, then it may be appropriate to have the name and phone number of the probation officer. This occurs frequently when treatment involves family reunification work subsequent to child abuse or domestic violence.

Case Example

LEGAL SYSTEMS

Child Abuse/Domestic Violence

Current: ☒ **No** ☐ **Yes:** ☐ **Physical** ☐ **Sexual** ☐ **Emotional** ☐ **Neglect** ☐ **Witnessed Violence**

Perpetrator(s): _____ Victim(s): _____

Relationship to Child: _____ Relationship to Child: _____

Description: _____

Report Filed: ☐ No ☐ Yes, When: _____ **CPS Involved:** ☐ No ☐ Yes

Caseworker: _____ **Telephone:** _____

CPS Response and Long Term Plan: _____

Impending Court Appearance: ☐ No ☐ Yes, Date: _____

    Purpose: _____

Domestic Violence Shelter: ☐ No ☐ Yes, Describe: _____

Caseworker: _____ **Telephone:** _____

Orders of Protection: ☐ No ☐ Yes, Describe: _____

Previous: ☒ **No** ☐ **Yes:** ☐ **Physical** ☐ **Sexual** ☐ **Emotional** ☐ **Neglect** ☐ **Witnessed Violence**

Perpetrator(s): _____ Victim(s): _____

Relationship to Child: _____ Relationship to Child: _____

Description: _____

Report Filed: ☐ No ☐ Yes, When: _____ **CPS Involved:** ☐ No ☐ Yes

Caseworker: _____ **Telephone:** _____

CPS Response and Long Term Plan: _____

Impending Court Appearance: ☐ No ☐ Yes, Date: _____

Purpose: _____

Domestic Violence Shelter: ☐ No ☐ Yes, Describe: _____

Caseworker: _____ **Telephone:** _____

Orders of Protection: ☐ No ☐ Yes, Describe: _____

Intergenerational History of Child Abuse/Domestic Violence: ☒ No ☐ Yes, Describe: _____

Legal System (Non-Criminal) (For all persons mentioned be as specific as possible about their relationships(s) to the child.)

Divorce: ☐ No ☒ Yes, Describe: <u>Mother divorced Steven's biological father when Steven was 2 years old.</u>

Current Custody Proceedings: ☒ No ☐ Yes, Describe: _____

Mediator/Attorney: _____ **Telephone:** _____

Past Custody Proceedings: ☐ No ☒ Yes, Description/Outcome: <u>Mother has sole custody of Steven and his sister. Biological father had no interest in maintaining contact with the children.</u>

Foster Placement: ☒ No ☐ Yes, Describe: _____

Adoption: ☒ No ☐ Yes, Describe: _____

Law Enforcement System (For all persons mentioned be as specific as possible about their relationship(s) to the child.)

Contact(s) <u>Not</u> Leading to Arrest: ☒ No ☐ Yes, Describe: _____

Arrest(s) <u>Not</u> Leading to Court Proceedings: ☒ No ☐ Yes, Describe: _____

Juvenile Offender System (For all persons mentioned be as specific as possible about their relationship(s) to the child.)

Arrests for Statutory Violation(s): ☒ No ☐ Yes, Description/Outcome: _____

Arrests for Misdemeanor(s): ☒ No ☐ Yes, Description/Outcome: _____

Arrests for Felony(s): ☒ No ☐ Yes, Description/Outcome: _____

Juvenile Hall Placement(s): ☒ No ☐ Yes, Describe: _____

Probation: ☒ No ☐ Yes, Describe: _____

Probation Officer: _____ **Telephone:** _____

Family Members Involved in Juvenile Justice System, Past or Present: ☒ No ☐ Yes, Describe: _____

Legal System (Criminal) (For all persons mentioned be as specific as possible about their relationship(s) to the child.)

Court Appearances for Misdemeanor(s): ☐ No ☒ Yes, Description/Outcome: <u>Father was convicted of driving under the influence when Steven was an infant.</u>

Court Appearances for Felony(s): ☒ No ☐ Yes, Description/Outcome: _____

Probation/Parole: ☒ No ☐ Yes, Describe: _____

Probation/Parole Officer: _____ **Telephone:** _____

Unlike many children who come for treatment, Steven's involvement in the CPS and Family Court systems was relatively limited and had little effect on his life. He is fortunate in this sense.

Medical System

The information in this section is used to conceptualize several types of systemic interactions. At one level, it is used to understand the mind–body interactions that may influence the child client's perception of his or her world. On a number of other levels, it is used to conceptualize the effect that medical problems may have had on the client's interactions with any of the other systems. Finally, it is used to understand the effect the medical system itself has had on the client and his or her functioning. This is another area in which it often pays for the play therapist to ask specific questions if nothing is mentioned in the open-ended interview. Often, a chronic illness becomes so integrated into a family's life that neither the child nor the caretakers will think to report it. Often, too, medications that the child takes on a semiregular basis will not be reported because the caretaker assumes that the medication has no bearing on the child's behavioral functioning.

This part of the Workbook is also used to record any recent changes in the child's physical condition. Symptoms such as weight loss or gain, finicky eating, eating disorders, insomnia, nightmares or night terrors, and fatigue can all be recorded here. This information can be used to assess the severity of various disorders (e.g., depression), to rule out disorders (e.g., anorexia), and to rule out potential biologic underpinnings to the current behavioral difficulties.

Case Example

MEDICAL SYSTEM

Allergies: ☒ **No** ☐ **Yes, Describe:** _____

Serious Accidents: ☒ **No** ☐ **Yes, Describe:** _____

Head Injury w/ Loss of Consciousness: ☒ **No** ☐ **Yes, Describe:** _____

Serious Illness: ☐ **No** ☒ **Yes, Describe:** <u>Viral encephalitis at 17 days of age. Hospitalized for 10 days.</u>

Chronic Illness: ☒ **No** ☐ **Yes, Describe:** _____

Hospitalizations: ☐ **No** ☒ **Yes, Describe:** <u>See above.</u>

Other Medical Problems: ☐ **No** ☒ **Yes, Describe:** <u>Steven has been treated for hyperactivity since he was 8 years old.</u>

Present Medications: ☐ **No** ☒ **Yes, Physician:** <u>Doug Ross, MD</u>

    Type, Dose, Frequency: <u>Ritalin.</u>

Eating Pattern: <u>Steven tends to overeat and has been overweight since the age of 6.</u>

Sleeping Pattern: <u>Within normal limits, no problems reported.</u>

Family History of Medical Problems: <u>None.</u>

Mental Health System

This part of the Workbook is used to document the client's and the family's concurrent and previous contacts with the mental health system. In addition, individual or familial substance use is recorded here.

Current and Previous Substance Abuse

Among mental health professionals it is generally agreed that the stress interview technique produces the most accurate reports of actual substance use patterns. This technique involves interviewing the client as if one assumes substance use occurs. The client is not asked whether he or she drinks, instead the client is asked whether he or she drinks every day or whether she or he drinks more than two drinks a day. The same format is used when asking about frequency and intensity of the use as well. For example, "do you drink more than three drinks a day?" or "Do you have more than four drinks at any one time?" The estimates the play therapist uses in the question should be high but not so high as to seem preposterous. The idea is to make the client believe that the play therapist would not be shocked by a positive response and to require the client actively to undo or correct the assumption underlying the question rather than passively deny having a problem. The same technique is used to inquire about the use of other substances.

Although many play therapists may be put off by the thought of interviewing children about their substance abuse it is naïve to think that such abuse does not occur in an unfortunate percentage of the population at a very young age. I have worked with clients who were using alcohol on a daily basis at the age of 9 and have heard of substance abuse in children as early as first grade. The 9-year-old's abuse was not detected until he was 13, at which time his behavior had deteriorated to

the point that he required 2 years of residential treatment. We strongly recommend making at least a minimal inquiry with clients over the age of 10.

Potential Interview Format: Caretaker The play therapist should begin by inquiring about the caretakers' alcohol and substance use following the guidelines suggested in the previous section. Having completed that portion of the interview, the play therapist can begin asking about the child's substance use.

- *Do you have any reason to believe that your child drinks alcohol or uses any other substances?*
- *Have you noticed significant shifts in your child's mood or behavior over the past few months?*
- *Have you noticed increased moodiness or sudden shifts in your child's behavior over the course of a given day?*

Potential Interview Format: Child

- *How often have you tried or drunk alcohol?*
- *How often do you have more than three drinks in one day?*
- *In what types of situations do you drink?*
- *Aside from medicines that your parents or doctor have given you, what other pills or drugs have you tried or used?*

Case Example

MENTAL HEALTH SYSTEM

Concurrent Outpatient Treatment: ☒ **No** ☐ **Yes, Describe:** _____

  Diagnosis: _____

  Facility/Therapist: _____

Previous Outpatient Treatment: ☒ **No** ☐ **Yes, Describe:** _____

  Diagnosis: _____

  Facility/Therapist: _____

Previous Inpatient Treatment: ☒ **No** ☐ **Yes, Describe:** _____

  Diagnosis: _____

  Facility/Therapist: _____

Psychotropic Medications: ☐ **No**   ☒ **Yes, Describe:** Steven is being treated by his pediatrician for hyperactivity.

  Current Medications: Type, Dose, Frequency: Ritalin.

  Prescribing Physician: Doug Ross, MD

  Previous Medications: Type, Dose, Frequency: Steven has been on Ritalin since he was 8 years old.

  Prescribing Physician: _____

Current Mental Health Difficulties and Treatment of Other Family Members: (For all persons mentioned, be as specific as possible about their relationship(s) to the child.) <u>None.</u>

History of Mental Health Difficulties and Treatment of Other Family Members: (For all persons mentioned be as specific as possible about their relationship(s) to the child.) <u>None.</u>

Current Substance Abuse: ☒ None ☐ Mild ☐ Moderate ☐ Severe: _____

    Substances Used/Frequency/Intensity: _____

    In Treatment: ☐ No ☐ Yes, Describe: _____

Previous Substance Abuse: ☒ None ☐ Mild ☐ Moderate ☐ Severe: _____

    Substances Used/Frequency/Intensity: _____

    Treatment: ☐ No ☐ Yes, Describe: _____

Current Substance Abuse and Treatment of Other Family Members: (For all persons mentioned be as specific as possible about their relationship(s) to the child.) <u>Whereabouts of Steven's biological father are unknown as is his present level of substance use.</u>

History of Substance Abuse and Treatment of Other Family Members: (For all persons mentioned be as specific about their relationship(s) to the child.) <u>Mother reports that Steven's biological father used alcohol to excess on occasion. He was charged with drunk driving once while still living in the home. His substance use did not interfere with his occupational functioning although it may have interfered with his interpersonal functioning.</u>

Four metasystems—Regional Culture, Dominant/National or Political System, World Community, and Historical Time—have been identified as potentially contributing to the presenting problem and/or being a resource in resolving the problem. These sections are included to stimulate the play therapist's thinking about their potential import, but need only be completed if the play therapist views them as particularly relevant to the problem dynamics or solution. Each of these systems plays a major role in creating the context of any child's life, but the degree to which they play a day-to-day role varies considerably. For example, 15 years ago, the Star Wars movies were a major phenomenon. Many children endlessly reenacted themes from the movies in their play sessions. For some, their fears and conflicts were channeled into movie-related content. Although their problems were neither caused by nor specifically related to the movie, it did create a time- and place-specific vehicle for the expression of these problems.

Regional Cultural System

Different areas of the United States have different regional cultures that have different beliefs, values, and even sociopolitical systems. The extreme variability in identifying, responding to, and intervening in child abuse cases serves as an excellent example. In California, the same incident may be considered a near crisis in one city or county and not worth reporting in another. The services available for children and families experiencing abuse vary widely and fluctuate over time as funds either become available or are withdrawn.

There is also substantial variability in the regional response to persons from different ethnic, racial, or cultural groups. For example, the Central Valley of California is quite ethnically diverse. However, its regional cultural value system is conservative and relatively intolerant of diversity. This certainly affects anyone who is not Anglo- or Euro-American and Christian who lives in this regional culture.

Dominant/National or Political System

Although the regional culture tends to have a more immediate effect on people's day-to-day lives, the dominant/national or political system can have long-term and profound consequences. For example, a lesbian couple raising a child in San Francisco will most likely find that the regional culture is quite supportive of their relationship to one another (legally recognizing domestic partnerships) and of their parental status (allowing for joint adoption of the child). However, they will live under the cloud of a state and national political system that, at times, seems bent on destroying them. In 1996 alone, California attempted to ban recognition of same-sex marriage and President Clinton vowed to sign a national Defense of Marriage Act which would have the same effect on a national level. Although living within such conflicting value systems is unlikely to have a readily identifiable effect on the family, it undoubtedly has consequences. Are the couple supported in their relationship and in their parenting on a day-to-day basis? Must they constantly seek out settings (schools, baby sitters, pediatricians, etc.) where they and their child feel safe? Must they be aware of teaching their child strategies for coping with the homophobia that exists in the world? These effects of the dominant culture tend to be pervasive and to create a context in which outsiders may be viewed with some initial suspicion and distrust.

World Community

As with the dominant/national or political system, the day-to-day effects of the world community on an individual child or family may be difficult to detect. The reality of the twentieth century is that the world has become a much smaller place where people of many different backgrounds and groups are forced to interact on a much more regular basis. For the most part, this is a good thing, allowing for the sharing of information and resources and encouraging a sense of mutual responsibility. But with the interaction comes a level of stress and potential for conflict previously unknown. Working to accept responsibility for the welfare of one's relatives can be difficult, accepting it for one's neighbors can be even more so, but accepting responsibility for disaster victims on the other side of the world can be truly overwhelming. Although world events do not generally have a specific effect on a family, they create a potentially stressful backdrop against which the family lives.

In some cases, world events do have a very direct impact on the children and families who come for treatment. Events that the play therapist may have pushed into the background of their own consciousness may take on traumatic proportions for their clients. One family was referred with when oldest son began doing poorly in school and showed signs of depression. During the intake it was discovered that the mother was profoundly depressed and that the son was one of her primary sources of support. The source of the depression was the fact that this family had come to the United States on vacation from Iraq just prior to the Gulf War. Once here, they were unable to return and found themselves with nothing but their travel clothes, isolated and afraid. Although they had, in many ways ad-

justed well, the continued separation from their extended family was intolerable and the mother suffered terribly when she learned that her own mother had died alone in Iraq. Although individual and family intervention is clearly necessary in this situation, it is also clear that the source of their problems is a world event with which anyone would have difficulty coping.

Historical Context

The historical context in which a family exists creates an even more abstract influence on their day-to-day lives than does being members of the world community. In some ways the Gulf War example just related is also an example of historical context. The family discussed is the victim of a specific historical event and their circumstances are, therefore, somewhat unique to a specific point in historical time. The world response to the problem of child abuse is an even better example. Less than 200 years ago, child abuse was not thought to be a problem per se. Children were the disposable property of their parents, who could raise them or use them in virtually any way they saw fit. Selling or indenturing a child was not outside the realm of parental rights. Within a matter of only a few generations in the United States, it has become generally unacceptable to beat children and nearly unacceptable to use corporal punishment. Because most parents rely to some extent on their own upbringing as a source of information about how to raise their children, such rapid social changes challenge them to act in ways that they may experience as directly contradictory to their own beliefs and upbringing. Generally, any type of rapid social change creates stress that may directly affect the day-to-day lives of children and families.

SUMMARY

In completing Parts I and II of the Workbook, the play therapist has gathered comprehensive intake data on both the child client and the systems in which that client is embedded. The Workbook format was designed to allow for very comprehensive data gathering from sources such as the child, caretakers, and other reporters in the child's world. Not all of the information will be relevant to all cases, and the play therapist is free to pick and choose the information to be gathered. We have attempted to guide this selection by specifically highlighting those areas that involve potential danger to the client and those we see as critical to a complete evaluation of any child. We have also attempted to describe how the information will be used in subsequent treatment planning so that the play therapist can determine whether or not it will be relevant in a given case.

Even though these data are quite comprehensive, it is often useful to supplement this information with data from more structured assessments. Such data may already be available in the form of evaluations completed by the school, a previous psychologist, and so forth. The play therapist may also want to gather data with instruments or methods particularly suited to his or her clientele or work setting. The next chapter presents an ecosystemic approach to assessment and a discussion of some of the instruments we find particularly useful.

· 5 ·

ASSESSMENT

OVERVIEW: WORKBOOK, PART III

Having obtained data and made observations from the intake interview, the therapist might determine that additional information is needed to develop an accurate case conceptualization and subsequent treatment plan. In this chapter, assessment refers to any strategy for obtaining case-related data that goes beyond the intake interview and Mental Status Examination. Assessment data can be obtained from three different sources.

First, data might already be available, in which case a signed Release-of-Information form is all that is needed to obtain this information. If the child is receiving any type of special education services through the schools, he or she is required, in California, to have an Individual Assessment Plan (IEP), which includes, at a minimum, cognitive and educational testing every 3 years. Previous residential treatment often includes a full psychological assessment. Also, in California, a child with significant developmental delays may have received an evaluation (and services) through the Regional Center programs. The therapist should be alert to likely sources of assessment data when completing the initial intake interview and obtain the necessary releases at that time so that assessments are not duplicated and information can be gathered as quickly as possible.

Second, the therapist may want to refer the client for an evaluation as part of the initial data gathering process. Formal testing may be requested to rule out

various problems or disorders. If biologic factors are a possible contributor to the problems, a referral for a medical or neurological assessment should be considered. This will either rule out biologic factors that will help in the differential diagnosis or will rule in biologic factors that can then be taken into account in the treatment planning process. Neuropsychological assessment may be used to better understand the unique ways in which the child processes information about the world as a result of neurological problems. Psychological testing is often done to assess global intellectual functioning, emotional functioning, personality functioning, and the child's level of contact with reality. Other relevant assessments for use with children may include, but are not limited to, a speech and language evaluation, educational assessment, and sensory–motor evaluation.

Finally, the therapist can collect the assessment data as part of the initial intake process. There are several considerations that should be explored before the therapist makes the decision to conduct the evaluation him or herself. First, does the therapist have the qualifications and training to administer the evaluation tools needed. Second, what is the potential effect on the future therapist–client relationship. The testing puts the client in an entirely passive stance for a sustained period of time. That is, the therapist assumes all responsibility for the structure and content of every session and limits the type of input the client may have. Many children experience this as being very similar to school and, therefore, not particularly pleasant. Third, during the course of testing the child may disclose a great deal of information very quickly. The pace of disclosure is generally much higher than it would be during the initial stages of treatment. As the treatment begins the child may become increasingly aware of how much the therapist already knows and feel vulnerable. The vulnerability may show up as attempts to avoid treatment altogether or to deny or undo the information that was disclosed Finally, if the treatment has already begun, the therapist needs to recognize that the therapeutic relationship may contaminate the assessment process. Children who are evaluated by their therapists often disclose much more during testing than they would if they were being assessed by a stranger. They feel safe with the therapist and, therefore, they do not censor what they say as much, significantly skewing their results. Or the child may interpret the evaluation as an attempt to trick him or her into disclosure when therapy has not worked and respond by shutting down even further.

Alternatively, some information is lost to the therapist when someone else does the assessment. Specifically, the therapist does not have access to all of the behavioral and observational data the examiner gathered in the course of testing the child. In effect, the therapist is left to examine the child's world through two sets of lenses, his or her own and the examiner's. As a message often gets distorted as it is relayed through more people, so are indirectly obtained test results subject to distortion. The pros and cons of the therapist serving as the examiner must be evaluated in the context of each specific case.

In the rest of this chapter, we address different assessment tools and approaches that can be incorporated into the intake process. Some of the assessment tools may be restricted for use by examiners with specific levels of education or may require specialized training. Where applicable, we note those restrictions and indicate appropriate referral sources. Some of the tools are not well known and therefore will be described in more detail, including information on how to obtain further information and training.

Although we refer to traditional assessment instruments, our focus is on assessment tools that we have found to be particularly useful in guiding the process of treatment planning. Experiential and play techniques are emphasized because of their obvious link to play therapy. Our focus for assessment is not on diagnosis or classification but on identifying the child's coping styles, strengths, weaknesses, intrapsychic processes and perceptions, interpersonal abilities, and so forth, as these are brought to bear in his or her functioning in the real world. For example, a traditional instrument for assessing overall cognitive functioning is a standardized intelligence test, such as the Wechsler Scales (Wechsler, 1989, 1991) or Standford-Binet (Thorndike, Hagen, & Sattler, 1986a, 1986b) which gives a global classification of the child's cognitive level relative to the child's age group. This is minimally useful for treatment planning. A pattern analysis of the scores may reveal more information about that particular child's cognitive strengths and weaknesses and how they affect his or her thinking and behavior which may be more useful in treatment planning (e.g., Kaufman, 1994). A more focused functional analysis of the child's behavior and the meaning of that behavior, using the Cipani Behavioral Assessment and Diagnostic System (C-BAD; Cipani, 1993), may provide more useful information for treatment planning than the standardized cognitive assessment.

There are many types of assessment tools available, ranging from those that are highly structured and standardized to those that create a loose framework for organizing clinical observations. Assessment tools also vary with respect to the data collection process involved, ranging from direct assessments of the child, to observation of the client or observation and testing of various family members, to indirect assessments, such as behavior checklists completed by those who know the child well. Direct assessments can also be part of a continuum from more objective (e.g., behavioral observations and standardized testing) to more subjective (e.g., interviews and projective and play techniques). Each of these dimensions should be considered when interpreting the results of any assessment data. If the data are to be used to guide the treatment planning and therapeutic process, the less standardized, more subjective tools may be particularly useful because they promote understanding the individual contextually and relative to the individual's own strengths and weakness. However, if the data are to be used as part of a formal evaluation for court, the more standardized tools may be more appropriate because they are more accepted in that setting.

Cultural Issues

Before moving into a discussion of the Workbook, Part III: Assessment Data we address issues involved in conducting culturally sensitive assessments (Dana, 1993). Several steps are suggested.[1]

Step 1: Self-Inquiry

Before engaging in the assessment and treatment of any clients, the therapist should examine his or her own

---

[1]These steps are adapted from Dana, 1993, and E. Davis-Russell, personal communication, November, 1994.

cultural identity and any personal values, beliefs, or presuppositions about the client based on the client's ethnicity, age, gender, socioeconomic status, sexual orientation, religion, physical size, and so forth. This is particularly important if the client's culture is different from that of the therapist, but it is also important even if we perceive it to be similar, because we may be at greater risk of imposing our own beliefs on clients who are like ourselves. The therapist also needs to be aware of the core values held by the mental health profession (refer to Chapter 2, "Diversity"), which are consistent with many of the values held by the dominant culture and inconsistent with some values held by other cultures. These values have the potential to influence the way the therapist structures the assessment situation (e.g., questions asked, assessment tools used, who is included, and so forth) and how he or she interprets the results. Finally, the therapist needs to consider whether or not he or she has the knowledge base and experience to do a competent job on this assessment. If not, the therapist needs to refer or obtain supervision from a supervisor appropriately trained in this area.

Step 2: Defining the Purpose

The purpose of the assessment should be examined, as there are culturally based assumptions inherent in some purposes, such as diagnosing or classifying. The most culturally sensitive purpose for assessment is to increase our understanding of the child. That is, what is happening and what has happened to this child that he or she is experiencing him or herself in this way, and is responding to his or her environment in this way, at this time? This is an ecosystemic approach, in that it takes into account the individual's experience relative to his or her intrapsychic understanding and ecosystemic context, including culture, development, and life history.

Step 3: Decisions about Assessment Tools

Before beginning the assessment, the therapist must determine the level of acculturation, that is, the degree to which the child (and family) identify with the dominant Anglo/Euro-American culture. This is important because many of the available tests rest on Anglo/Euro-American-centered assumptions about mental health and these assumptions determine both the content of the tests and the interpretations of the data. In addition, most instruments are normed on predominantly Anglo/Euro-American populations, and even if different ethnic subgroups are proportionally represented, the results do not capture their experiences within their culture.

Note that level of acculturation is different from immigration status, although they are related. Level of acculturation refers to the degree to which the child and family identify with and relate to the values of the dom-

inant Anglo/Euro-American culture. It is possible that a relatively recent second-generation family from Mexico has fully embraced the dominant Anglo/Euro-American culture values, beliefs, and behaviors, whereas an African American family who has lived in the United States for many generations may have a stronger identification with an Afrocentric world view based on African cultural values. One useful strategy is to evaluate the degree of acculturation along two dimensions: (a) the degree to which the individual (or family) identifies with the dominant Anglo/Euro-American culture, and (b) the degree to which the individual (or family) identifies with their own culture. This leads to four categories of acculturation. The assimilated category represents those people who have embraced the dominant Anglo/Euro-American values and culture and are minimally identified with their own culture. The traditional category includes those people who are minimally identified with the dominant Anglo/Euro-American culture and are strongly identified with their own culture. Bicultural individuals are strongly identified with both the dominant Anglo/Euro-American and their own culture, whereas those in the alienated category are not identified with either the dominant culture or their own culture. Dana (1993) discusses several tools and methods that can be used to assess the level of acculturation, particularly for Hispanic and African-American clients. Cappelletty (1987) developed an acculturation instrument for Southeast Asian populations. Once the level of acculturation has been determined, this information is used to decide which assessment tools to use. Table 5.1 summarizes this decision-making process.

Step 4: Interpretation

The last step is to identify potential problems in interpretation, including misdiagnosis, overestimation, underestimation, or neglect of psychopathology, as well as misunderstanding of meanings for that child and family. It is important to integrate and interpret the results from an ecosystemic perspective, with culture as a major determinant.

In the following discussion, we illustrate the use of the Workbook Part III: Assessment Data using the case of Steven Johnson. Consistent with the rest of the Workbook data, the assessment section moves from the individual level of assessment through the dyadic level and ends with the family/social level. All of these assessments are optional in the intake process, and if no assessment data is available, this section of the Workbook is completed by putting NA (none available) in the appropriate fields. For this reason, we have left this section of the Workbook relatively unstructured. The

TABLE 5.1 Level of Acculturation and Assessment Tools

Level of acculturation	Identification with Euro-American culture	Identification with own culture	Appropriate assessment tools
Assimilated	High	Low	• Existing standardized measures
Traditional	Low	High	• Existing measures not appropriate • Use culture-specific measures if available combined with culturally sensitive clinical interview
Bicultural	High	High	• Discuss with client/family • Use both existing standardized measures and culture-specific measures
Marginal	Low	Low	• Most difficult to assess • Use clinical interview

organization of the case example is specific to Steven Johnson's assessment data.

DATA SOURCES

The first component of the Workbook assessment section identifies the sources of the data. Under Tests and/or Measures Administered, the date of the assessment, the source (who completed the assessment), and the specific measures and procedures should be clearly indicated. If the data were directly gathered by the therapist, as well as from other sources, this should be noted. Where the data source is not based on a test or measure but rather on observation, organized by using a framework such as O'Connor's (1991) description of a Developmental Context for Play Therapy, this should be indicated on the Other Data Sources line.

Case Example

III. ASSESSMENT DATA

DATA SOURCES

Tests and/or Measures Administered: 6/93: Comprehensive physical, cognitive, educational, and language evaluation completed by diagnostic team at medical center. Specific tests included Weschler Intelligence Scale for Children-Revised (WISC-R), Peabody Individual Achievement Test (PIAT), Detroit Test of Learning Aptitude (DTLA), Screening Test for Auditory Processing Disorders (SCAN), Clinical Evaluation of Language Functioning (CLEF-R), Bender Test of Visual-Motor Integration (Bender), Nonmotor Test of Visual Perceptual Skills (TVPS) 9/93: Therapist administered Developmental Therapy Objectives Rating Form (DTORF) and Personality Inventory for Children (PIC) to mother, and projective drawings, Robert's Apperception Test for Children (RAT-C), and Rorschach Ink Blot Test (Rorschach) to Steven.

Other Data Sources: Symbolic play observations during the play interview were used to rate Steven on his developmental level of representational play using the Westby Symbolic Play Scale

ASSESSING INDIVIDUAL FUNCTIONING

Three general goals in individual assessment are to determine the levels of developmental functioning, to identify clinically relevant disorders that may be present, and to understand the individual styles and meanings that the child uses to make sense of his or her experience in the world. Development refers to normal processes that may be advanced, consistent with, or delayed relative to other children of similar ages. Often the term developmental functioning is associated only with cognitive development. Although the child's level of cognitive functioning is critical for treatment planning, the child's level of social–emotional functioning is often even more so. Social–emotional functioning captures several dimensions of experience, including the child's behavior, communicative abilities (language), social relating, and emotional functioning. We exist both in our intrapsychic experience of the world and in our interactional experience with others. Our subject-dependent and interpersonal realities are intertwined largely through our social–emotional experiences and our attempts to understand those experiences.

Not only do specific developmental delays become a focus of treatment, but the general levels of social–emotional and cognitive development must be considered when designing the treatment plan and interventions. "The formulation of an adequate play therapy treatment plan requires that you also have a sense of the child's overall developmental level across her full range of functioning" (O'Connor, 1991, p. 149). Information about a child's current cognitive developmental level is useful in play therapy treatment planning for at least four different reasons:[2]

• The child's current level of cognitive functioning gives some sense of how that child has processed life experiences to date. A 12-year-old child whose cognitive functioning is still preoperational organizes his or her life experiences much differently from a 12-year-old who is already using abstract reasoning processes.
• The play therapy process and content can be adjusted to the child's level to maximize the child's learning in sessions.
• Knowing the child's level of cognitive functioning allows the therapist to develop appropriate expectations about the child's behaviors both in and out of sessions.
• The therapist can use this knowledge to facilitate understanding of the child's behavior by others in his or her ecosystem, such as parents, foster parents, or teachers.

Assessment can be used to identify clinical disorders related to behaviors and intrapsychic processes that are atypical regardless of age. Level of depression, psychotic processes, attention deficits, and conduct disorder behaviors are areas often assessed in children. However, the degree to which some behavior is labeled as pathologic is sometimes developmentally deter-

mined. For example, oppositional and defiant behavior is diagnosed as a clinical disorder in the DSM-IV when it occurs after the age of 5 or 6, but is seen as a typical, developmentally appropriate behavior in younger children. From an ecosystemic perspective, treatment planning is facilitated if we treat oppositional behavior as a delay in social–emotional functioning rather than a clinical disorder, while recognizing that it may be related to a clinical disorder.

The first two assessment goals essentially compare the functioning of the child to other children of a similar age and background. The third goal of individual assessment focuses on the unique way in which this child experiences, makes sense of, reacts to, and interacts with his or her world based on past experiences, developmental functioning, and the current ecosystemic context. This focus is particularly critical to the development of an individualized play therapy treatment plan.

The general categories of assessment tools used in individual assessment are described here. We describe in greater detail a few of the instruments that may be less well known and that we have found to be particularly useful in our practices. The following resources on assessment provide a more comprehensive list of available instruments for assessing children and families: Fischer and Corcoran (1994), Friedman and Sherman (1987), Grotevant and Carlson (1989), Holman (1983), Johnson (1976), Kestenbaum and Williams (1988), Southworth, Burr, and Cox (1981), Touliatos, Perlmutter, and Straus (1990), and Weaver (1984). Schaefer, Gitlin, and Sandgrund's (1991) edited book, *Play Diagnosis and Assessment,* is a particularly excellent resource for play therapy treatment planning.

In the following descriptions, Steven Johnson's data have been used to illustrate the instrument's use where appropriate. His assessment data are presented in its Workbook form later in the chapter.

Standardized Instruments

Standardized instruments, such as intelligence tests or personality tests, compare the client's performance to a normative group. These instruments may be useful in determining whether or not the child's functioning or behavior is discrepant from most children of a similar age and background, and, if so, in what direction. These instruments may also provide diagnostic or clinical categories based on the pattern of scores. Standardized instruments are particularly vulnerable to cultural bias and distortion issues related to the nature of the normative population and to psychometric concerns such as whether or not the construct being examined is comparable across cultures (Dana, 1993).

---

[2]This list is adapted from O'Connor, 1991, p. 147.

Weschler Intelligence Scales for Children—Third Edition (WISC-III)

The Weschler Intelligence Scales are among the most widely used assessment instruments for determining a child's intellectual abilities and particular strengths and weaknesses in cognitively understanding his or her world (Cohen, Swerdlik, & Smith, 1992). The Wechsler Scales provide an estimate of global intellectual ability (Full Scale IQ), verbal intellectual ability (Verbal IQ), and nonverbal intellectual ability (Performance IQ). Test results can also be examined to determine whether there is a pattern in the subscale results that might facilitate understanding how a particular child processes information. Kaufman's (1994) book, *Intelligent Testing with the WISC-III,* is a useful guide that presents many different approaches to examining the pattern of responses on the WISC-III. The case example of Steven Johnson demonstrates a situation in which intelligence testing was particularly useful in understanding the functioning of this child.

> Steven's WISC-R[3] results were as follows: FSIQ = 80 indicating below average cognitive abilities; VIQ = 85 with intertest scatter and PIQ = 78. Examination of intertest scatter with Cattell's (1971) Crystallized vs. Fluid dichotomy revealed a significant difference. Fluid mean = 6.2 (A-5, C-5, BD-6, PC-7, PA-7, OA-7) and crystallized mean = 9.3 (I-11, S-9, V-8). Fluid intellectual abilities develop through incidental learning and involve problem solving through flexibility and adaptation, while crystallized intellectual abilities involve skills and knowledge acquired through direct, deliberate training or education. Fluid intellectual abilities are more vulnerable to neurological injury. Deficits in fluid intelligence contribute to problems in learning social skills that are largely dependent on incidental learning.

Personality Inventory for Children

The Personality Inventory for Children (PIC; Witt, Lachar, Kinedinst, & Seat, 1977) is a test that is similar to the MMPI-2 (Hathaway & McKinley, 1991) but which can be used to evaluate younger children by having it completed by the caregiver. It has three validity scales and a scale that indicates the need for further assessment if elevated, thus providing an overall screening function. Three scales relate to different dimensions of cognitive functioning (Achievement, Intellectual Screening, and Development). Clinical dimensions include Depression, Somatic Concern, Delinquency, Withdrawal, Anxiety, Psychosis, and Hyperactivity. Family functioning (Family Relations) and peer functioning (Social Skills) are also assessed. Thus, this single instrument covers many relevant areas of developmental, intrapsychic, and interpersonal functioning.

> Steven's PIC results indicated significant problems in almost all areas, including cognitive functioning (elevated Achievement, Intellectual Screening, and Development), as well as depression, anxiety, angry defiant behavior with impulsivity, and poor judgment (elevated Delinquency), and atypical behaviors (elevated Psychosis). The family relations scale was also elevated indicating the presence of family conflict.

Developmental Assessment Tools

Developmental assessment tools often provide an estimate of the child's developmental age and typically anchor the child's performance relative to a developmental continuum of tasks. These are particularly useful for two reasons when compared with the standardized instruments. First, framing a 10-year-old child's behavior as similar to that of a preschool-age child rather than as significantly deviant from the normal 10-year-old provides a way to anchor the treatment to this developmental level rather than just focusing on deviant behaviors. Second, by defining a continuum of developmental tasks and identifying where that child falls on the continuum, treatment can be designed to promote the child's movement along this continuum. This strategy is particularly relevant when considering social–emotional functioning. Because developmental instruments are more functionally based than standardized instruments, they are potentially less culturally biased, though there are still concerns related to the interaction between development and its expression within a particular culture.

Developmental Teaching Objectives Rating Form–Revised (DTORF-R)

The Developmental Teaching Objectives Rating Form (DTORF-R; Developmental Therapy Institute, 1992; Wood, 1992a, 1992b) is a developmental assessment tool that focuses on social–emotional functioning. We have found it to be particularly useful for treatment planning. The DTORF-R uses ordinal scales to assess a child's social-emotional development across several domains, including Behavior, Communication, Socialization, and Academics (Wood, Combs, Gunn, & Weller, 1986; Wood, 1996). For our purposes, we limit the use of the DTORF-R to the first three domains and typically assess Academic functioning with more standardized and fine-tuned instruments, or we obtain the academic data from other sources. The DTORF-R contains hierarchically arranged, operationally defined developmental objectives spanning from birth to age 16. The items are broken down into stages representing different developmental ages: Stage I (0–2), Stage II

---

[3]The current version of the Weschler Intelligence Scales for Children is the third version (hence the III), but at the time this client was tested, the second version or revised version (hence the R) was in use.

(2–6), Stage III (6–9), Stage IV (9–12). The rater interviews an informant who knows the child well (preferably a caregiver or teacher or both) and identifies whether or not the child has mastered each objective consistently at least 80% of the time in most settings. The rating starts with the developmentally lowest item and continues until two items are identified in each domain that the child has not yet fully mastered. These items then become treatment goals.[4]

Stevens DTORF-R results were as follows (i.e., tasks to be accomplished):

Behavior Goals:

B12—Participates in individual movement activities with a group without loss of control (e.g., waits turn, does not intrude).
B13—Takes personal initiative to spontaneously participate in social or classroom activities that are expected of him.

Communication Goals:

C9—Develops internal language (e.g., receptive vocabulary and representational concepts) no more than 2 years delayed.
C12—Can describe characteristics of self to others.

Socialization Goals:

S16—Participates in peer sharing activities with adult guidance
S17—Engages in interactive play with peers.

Discussion:

All of these goals are in the upper end of the Stage II goals, indicating that even though Steven is 12 years old chronologically, his social–emotional functioning is similar to that of a 4- to 6-year-old child.

Checklists and Rating Scales

Checklists and rating scales are used to measure specific behaviors, thoughts, feelings, experiences, and so forth. Some rating scales are standardized and compare the child's behavior or performance to a normative group. Many, however, are criterion referenced, that is, they are based on some preestablished criterion and the degree to which a certain score on the checklist or rating scale indicates that the child demonstrates that characteristic or style. The Conners Ratings Scales (Conners & Barkley, 1985) are some of the most widely used scales for assessing hyperactivity and conduct problems. Rating scales can be completed by the child, caregivers,

teachers, and other relevant people, providing an ecosystemic view of the problems. Cultural appropriateness depends on the degree to which the criterion has been examined within a specific cultural context.

Dean Behavioral Checklist for Child and Adolescent MPD

Trauma and abuse are frequently found in the histories of children seen in play therapy. There is increasing recognition that dissociative phenomena are present in children even though they may not be as clearly defined as when reported by adults. The Dean Behavioral Checklist (James, 1989) provides a way to assess dissociative phenomena on the basis of the child's behaviors in multiple settings and his or her drawings.

Functional Behavioral Analysis[5]

Functional behavioral analysis is a form of behavioral assessment that targets the function of the child's behaviors rather than targeting the problem behaviors without identifying the function of those behaviors. Functional behavioral analysis is consistent with our ecosystemic perspective in that it addresses the purpose of the child's behavior within that child's ecosystemic context. However, it places minimal emphasis on the role of intrapsychic experience and expectations. Thus, we would combine this type of assessment with data from the interviews or projective and play assessments to generate a more comprehensive understanding of the child's behavior. Currently, there are several sources that provide strategies for conducting a functional analysis and for designing behavioral interventions based on that analysis (Cipani, 1989, 1993; O'Neill, Horner, Albin, Storey, & Sprague, 1990). Cultural sensitivity is maintained when the function of the behavior is understood from the perspective of the child's cultural context, thus the responsibility for cultural appropriateness lies with the examiner.

Cipani Behavioral Assessment and Diagnostic System (C-BAD)

The Cipani Behavioral Assessment and Diagnostic System (Cipani, 1993) is a four-category functional diagnostic system to prescribe behavioral interventions based on the function of the child's behavior. A functional analysis attempts to identify the function of the problem behaviors in terms of its maintaining contingency or contingencies and then to design interven-

---

[4]Refer to O'Connor (1991) for a detailed description of the DTORF and its use in treatment planning.

[5]Thank you to Ennio Cipani for contributing to this section on functional behavior analysis.

tions that target the function of the child's behavior and the contingencies that maintain it.

Projective Instruments and Projective Play Techniques

Projective instruments and projective play techniques, such as projective drawings (Cantlay, 1996), the Rorschach Ink Blot Test (Exner, 1993; Exner & Weiner, 1994), storytelling techniques (Teglasi, 1993), and puppet play interviews (Irwin, 1991), can be particularly useful for gathering information about how the child perceives his or her experiences and relationships and organizes his or her intrapsychic world. The primary purpose of projective assessment is to provide a description of the individual child's functioning within his or her current life experience, including cultural context, rather than to compare the child's functioning to a normative group, although some projective instruments also have a normative component. When projective instruments are used appropriately, it is possible to reduce significantly the effect of cultural bias. However, projective instruments place a greater responsibility on the examiner to have the cultural knowledge necessary to interpret the results in context and to be aware of the cultural biases that may be inherent in the theoretical model used to interpret the meaning of the results (Dana, 1993).

Children's Projective Drawing Battery

The Children's Projective Drawing Battery (Sullivan, 1996) is designed to gather information about the child's self-perceptions (Draw-A-Person), perception of relationships with caregivers (Mother-Child Father-Child Drawing), family relationships (Kinetic Family Drawing), and perception of environment, especially home (Draw-A-House). This battery is particularly useful because it provides a view of the child's world across several different systems.

Robert's Apperception Test for Children (RAT-C)

The Robert's Apperception Test for Children (McArthur & Roberts, 1982) is a storytelling test for children ages 6 to 16 that shows a variety of children and adults in a number of different situations. Storytelling tests are all based on the projective hypothesis, that is, the assumption that people will attempt to structure any minimally structured stimuli they encounter and that the structure they impose reflects the structure and functioning of their own personality. Each of these tests also looks at the way in which the respondent describes interpersonal interactions. Thus, storytelling tasks have the potential to provide an un-

derstanding of the way the child organizes his or her experience of his or her self-perception and interpersonal relationships. Use of the RAT-C or other storytelling assessment tool requires training in the use of projective assessment techniques.

> Steven's RAT-C results combined with his other projective test results (drawings, Rorschach) indicate that he struggles with control of his impulses, has difficulty interpreting his social environment accurately, and at times demonstrates illogical reasoning processes. These cause him to experience high levels of anxiety, particularly in novel situations in which the demands of the new experience feel overwhelming in comparison with his abilities to make sense of the situation. Social situations in particular are difficult for him to accurately comprehend. He expresses his anxiety through physical symptoms such as overeating. He tends to constrict his emotional responses, thus he doesnt let others know that he is having difficulties until he becomes overwhelmed, at which point he responds with a primitive anger and strikes out at whomever he perceives to be the immediate source of his frustration. When the demands of his environments (academic and social) are clear and comprehensible to him, he is able to be relaxed and friendly in his interactions with others.

Semistructured Clinical Interviews and Play Interviews

Semistructured clinical interviews and play interviews range from highly structured diagnostic interviews (Orvaschel, 1988) to less structured approaches that provide a way to organize interview data, observations, and play interactions in a clinically meaningful way. The Mental Status Examination (MSE) is the best known tool in this category. Another organizing framework is Greenspan's (1992) Functional Emotional Assessment Scale, which organizes observations of behavior and interactions to determine an infants or preschoolers level of emotional development. O'Connor's (1991) description of a developmental context for play therapy also provides an organizing framework for determining a child's level of cognitive and social–emotional functioning and is briefly described in Chapter 9, "Session Activities." Developmental play interviews also provide useful information about the child's level of representational play (e.g., Westby, 1991) and an integrated assessment of cognitive, social–emotional, communication, and sensorimotor developmental functioning (Linder, 1993). Diagnostic play interview scales can be used to assess clinically focused concerns such as thought disorder (Caplan & Sherman, 1991), hyperactivity (Mayes, 1991), autism (Siegel, 1991), and the effects of trauma (Nader & Pynoos, 1991). The cultural appropriateness of any of these interviews depends on both the sensitivity of the content and the examiners understanding and interpretation of the child's behavior with respect to its meaning in the child's cultural context.

Westby Symbolic Play Scale

Representational play refers to a child's ability to engage in symbolic or pretend play. This is an important developmental skill, because it is through symbolic play that children communicate and develop their understanding of their experiences and relationships in the world. Westby's (1991) Symbolic Play Scale provides a way to evaluate a child's level of representational play based on a play interview. Representational play develops across several dimensions in specific stages over time. Although Westby identifies five dimensions of symbolic play, we find these three the most clinically useful: (a) decontextualization, or the ability to move in the play from life-size realistic props to miniature toys or no props; (b) play themes, from everyday activities to totally invented situations; and (c) organization of play themes, from limited symbolic actions to sequentially organized play. Children begin to develop representational play abilities around 17 to 19 months, and have moved through all of these stages by age 5, though their representational abilities continue to develop throughout their lives. Specifically, by age 5, the child's play should be completely decontextualized with little or no need for props. Thematic content can include events that the child has neither participated in nor observed, which allows the child to integrate information from his or her own experiences in novel ways to develop alternative ways of experiencing his or her world. This is a critical skill for play therapy. The representational play should be highly organized, with planning of the sequences.

Based on Steven's initial play interview, his developmental level of representational play is estimated to be similar to that of a 3- to 3½-year-old. While he is able to decontextualize his play by using small toy figures, his play was minimally organized with little planning and the themes were limited to events in his life with little elaboration. This concreteness and paucity in the content and organization of his representational play is consistent with that seen in children with neurological problems.

We have identified the following core areas as being most relevant in assessing the child's individual functioning: cognitive, emotional, behavioral, and physical. Cognitive functioning is addressed first because the child's level of cognitive functioning determines the way in which that child processes his or her behavior, emotions, and interpersonal relationships. A child whose cognitive level is still preoperational, regardless of his or her chronological age, is going to have difficulty structuring experiences and planning behavior in a logical and organized manner. Information that may be addressed in this category includes the child's intelligence, cognitive and coping styles, intrapsychic models, language development and communication abilities, and academic skill areas. There are certainly other aspects or ways in which the cognitive domain can be approached and evaluated. Emotional functioning is next because it is inextricably tied to the child's intrapsychic models and organization of his or her life experience. Behavioral functioning is the most visible manifestation of the child's developmental and clinical functioning, and the physical domain may reflect the child's development in other areas and/or address biologic contributions to the child's functioning. We recognize that these areas are interdependent; thus, the data must be integrated for a full understanding of the child.

Steven Johnson's case material has been previously presented as it related to the specific categories of tests and techniques. Now, this case material is integrated into the structure of the Workbook.

Case Example

INDIVIDUAL DATA

List the source of the data reported in each of the following sections. For example: Data regarding a child's intellectual functioning may have been obtained from an intelligence test, school records and their scores on various projective instruments.

Cognitive Functioning (Including, if relevant, intelligence, learning styles, language and all academic skill areas.) **:**

Intellectual Functioning: WISC-R: FSIQ = 80; VIQ = 85 with intertest scatter; PIQ = 78. Below average cognitive abilities. Examination of intertest scatter with Cattell's (1971) Crystallized vs. Fluid dichotomy revealed a significant difference Fluid mean = 6.2 (A-5, C-5, BD-6, PC-7, PA-7, OA-7) and Crystallized mean = 9.3 (I-11, S-9, V-8). Fluid intellectual abilities develop through incidental learning and involve problem solving through flexibility and adaptation, while crystallized intellectual abilities involve skills and knowledge acquired through direct, deliberate training or education. Fluid intellectual abilities are more vulnerable to neurological injury. Deficits in fluid intelligence contribute to problems in learning social skills that are largely dependent on incidental learning.

Representational Play: Westby Symbolic Play Scales: Based on Steven's initial play interview, his developmental level of representational play is estimated to be similar to that of a 3 to 3-1/2 year old. While he is able to decontextualize his play by using small toy figures, his play was minimally organized with little planning and the themes were limited to events in his life with little elaboration. This concreteness and paucity in the content and organization of his representational play is consistent with that seen in children with neurological problems.

Academic Functioning: PIAT: Reading - grade 5.0; Spelling - grade 4.2; Math - grade 3.5; General Information grade 4.3

Language Functioning: Language Evaluation: SCAN: Auditory processing difficulties; deficits in auditory attention (age equivalent of 4-6 on Detroit Tests of Learning Aptitude (DTLA)); Expressive and Receptive Language Delays (age equivalents of 6-1 on Clinical Evaluation of Language Functions (CELF-R)).

DTORF-R Communication Goals: Both are higher Stage II Goals indicating that his communication abilities are similar to that of a 4 year old child. He has limited use of representational language to organize his intrapsychic sense of himself and his world.

C9 - Develops receptive vocabulary (e.g., representational concepts) no more than two years delayed.

C12 - Can describe characteristics of self to others.

Emotional Functioning : Steven's personality and projective test results (RAT-C, drawings, Rorschach, PIC) indicate that he struggles with control of his impulses, has difficulty interpreting his social environment accurately, and at times demonstrates illogical reasoning processes. These cause him to experience high levels of anxiety, particularly in novel situations in which the demands of the new experience feel overwhelming in comparison with his abilities to make sense of the situation. Social situations in particular are difficult for him to accurately comprehend. He expresses his anxiety through physical symptoms such as overeating. He tends to constrict his emotional responses, thus he doesn't let others know that he is having difficulties until he becomes overwhelmed, at which point he responds with a primitive anger and strikes out at whomever he perceives to be the immediate source of his frustration. When the demands of his environments (academic and social) are clear and comprehensible to him, he is able to be relaxed and friendly in his interactions with others.

Behavioral Functioning: Both of Steven's DTORF-R Behavioral Goals are Stage II indicating that his behavior is similar to that of a 4 year old in terms of his impulse control and ability to recognize what is expected of him in different situations.

B12-Participates in individual movement activities with a group without loss of control (e.g., waits turn, doesn't intrude).

B13 -Takes personal initiative to spontaneously participate in social or classroom activities that are expected of him.

Physical Functioning and Motor Development : *Visual-Perceptual Skills*: Steven's visual-motor integration (Bender) and nonmotor visual perceptual skills (TVPS) were both significantly delayed with developmental ages ranging from 5-1/2 to 7-1/2 on the different tasks. This suggests that neurological inefficiencies contribute to problems in Steven's overall functioning.

ASSESSING INTERPERSONAL FUNCTIONING

Dyadic, family, peer, and other systemic assessment tools are less well known than individual assessment tools. The Marschack Interaction Method (MIM; Jernberg, 1991) is one of our favorite techniques because it captures the interactive processes between a caregiver and a child, although it can be adapted to families or couples as well.[6] Other useful systemic assessment tools include family projective play techniques (e.g., Ross, 1991; G. Smith, 1991), family play interviews (e.g., Stollak, Crandell, & Pirsch, 1991), parent–child interaction scales (e.g., D. Smith, 1991), and peer interaction scales (e.g., Pope & Bierman, 1991).

Marschak Interaction Method (MIM)

The Marschak Interaction Method (Jernberg, 1991) is used to assess the parent–child attachment relationship. Between the 1960s and 1970s, Mary Ann Marschak conducted many anthropological studies on different styles of parenting and parent–child interactions among different cultural groups, as well as among parents who had children with emotional or cognitive disorders. Consistent across these studies was her finding that regardless of the cultural group or childhood disorder,

the intensity of the child's emotional tie to the parent was due in part to the behaviors of the parent, particularly the parent's affective quality (Jernberg, 1991).

Jernberg (1991) expanded the MIM into a clinical assessment tool to assess the quality of the parent–child attachment. Although not directly linked to Bowlby's attachment theory, Jernberg clearly identified attachment as a central construct of the MIM, particularly with respect to the parent's ability to reduce stress, be playful, and be affectively attuned to the child. The therapist videotapes the parent and child engaging in several predetermined tasks, then reviews the videotape with the parent. Tasks have been identified for infants, preschoolers, school-aged children, and adolescents, as well as a prenatal MIM (Jernberg, 1988, 1991).

The MIM has no standardized coding system. Rather, the interaction is clinically evaluated with respect to the parent's ability to guide purposive behavior, alert the child to the environment, reduce stress, give affection, and behave playfully (Jernberg, 1991). A 10-point Likert format checklist has been designed to assist in evaluating videotape on the preceding dimensions, but no normative, reliability, or validity data are available at this time. However, the MIM has excellent face validity and has been accepted as evidence in juvenile and family court proceedings in the Chicago area.

Case Example

INTERPERSONAL DATA

List the source of the data reported in each of the following sections. For example: Data regarding a child's peer social functioning may have been obtained from a parent rating scale, a sociogram and the child's responses to projective instruments.

Dyadic Functioning (Specify dyads assessed.): <u>None.</u>

Family Functioning: <u>Elevated scores on the Family Relations scale of the PIC suggest that family conflict is or has been present and that parental inconsistency in setting limits may contribute to the development of the child's behavioral problems.</u>

Social Functioning (Including, if relevant, both extrafamilial and peer interactions.): <u>Both of Steven's DTORF-R Socialization Goals are higher Stage II goals indicating that his social functioning is similar to that of a 4 year old with emerging abilities in interacting and engaging successfully with peers: S16 - Participates in peer sharing activities with adult guidance. S17 - Engages in interactive play with peers.</u>

SUMMARY

The purpose of this chapter was to show the use of assessment data in treatment planning from an ecosys-

temic perspective and to show the use of the Play Therapy Treatment Planning Workbook for organizing these data. As discussed earlier, the information that can be presented in the assessment section of the Workbook is diverse, and thus we have intentionally left it relatively unstructured.

[6]Training and information on the MIM can be obtained from the Theraplay Institute in Chicago.

·6·

CASE CONCEPTUALIZATION

In Chapters 4 and 5, the play therapist was oriented to the process of gathering intake and assessment data. In this chapter, the focus is on the process of organizing that data into a comprehensive case conceptualization. This involves completing Appendix Parts A1 through A4 as described in this chapter, and then completing Workbook Parts IV and V. For each of these parts, we present a theoretical rationale, general instructions, and the continuation of the case of Steven Johnson.

OVERVIEW

Having gathered a large quantity of information about the various systems involved in the case, the play therapist is ready to proceed with organizing and integrating the data. This is the purpose of the Appendix. It is used by the play therapist to develop ideas and hypotheses about the case. The hypotheses generated here will be evaluated, synthesized, organized, and presented in their final form in Workbook Parts IV through VIII. The Appendix simply provides a structure that facilitates the therapist's thinking about the case in a manner consistent with Ecosystemic Play Therapy Theory. It is not a formal part of the treatment plan and many therapists may wish to exclude it from the child client's chart so that they feel truly free to engage in creative speculation without fearing they will be held accountable for every detail.

The entire intake and treatment planning process can be likened to the process of assembling a complex jigsaw puzzle. The analogy works best if one imagines a puzzle similar to the one we recently saw assembled. It was a three-dimensional jigsaw puzzle out of which was built a movable Ferris wheel. There were several ways it could be put together, but it worked best when assembled in a certain order. The child's life situation can be thought of as being quite similar, in that it is made up of a large number of interlocking "pieces." These pieces may go together in a number of workable configurations, but there is often a way to optimize the child's functioning. This is the overarching goal of Ecosystemic Play Therapy.

During the intake and assessment phase, the play therapist locates as many of the pieces of the puzzle as possible and attempts to make sure they are all oriented correctly. During the process of formulating the case conceptualization, the play therapist attempts to discern the current relationships between the pieces of the child's life, the way they are put together, and then to develop hypotheses about the way these currently function. In this process it is essential that the play therapist develops as clear an understanding of the way the child views the world as possible. In the previous discussions about diversity, we talked about the "lenses" through which individuals view their world. We noted that these lenses are the result of accumulated experience and that they significantly affect the way in which

APPENDIX: Data Integration and Hypothesis Formulation

A1. DEVELOPMENTAL INTEGRATION OF INTAKE INFORMATION

Age	Cognitive Stage	Individual History	Family	Social
<Birth			Parental Conflict/ Separation	
Birth				
1		Developmental Delays in all areas of Functioning	Death of Maternal Grandmother	
2		↓	Parental Divorce	
3		↓		
4		↓		
5		↓	Stepfather joined family	
6		↓		
7		↓		
8		↓		
9		↓		
10		↓		
11		↓		
12	Concrete Processing of Information	↓	Mother and Stepfather Separated	Middle school peers less tolerant of immature behaviors

Age	Educational	Legal	Medical	Mental Health
<Birth				
Birth			Encephalitis at 17 days old	
1				
2		Parental Divorce (no custody battle)		
3				
4				
5				
6	Learning problems identified - began receiving spec ed assist.			
7				
8				
9				
10				
11				
12	Moved to new school as entered middle school/ Problems with behavior			

individuals define and attempt to solve problems. Before beginning treatment, the play therapist needs to make every effort to see the world through the child's lenses to have a clear understanding of where the treatment needs to begin. The play therapist then develops hypotheses about alternative ways the pieces of the child's life could fit together to function more effectively. These become the basis for the development of the treatment plan, which will be discussed in the next chapter.

APPENDIX, PART A1: DEVELOPMENTAL INTEGRATION OF INTAKE INFORMATION

The first step in organizing the intake data is to put everything that has occurred in the child's life into developmental context. The grid provided in the Appendix, Part I, is designed to facilitate that process by giving the play therapist a visual anchor for subsequent hypothesis generation. The grid is quite easy to complete and need not be filled out in detail.

The second column, Developmental Stage, is used to list the anchor points for the developmental model that the play therapist is using and to adjust those anchors based on what is known about the child's current functioning. For example, therapists using a Piagetian framework (Piaget, 1952, 1959, 1967) know that the sensorimotor period usually lasts from birth to about age 2 and is followed by the preoperational period from age 2 to 6. Those anchor points could be entered in the second column if the child's overall development is currently consistent with age expectancies. If, however, the child is currently 4 years old and shows no signs of engaging in preoperational thinking, then the anchor points for the stages need to be adjusted to indicate that this child is still in the sensorimotor stage in spite of his or her age. Anchoring the child's developmental progress is critical, because hypotheses about the child's reactions to various life events will be based on the developmental level he or she was in rather than his or her age at the time.

The rest of the columns are completed using data gathered during the various systems reviews that were completed during the intake. See Figure on pages 88–89.

APPENDIX, PART A2: DEVELOPMENTAL DESCRIPTION OF THE CHILD

The overall goal of this part of the Appendix is to form a comprehensive, developmentally based picture of the child's present functioning. This information is crucial to the goal development and treatment planning process. The point of lowest current functioning is used as the starting point for the play therapy. The child's optimal level of functioning, the level one would want the child to achieve given his or her capacities and context, serves as the overall goal or ideal end point of the play therapy. Activities are selected on the basis of, among other things, the capacity of these activities to transition the child between the point of current functioning and the target or goal.

Developing a good, norm-referenced description can be difficult if the child is functioning at a level with which the therapist is unfamiliar. It can also be difficult if the therapist's primary daily interactions with children involve only children in treatment. When this is the case, it becomes easy to lose sight of what should be considered developmentally appropriate behavior. If the therapist regularly administers a developmental rating instrument such as the DTORF-R, (Wood, 1992b) it can help keep his or her reference point accurate. There are also some excellent tables describing normative behavior for children at different ages (Caplan, 1973; Caplan & Caplan, 1977, 1983; Linder, 1993). *The Clinical Interview of the Child* (Greenspan, 1991, pp. 64–77), also contains a set of tables that focus on the neurological and social–emotional development of children ages 1 through 10.

Developmental Level

General

In this section, the play therapist records his or her overall impression of the child's present level of functioning. Does this child impress one as being much younger than his or her chronological age? Conversely, does the child seem older? Does the child's developmental functioning fluctuate over time or across situations? This description will give the play therapist some sense of how others are likely to perceive the child and, in turn, a sense of how the child is likely to respond. Understanding how the child is perceived by others may give clues as to why the child's needs are not getting met effectively or appropriately. For example, teachers often overlook the intellectual abilities of children who present as socially and emotionally immature, so that the child ends up receiving very little reinforcement for academic performance. On the other hand, teachers also tend to overlook the peer relationship problems experienced by children who present as much older than they really are. These children socialize well with adults but have difficulty getting their needs met through peer interactions.

Interpersonal

Once an overall developmental description of the child has been created, it is also important to note whether or not this developmental level is consistent across various interpersonal interactions in which the child engages. Children of alcoholics may sometimes appear very dependent and needy when they feel comfortable with an adult outside of their family. These same children may switch to being overly mature and caretaking when interacting with their alcoholic caregiver. Again, awareness of these variations will help the play therapist understand the strategies the child is currently using in attempts to get his or her needs met.

Case Example

A2. DEVELOPMENTAL DESCRIPTION OF THE CHILD

DEVELOPMENTAL LEVEL

General: (What is your overall impression of this child's current functioning? Do you think others would perceive him or her to be developmentally on, above or below age level?) Steven's overall functioning is like that of a much younger child. Both adults and children perceive him to be very immature.

Interpersonal: (Does this child's functioning change depending on the developmental level of the person(s) with whom he or she is interacting?) Steven's interpersonal functioning is developmentally lower than his overall functioning. This is consistent whether he is interacting with children or adults. The more structured the situation and the more specific the demands the better his functioning.

Cognitions

In this section of the Appendix, the play therapist develops hypotheses about the child's cognitive capacities and the interaction of those capacities with the presenting psychopathology. It is the first relationship between the pieces of the puzzle that needs to be surmised. It will not be possible to engage the child in therapeutic problem solving in play therapy if the play therapist does not understand how and what the child currently thinks about the problem and how he or she currently engages in problem solving.

Functional Level

Here, the play therapist formulates a description of the child's overall intellectual functioning. Although IQ is somewhat important in this context, it is the developmental level at which the child is functioning that is most important. A child who is functioning in the preoperational stage will need more experiential as opposed to cognitive activities in session in order to engage in functional problem solving, even if his or her IQ is 145. It is also important to note whether the child's cognitive functioning is stable over time and across situations. In much the same way that the developmental level of children's behavior may be situation-dependent, so, too, may their cognitive skills. When there is a problem in this area it most often shows up as difficulty processing emotionally loaded material. A very bright child who is capable of fairly abstract discussions about a computer's ability to "think" may find it difficult to engage in any but the most concrete descriptions of his or her emotional experience or to track comments the play therapist makes about that experience.

Significant Organizing Beliefs

This refers to those thoughts or beliefs the child has that are so powerful that they have come to organize the child's world view. These beliefs are significant elements of the "lens" through which the child sees others and their behavior. This is the point at which the play therapist begins his or her attempts to see the world the way the child sees it. The thoughts and beliefs noted here may have been stated by the child but much more often the play therapist will be developing hypotheses about how the child thinks. In essence, the play therapist is answering the question If I had lived this child's life and were functioning at his or her current developmental level, what would I believe about the world?

Some of these hypotheses will be easy to derive, whereas others will take both some creativity and empathy on the therapist's part. Piaget (1959) notes that once people leave a cognitive developmental stage as the result of maturation they can never return. That is, adults lose their capacity to think like children—an adult cannot fully understand an event in the same way a child understands it. We do not believe this to be necessarily the case. Either by empathy or projection or simply as the result of accumulated experience with children, some adults seem quite able to anticipate the way a child will understand a given event. Therapists who have this skill are truly gifted. What is critical here is that the therapist gives himself or herself permission to view the world in ways that may not seem logical or realistic and allows himself or herself to adopt a child's perspective.

It is fairly easy to hypothesize that children who have been physically or sexually abused are likely to believe that all adults are potential abusers. It may be a little harder to hypothesize that a child who was 3 years old when his or her sibling died shortly after birth may believe that he or she caused the death by wishing the child had never been born because he or she did not want to cope with the competition of a younger sibling. And it may be even harder to hypothesize that very young children who were abused at their day care center may believe that their parents wanted them to be abused because, after all, the parents were the ones who took them to day care and who, being omniscient, must have known what was going to happen. These are all examples of the types of hypotheses the play therapist will be developing in this section.

Once formulated, the hypotheses are used as another clue to understanding why the child uses the strategies he or she uses in attempts to get his or her needs met and why these strategies are not proving to be effective.

Case Example

COGNITIONS

Functional Level: (Describe overall cognitive functioning as well as any changes that occur when the child is working with emotionally loaded material versus more concrete material.) Steven's overall intellectual functioning is below average. In addition, he handles structured, well-defined information such as learning to read (crystalized intelligence) much better than incidental learning (fluid intelligence) which is required for successful negotiation of interpersonal relationships. Most children learn to modulate their emotions and to interact effectively through recognizing subtle social cues in the environment. Thus his reasoning and judgment are significantly impaired in situations which are not clearly defined and which require flexible problem-solving skills. His problems are compounded by emotional interference because he becomes easily overwhelmed and anxious when he doesn't understand what is expected of him. Emotional lability and attention deficits (probably neurologically based) also interfer with effective cognitive functioning.

Significant Organizing Beliefs:

1. Steven believes that he is stupid.

2. At times Steven reverses the above belief and attributes the problems he experiences to the fact that he is not stupid but others do not understand him.

3. Believes that his mother had his stepfather leave because his expectations of Steven's behavior were too high. Steven is ambivalent that this occurred, but believes it was the right thing for her to do.

Emotions

Although the problem solving that will occur in the course of the child's play therapy is largely a cognitive endeavor on the part of the play therapist, it is usually a combined cognitive and experiential endeavor for the child. Young children may understand very little of the problem-solving process in which they have been engaged. They may only know that they feel better. Emotions are, therefore, a critical way of assessing whether or not the play therapy is having a positive effect. But, even more importantly, effective problem solving cannot take place if the emotions of all concerned are not considered at every step in the process.

Type

This refers to the overall categories of emotion that the child is known to exhibit based on either observation or report. We generally consider four categories: anxiety-related emotions, depressive feelings, angry and aggressive feelings, and positive feelings. Is the child capable of all of these? Which type is predominant? Of the unpleasant affects, which one(s) does the child experience as most aversive? Does the balance of the child's emotions lean toward the pleasant or the unpleasant? With respect to a positive treatment outcome, it is important that the child has or develops the capacity to experience all types of affects in situationally appropriate ways.

Repertoire

By report or by observation, what different emotions in each category are a part of the child's repertoire? Younger children typically exhibit a smaller repertoire of intensely expressed emotions. A toddler is not likely to appear annoyed in response to a small frustration and enraged in response to a larger frustration, rather he or she is likely to exhibit rage in both cases. When you are 2 years old, everything seems to be a life-or-death crisis. As children develop more elaborate cognitive skills they can better understand their experiences and adjust their emotions accordingly. Developmental delays, aversive experiences, and psychopathology all are likely to restrict a child's affective repertoire. Having a good repertoire of emotional responses allows the child to fine tune his or her problem solving and elicit better responses from others and the environment.

Range

This refers to both the range from unpleasant to pleasant affects and the range of intensity of those affects. Is the child capable of having both very unpleasant and very pleasant affects? Within any one category of affects, what range of intensity is the child capable of experiencing? That is, can the child experience small pleasures as well as near manic excitement if the situation warrants? If the child is to function well in the world, he or she needs to be able to modulate affect in a way that its intensity matches the situation triggering it. Children who either over- or underreact emotionally are rarely able to get their needs met consistently and appropriately.

Reality Base

This does not refer to the child's ability to differentiate reality from fantasy, rather it refers to the degree to which the emotions the child displays fit, in both type and intensity, the situation that evoked them. The de-

gree of disparity between children's experience and their feelings gives the play therapist clues about three important areas of the child's psychological functioning. These are the child's ability to experience, identify and express emotions. Although problems may arise with any one of these functions, it can be difficult to sort out which one or combination is causing the problem. Obviously, a child whose capacity to experience emotions seems fundamentally limited, as often is the case with autistic children, will have difficulty identifying and expressing affect. One clue to look for when interacting with children is whether or not they show any physiologic manifestations of an emotional response to a given situation.

Some children manifest major physiologic and behavioral responses to events that are easily interpreted as emotional reactions but seem unable, rather than unwilling, to label those responses. This frequently has been the case with many of the children in residential treatment with whom I have worked. There was one boy, who stands out in my mind because he would become furious at some action taken by another child. He would clench his fists, tighten down every muscle in his upper body, and twist his face with anger, appearing truly fearsome, and hold there for several seconds before lashing out. If you could catch his attention in those few seconds he would deny being angry. If you directed him to look at his hands and the way he was standing because he certainly looked angry, he would look down and suddenly appear confused. It was as if he had been totally unaware of his body until that moment. He was able to see that he looked angry and had no trouble saying it once he saw it, but he clearly needed help learning to identify it spontaneously.

Other children experience a variety of emotions and are able to identify them but then are unable or unwilling to express them. For many of these children, the problem is a long-standing belief that there is no point in expressing your emotions because no one will respond to them appropriately anyway. For example, most abused children are not likely to tell their abuser that his or her behavior makes them angry for fear that this will only evoke more abuse. These children do not see that emotional expression is one of the key elements in getting one's needs met effectively and appropriately. Their bad experiences in the context of some interactions have generalized to many of their interactions. There is another group of children, though, whose emotional expression is not blocked by either experience or defensiveness but rather by the lack of a vocabulary sufficiently sophisticated to convey their experience. These children often make very rapid gains in resolving psychopathology when provided with the necessary tools through direct education.

Case Example

EMOTIONS

Type: Steven's mood is highly dependent on the cognitive frame he places on his current situation. When he doesn't feel threatened by expectations in his environment, his mood is generally positive and happy. When he is internalizing others' criticisms then he becomes very upset and and potentially self-destructive. When he externalizes others' criticisms as being inappropriately high he becomes very angry and will act out. The latter serves him better as he seems able to return to a generally positive mood once he has acted out because in the long run it tends to force others to reduce their expectations.

Repertoire: His repertoire is limited because of his limited understanding of the subtle nuances of affective communication.

Range: Full range of affect that tends towards extreme emotions when he feels threatened or overwhelmed

Reality Base: Steven's limited social understanding interferes with his accurate perception of appropriate affective responses to situations.

Psychopathology

This section was designed to be consistent with Ecosystemic Play Therapy Theory as presented in Chapter 1. In that chapter, psychopathology was defined as the child's inability to get his or her needs met effectively and in ways that did not interfere with others getting their needs met. Here, the play therapist considers three perspectives on psychopathology as it manifests in the case: first, those needs that the child has that are not being met effectively; second, those needs that the child has that are being met inappropriately in that they interfere with others getting their needs met; and, third, those needs that others in the child's ecosystem have that are being met in a way that interferes with the child's needs being met.

Needs Not Met Effectively

In this section, the play therapist identifies those needs that the child has that are either not being met at all or that are not being met in ways that are qualitatively or quantitatively satisfactory to the child. The play therapist does not consider here whether or not those needs are realistic from an outside perspective, only that these needs exist. For example, if the child desperately wants to spend 24 hours a day in close physical proximity to his or her mother in order to feel secure, this is clearly unrealistic. However, it is a good reflection of the intensity of the child's attachment needs and the degree to which those are not being met.

Needs Not Met Appropriately

Here, the play therapist lists those needs the child is meeting or getting met by engaging in behavior that prevents others from getting their needs met. If the preceding child refuses to allow the mother any time alone, even to go to the bathroom, then the problem should be listed here because of the fact that the mother clearly cannot get her own needs met in such a situation. Similarly, the child whose need to feel safe and powerful drives him or her to beat up other children at school is getting his or her need for power met at the expense of others feeling safe. This should be listed here as well.

Others' Needs Not Met Appropriately

The play therapist identifies those persons or systems whose needs are being met in ways that directly interfere with the needs of the child. The needs of the father whose needs for intimacy and control lead him to abuse his daughter sexually should be listed here. The needs of a school system not to identify a child as in need of a specific type of service because they cannot afford to provide the service should also be listed here.

The issue of how or why these needs are not being met is not addressed in this section. The factors that created or maintain the problem situation are described in Part A3, Etiologic Factors, and Part A4, Maintaining Factors.

C a s e   E x a m p l e

PSYCHOPATHOLOGY

Individual (Client) Need(s) Not Being Met Effectively: <u>Steven does not feel competent or capable.   Steven is unable to develop adequate peer relationships.</u>

Individual (Client) Need(s) Not Being Met Appropriately in That These Interfere with Other's Needs Being Met: <u>Steven's acting out and encopretic/enuretic behaviors interfere with others being able to learn. Steven's acting out and immature behaviors create a source of embarrassment for his sister. Steven's acting out and immature behaviors create a source of conflict in the home.</u>

Others' Need(s) Not Being Met Appropriately in That These Interfere with Child's Needs Being Met: <u>None</u>

Response Repertoire

Up until now, the play therapist has been looking at elements of the child's cognitive and emotional response to his or her world. This section provides the therapist with an opportunity to formulate a more generalized description of the child's overall response style. The terms *autoplastic* and *alloplastic* are taken from the psychoanalytic literature (Ferenczi, 1919) and refer to two opposing styles of responses that persons may engage in when faced with a situation in which their needs are not being met. The word *plastic* refers to change, *auto* refers to self, and *allo* refers to other. In such situations, children with autoplastic styles tend to try to modify their own behavior in an effort to get their needs met. These children will often try to placate their abusers or to behave in ways they hope will not trigger abuse. When they are not getting their needs met, children with an alloplastic style expect others to change. Often they will act out in an effort to force the other person to change: If you do not give me what I want, you will suffer. Most children have a dominant style but may use each mode of responding in different situations. An abused child may appear entirely autoplastic when the abuser is nearby but use primarily aggressive, alloplastic strategies when interacting with children who are younger or smaller than themselves. Adults tend to excessively reinforce children's use of an autoplastic style because it means the child will rarely act out in intrusive or aggressive ways. Most of us are perfectly willing to allow the other person to change when we are faced with a problem. Even play therapists must be vigilant to the possibility that they are expecting the child to do too much of the changing required to resolve a problem situation.

Children who are able to get their needs met consistently and appropriately may show a dominant style of responding but will be able to use the two styles in situationally appropriate ways. That is, they will attempt to change their own behavior when they become aware that something they do interferes with getting a positive response from another person.

> You know I realized that Mom never says yes to anything I ask for when she is walking in the door on her way home from work. Lots of times she says yes to the same requests if I leave her alone for about a half an hour after she gets home. From now on I'll just keep playing when she first gets home and ask for things later.

This same child may be able to use an alloplastic approach in a situation in which getting his or her needs met is being blocked by the inappropriate behavior of others.

> I was playing just fine and not bothering anybody until John came over and messed up the castle I was building out of blocks. It wasn't fair that he did that. I'll ignore it this time but if he does it again I'll tell the teacher. And . . . if he does it again after that I'm going to hit him so hard he won't even think about doing it again.

In this last response, the child has actually come up with a series of responses that range from autoplastic (ignoring) to aggressively alloplastic. A child with a flexible response style is much more likely to get his or her needs met consistently and appropriately.

The play therapist needs to keep in mind that response style is not the same as the concept of locus of control (Phares, 1976) and that these two variables should both be considered in conceptualizing the child's problem-solving capacity. Locus of control refers to children's perception of where the power to change a problem lies. Those children with an internal locus of control believe they have the power to initiate change, whereas those with an external locus of control believe others hold that power. Although locus of control is a somewhat useful concept for organizing one's thoughts about a child's organizing beliefs and response style, we have not specifically included it in the Workbook because research has shown it to be a highly situation-dependent variable (Phares, 1984). That is, children do not have a solidly internal or external locus of control. Rather, they may have an internal locus for academics and an external locus for abuse experiences. A child might even have an internal locus of control for academics ("I am a smart and capable student") and an external locus for mathematics ("I could do much better in math if only I had a better teacher"). The question the play therapist needs to consider is whether the variability in the child's attribution fits the situation and enhances problem solving or runs counter to the situation and interferes with problem solving.

As with response style, most children have a dominant perception with respect to the locus of control that is modified depending on the situation in which they are involved. When faced with an insoluble problem, most children initially assume an internal locus of control and believe they can figure out a solution. As time passes and the problem remains unsolved it will take different children more or less time to shift to an external locus of control and admit they cannot solve the problem. Children who get their needs met effectively and appropriately are good judges of the locus of control in different situations.

Certain combinations of locus of control and response style can result in very pathologic behavior on the part of the child. A child who has a predominantly autoplastic response style and assumes an external locus of control is a likely candidate for significant depression. These children assume they are the ones who can or should change when faced with a problem (or that others will not change), but they do not believe they have the power to actually effect resolution of the problem. Helplessness and hopelessness often result from this combination. At the opposite end of both continua is the child with an alloplastic response style and an internal locus of control. These children believe others must change in order to meet their needs and that they have the power to force those changes. These children are rarely attuned to the needs or emotional states of others and can be violently aggressive when frustrated.

Given these observations, the goal of the play therapy will be to move the child to a point where he or she has a reasonably flexible response style and is a good judge of locus of control across a variety of situations.

Case Example

RESPONSE REPERTOIRE

Dominant Approach to Problems: ☐ **Autoplastic**   ☒ **Alloplastic**

Autoplastic: (Describe those situations to which the child is most likely to make an autoplastic response.)

When pushed to the point that he believes others will not modify the situation that is distressing him no matter how much he tantrums then Steven becomes very withdrawn.

Alloplastic: (Describe those situations to which the child is most likely to make an alloplastic response.)

When the academic or social demands of a situation become more than Steven can manage he believes others should modify their expectations. When they do not do this spontaneously he uses severe temper outbursts to push their compliance.

APPENDIX, PART A3:
HYPOTHESIS DEVELOPMENT—
ETIOLOGIC FACTORS

The overall purpose of Appendix Part A3 is to answer the question How did this client come to be the child described in Appendix Part A2? That is, what was the cause of both the developmental problems and the problems related to the gratification of needs that have been identified to this point?

Underlying this question is the assumption that it is often easier to do effective problem solving if one knows the origins of the problem. Identifying the source of the problem is very different from laying blame for the problem. Blaming is generally a hostile and fairly unproductive strategy with respect to problem solving. Hence the common popular complaint against psychotherapy that "everything is always the mother's fault." Even if and when this were true, the problem may be no closer to resolution. Identifying the origins of the problem also does not assume that the original problem can, or necessarily should, be resolved. A death in the family may have caused great trauma, but the fact of its occurrence cannot be changed. The hope is that by identifying the sources of the presenting problems a plan can be developed that will minimize the interference of those original variables on the child's present ability to get his or her needs met effectively and appropriately.

Child Factors

Endowment

Here, the play therapist takes into account the fact that children are not all born equal. Children come with patterns of strengths and weaknesses that play a significant role in their functioning across their life spans. Hypotheses need to be developed about the role factors inherent to the child played in creating the present pattern of functioning and related problems. Hypotheses should be developed that not only cover the role of any deficits or dysfunctions, but also the role or roles of any particular strengths. The role of the child's intelligence should be examined, as well as genetic or congenital disorders, neurologic functions, temperament, and, potentially, even the impact of the child's appearance. In other words, does the child have any characteristics that significantly affect his or her ability to engage in effective and appropriate needs gratification?

Case Example

A3. HYPOTHESIS DEVELOPMENT: ETIOLOGIC FACTORS

Develop hypotheses regarding the bases for the child's present level of function/dysfunction.

CHILD FACTORS

Endowment: Steven's neurologic deficits secondary to the viral encephalitis he had at 17 days of age are the major contributor to Steven's deficits in all other areas. His most dominant problem is his extreme difficulty with both incidental learning and creative or flexible thinking. While this contributes to poor school performance it most significantly interferes with his social functioning. Social interaction requires the ability to read incidental cues and to respond to constantly shifting situational demands which Steven is unable to do. The limited flexibility in his thinking also makes it very difficult for him to engage in any functional problem solving so that he tends to resort to toddler-like tantrums. Steven responds best when the environment is very structured, the expectations are clear and he receives direct and concrete feedback regarding the appropriateness of his behavior. At this time it is unclear how readily Steven will internalize these structures and be able to function adequately in new or novel situations and interactions in the future.

Developmental Response

This section of the Appendix is often one of the more difficult for therapists to use. The goal is to develop hypotheses about the interaction of specific events that have occurred in the child's life with the developmental period during which these occurred and the subsequent contribution of these to the child's present functioning. That is to say, we know that a child whose parents divorce when he or she is 2 years old is not affected by the event in the same way as is a child who is 6 or 7 when the divorce occurs. Children's developmental level at the time an event occurs will have an effect on the way they understand the event, their perceptions of the locus of control for that event, their perception of their role in the event, and the potential solutions they see as being available to them.

When an event is particularly traumatic, children may arrest at the developmental level at which they were functioning, either with respect to their understanding of and response to that event or globally. I had an adult client who was horrifically abused starting at age 4. As an adult, she reached very high levels of cognitive and social functioning except for marked problems when anyone approached anything related to her abuse experience. Relative to the actual events, she was unable to engage in any abstract reasoning and even tended to use simpler more concrete language. Until some of the powerful emotions that had blocked de-

velopmental progress in this one area could be neutralized, she was unable to engage in any functional problem solving with respect to the impact of these events on her present functioning.

Case Example

Developmental Response: For the most part the impact of Steven's endowment-related problems greatly overshadow the impact of any of the other events in his life. Only one event seems to have played much of a role. Some of Steven's difficulty responding to limits appropriately and his tendency to use toddler-like tantrums may be related to the death of his maternal grandmother when he was about 18 months old. It is suspected that his mother's emotional availability was somewhat limited at this time and that Steven responded with intensified control issues and behaviors.

Ecosystemic Factors

For each of the major systems in which the child is embedded, the play therapist needs to develop hypotheses about the role those systems played in creating the child described in Part II. Again, the focus is not just on the degree to which each system contributed to areas of difficulty, but how or what each contributed to the strengths the child currently manifests.

Family

Of primary interest is an assessment of the role of the attachment relationship with the primary caretakers. As this relationship sets the stage for all future interpersonal transactions, its role in the child's life cannot be overestimated. If there were problems, these must be addressed before the child can be expected to function adequately in the present. Here, the play therapist also considers the roles played by siblings, the nature of the marital relationship, and the nature of the family as a whole.

Peers

The role of peers in creating problems for children is often overlooked or minimized as the play therapist focuses on the nature and role of the family. Children's peers have an amazing capacity for creating psychopathology that is sometimes very resistant to change. Cases in which the child has become the scapegoat for his or her peer group are particularly good examples. The negative appraisal rendered by peers often becomes a painfully ingrained part of the child's self-perception. As these children are able to use play therapy to develop skills to alter their behavior when interacting with

peers, they are often devastated to find that their peers do not change their perceptions so readily. This even applies to obvious changes in the child's physical characteristics. Many a child who has worn glasses in elementary school and goes on to wear contact lenses in high school finds that the nickname "four-eyes" persists long after the glasses have disappeared.

Other

As easy as it is to overlook or minimize the role of peers in creating a child's psychopathology, it is also easy to overlook the role of other nonfamily systems. Many children raised in very healthy families become symptomatic when exposed to iatrogenic systems. Schools, hospitals, courtrooms, and the like have all been known to have negative effects on children, sometimes in the most indirect or unintentional ways.

Take, for example, the plight of an African-American child who is school-phobic for developmental and attachment reasons. This child cannot be expected to do very well in play therapy if there are ongoing problems in the community that are currently being manifested in the form of hooded Ku Klux Klan members marching outside his or her school. Similarly, media coverage of a father who kills his family and then himself while on a drunken binge is likely to have more serious negative consequences for children whose parents abuse alcohol than for those whose parents abstain. Although adults often think children do not pay attention to events distant from their own lives, this is rarely the case, and therapists need to be attuned to the potential impact of distant and very abstract factors on the welfare of their clients.

Case Example

ECOSYSTEMIC FACTORS

Family: Steven's brush with death in infancy seems to have triggered a long-term protective response from his mother. This has been a benefit in that Steven's mother and sister have served as stable supports within his family and tempered the impact of most other life events. To some extent this has also been a problem in that Steven's mother tends to be very protective and to make allowances for Steven's behavior rather than developing appropriate expectations and setting clear limits.

Peers: None.

Other: Educational, Medical, Legal, Cultural, Historical: Although Steven's mother began reporting her observations of Steven's deficits to the medical system very early in his life these observations were largely ignored. That system's failure to respond meant that no resources were made available to either Steven or his family until he was 6 years old and the school system began noting significant deficits.

APPENDIX, PART A4: HYPOTHESIS DEVELOPMENT— MAINTAINING FACTORS

The subsections of Part A4 almost exactly duplicate the ones of the preceding part. Here, however, the play therapist is developing hypotheses about the role each of the variables plays in *maintaining* the present problems. That is, the way in which each continues to interfere with the child's ability to engage in effective and appropriate needs gratification. These hypotheses will identify those systems that must be altered to facilitate the child's future health and development as well as those that will serve as potential resources. These hypotheses will also help the play therapist identify systems that are most likely to resist the changes the child will be making. Those systems will have to be blocked in some way or provided with other sources of gratification if the child is going to have a chance of changing. For example, a mother who has relied on her child as her emotional confidant to the point that it has interfered with the child's ability to develop peer friendships is not likely to be happy when the child wants to stay after school to play on a sports team. If she cannot find someone else to meet her need for an emotional confidant, she is likely to sabotage the treatment and attempt to block the child's progress.

Child Factors

Endowment

The play therapist formulates hypotheses about the degree to which factors inherent to the child contribute to maintaining the child's difficulties or prevent resolution of the problems.

Case Example

A4. HYPOTHESIS DEVELOPMENT: MAINTAINING FACTORS

Develop hypotheses regarding factors maintaining the child's present level of function/dysfunction.

CHILD FACTORS

Endowment: Steven's neurologic deficits remain unchanged and continue to play a very significant role in his present difficulties. Although he has been able to achieve some level of cognitive competence in structured learning situations, the demand for more abstract and creative learning abilities will increase as he gets older, and it is unlikely that he will be able to meet these demands.

Developmental Response

The play therapist formulates hypotheses about the degree to which specific events that have occurred in the child's life, and the developmental period during which these occurred, continue to create difficulties in the child's life or prevent resolution of the problems. In the etiology section, the play therapist considered what early life events set the presenting problem in motion; in this section, the issue is the degree to which those early life events perpetuate the problems. For a girl who was molested the experience may have played a significant role in the etiology of her fear of men and her later fear of social interactions in general. In this section, the play therapist must consider whether or not the molest experience is still an active issue, the resolution of which would enable the child to engage in more effective problem solving. That is, will changing anything about the child's intrapsychic response to that event change her present behavior, or has the event become so layered over with later experiences and thoughts as to have been rendered essentially meaningless?

C a s e   E x a m p l e

Developmental Response: <u>The impact of Steven's neurologic deficits continue to be the predominant factor in maintaining his present functioning. The degree to which he sees himself as unable to function without his mother's input and the intensity of his toddler-like tantrums in response to stress are the result of an interaction between his actual neurological vulnerabilities and his mother's response to his illness (overprotectiveness), and that she accurately perceives that he is vulnerable and continues to respond by overprotecting him.</u>

Cost/Benefit of Beliefs, Emotions, and Behavior

This is the only section that is different from Part III of the Workbook Appendix. In this subsection, the play therapist develops hypotheses as to what the child gains and loses by functioning in the way he or she currently functions. The play therapist should also consider the degree to which the child is aware of the gains and losses. For example, parentified children are often unaware of the fact that they are losing out on their childhood. After all, it is difficult to realize that one is missing something that one never had. Because many of these children have been their parent's intimates since a very young age, they do not realize that they are missing out on the carefree pleasures of childhood and the development of peer friendships. On the other hand, they are often acutely aware of what they gain by being parentified. They know that they have considerable power, are greatly admired by adults who see them as very well behaved, and may have many adult privileges. These children often see other children as immature and unworthy of their time or interest. When this is the case, it can be difficult to find a way to help the child relinquish his or her current role.

Similarly, abused children who act out in ways that often trigger aggression from others may have difficulty focusing on what they lose as a result of their behavior. What they tend to be aware of is the fact that, at least intermittently, their aggression gets them what they want, and we all know the power of an intermittent reinforcement schedule. They are also partially aware of the power their aggression gives them over others. They may even perceive that it is better to provoke abuse at a point when you feel ready to cope with it rather than to let it happen to you at random. These children usually do not see any point in avoiding behavior that makes others angry, in as much as they believe they will be abused no matter what they do. They feel they might as well act out.

Keep in mind, if a thought, emotion, or behavior persists over time, the child's experience is that he or she gets more from it than he or she loses no matter what the result may look like from an outside observer's point of view. In Chapter 1, this was referred to as the child's subject-dependent sense of the adaptiveness of the behavior. Very often both therapists and lay persons will get caught up in the notion that children act out to "get attention," even if that attention is very negative. This notion runs counter to all behavioral principles, as there are no examples of animal behavior modification that suggest that one could train an animal to engage in aggressive or any other behavior just so that the experimenter will come over and beat it. When children's acting out appears to bring them nothing but grief, the most likely explanation for the continued behavior is either that it is intermittently reinforced or that it gives the child some sense of power and control. If every 10th or even every 50th temper outburst results in the child actually getting what he or she wanted, then temper outbursts are likely to continue and to be difficult to extinguish. Similarly, if being aggressive sometimes controls the timing or intensity of the child's abuse by others, then that behavior is likely to continue because it provides the child with at least a modicum of power with which to counteract feelings of helplessness. What is important here is the fact that when a behavior persists in spite of what appear to be very dire consequences, the play therapist must look hard to discover the powerful reinforcer that makes these children willing to tolerate the unpleasantness or even the pain they regularly experience.

To develop an effective treatment plan, the play therapist will have to consider how to help child clients

1. develop alternative strategies to maintain the benefits they gain from their current thoughts, emotions and behaviors;
2. recognize their current cost benefit ratio so that they will be willing to trade some of their old benefits for new ones if this means they will also lose some of the unpleasant consequences that accompany the old behavior; and
3. recognize the costs of, and the needs that go unmet on account of their current behavior and develop

strategies for tapping previously unknown resources and emotional supplies.

It is also important to keep in mind that none of what we have described here is meant to imply that children are consciously aware of any of the strategies they use in their attempts to get their needs met. In fact, it is more likely that they are unaware of both the intrapsychic and behavioral strategies they use. Unfortunately, the nature of written language is such that it makes concrete even the most abstract and hidden of human operations. When we say "children enjoy being parentified and will resist attempts to change their status," the nature of the phrase implies that children consciously know they are parentified, know that they enjoy this, and know they do not want to change. In reality, all or none of these implied factors may be true. Fortunately, the issue of conscious awareness only affects the play therapy in one way. If children are completely unaware of the nature of their motivations and methods, then creating some degree of awareness becomes an early treatment goal. If they are aware, then this step is simply skipped and the play therapy moves directly to more focused problem solving.

Case Example

COST/BENEFIT ANALYSIS OF BELIEFS, EMOTIONS AND BEHAVIOR

It is very painful for Steven when he becomes aware of the nature and extent of his cognitive and social deficits. It appears to be so painful that he cannot tolerate it for very long and begins to blame others for having inappropriate expectations of him. Once he can blame others he becomes enraged and acts out. In the short run the acting out causes him a great deal of distress because others become very angry with him or tease him. However, in the long run the benefit of the acting out is that others do reduce their expectations and his overall anxiety and negative self-evaluation are reduced. The acting out also drives most others away thereby reducing his social anxiety. At the same time the acting out tends to pull his mother closer to him because she feels the need to protect him.

Ecosystemic Factors

Family

Note the degree to which the family and its individual members work to maintain the problem or resist its resolution. What do any of the family members gain as a result of the child having the presenting problem? What will any of the family members lose if the child were to become healthy? Although the primary focus of this section is on the degree to which families may interfere with children's progress, the play therapist

should also note the family's potential to serve as a resource and supporter of change.

Peers

How do the child's peers work to maintain the problem or resist its resolution? What do any of the child's peers gain as a result of the child having the presenting problem? What will any of the child's peers lose if the child were to become healthy? Although the primary focus of this section is on the degree to which peers may interfere with children's progress, the play therapist should also note the peers' potential to serve as a resource and supporter of change.

Other

Note the degree to which other systems in which the child is involved work to maintain the problem or resist its resolution. What do any of these systems gain as a result of the child having the presenting problem? What will any of these systems lose if the child were to become healthy? Although the primary focus of this section is on the degree to which these systems may interfere with children's progress, the play therapist should also note the potential of various systems to serve as a resource and supporter of change.

Case Example

ECOSYSTEMIC FACTORS

Family: Steven's mother's ongoing protectiveness and tendency to expect very little of him contributes to his resistance to the demands placed on him by others and to the degree to which he sees himself as dependent on her.

Peers: Peers have become increasingly intolerant of Steven's immature and inappropriate behaviors. When he attended a smaller elementary school, his peers left him alone for the most part. But last year after his move to a larger middle school, peers more actively teased and rejected him. It should be noted that the chronically poor response Steven gets from both other adults and peers has tended to crystalize his negative pattern of behavior.

Other: Educational, Medical, Legal, Cultural, Historical: As mentioned above Steven's specific cognitive deficits make it very difficult for him to function adequately in both acacemic and social situations. None of the systems with which he interacts seem to recognize Steven's extremely high needs for environmental structure. When his interactions are appropriately structured he is able to use the cognitive skills he does have to learn and to behave more appropriately. External structure, clear expectations and direct, concrete feedback about the appropriateness of his behavior is required in all situations.

After completing Parts A1 through A4, the play therapist is ready to return and complete Parts IV through VI of the Workbook. To do this, the play therapist relies on the work done in the Appendix. The ideas developed there must be validated, synthesized, organized, and translated into prose for inclusion in the body of the Workbook.

The process of evaluating the validity of the ideas the play therapist has developed in the Appendix is fairly straightforward and does not require the use of complex processes or statistical analyses. First, the play therapist scans the material in the Appendix for face validity. That is, the material should seem logical and reasonable to another play therapist with the same level of training. A common question attorneys ask mental health professionals in court is Could another play therapist with your level of training come up with a different set of hypotheses when reviewing the same information? If the answer is yes they could, then the therapist should be prepared to defend his or her interpretation of the data. Second, the information should be scanned for consistency with the theoretical model being used. If there are data that do not fit, there are problems with either the data or the model that must be resolved. Finally, ideas that were entertained along the way but which now seem inconsistent with the remainder of the data should be evaluated further or discarded. Amorphous suspicions of abuse often fall into this category. For example, at some point in the case the play therapist may entertain the idea that abuse may have contributed to the problem but uncovers absolutely no substantiating evidence, concrete or otherwise. Before proceeding with the completion of the Workbook, the play therapist should decide whether any of these ideas needs more comprehensive evaluation or whether they should be dropped. Obviously, if the ideas have, at any point, reached the level of reasonable suspicion, then a report must be filed and investigated by the proper authorities.

Synthesis and organization of the intake information from Parts A1 through A4 of the Appendix is developed and presented in prose in Parts IV and V of the Workbook.

WORKBOOK, PART IV: DIAGNOSIS

Although Ecosystemic Play Therapy Theory defines psychopathology in a particular way, Part IV defines psychopathology in a way that meets the needs of traditional mental health practices and most third-party payers. The format used is the five axes system that is described in the Diagnostic and Statistical Manual IV (DSM-IV) (American Psychiatric Association, 1994). (See the DSM-IV for a complete description of its use and content.) Although most therapists are not quali-

fied to make initial medical diagnoses, they can and should convey existing diagnoses that affect the child's present psychological functioning on Axis III of the diagnosis section.

Finding suitable diagnostic categories for the problems and symptoms seen in young children can be a frustrating experience for therapists. The DSM-IV still has not reached a high enough level of sophistication for the complexities of children's experience or developmental variability. If the nature of your practice does not limit you to using DSM-IV diagnoses, we have found *Diagnostic Classification: 0-3. Diagnostic Classification of Mental Health and Developmental Disorders of Infancy and Early Childhood* (National Center for Clinical Infant Programs, 1994) to be very useful. It provides a much more comprehensive view of children's difficulties that lends itself more readily to conceptualization.

Case Example

IV. DIAGNOSIS

Axis I (Clinical Disorders): 315.1 Mathematics Disorder (2.5 grade delay);   315.31 Mixed Receptive-Expressive Language Disorder;   315.9 Learning Disorder NOS (less severe general delays in all areas of learning including reading, writing, and spelling);   314.01 Attention-Deficit/Hyperactivity Disorder, Combined Type (partial remission with medications);   312.9 Disruptive Behavior Disorder NOS (age inappropriate temper tantrums);   307.7 Encopresis w/o constipation and overflow incontinence;   307.6 Enuresis (Diurnal Only)

Axis II (Personality Disorders & Mental Retardation): V71.09 No Diagnosis

Axis III (General Medical Conditions): 049.9 History of viral encephalitis at 17 days old

Axis IV (Psychosocial & Environmental Problems): Disruption of family due to stepfather's separation from mother

Axis V: Current GAF: 50   **Highest GAF in past year:** 50

WORKBOOK, PART V: CASE FORMULATION

By this point the play therapist should have a comprehensive understanding of the case. In Part V, Case Formulation, the play therapist presents a thumbnail description of the case, in prose, that summarizes and integrates all of the case data, information, and ideas generated in the Appendix. The case formulation can be organized with the following outline or checklist:

- An overall description of the child, including mental status and present developmental level

- A clear, operationally defined, description of the presenting problem(s) and how it relates to those needs the child has that are going unmet or that are being met inappropriately
- A description of the origins of the psychopathology
- A description of the factors currently maintaining the psychopathology
- A statement of the overall goal and expected outcomes for the case if treatment (as described in the Workbook, Parts VII and VIII) is implemented

Every attempt should be made to keep the case formulation brief and focused. The play therapist should try to cover each of the areas in no more than one to four sentences. An overall goal of about a half page of single-spaced type is recommended. The case formulation can be thought of as being similar to the abstract of a research article. It may be the only part that is read so it should convey the case thoroughly and accurately without burying the reader in, albeit relevant, details.

Case Example

> **V. CASE FORMULATION** (This should be an integration of the case data and a description of the primary hypotheses to be addressed in treatment.)

Steven is a 12-year-old whose social-emotional functioning is more like that of a preschooler. His immature behaviors, encopresis and enuresis, and temper tantrums interfere with developing any positive relationships with peers and at this point are interfering with his functioning at school. He experiences social isolation, rejection, and limited competence in his functioning that contribute to feelings of sadness and anger. The primary source of his problems is probably neurological deficits secondary to having a viral encephalopathy at 17 days of age. The primary deficits are in his ability to engage in flexible problem solving and incidental learning, in particular, recognizing social cues such that he can learn to respond appropriately in social situations. His mother's fear that he would die as an infant and her ongoing awareness of his developmental problems contribute to her overprotective stance. This is compounded by the loss of her mother when he was 18 months old, during which he probably entrenched his use of tantrums as a coping strategy in an effort to keep her engaged and he continues to use this strategy. Successful treatment will require changes in both Steven's behavior and skills and in his environment's (school, family) understanding of and response to his behaviors.

After developing a comprehensive, hypothetical conceptualization of the nature of the child's ecosystem, the play therapist is now ready to map out a tentative treatment contract and plan.

TREATMENT PLANNING

Treatment planning has four components. First, the play therapist must develop accurate, comprehensive treatment goals that are consistent with the case formulation and the theoretical model being used. Second, the play therapist must find a way to work with both the child client and his or her caregivers to develop a treatment contract that will address each party's needs in a way that will keep them actively engaged in the treatment process over time. Third, the play therapist must organize the treatment goals and the treatment contracts into a realistic and sequential treatment plan. Finally, the play therapist must devise both experiential and cognitive/verbal interventions that will move the client toward the treatment goals. This chapter addresses the first three components of this process. The principles used to devise specific interventions and ex-

amples of such interventions are presented in the next chapter.

APPENDIX, PART A5: GOAL DEVELOPMENT, SYNTHESIS, AND TREATMENT PLANNING

In Part A5 of the Appendix, the play therapist lists all of the goals that might contribute to the child's ability to engage in effective and appropriate needs gratification. These goals are derived from a number of sources contained within the workbook. The general types of treatment goals are listed in the following table along with the sources of these data as found in the Workbook and Workbook Appendix.

Goal type	Source
1. Reduction or alteration of the specifics of the presenting problem.	Workbook, Part I: Presenting Problem
2. Optimize child's ability to get his or her needs met effectively and appropriately. This includes teaching the child functional problem solving.	Appendix, Part A2: Psychopathology
3. Optimize child's developmental functioning.	Appendix, Part A2: Developmental Level
4. Optimize child's ability to use his or her cognitive skills across situations, no matter how emotional.	Appendix, Part A2: Cognitions
5. Correct any erroneous beliefs that currently interfere with the child's ability to meet Goal 2.	Appendix, Part A2: Significant Organizing Beliefs
6. Problem solve for strategies to minimize the power of previous experiences or trauma to interfere with the child's ability to meet Goal 2.	Appendix, Part A3: Developmental Response
7. Problem solve for strategies to circumvent any beliefs that the child hold's that are not incorrect per se but which interfere with the child's ability to meet Goal 2.	Appendix, Part A3, Developmental Response

Goal type	Source
8. Ensure that the child is able to experience, identify, and express affect.	Appendix, Part A2: Emotions
a. Ensure that child is able to recognize physiologic cues and identify these as affects.	
b. Enable child to experience a broad range of affective experiences (type and intensity).	
c. Ensure that child has words and strategies for expressing affect.	
d. Enable child to use his/her own and others' affects in problem solving.	
9. Ensure that child had a balanced, situation-specific, response repertoire (autoplastic vs. alloplastic).	Appendix, Part A2: Response Repertoire
10. Problem solve for strategies to help the child minimize or maximize the effect of his or her endowment.	Appendix, Part A2: Endowment
11. Ensure that the child is able to use good judgment with respect to evaluating locus of control in a variety of situations.	Appendix, Part A2: Response Repertoire
12. Problem solve for strategies to minimize the degree to which other systems interfere with the child's ability to meet Goal 2.	Appendix, Part A3 & A4: Ecosystemic Factors
13. Problem solve for strategies to maximize the degree to which other systems enable the child to meet Goal 2.	Appendix, Part A3 & A4: Ecosystemic Factors
14. Optimize the child's primary attachment.	Workbook, Part II: Dyadic System & Part III: Dyadic Data
15. Problem solve for strategies to improve the cost/benefit ratio created by the child's present patterns of behavior and systemic interactions.	Appendix, Part A4: Cost/Benefit Analysis
16. Problem solve for strategies to ensure that others' needs are met so that they are able to accept the changes the child makes in play therapy and are willing to keep the child involved in the treatment process.	Appendix, Part A2: Psychopathology

When listing goals, the play therapist should strive to be all inclusive whether or not the goals derived will, or should, be addressed in the play therapy. The idea here is to take a truly ecosystemic perspective in an attempt to understand which factors or systems should or could be changed to maximize the child's functioning. Even pragmatism or realism need not be a primary concern at this point in the process. For example, therapists sometimes leave out goals that involve the biologic parents when children are in long-term foster care, and instead focus on helping these children adjust to the demands of their current placement. This may be a realistic approach, but it circumvents two possibly useful outcomes. A treatment plan that involves the biologic parent or parents might allow this child to return home earlier and minimize the negative impact of long-term placement. Alternatively, such a plan may provide documentation that the biologic parents are unable or unwilling to act in the best interests of the child and cause the system to move to terminate their parental rights, freeing the child for adoption. Although this may not be an ideal outcome, it does, as with the first, allow the child to potentially avoid long-term foster care.

Column B

After developing a comprehensive list of treatment goals, the play therapist can next cluster those goals by type in Column B. This will sort out the priority of the different goals, the potential interrelationship of the goals, and the sequence in which they should be addressed. We have suggested six categories:[1] safety/crisis, secure base, developmental, problem/content, coping, and systemic but the play therapist may certainly adapt or modify these as needed.

• *Safety/crisis* are goals that involve imminent danger to the child or others, or those that are so catastrophic in nature that they supersede all other treatment goals.

• *Secure base* includes goals that focus on establishing basic trust and attachment. Children with severe abuse and neglect histories, for example, cannot work effectively on some of the content-specific treatment goals until they have established a secure emotional attachment to at least one adult in their environment. Without this type of secure base, it will be impossible for them to move on and develop any other mutually satisfying social relationships with adults or peers.

• *Developmental* goals involve bringing the child's current developmental functioning into line with his or her potential. These often include the development of skills that are considered universally necessary for a child of a given age, such as the ability to share.

• *Problem/Content* goals are found in most traditional play therapies. These include such things as working through grief reactions to the death of a parent or resolving the anger still felt toward a sibling who is intermittently abusive and problem solving a way to prevent future abusive episodes. They require that the child address a content area in order to break set and engage in more effective problem solving.

• *Coping* goals require the development of child- or situation-specific coping skills. Although all children must learn to share (a developmental goal), only some children need to learn to cope with being teased because they wear glasses (a coping goal).

[1]The authors acknowledge the contribution of Scott Van de Putte, Ph.D., in the development of this strategy for clustering treatment goals.

• *Systemic* goals include all goals that address changes that need to be made in the systems (from the dyadic level on up) in which the child is embedded to facilitate the child's optimal growth and development.

Column C

The next step is to identify those goals that can be reasonably addressed in play therapy and those that would be best addressed elsewhere. This is done in Column C. To determine the best venue for addressing each goal, the play therapist considers not only the nature of psychotherapy but also the best interests of the child and the systems in which he or she is embedded. It may be fairly easy for the play therapist to help a child who is undergoing medical treatment to negotiate the medical system. However, if this child is likely to face future medical intervention it may be best to mobilize resources within the medical system that can meet the child's needs or to train the parent to be a medical advocate for the child.

This issue becomes particularly significant when the development of attachment is a treatment goal. Should the play therapist ever serve as the child's primary attachment object and, if so, under what circumstances? We have talked about the critical importance of attachment in the child's future development and health, but it seems that the play therapist is rarely the person with whom the child should initially master this relationship. First, the play therapist is not available for a sufficient number of hours each day to make genuine attachment a reasonable goal. Even if the child is in residential treatment, his or her access to the play therapist is limited. Second, the play therapist is not likely to be available to the child over an extended period of time. In fact, as managed care becomes ever more a reality, the duration of the therapist's availability continues to shrink. And, last, the play therapist is not engaged in a "real" relationship with the child, so that the attachment relationship will be missing some critical elements. The most important of these is the fact that any attachment relationship the child forms with the play therapist is not reciprocal. That is, as play therapists enter the play therapist role they set aside their own needs in order to be fully engaged in helping children learn to meet their own needs. Therapists may demand appropriate behavior of the child client but they do not and should not demand emotional reciprocity. However, emotional reciprocity is an essential element of a positive attachment relationship. A caretaker engages the child in an attachment dance that "is always in motion. The dance may be graceful, with each person responsive to his or her own and to the other's varying rhythms over time." (James, 1994, p. 5). For these reasons, the play therapist should always attempt to find a person who will be consistently available to the child to serve as the focus for the development of attachment. Only when no other person is available should the play therapist serve as a transitional object until a more suitable person can be identified. However, even in such unusual cases, the play therapist should proceed with extreme care.

Column D

In Column D, the play therapist prioritizes goals. The play therapist may use any system for numbering or ranking goals that he or she prefers. We often number goals and may assign the same number to more than one goal, indicating that these might be best accomplished in clusters. Some therapists prefer to assign goals a high, medium, and low priority ranking. When prioritizing goals, those that involve a danger to the child client or to others will receive the highest priority. Next, those goals that reflect the lowest area of the child's developmental functioning have the highest priority. Whenever the child's development is uneven, the treatment should first focus on raising the lowest areas before addressing goals that are closer to age level. With respect to the remaining goals, there are several places the play therapist can look to determine the priority. In the case of conceptualization, the play therapist has laid out how the elements of the case fit together, and the sequence in which the pieces should be repaired or rearranged may be obvious from that description. In Appendix Part A3, etiologic factors were delineated, and it may be that these need to be addressed before the child can make any future gains. To use a construction analogy, there is no sense in extensively remodeling a house that has a shaky foundation. In Appendix Part A4, maintaining factors were delineated. Some of these may be considered to be of high priority if they will prevent the child from engaging in any alternative behaviors. To continue the construction analogy, there is no sense remodeling a house that is currently on fire.

Goals may be of equal priority but need to be addressed within different systems. If a child is having nightmares because of mistreatment currently being suffered at the hands of a teacher, a high priority *play therapy goal* may be the reduction of the anxiety and nightmares, and a high priority *school system goal* may be the transfer of either the child or the teacher. Finally, not all goals need to be prioritized at the outset. Many times, smaller and lower priority goals simply drop out as the child becomes better able to engage in functional problem solving.

Column E

In Column E, the play therapist identifies the system or systems in which the goal would be best addressed.

Both idealism and reality should be used here. The ideal system in which to address a goal should be considered first. For example, the social services or court system might be the best place to address the needs of a child who has been placed in 10 foster homes in 2 years. In spite of the fact that these systems are highly resistant to change, it does not mean that one should not try. It may be possible to have a legal advocate appointed to protect the child's rights in future placement hearings. It may also be possible to get the American Civil Liberties Union to file suit on behalf of foster children in a given county, triggering a complete reorganization of the system. Not every case will warrant such dramatic interventions and not every play therapist will be willing to attempt them, but it is important that the possibility not be overlooked in favor of a pragmatism that gradually succumbs to cynicism.

Reality must of course be considered when the treatment plan is actually initiated. Which system or systems are most accessible to the play therapist? Which system or systems are most likely to change? Is there one system which, if changed, would cause a ripple of change in other systems? All of these issues can be reflected in the systems identified in Column E and in the ranking of these in Column D.

Column F

In Column F, the play therapist indicates the type or modality of intervention that would be the most likely to produce the desired changes in the targeted systems. Multiple types of interventions may be appropriate and these can all be listed. It may also be appropriate to sequence interventions within a system, and this, too, can be indicated. For example, although family play therapy may be a goal, several members of the family might benefit from completing some individual work before engaging in family sessions. The child might also benefit from attending a peer group simultaneous to the implementation of the family work. This sequencing can also be reflected in Column E. The different treatment modalities and their implementation are discussed at some length in Chapter 8.

It is important to note that all of the information included in Columns B through E is tentative and probably quite idealistic. The data are the result of play therapists brainstorming on an optimal package of comprehensive interventions. It is better to have too many ideas about how to intervene in a given case then to have too few. As these goals are organized and sequenced in Workbook, Part VIII: Detailed Treatment Plan, the chaff will be separated from the grain and a solid, realistic plan will emerge.

Case Example

A5. GOAL DEVELOPMENT/SYNTHESIS AND TREATMENT PLANNING

A. Develop goal statements specific to the factors identified in Section VI and VII.
B. Indicate the category into which the goal falls
   S = Safety/Crisis, **SB** = Secure Base, **D** = Developmental, **PC** = Problem/Content, **Sy** = Systemic, **C** = Coping, etc.
C. Check those goals to be addressed in context of psychotherapy.
D. Number or rank the goals in order of priority.
E. Determine the system or context in which each of the treatment goals should be addressed.
   I = Individual, **F** = Family, **P** = Peer, **S** = School, **M** = Medical Setting, **MH** = Mental Health Setting, **C** = Community, etc.
F. Determine the interventions to be used in the course of the treatment.
   R = Referral, **IP** = Individual Psychotherapy, **FT** = Family Therapy, **PG** = Peer Group Therapy, **Fi** = Filial Therapy, **C** = Consultation, **Ed** = Education, **Ev** = Evaluation, **A** = Advocacy, etc.

A: **Comprehensive Goal List**	**B**	**C**	**D**	**E**	**F**
1. Reduce potential for suicidal ideation by decreasing Steven's sense of failure and increasing his ability to handle frustrations	S	X	1+	I,F	IP,FT
2. Develop more mutual goal-corrected relationship between Steven and mother to promote his awareness of other's needs and feelings	SB	X	2	F	FT
3. Utilize Steven's sense of security in the relationship with his mother to facilitate his exploration of alternative ways of behaving	SB	X	3	F	FT

A: Comprehensive Goal List	B	C	D	E	F
4. DTORF, B12, Participates in individual movement activities with group without loss of control (waits turn, etc., doesn't intrude)	D	X	4	S, MH	C,PG
5. DTORF, B13, Personal initiative to spontaneously participate in social or classroom activities which are expected of him	D	X	5	S, MH	C,PG
6. DTORF, C9, Develops internal language (receptive vocabulary/representational concepts) no more than 2 years delayed.	D	X	2	S, MH	C,IP
7. DTORF, C12, Can describe characteristics of self or others	D	X	2	MH	IP,PG
8. DTORF, S16, Participates in a peer-sharing activity with adult guidance	D	X	5	S, MH	C,PG
9. DTORF, S17, Interactive play with peers	D	X	5	S, MH	C,PG
10. Steven will improve his ability to engage in symbolic play and to utilize symbolic play as a medium for him to practice and process situations in his life.	D	X	2	MH	IP
11. Increase Steven's understanding of the nature of his cognitive deficits	P	X	3	MH	IP,FT
12. Help Steven develop coping strategies to compensate for cognitive deficits	P/C	X	4	MH, S,F	IP,FT,PG,C
13. Increase Steven's ability to differentiate between problem situations that are triggered externally (e.g., when other's expectations are inappropriate) versus those triggered by his inappropriate behavior. This will improve his ability to determine when an alloplastic versus an autoplastic response would be most effective.	C	X	4	MH, S,F	IP,FT, PG,C
14. Decrease Steven's use of temper tantrums as a primary response to frustration and anxiety by	P	X	1+	S	C
a. decreasing his experience of frustration in his environment	SYS		1	S	C
b. decreasing the environmental reinforcement for tantrumming (e.g., avoidance of work)	SYS		1	S	C
c. increasing his use of alternative strategies to getting his needs met	C	X	3	S, MH	C,IP, FT,PG
15. Decrease Steven's use of withdrawal as a primary response to social anxiety by	P	X	1+	S	C
a. increasing his experience of positive social interactions by providing high environmental support	SYS		1	S	C
b. decreasing the environmental reinforcement for withdrawal (e.g., avoidance of resolving a social conflict)	SYS		1	S	C
c. increasing his ability to recognize, interpret, and appropriately respond to social cues in interactions with both adults and peers	C	X	3	S, MH	C,IP, FT,PG

A: Comprehensive Goal List	B	C	D	E	F
16. Eliminate Steven's encopretic and enuretic behaviors in response to anxiety by	P	X	1+	S	C
a. decreasing his experience of anxiety in his environment	SYS		1	S	C
b. increasing his desire to avoid encopretic and enuretic incidents through behavioral management strategies	SYS		1	S	C
c. increasing his use of alternative strategies to cope with anxiety and frustration	C	X	3	S, MH	C,IP, FT,PG
17. Help family and school understand the nature of Steven's cognitive deficits	SYS	X	4	S, MH	C
18. Increase mother's ability to create realistic expectations for Steven's behavior, to communicate these clearly and to impose appropriate limit setting	SYS	X	4	F	C,FT
19. Increase the ability of school personnel to create realistic expectations for Steven's behavior, to communicate these clearly and to impose appropriate limit setting	SYS		5	S	C

WORKBOOK, PART VI: TREATMENT CONTRACT AND GENERAL PLAN

This portion of the Workbook is designed to cover two critical elements of the Ecosystemic Play Therapy process as well as some pragmatic professional practice concerns. The critical elements are the specific treatment contract and a thumbnail sketch of the intended intervention. This thumbnail sketch is limited to a description of the treatment modality, the anticipated number of sessions, and any planned collaborative interventions. Most regulating agencies and third-party payers require just such a description early in the treatment process, often before they will approve payment for any sessions. This limited description can often be developed by the end of the first or second session with the child and family. However, it may take a little longer for the play therapist to devise a more detailed plan. Therefore, the comprehensive plan is placed separately in Part VII of the Workbook.

Treatment Contract

During the course of the intake, the play therapist will have worked with the child client and the child's caretakers to define the presenting problems from their perspectives. During the course of developing the treatment goals, the play therapist will have defined the needs of the child and the caretakers/family from the perspective of Ecosystemic Theory. The goals derived from these two independent processes may or may not mesh well. The parents may be convinced that the child is willfully bad and in desperate need of being brought under rigid, even punitive, control. The child may feel that there is no problem at all except for the fact that his parents are constantly giving him a bad time of it and now dragging him to a play therapist to prove that he is a bad child. The play therapist may have hypothesized that the child's needs for attachment are not being adequately met, and that, subsequently, parent–child interactions have degenerated into near constant power struggles. If play therapy is to proceed and to be effective, these highly disparate viewpoints will have to be brought together in such a way that both the child and the parent believe their needs for an improvement in the current situation will be addressed. This is the role of the treatment contract. It creates the basis for the working alliance. Play therapist, child, and caretaker do not all have to like each other, but they do have to agree to work together toward a mutually agreeable goal.

As the term is used here, treatment contract does not refer to the number of sessions or the type of intervention to be used. Rather, this treatment contract specifically delineates the needs that will be more consistently and appropriately met once the treatment is completed. The contract may be worded in terms of these needs or it may be worded in terms of symptom reduction. In either case, both the child and the caretaker or family must have a solid sense of what it is they are to gain by subjecting themselves to treatment.

In Ecosystemic Play Therapy, the treatment contract

with the child is critical to the success or failure of the entire intervention. If children cannot see how they will directly benefit from participating in treatment, they will not have the motivation necessary to see it through. Adults understand the concept of enduring temporary pain to access long-term gains but most children do not. They do not see how or why potentially painful self-reflection will help them in the long run and they strive to avoid it in much the same way that most children avoid inoculations for disease. Unless their behavior is very egodystonic, most children also experience behavioral goals as criticisms of their present functioning. A child might very much want to stop wetting the bed, but allowing someone to set that as a treatment goal means having to admit that it really is a problem, that it upsets him or her, and that every time the child wets the bed after the goal is set he or she has failed. Many children simply do not have the ego strength needed to withstand the temporary setbacks that often accompany even the most successful play therapy. On the other hand, most children will work very hard in a situation that they perceive to be entirely focused on meeting their needs. The child who bed wets may be better able to tolerate an intervention aimed at reducing his or her feelings of shame. In the first case, the child may quickly decide that he or she wants to avoid all problem solving and stop reporting accidents to the play therapist. In the second, the child may be able to be engaged in role plays in which he or she pretends to wet, is teased, and problem solves ways of maintaining his or her self-esteem. With this feeling of safety, he or she may be better able to tolerate problem solving related to the wetting itself. The outcome of these scenarios may be exactly the same but the focus along the way is quite different.

Because children do not come to play therapy on their own, the play therapist must also consider a treatment contract that addresses the needs of those directly involved in the child's life. No matter how good the child feels about the progress in play therapy the treatment is in jeopardy of being discontinued if the primary caretaker does not experience the changes being made as progress. One often hears this complaint from parents in one of two forms. One form includes complaints of, "I don't see how just playing is ever going to solve any of the problems we are having at home." The other form includes statements such as, "Johnny sure likes coming here (or seems happier) but he is still fighting with his sister (or whatever the presenting problem was)." The latter may even be accompanied by reports of a problem that was either omitted or minimized at the time of the intake. Both types of complaints should be taken as clues that the caretaker's needs are not being met and the continuity of the treatment is in jeopardy.

It is not necessarily the therapist's place to be direct-ly involved in helping the caretakers get their own needs met. This important issue can be addressed in one of seven ways. First, the caretakers may only need to be involved, at least indirectly, in the child's treatment to keep abreast of the process and progress of the play therapy in order to feel that their needs are being addressed. Regularly scheduled feedback and planning sessions may be effective in such cases. Second, the caretakers may need to be directly involved in the child's play sessions. This can be done either through Filial Play therapy (Guerney, 1976, 1983b; VanFleet, 1993, 1994) sessions or by involving the parent directly in the playroom. In the playroom, the parent might take the role of passive observer, might become directly involved in the play, or even become directly involved in the treatment process as a co-play therapist. Third, the play therapist could choose to involve the family in family play therapy. Fourth, the caretakers may need conjoint/collateral sessions in which they can discuss parenting and behavior management strategies so that they feel better able to cope with the child between play sessions. Fifth, the caretakers may need treatment of their own to address issues that have little or nothing to do with their interactions with their children. These sessions might be either individual or marital sessions. Sixth, the caretakers may need to be assisted in accessing support within other systems to be better able to cope with the stress they are experiencing. Caretakers whose child is having severe school difficulties may need an advocate who can help them activate all of the services their child is due by law. And finally, caretakers may need to be directed to find social supports of their own that will be available to them on a regular basis. There is some danger that the play therapist will become the wise friend. When extended family support is available, this role was often served by grandparents or aunts and uncles. These people had accumulated childrearing experience and served to provide both cognitive and physical support to the parent. As individuals become more isolated within our society they often try to make do without these supports only to find that raising even one child, let alone several, can be a daunting task. The play therapist should endeavor to steer the parent toward whatever sources of support that will prove both beneficial and reliable. This will help to ensure that the caretakers are able to be fully available to their children.

Treatment Objectives

This is a relatively global statement or series of statements about what is to be accomplished over the course of the therapy. The presenting problem should certainly be addressed here. Specific goals are delineated in the Workbook: Part VII: Detailed Treatment Plan.

Treatment Modalities and Number of Sessions

A brief list of the treatment modality(ies) can be derived from those the play therapist has identified in Part A5 of the appendix, Columns E and F. Column E indicates the system in which the intervention will be best carried out. Column F gives the type of intervention. At this point, play therapists need to make some decisions about what will actually be done. Some of these decisions may be pragmatic. It might be great for a client to have certain goals addressed in a peer group in a school setting, but this does not mean such an intervention is possible. Here, the therapist indicates what will actually be done to address the treatment objectives. The anticipated number of sessions can either be arbitrarily established, as in the case of some managed care limitations, or be based on the number and type of goals that would be addressed in an ideal situation.

Collaborative Interventions

A description of any planned collaborative interventions can also be derived from those listed in Part A5 of the Appendix, Columns E and F.

Case Example

VI. TREATMENT CONTRACT & GENERAL PLAN

Contract with Child: Therapist will help Steven figure out how to keep people from being mad at him so much and help him feel less sad. Client agrees to come to sessions and spend part of the time talking about how he gets along with others even though it is very difficult for him to talk about these things and he would prefer to just play. We also will "just play" for a significant amount of the session.

Contract with Caregivers(s)/Family: Mother agrees to meet with therapist alone or with son to identify ways in which she can help him feel less sad and to help him learn to behave in ways that don't cause others to tease or reject him.

Contract with Others: The School District agrees to be involved with the planning process when Steven is to be reintegrated into that school system so that the environment and people there may optimally assist Steven in handling the interpersonal and academic demands of this setting more appropriately

Treatment Objectives: 1. Eliminate use of temper tantrums and social withdrawal as ways to cope with anxiety and frustration; 2. Eliminate encopresis and enuresis; 3. Develop compensatory strategies for cognitive deficits; 4. Improve social skills.

Treatment Modality(ies): Steven will be involved in a diagnostic residential treatment program for six months during which he will be at the program during the week and at home on the weekends. Treatment will include individual play therapy 1-2x/week, collateral sessions with his mother, conjoint family sessions with both he and his mother, and later, peer group therapy once/week.

Anticipated Number of Sessions: Six months (approximately 25-40 as needed)

Collaborative Interventions (Evaluation, Education, Consultation, Advocacy, etc.)**:** Regular collaboration, consultation and training with the teachers, support staff (e.g., speech and language therapist, motor specialist, etc.) and dormatory staff. Consultation with the school district approximately one month before Steven's scheduled re-entry into that system. Consultation with physician regarding medication management as needed.

Signature: _____ **Position:** _____ **Date:** _____

Signature: _____ **Position:** _____ **Date:** _____

WORKBOOK, PART VII: DETAILED TREATMENT PLAN

To this point the play therapist has gathered case information, organized and synthesized it, and developed treatment goals consistent with Ecosystemic Play Therapy Theory. In the process of developing the treatment contract, the play therapist has attempted to integrate the goals of the child and the caretakers into the overall list of treatment goals in such a way that the child and caretaker see play therapy as having something to offer them directly. Except for the focus on the inclusion of variables external to the child, the process of formulating the case and developing the goals may not seem dramatically different from the methods used in other theoretical models of play therapy. Many play therapists conduct comprehensive intakes and develop specific treatment goals. What substantially differentiates Ecosystemic Play Therapy is the emphasis on the development of a treatment plan that will move the child from his or her present level of functioning to his or her optimal level of developmental functioning in a series of preplanned steps.

The bulk of the treatment plan focuses on individual, dyadic, sibling, family, or peer play therapy, or some combination or sequence of these. The treatment plan may also include plans for interventions at the level of any of the systems in which the child is embedded that impinge on the presenting problem. Not only is the treatment planned, but the play therapist takes an active role in implementing that plan, moving the child along the developmental continuum and engaging him or her in active problem solving. The next section describes the elements of the treatment plan; Chapter 8 focuses on the actual implementation of the plan.

The treatment plan is a map for the planned exploration and development of essentially unknown territory. It is based on theory and the available data, but it may need to be modified along the way if additional data are uncovered that indicate the terrain is not as it was thought to be. There are pros and cons to using such an independently made map. To examine these, let us continue with the explorer analogy.

A land developer who wants to go into unknown territory and develop it for use can work one of three ways. The developer could use satellite pictures of the area to be developed and create a development plan from a theoretically based, scientific interpretation of those pictures without ever traveling to the actual site. This type of strategy is sometimes used by behavior therapists. They gather a comprehensive picture of the client's life and behavior and then create a theoretically derived intervention plan without actually talking to the client. This approach makes a great deal of sense when the client is unable to serve as a source of data, such as when the client is autistic. The disadvantage to the plan is the fact that a key element operating out of direct sight may render the plan ineffective. The local population may have known all along that one section of the land is quicksand even though it looks just like the rest. The child may have known a particular intervention would not work because he or she may not want the seemingly obvious target outcome.

Another strategy our developer might use is to go to the area to be developed and find a well-traveled local to serve as a guide. The development plan would then be based on the information provided by the guide. This type of strategy is often used by child-centered play therapists. Its obvious advantage is that it works with on-site information and virtually ensures that the development will meet the desires and needs of the local population. But what if one section of the land is reported to be dangerous, even volcanically active, an area no local has visited for hundreds of years because of local myths about people who were lost there forever? The developer would avoid the area as well, never knowing whether or not it could have played an integral part in the overall plan. Many client-centered play therapists face just this dilemma when working with traumatized children. Should frightening aspects of the child's psyche and experience be avoided just because the child has always avoided them. What if the child is never ready to explore or develop these areas? With this strategy, the play therapist is dependent on the knowledge and skill of the child. It may work well with children whose problems are relatively encapsulated and whose overall functioning is quite good, but it seems risky with more damaged or impaired clients.

The strategy used in Ecosystemic Play Therapy is a combination of both strategies. The play therapist is encouraged to take a satellite picture of the situation *and* to gather data from the local residents (the Ecosystemic intake), to interpret it using theoretically based principles (the case conceptualization), and to create a development (treatment) plan that is used to guide interactions with local resident(s) (the child and caretaker(s)) so as to create a development (treatment outcome) that optimally utilizes the land in a way that allows the local residents to consistently and appropriately get their needs met.

The next sections discuss the goals commonly associated with each phase of the play therapy treatment process. The play therapist will need to integrate these goals with the case-specific goals to develop the detailed treatment plan. We also continue to illustrate the treatment planning process with material from the case of Steven Johnson.

Stage I: Introduction and Exploration

During this phase, the therapeutic relationship is established and the parameters for work on the treatment contract are delineated. The child comes to have a sense of the play therapist, the playroom, the toys, and the process of the sessions. Although children may engage in some testing of limits during this phase, their exploratory behavior is generally geared more toward familiarizing themselves with the play therapist and the environment. For many children, this phase of the play therapy can be accomplished in less than a single session. For those who have been traumatized or damaged in the course of their previous interactions with others, this phase may take longer. The more skeptical a child is about the degree to which play therapy can truly be of any value, the more the play therapist should focus on the treatment contract and its implementation. Nothing will encourage the child to accept play therapy like an initial, even if minor, success.

Case Example

VII. DETAILED TREATMENT PLAN	**CASE NAME:** STEVEN JOHNSON

Stage I: Introduction & Exploration: (Anticipated Number of Sessions: **1**)

Stage Goal(s): Minimize Steven's initial anxiety in the novel social situation of therapy by providing very clear structure, expectations and limit setting. Encourage the development of a positive emotional attachment to the therapist to help Steven mediate those times when he experiences the limit setting done by the therapist as being withholding or critical and he experiences the therapy setting as supportive. Because Steven had been included in an early family interview he seemed to have associated the therapist with his mother and to have developed a positive response to her. Therefore, it was anticipated that this phase would be fairly brief.

Participants: Steven

Materials: Long white paper, colored marking pens, realistic size pretend toys like telephones, pretend food

Experiential Component(s): The experiential activities are designed to actively engage Steven, to provide an affirming experience, and to introduce him to pretend play activities as a way to develop his representational play skills. Because he is functioning much like a preschooler emotionally, the first activity will be a full body drawing (Jernber, 1979) which focuses on his positive attributes. Because of his neurological deficits, the pretend play will be largely structured by the therapist and will focus on real-life activities such as going on a picnic.

Verbal Component(s): Verbally introduce structure of future sessions which will include a conjoint component with his mother initially, followed by pretend play activities. Discuss three rules of playroom: 1. Don't hurt yourself, 2. Don't hurt anyone else, and 3. Don't hurt the room or objects in the room.

Collaborative Component(s): (Advocacy, Consultation, Education, Evaluation) Meet with mother individually. Acknowledge Steven's needs and problem-solve ways to structure the environment at home to reduce some of these problems. Meet with teachers and counselors in residential education program to help them understand the reasons for Steven's problem behaviors and to consult with them on ways to structure the classroom and dorm settings to reduce these problems.

Stage II: Tentative Acceptance

During this stage children have accepted that the play therapy will prove beneficial and appear to be cooperating with the process. In reality, they are waiting to see when and how the play therapy will duplicate the negative experiences they have had in the past with respect to getting their needs met effectively and appropriately. When will the play therapist set limits on the child's desire to be in control, creating anxiety and causing the child to want to withdraw from treatment? If the child risks expressing a need, will the play therapist gratify it? And if not, why not? When will the play therapist prove that he or she is no better at understanding the child's needs than anyone else has been in the past? Although these questions may not be conscious on the child's part, they are there like so many land mines waiting for the unsuspecting play therapist. These mines are present in the healthiest of children re-

ferred to treatment as they derive from past experiences when the child was unable to get his or her needs met effectively and appropriately. Although the play therapist does not want to aggravate the child intentionally, he or she needs to be aware that disappointment is inevitable and a healthy part of the play therapy process. Change is always at least a little anxiety producing, and, at some point, most of us begin to resist no matter how much we want to go along with the process. Once this resistance begins, the Tentative Acceptance phase has come to an end.

Case Example

Stage II: Tentative Acceptance: (Anticipated Number of Sessions: **4**)

Stage Goal(s): Primary focus will be the development of enhanced interpersonal communication strategies to set the stage for subsequent problem solving. Increase recognition of affect and ability to express it. Gradually increase expectations of Steven's behavior and interaction.

Participants: Steven & Mother for 1st half, Steven alone for second half.

Materials: Representational play materials (e.g., puppets, toy animals), small white paper and color crayons

Experiential Component(s): Pretend play using different mediums which pull for relationship interactions; Color-Your-Life activity to promote affective communication about events in his life.

Verbal Component(s): Introduce Good-Feeling Bad-Feeling (GFBF) Game (Ammen, 1993) as a way to use Steven's already secure relationship with his mother to develop his affective communication skills.

Collaborative Component(s): (Advocacy, Consultation, Education, Evaluation) Meet with mother individually and begin to transition from focus on Steven's needs to helping mother recognize and address her own needs and the importance of addressing these in her daily life. Meet weekly with residential program teachers and counselors to monitor Steven's behavior and functioning in the program and to consult with them on ways to increase their expectations of him in a clear but supportive manner.

Stage III: Negative Reaction

During the Negative Reaction phase, the child actively resists the play therapy process. Usually, the onset of this phase is triggered by anxiety that is stirred up in the course of the play therapy process. By this point, the play therapist and child have generally been able to identify one or more problems that the child would like to resolve. For some children just the process of admitting that there are indeed problems that they find distressing is enough to create so much anxiety that they withdraw from the process.

> Before I came to play therapy I played the role of the class clown and had weird random anxiety attacks. Play therapy has made me aware that my anxiety is not random but rather

the result of the fact that I do not like being the class clown. I just do it to mask being teased for wearing both glasses and braces. Now I'm anxious all of the time instead of just once in a while. I do not want to do this anymore!

For other children, it is not the fact of identifying the problems but the idea of having to change their behavior that is anxiety producing.

> Before I came to play therapy I was sad that I was so shy but I wasn't ever really too worried about it. Now I keep thinking about trying to talk to other kids. I want to but it makes me so scared I feel like I am going to be sick. I think I'll just go back to being shy.

For still other children, it is the failure of one or more of their first attempts at change to meet their needs more effectively that creates frustration and anxiety and a subsequent desire to withdraw from treatment. These reactions may range in intensity, from so subtle and mild that they are hardly noticed by the play therapist to full blown rage episodes that result in physical aggression. The former is most likely to be seen in children who are relatively healthy and who are addressing relatively recent and probably transient stress in their play therapy. The latter is most often seen in children who have suffered marked abuse over a long period of time and who have little expectation that anyone in their environment can or will ever meet any of their needs.

Some therapists who have seen children have severe acting out reactions during the negative reaction phase of play therapy question whether or not such crises are a necessary part of treatment or whether they could be avoided. This question is often framed in the context of a child-centered play therapy versus directive play therapy theoretical debate. That is, would children have a less pronounced negative reaction if they were allowed to move at their own pace instead of being paced by the play therapist? This may indeed be the case, as there are many more discussions about severe negative reactions in the literature on approaches such as Theraplay (Jernberg, 1979) than there are in the client-centered literature. If this is true, then why not use a client-centered approach? Two issues must be considered in answering this question. The first is the degree to which issues of control (self and other) are central to a particular client's psychopathology. In cases in which the child never learned to trust others to use their control to the child's best interest, a child-centered approach seems inappropriate. The child needs to experience situations in which he or she benefits from allowing others to be in control. In the course of the child's first few attempts to allow others to be in control, it is likely that there will be some degree of power struggle no matter how much the child has come to trust the adult and no matter how much the child wants the experience of being taken care of. These power struggles need not be pitched battles but they are likely to be at least somewhat difficult. The other issue to consider is that of time. Healthy children should be developing quickly and if their psychopathology is interfering with that process they are rapidly losing ground relative to their peers. More severely damaged children may eventually benefit from a child-centered approach, but can they afford the time it takes? Obviously, the question of which approach is more effective should not be answered on the basis of either a theoretical argument or a pragmatic one. Rather, it is a question that speaks directly to the need for play therapy process and outcome research.

C a s e   E x a m p l e

Stage III: Negative Reaction: (Anticipated Number of Sessions: **4**)

Stage Goal(s): As the sessions begin to address more directly Steven's problems outside of session it is anticipated that Steven will begin to resist and display some of his problematic behavior. The goal of the therapist is to structure the session such that Steven's anxiety is acknowledged, yet some of the problems are still addressed in spite of his attempts to resist. Two factors should contribute to a successful resolution of this stage: (1) that he experiences positive affirmation and support from both the therapist and his mother during these problem-solving processes, and (2) that he experiences a positive resolution to a problem as a result of the problem-solving process.

Participants: Steven & Mother for 1st half, Steven alone for second half.

Materials: Representational play materials

Experiential Component(s): Continue to develop Steven's symbolic play abilities through representational play. Link play situations to problematic events occurring in residential program. Reflect on problem areas and on his resistance to address these problem areas as these are presented in the experiential interactions.

Verbal Component(s): Use GFBF with Steven and mother to continue to develop affective communication. Introduce problem-solving component of GFBF game particularly related to his behaviors at home.

Collaborative Component(s): (Advocacy, Consultation, Education, Evaluation) <u>Individual sessions with mother to help her recognize that one of her needs is to grieve the loss of her hopes for a normal child and its effect on her own life. This will be difficult because it will cause mother to recognize those aspects of the problem that were out of her control and less likely to change. At the same time, the grieving process should free her to give up some of the highly protective stance she adopted when Steven was sick as an infant. Continue to meet weekly with residential program teachers and counselors to monitor Steven's behavior and functioning in the program and to consult with them on ways to increase their expectations of him in a clear but supportive manner. Prepare them to cope with some regression in his gains and negative affect during this stage of treatment as he becomes more aware of his problems.</u>

Stage IV: Growing and Trusting

After negotiating at least one difficult interaction and discovering that the play therapist is willing and able to work to ensure that their needs are met, children dive into play therapy with renewed enthusiasm. It is during this phase of treatment that the majority of the therapeutic gains occur. Children who have entered into this stage are ready to hear/accept the underlying causes of their difficulties and to work directly on addressing these. They now see that it is possible to get their needs met more effectively and appropriately and they are eager to make changes. The excitement will ebb and flow as the child faces resistances and setbacks from both within and without, but there will be overall forward progress.

During this stage the play therapist is working with the child on active problem solving. Initially, this work is focused on what occurs within session or on issues brought to session by the child. As the play therapy progresses it is important that the process become focused on problem-solving issues and events outside of the play therapy. Without this shift, the improvements that the child makes are less likely to generalize outside of the play room. As the play therapy moves toward termination, the work of play therapy should become progressively more pragmatic and less intrapsychic. The child must be able to get his or her needs met effectively and appropriately in the world if development is to proceed normally and future psychopathology is to be avoided.

Case Example

Stage IV: Growing & Trusting: (Anticipated Number of Sessions: **25-30**)

Stage Goal(s): <u>Focus on all aspects of problem solving in both individual and dyadic play sessions. Help Steven understand the nature of his deficits and develop coping skills to compensate for these deficits. Begin development of some peer interaction skills.</u>

Participants: <u>Steven & Mother for 1st half, Steven alone for second half; Peer Group Therapy once/week</u>

Materials: <u>Representational play materials, structured games</u>

Experiential Component(s): <u>Continue to use representational play to help Steven understand problem situations and to communicate and problem-solve alternative ways to deal with these problems. Begin to introduce more cooperative and rule-based activities to develop his social interactional skills with the therapist. Introduce developmentally based peer group therapy approximately half-way through this stage, starting with highly structured individual and group activities and moving towards less structured interactive play activities (see O'Connor, 1991, 1993a)</u>

Verbal Component(s): <u>Continue to use GFBF with Steven and mother to develop affective communication and problem-solving skills particularly related to his behaviors at home. Gradually increase Steven's verbal problem-solving and communication during the play therapy.</u>

Collaborative Component(s): (Advocacy, Consultation, Education, Evaluation) <u>Now that mother is better able to put her experience of loss into perspective she should be able to focus on his present needs and to engage in needed problem solving. Individual sessions with mother now more focused on helping her to increase her expectations and encourage Steven to develop more appropriate ways of getting his needs met. Towards end of this stage reduce frequency of meetings with mother and help her become involved with a support group for parents with children with learning or neurological problems. Continue to meet weekly with residential program teachers and counselors to monitor Steven's behavior and functioning in the program and to consult with them on ways to increase their expectations of him consistent with his increased understanding and skills.</u>

Stage V: Termination

This is a difficult stage in treatment for children especially if they have developed a significant attachment to the play therapist. The more task-oriented the play therapy has been, the more termination will make sense to the child and the easier it will be to accomplish emotionally. When the relationship has been the primary focus of the play therapy termination seems like a negative consequence imposed for having emotionally and behaviorally improved. The child came into session troubled, but the play therapist allowed and nurtured a relationship and the child gradually improved. Now that the child is doing well, the play therapist announces that the relationship is to end and, not surprisingly, the child often regresses. When children have been problem-focused for the duration of the play therapy, termination is a signal that they have achieved their goals and are able to get their needs met effectively and appropriately without the play therapist. In such a case, the relationship with the play therapist was *seen by the child* as a means toward an end, not an end in and of itself.

Irrespective of the nature of the play therapy, all children typically display some sort of regression in the face of termination. For children for whom attachment or separation/individuation was a significant issue, termination is likely to be particularly difficult, as it reactivates the very problems that brought them to play therapy. For these children termination should be a fairly drawn out and gradual process accompanied by considerable problem solving. For other children, the idea of facing the world without the support of the play therapist can be quite overwhelming and their symptoms return in an attempt to keep the play therapist engaged. These children usually respond to direct problem solving of the termination anxiety and to assurances that they are ready to make it on their own with the support of the adults and peers in their environment.

In either case, it seems beneficial to try to accomplish three tasks over the course of the termination period. The first is to review the course of the child's play therapy, the problems that have been faced, and the strategies the child used to address these. The second issue is to ensure that generalization of the gains the child has made in play therapy takes place. Often this involves helping the child identify people in the environment who will take the therapist's place as the play therapy draws to a close. Two sets of individuals need to be identified. One set includes those persons who are capable of helping the child problem solve in new or difficult situations. The other set includes those people who are willing and able to serve as potential resources for the child. These are people the child can approach to get his or her needs met. This latter group should be as diverse as possible so that the child's chances for success in any given situation are quite high. This group should definitely include peers, no matter how young the child. Finally, the play therapist needs to help the child celebrate the gains he or she has made over the course of play therapy. If even a little progress has been made there is cause for celebration. Often both the transfer to other persons as resources and the celebration of the child's gains can be accomplished by gradually including others in the child's sessions as termination approaches, culminating in a party attended by those central to the child's emotional life.

Case Example

Stage V: Termination: (Anticipated Number of Sessions: **5**)

Stage Goal(s): Help Steven prepare for the transition from the residential education program and termination from therapy, and to differentiate this experience from his first transition from elementary school to middle school. Help him generalize his problem-solving skills and compensatory skills by including him in the transfer planning process with his new school.

Participants: Steven & Mother for 1st half, Steven alone for second half; Peer Group Therapy once/week; one family session with Steven, mother, and sister prior to his return home.

Materials: Representational toys, games

Experiential Component(s): Through representational activities help Steven recognize the gains Steven has made in his coping and problem-solving skills. Use representational play to problem-solve the transition to his new school and termination with the residential program. Incorporate graduation activities into the peer group therapy.

Verbal Component(s): Continue to use GFBF with Steven and mother using it now to focus on affective communication and problem-solving related to his transition to a new school and return to living full-time at home. Incorporate sister into this anticipatory problem-solving process during family therapy session.

Collaborative Component(s): (Advocacy, Consultation, Education, Evaluation) Individual sessions with mother focusing on the gains she has made in her parenting skills and anticipatory problem-solving regarding the changes in her life which will occur when Steven returns home full-time. Also help her grieve the loss of the therapy relationship and to differentiate this loss from the other losses in her life, particularly her mother. Assist her to develop a relationship with other support services (particularly at Steven's school) to replace what she was deriving from the problem solving and relationship of the therapeutic interaction and encourage her to remain involved in the parent support group. Continue to meet weekly with residential program teachers and counselors to monitor Steven's behavior and functioning in the program and to consult with them on how best to facilitate his transition/termination process and to generalize his gains. Meet with teachers and counselors at his home school to develop a transition plan and to help them understand the nature of his problems and the types of support and structure he needs to be successful in an academic setting. Identify strategies to address both academic setting and peer group interactions. Include Steven in the final stage of this planning process with the school.

Signature: _____ Position: _____ Date: _____

Signature: _____ Position: _____ Date: _____

SUMMARY

In Chapter 6 we presented a strategy by which the play therapist develops a comprehensive, theoretically grounded conceptualization of the child's case. Here, we presented a strategy for developing and organizing specific treatment goals. We then combined the case conceptualization with the organized treatment goals to develop (1) a treatment contract that addresses the needs of the child and the significant others in the child's life; (2) a global play therapy treatment; and (3) a detailed session-by-session play therapy treatment plan that takes into consideration the specifics of the case and the natural evolution of the play therapy process across the stages of treatment. In the next two chapters we present strategies for developing this detailed treatment plan and give examples of specific session activities that address both general developmental as well as content-specific treatment goals.

·8·

INTERVENTIONS

OVERVIEW

At this point, the reader has been guided through all of the Workbook except for the decision making process involved in selecting and designing specific experiential and verbal play therapy interventions. Once these are identified, they can be incorporated into the Detailed Treatment Plan in Part VII of the Workbook as was illustrated in the last chapter case example. Before we can go on to discuss the planning of specific session activities we need to discuss the general or overarching elements of any and all Ecosystemic Play Therapy interventions. Once these are understood the number of excellent play session activities the play therapist can invent is limited only by his or her creativity.

First, we review the Ecosystemic Play Therapy definitions of psychopathology and cure. Second, we discuss the range of treatment modalities available to the Ecosystemic Play therapist for addressing any and all treatment goals. Third, we examine the play therapy process in terms of two critical factors: the role of the play therapist–child relationship and the role of problem solving. Fourth, we address some of the issues involved in planning activities for specific therapeutic content areas. Finally, we present a brief discussion of activities specifically aimed at helping the child transition through the various play therapy treatment stages. The next chapter includes general descriptions of children's functioning at each of the first three develop-

mental levels and provides 25 sample session activities geared to each of the three levels.

Psychopathology

We have defined psychopathology in a specific and somewhat unusual way. Specifically, we have stated that psychopathology can be said to exist when an individual is unable to get his or her needs met consistently or is unable to do so in ways that do not substantially interfere with the ability of others to get their needs met. This definition maximizes the focus on the child's needs without necessarily implying that there is anything "wrong" with the child, or anyone else for that matter. It also minimizes the chance that treatment will be initiated solely to make the child or his or her behavior more pleasing to others. Children who do not want to change are not suitable candidates for play therapy or any other form of treatment. However, most children are quite willing to change if it means that the amount of gratification they receive will increase and that the number of negative responses they endure will decrease.

When children are unable to get their needs met effectively and appropriately, five sources of potential interference are considered.

1. Constitutional/inherent factors, such as limited cognitive functioning, neurologic, genetic, and biologic disorders.

2. Developmental factors which may cause interference on two levels
   a. Children have limited cognitive, emotional, and social resources. This is not their fault, it is simply a reality of their developmental progress. A child who is either 2 years old or functioning like a 2-year-old cannot be expected to be consistently effective in managing his or her interactions with others. The child's ability to conceptualize a need, to communicate it, and to activate the resources to meet it are all limited.
   b. Children can experience developmental delays. These may result from problems inherent to the child, problems in the environment (inadequate stimulation), or, most often, an interaction of the two.
3. Dyadic interference refers to interference created through the child's interactions with specific people in his or her ecosystem. This type of interference may include situations in which the child, the other person, or both have inherent difficulties that make for problematic interactions. Many times, however, both individuals are basically intact and the problem lies in the interaction itself.
4. Systemic interference refers to those factors that are not person-specific and which may arise from any of the systems in which the child is embedded.
5. Metasystemic interference is much more difficult to focus on, in that it derives from sources like cultural and political influences that may have multisystemic origins. Concepts such as bigotry fit into this category.

The reader may, quite rightly, note that this definition of psychopathology seems inherently biased toward a Western culture world view given its emphasis on the needs of the individual. Although the model can be readily used within a Western frame of reference, the individualistic bias is not inherent in the model. The second part of the definition notes that the individual must be able to get his or her needs met in ways that do not substantially interfere with the ability of others to get their needs met. It is at this level that the critical element of creating balance among the systems comes into play. When working with an Anglo- or Euro-American family, emphasis may be placed on the needs of individuals over the needs of the family as a whole. One characteristic of these groups is the valuing of separation–individuation among its members. Children are expected to create independent households as soon as possible after reaching adulthood. In an Asian-American family, there may be substantially more emphasis placed on the health of the family over the needs of any individual member. The play therapist must

help the child learn to achieve a satisfactory balance between the familial and sociocultural needs and his or her own needs. Achieving such balance becomes even more crucial when there are differences between the cultural systems to which the child is exposed and the cultural base of the family. Similarly, the child or the family who is different from the dominant culture on any particular dimension will need to learn how to get their needs met in ways that do not create unnecessary conflict with the dominant system. The play therapist becomes a key player in helping clients establish a successful balance, preferably in ways that do not require either individuals or groups to subjugate their needs or lose their cultural values.

Concept of Goal or Cure

Given the preceding definition of psychopathology, the overall goal of Ecosystemic Play Therapy is to help children learn how to maximize their ability to get their needs met consistently and appropriately given the context of their developmental potential and their environment. The play therapist assists the child in navigating this process, depicted in Figure 8.1. Thus the play therapist designs interventions that help children

- recognize their own needs,
- identify potential resources for meeting those needs and potential sources of interference,
- develop strategies for activating resources and minimizing interference,
- tolerate frustration, and
- value and accept gratification once it is received.

Simultaneously, children must learn to recognize others' needs and to learn strategies for balancing those needs against their own. This aspect feeds into the part

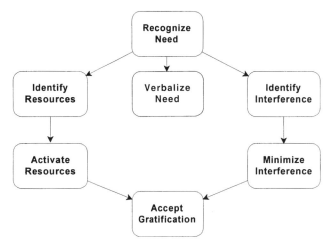

FIGURE 8.1 Concept of goal in Ecosystemic Play Therapy.

of the definition of psychopathology that specifies that children must be able to get their needs met in ways that do not interfere with others getting their needs met.

Although all of the interventions the play therapist designs will be experiential in nature, these will be supported by a strong cognitive/verbal component. The focus of the cognitive/verbal component is the child's development of problem-solving skills. The cognitive/verbal problem solving within the play therapy is enhanced by the effective use of interpretation and functional problem solving.

INTERVENTION MODALITIES

One feature that differentiates Ecosystemic Play Therapy from other play therapy models is the therapist's focus on maintaining a systems perspective. This does not mean that the Ecosystemic Play therapist will necessarily intervene at a systems level, only that the interaction of a given child client and the systems in which he or she is embedded will be taken into consideration at all points in the play therapy. In other words, the play therapist evaluates the potential role of all systems when answering the two key questions that guide the course of Ecosystemic Play Therapy: (a) Why are the child's needs not being met effectively and appropriately? and (b) What can be done to maximize the child's ability to get his or her needs met effectively? This means that treatment goals may include making changes in systems that are quite distant from the child or that are not directly available to the treatment process. This does not mean that the play therapist will necessarily intervene in these systems directly, if at all. However, it does mean that the play therapist will seek to activate persons or systems who can or should make the changes necessary for the child's mental health and optimal development.

When it comes to systemic work, two different approaches are espoused in the literature. The most traditional family systems view posits that the only interventions that should be conducted are those that include the entire family. The extension of this view suggests that if the child's primary problems are being caused by his or her teacher, then the only intervention that should occur is to work through the school system to change the teacher or the teacher's behavior. On at least two levels this approach makes sense. At least conceptually, the most efficient change will occur when an intervention is focused directly at changing the most problematic system. Indeed, where possible, such interventions often result in many of the other smaller problems being resolved as well. Also, systemic change places the least burden on the individual. It is sometimes much easier to motivate a group of people to make needed changes in a system than it is to motivate individuals to change themselves. In the former situation, no one needs to feel at fault and there is the strength of the team to draw upon in making changes. In the latter, the individual tends to feel somehow at fault and he or she must often work alone to make the changes.

Although these are excellent goals, there are also potential problems with routinely intervening at only the systems level. Such interventions sometimes minimize the very genuine problems an individual may bring to a situation. The system may keep trying to change in an attempt to manage an individual who manifests inherent sources of psychopathology. This can result in significant stress for the other members of the system and diffuse the responsibility the one individual has for the problem at hand. The other side effect of systems level intervention is that the individual may not learn any specific coping skills in the process. The child who is faced with a very disturbed teacher whose parents are able to have the teacher removed from the classroom learns that telling your parents is a good problem-solving strategy but does not learn much else.

A different view on conducting systems interventions is the notion that effective change in entire systems can result from changing a single element or individual in that system. The behavior of the problem teacher could also be changed by training one child to respond differently to the problem. Such a change in the child's behavior might include everything from teaching that child how to get his or her needs met by circumventing the teacher's problem behaviors to coaching the child on how to lead a classroom rebellion that draws needed attention to the scope of the problem. In this case the child would learn strategies for directly managing the problem. The child will be substantially empowered and is likely to be able to address similarly problems in the future.

Unfortunately, much of the mental health intervention literature makes it seem as though the two views on therapeutic intervention are diametrically opposed. One either believes in systemic intervention *or* one believes in individual intervention. This dichotomy runs directly counter to the basic principles of Ecosystemic Play Therapy. The goal here is to work from as many directions and at as many levels as possible, ensuring that both necessary individual and systemic changes are made. In determining a suitable point of entry into the child's ecosystem there are several factors the play therapist may consider.

1. Who in the system is the most distressed and, therefore, the most willing to work toward change?

2. Who is most accessible (logistically) to intervention?
3. Does the way in which various individuals (including the play therapist) and systems have defined the problem(s) suggest a likely point of entry?
4. What types of intervention is the play therapist most comfortable/expert in implementing?
5. What types of intervention are pragmatically possible given financial, temporal, and local considerations?

Direct Therapeutic Intervention

This section discusses all of the psychotherapeutic interventions that the play therapist conducts directly with clients in the traditional forms of play therapy. For the most part, these are interventions conducted in the therapist's office with individuals, families, or small groups. The goal of these interventions is to address the psychopathology either of individuals or of the smaller systems in which they are directly embedded. Direct intervention may be either problem-focused or aimed at global improvement in the child's developmental functioning and his or her ability to get his or her needs met effectively and appropriately. These interventions typically involve only peripheral contact with others in the child's world. Such interventions do not necessarily assume that broader systemic changes need to be made. Rather, they assume that the individuals or small systems can be helped to function better independent of changes in any other system. That is, changes in the individual may bring about the necessary systemic changes.

Individual

Work with individual children characterizes the vast majority of the play therapy literature. For an extensive, though not exhaustive, bibliography of play therapy literature the reader is referred to *The World of Play Therapy Literature* by Landreth, Homeyer, and Bratten (1993).

Individual work is the most appropriate form of intervention when the problem is such that changes in the child's problem-solving abilities will directly improve the child's ability to get his or her needs met consistently and appropriately. This may be the case whether the psychopathology is created by individual, dyadic, or systemic factors. It is the therapist's estimate of the child's responsibility and ability to make the necessary changes that determines the approach, rather than the source of the problem per se. Although it might be most efficient to have a child who exhibits significant individual psychopathology make changes in his or her be-

havior, the very problems that make change desirable may also make it highly unlikely. For example, even though it would be nice to have an autistic child learn better social skills, the very nature of the disorder makes the development of substantial social skills extremely difficult. Alternatively, even though it would be nice to have the Child Protective Services system in the United States make some substantial changes, it is unlikely that these will occur in such a way as to affect the immediate needs of a given client. The play therapist must, however, be careful not to expect the child to change to meet the needs of that system in ways that are beyond the child's developmental capacities.

Dyadic

Work with dyads, usually the child and primary caretaker, has been prevalent in the field of play therapy for many years and yet makes up only a relatively small part of the play therapy literature. Several key authors in this area include: Ammen (1993), Harvey, (1994), James (1994), and Jernberg and Jernberg (1993).

Dyadic work is useful for directly training both child and caretaker in the process of learning to balance individual and systemic needs. Both can be taught how to get their own needs met through the interaction and how to work together to get dyadic needs met in the context of other systems. Because so much of children's social learning happens within their dyadic interactions, this type of play therapy is often included as at least some portion of an Ecosystemic Play Therapy treatment plan.

Family

Within the play therapy literature, family play therapy probably receives the least attention. Several key authors on this topic include Shlomo Ariel (1992), Eliana Gil (1994), Guerney and Guerney (1987), and the edited book on *Family Play Therapy* by Schaefer and Carey (1994), which brings together many of the earlier writings integrating play and family therapy.

As with dyadic play therapy, family play therapy is an excellent way for the child and family members to learn about balancing their individual needs against those of others and of the family as a whole. The value of family play therapy does not automatically depend on the family being the source of the psychopathology. Rather, it is an intervention mode that is also useful when the family needs to work together to meet the needs of an individual member who is in distress or when a family needs to work as a team to get its needs met in the context of a larger system. It is important to note that a family perspective can be maintained in play therapy even if all of the members do not participate. Doing so simply requires that the needs and values of those members not present are considered in the course of any problem solving by those members who are present.

Peer

Although there appears to be more literature on group play therapy than on either dyadic or family play therapy it is still a relatively limited body of work. Key authors on group play therapy include: Nardone, Tryon, and O'Connor (1986), O'Connor (1993a), Rubin and Tregay (1989), and Van de Putte (1993).

Peer-group work with children is probably not done nearly as often as it should be. Although it is critical that children learn to get their needs met effectively through their interactions both within and outside of their families, it is peer interaction that forms a substantial portion of their day-to-day lives. Both therapists and children tend to overlook the child's peers as both a source of substantial interference and a source gratification in meeting an individual client's needs. Certainly, by school age, peer interaction should provide children with a substantial quantity of their social and emotional gratification. Many a child has withstood incredible trauma at home because he or she had the support of significant peer friends. If a child has had trouble learning to get his or her needs met at home, then it is highly likely those difficulties will also be experienced in peer interactions. It is also likely that simply learning how to get his or her needs met in interactions with adults or family members will not necessarily generalize to peer interactions. Therefore, a course of peer group play therapy is often highly valuable for children who have completed a course of individual play therapy.

Indirect Therapeutic Intervention (e.g., Filial)

The entire field of play therapy actually traces back to a case in which an indirect intervention was used, namely, the case of Little Hans (Freud, 1909). Freud never actually treated Hans directly; rather, he advised Hans' father, who implemented the actual intervention. The use of caretakers as primary therapist has continued in one form or another since that time. Major proponents of such work are Guerney (1976, 1983b) and Van Fleet (1993).

Indirect intervention is often most helpful when there are substantial resources in the environment that can be activated without directly involving the child in play therapy. Such interventions can often be highly cost effective. If a mother can be trained to have signif-

icantly health-promoting interactions with one of her children, she can carry out the intervention many hours a day compared with the limited time available to the play therapist. Furthermore, training her to interact more effectively with one child is likely to generalize to her interactions with her other children, so that several children are reached without requiring any direct intervention. When one is able to conduct such interventions with classroom teachers the impact is even broader. Unfortunately, there is some tendency on the part of therapists to devalue the treatment potential of various adults in the child's day-to-day environment. Although it may be true that these adults do not have the same training that the play therapist has, they can often more than make up for the lack of intensity or focus in their interventions with the sheer amount of contact they have with the child over the course of a given period of time.

Education

Teaching interventions may be implemented both within play therapy itself or as a relatively independent adjunct to the treatment process. In either case, the typical content covered includes either factual information or specific skills. In the context of play therapy, the educational mode is one way to provide children with information that may be critical to their ability to engage in critical problem solving. Similarly, as an adjunct to treatment, it may provide other persons in the child's environment with information they need to be better able to manage children and address and meet their needs.

The play therapist needs to be somewhat cautious in taking on the role of educator within the context of play therapy, as that role is somewhat in conflict with the role of play therapist. To review, the role of play therapist is to help the child break set and engage in functional problem solving to facilitate the child's ability to get his or her needs met consistently and appropriately. Although the play therapist may be quite directive in structuring the session, the process epitomizes cooperative work toward improving the quality of the child's life. The role of educator usually places the therapist in an authority position as an expert who possesses knowledge that the student does not have. The educator actively provides information and the student passively receives it. If the play therapist is successful in moving the child into the student role, it can be quite difficult to move him or her back into a cooperative stance. There is also the risk of activating all of the child's feelings about school and academics. For some children this may be a negative association involving fear of failure and diminished self-esteem. Even for children who have positive feelings about school, the desire to please others or to become competitive may take over and interfere with the play therapy process. The various ways in which play therapists can effectively use education in the context of play therapy are discussed at some length in connection with problem solving later in this chapter.

Consultation

Consultation defined generally is "a problem-solving interaction between professionals from differing fields" (Conoley, 1981b, p. xv). The use of a consultation model generally incorporates both psychotherapeutic and educational elements. Consultative activities range from providing mental health or behavioral consultation to another professional about a specific child to providing organizational consultation to a system involved with a child, such as a school (e.g., Conoley, 1981b). The system usually has recognized that a problem exists and invites the play therapist to assess the problem and suggest potential intervention strategies. However, if the play therapist has a client whose problems are adversely impacted because of the way the client is being handled in another system (e.g., school), then the play therapist may initiate the offer to consult with individuals in that system. Usually, the play therapist does not implement the interventions him or herself. Instead, the system intervenes in the problem from within with the information and guidance provided by the play therapist as a consultant.

Advocacy

When taking on an advocacy role, a therapist directly intervenes in a system for an individual or subsystem that is unable to act for itself. The need for advocacy comes up much more often in work with children than it does in work with adults simply because children are, by nature and by law, dependent on adults for their care and well-being. There are a number of issues to consider to be an effective child advocate (see also Conoley, 1981a; Young, 1987).

The initial decision to take on an advocacy role for a given child or family should not be made lightly. When the play therapist becomes an advocate, the implicit communication made to the clients is that they are not able to take care of the problem on their own. Related to this is the degree to which the client's dependency on the play therapist is increased. Although it is true that all children are dependent on their caretakers, such dependency can hamper the therapeutic relationship. One of the most common transference problems that is triggered when the play therapist becomes an advocate

is the activation of the child's fantasies of having the play therapist as a caregiver. After all, ideally it is the caregiver who most often takes on the advocacy role in the life of a healthy child. Even then most parents are aware that there are times when it is best not to intervene but to let children address the problem on their own. Therefore, a critical element of the play therapist's initial decision should be consideration of whether or not there is another person or persons who can or should be serving in the advocacy role. Other appropriate advocates include teachers, school administrators and counselors, physicians, social workers, and attorneys, among others.

When it becomes apparent that the child or family is in need of an advocate, it is important for the play therapist to be aware of both local and indigenous resources. For example, the most appropriate advocate for children who are abused varies from one region to another in the United States. In some areas, this function is served by a social worker who is directly affiliated with a Child Protective Services agency that may, in turn, be related to the welfare system or to the legal system. In other areas this function may be served by a caseworker operating through the medical system or even through the educational system. Many areas offer very specific services for a variety of clients. These services may be more or less well publicized or easy to access. Therapists also need to make efforts to remain current on the services available as these tend to come and go over time. This is especially true of grant-funded programs.

Aside from being aware of and able to access local resources, it is important for therapists to make themselves aware of resources that are indigenous to the group or groups of which the child or the family is a member. These resources might include ministers, community leaders or councils, shamans, curanderos, and so forth. Resources can also include extended family members or individuals in the community who have natural helping skills. The use of such advocates can be important for children or families who are members of a group that has experienced some history of oppression. On the one hand it reinforces the connection to the larger group or community and enhances the sense of identification. On the other hand it creates the opportunity for empowerment within the context of the group. This can benefit the child, the family, and the group or community.

If a play therapist decides to become the child's advocate in a given situation, it is also important for the therapist to understand the workings of the system within which he or she will be advocating and how to obtain and wield power within that system. For example, if a therapist plans to advocate for the child within the medical system, it is important to understand that this system is hierarchical and, in many ways, a patriarchal system. Physicians hold all of the power in the system and most are still male, although that is gradually changing. To make changes in that system, it is important to have a physician as an ally because outsiders tend to have little power or even access to the system. The Child Protective Services system is another good example. In most areas, the Child Protective Services system is unusually organized in that the caseworkers function quite independently and have a great deal of decision-making power. However, their power can be annulled by the action of a judge or attorney who may have only been involved in the case for a brief period. Some mental health practitioners have been angered by these sudden shifts in case management, wrongly viewing the change as capricious and even malicious behavior on the part of the caseworker instead of understanding the limits of that person's power. In such situations it may be time to engage others in attempts at advocacy.

The primary power that therapists have in any system is their training and subsequent role as an expert. This means, unfortunately, that not all play therapists will be equally strong advocates. Older and more experienced therapists will have more powerful voices in their advocacy work. The other source of power that therapists have is their understanding of the system and their strategies for disrupting it. These strategies should be used sparingly, and only when all efforts to work cooperatively have failed. An example follows.

A child was referred to psychotherapy to prepare her for radical surgery that would drastically alter her functioning on a day-to-day basis. Not all of the results of the surgery would be experienced by the child as necessarily positive. When the mother brought the child to the session she reported that the surgery was to be scheduled as soon as possible, possibly within 2 to 3 weeks. Because of various pragmatic problems, this meant the play therapist would have no more than one or two sessions in which to complete the preparatory work. The mother felt that she was completely at the mercy of a large, complex medical treatment team, so the play therapist decided that it was important to advocate for a longer delay before the surgery was initiated. Knowing how hierarchical most hospitals are, the play therapist decided to attempt advocacy with the primary physician. Direct contact with the physician simply yielded the information that, because three surgical teams from different specialties at major teaching hospitals were involved, the surgery would have to take place whenever the teams' availability could be coordinated. The physician did not even entertain the possibility of changing the schedule to meet the child's needs. The play therapist next contacted the physician's nurse. As it turned out, in this system, management of the physician's schedule was entirely her responsibility. She reported that although it was difficult to coordinate the three teams, it would actually be easier if she had more time. She was more willing to schedule the surgery for 8 weeks later and, in addition, to provide substantial information about the nature of the child's medical problems and the surgery for the play therapist to use in designing the intervention. In this case, the hierarchical nature of the system was bypassed in a way that did not undermine the authority of the physician and enabled the child's needs to be met.

Consistent with the idea that therapists should be cautious in making the initial decision to become the child's advocate, it is equally important for them to monitor both their professional boundaries and the need for them to remain in the advocate role. No matter how good a play therapist is at advocating for a child's needs in the medical system, the play therapist is not a physician and needs not only to allow the physician to function in his or her professional role but actually needs to provide an appropriate level of professional support to enable the physician to perform well and meet the child's needs. Similarly, although it may be important for therapists to take on the advocacy role at some point in the treatment process, it is rarely appropriate for them to remain in that role for any length of time. Therapists need actively to seek out persons who can serve as the child's advocate on a day-to-day basis and who will be accessible long after the play therapy has come to an end. This not only benefits the child but also helps prevent therapists from becoming stretched so thin in the performance of their jobs that they suffer burnout.

Having discussed some of the most common ways in which Ecosystemic Play therapists can intervene to promote children's health, we now turn our attention to the process that occurs when the child is directly engaged in a play therapy session.

THERAPY PROCESS

There are two key elements that appear to make play therapy successful. One element is the development of a relationship between the child client and the play therapist. The other is the ability of the child and play therapist to engage in effective problem solving that enables the child to get his or her needs met more effectively and appropriately. Although both of these elements can be effective on their own, they seem to work optimally in combination.

The Child–Play Therapist Relationship

Overview

A great deal has been written about the importance of the relationship between the child client and the play therapist (e.g., Moustakas, 1959). The theoretical importance ascribed to the relationship varies widely. On one end of the continuum, the child-centered therapists view the relationship as having curative power in and of itself (Axiline, 1947; Guerney, 1983a; Landreth, 1991). On the other end, both psychoanalytic (Freud, 1928; Bornstein, 1945) and behavioral (Bixler, 1949) therapists suggest that the primary use of the relationship is to make the child less resistant to the more unpleasant aspects of the play therapy process, such as interpretation or limit setting. As we have on other dimensions, we tend to integrate these diverse perspectives and suggest that the existence of a relationship between the child and the play therapist enhances the effectiveness of the play therapy along two dimensions: the working alliance and the therapist's function as a model and source of reinforcement.

Working Alliance

Children are not naturally motivated to come into play therapy or to engage in either self-examination or change. They do not understand either the pragmatics or the nature of the play therapy process. They are, however, usually motivated to work with an adult who is interested in them and who is emotionally and physically available. At least initially, the child works with the play therapist because the play therapist seems likable and there is no particular reason not to cooperate.

The therapeutic relationship provides stability for the child when the play therapy does not go smoothly. This may be the case when the content of the sessions is painful and something the child would rather avoid. This may also be the case when the changes the child hoped for do not come about. The latter is often a part of working with abused children or with children caught in hostile custody disputes. These children may make heroic efforts to get their needs met more effectively and appropriately only to find their efforts thwarted or even punished by those around them. Often it is their emotional connection to the play therapist that serves as their only motivation to continue to try to make their situations better.

Modeling and Reinforcement

The existence of a relationship enhances the therapist's viability as a model. Children are much more likely to imitate the behavior of someone they like and feel close to than they are to imitate the behavior of a stranger. Again, the relationship enhances the effectiveness of the play therapist as an agent of change.

The emotional tie that the child has to the play therapist also makes the play therapist a powerful source of direct reinforcement. This is an issue that therapists tend to overlook as they search for ways to motivate their child clients to change. An approving word or look from the play therapist can have an enormous effect on a child and can serve to motivate the child to try out behaviors that might otherwise seem too risky. Direct verbal reinforcement can quickly shape a child's behavior in the target direction. However, the play therapist usually should avoid directly meeting the child's needs, especially for an extended period of time. The primary reason for this is children's limited access to their therapists and their need to learn how to get their needs met on a day-to-day basis in their real worlds. Other reasons are discussed at greater length in the next section on the nature of the child–play play therapist relationship.

Nature of the Relationship

Although a great deal has been written about the therapeutic value of the child–play play therapist relationship, much less has been written about the actual nature of the relationship. We characterize the relationship as a highly specialized one that differs substantially from other relationships the child will have. These differences seem critical to both the welfare of the child and the effectiveness of the play therapy process. Child-centered therapists often use the term *real* when describing the child–play play therapist relationship. The play therapist is advised to be genuine or *real* in his or her interactions (Moustakas, 1959). This advice is differentially interpreted by play therapists and results in some interactions we view as potentially problematic.

The play therapist should be genuine with the child in the sense that he or she is truthful and direct with the client. The child should know what the play therapist and process of play therapy are about and understand how he or she is to benefit from the process. However, we would argue against the play therapist being genuine with the client in the sense of being self-disclosing. This limitation is based on several issues. First, the purpose of the play therapy is to address the client's, not the therapist's, psychopathology and as such the child probably does not need to know about the therapist's experiences and emotions in order to problem solve effectively. There seems to be substantial risk that the therapist's disclosure of his or her own content will interfere with his or her focus on the child's content. Second, the power of the play therapist in the session places undue weight on both his or her person and his or her thoughts and feelings. Therefore, when the play therapist expresses specific thoughts or feelings, the child is likely to be tempted to match these even if they do not necessarily match his or her own experience. Finally, the role of the play therapist is to focus on helping the child problem solve. When the play therapist discloses too much of his or her own material, the tables are likely to turn as the child attempts to help the play therapist problem solve. This can often be seen in a situation that is largely unavoidable. When the play therapist comes to the session sick or injured, with symptoms that are readily observable, he or she directly communicates his or her "problems" to the client. Many children become distressed at this change of roles and will either begin to act out or will suddenly move to begin taking care of the play therapist. In both cases, the child is no longer focused on his or her own problems but rather on those of the play therapist. For these reasons, we see the nature of the relationship between the child and the play therapist as being restricted in some very critical ways.

Probably the most significant restriction on the child–play play therapist relationship is that it is not a mutual relationship. This differentiates it from virtually every other relationship in which the child will become involved. The play therapist is available to the child 100% of the session. This means that the play therapist suspends his or her needs for that time in order to be fully able to work with the child on getting his or her needs met. The play therapist does not expect nor allow the child to meet either the therapist's emotional or physical needs. Play therapists do not need children to tell them they are doing a good job or that they are important. Nor do therapists need children to nurture them in any sort of direct way. The needs at issue in the session are those of the child.

Gifts

In keeping with the notion of focusing on the child's rather than the therapist's needs, the play therapist does not accept gifts from the child except in very limited situations in which small items are exchanged in the context of addressing a specific therapeutic goal. Here is an example of how a gift exchange might be incorporated into the play sessions. Joe was a child who had routinely been in the position of having to meet his mother's needs. Joe's play therapist knew that Joe would still be in play therapy at Christmastime and that Joe had been very disappointed by the outcome of this holiday in the past. Several weeks before Christmas, Joe began asking the play therapist what gifts the play therapist would like to receive. The play therapist made it very clear that it was not Joe's role to take care

of him because the play therapy was to help Joe learn how to get his own needs met. This caused Joe to begin writing out lists of the gifts he would like to receive. This content took longer for the play therapist to process but the focus was on the importance of Joe getting what he wanted outside of session so that he could affect not just this Christmas but future Christmases when the play therapist would not be available. They began to work on strategies for preventing Joe from having another disappointing Christmas at home. As this process proceeded, the play therapist made it clear that he would not be giving Joe a Christmas present but that they would complete a special activity in the final session before the holiday. In that session, the play therapist initiated an activity in which he and Joe made cards that they exchanged at the end of the season. The focus of the activity was the need to exchange information about what each person wanted to have included in their card so that neither would be disappointed. This exchange between equals provided Joe with both a corrective experience and with an opportunity to practice his skills at getting his own needs met in a non-threatening way.

Gift exchange is most likely to be counter-therapeutic in one of three situations. One is when the gift creates a situation in which the child is placed in the position, in reality or in effect, of taking care of the play therapist. This can be the case when the child perceives the play therapist to like or need something in particular and goes about obtaining it for the play therapist. This type of gift giving may re-create aspects of the child–caretaker relationship in which the child felt that his or her needs would not be met unless he or she was able to gratify the caretaker first. It also reverses the balance of the therapeutic relationship and diminishes the chances that children will be able to trust that the play therapist is really there to help them learn to get *their* needs met consistently and appropriately. The second type of gift exchange is one that sets the child up for unrealistic expectations. The child gives the play therapist a gift hoping that the play therapist will take on a caretaker role and give the child gifts for holidays and birthdays. The gift may represent the child's attempt to seduce the play therapist into taking on the role of caretaker in reality. This is not uncommon among children whose parents are seriously dysfunctional who find the experience of the therapist's attention in play therapy so rewarding that they come to fantasize about having the play therapist as a caretaker. The last problem is when the gift giving is actually initiated by the play therapist in response or reaction to his or her own needs. Such situations can be motivated by anything from rescue fantasies to indirect expressions of hostility toward the child's parents as a way of outdoing or outshining them in the child's eyes. Needless to say, the play therapist must be vigilant against any such manifestations of countertransference.

As just discussed, the play therapist must guard against both accepting gifts and direct gratification from the child and should use extreme caution with respect to gratifying the child's needs on any more than a very limited basis. The play therapist is only available to the child on a limited basis and, therefore, the child must find others in the environment who are able and willing to meet his or her needs on a consistent basis. Furthermore, the lack of reciprocity in the relationship can create for the child a skewed view of the way adult–child interactions ought to proceed. Recall that therapist's suspend their own needs for the duration of the session and focus solely on the needs of the child. If the play therapist not only engages in problem solving relative to those needs but actually goes on to meet the need as well, the child is put in an unrealistic one-way relationship. The play therapist has no needs and is solely focused on the child. Any child who did not see such a play therapist as an ideal potential caretaker is clearly missing something. No caregiver can compete with such a play therapist nor should they be put in a situation in which such a comparison is easily made. In the caregiver–child relationship, the child must learn to manage a certain mutuality and reciprocity of needs. The solution is not to create an "as if" caregiver–child relationship between the play therapist and the child so that the child comes to learn about the nature of caregiver–child relationships. The solution is to focus the problem solving done by the play therapist and the child in the session on making the real-life caregiver–child relationship more satisfying for the child.

There are very few situations in which the play therapist will have to engage in more direct gratification of the child's needs than is usually desirable. These all have in common the near total emotional or physical absence of the child's primary caretaker. Children in abusive or alcoholic homes, as well as those recently placed in foster or residential care, may meet these criteria. Children whose caretaker is struck with a sudden physical or emotional illness or trauma may also qualify. There is, quite literally, no one available to meet their needs at the time. In such cases, the play therapist may need to serve as a *temporary* transitional object to whom the child can attach while a more suitable and stable caretaker is identified.

Summary

In summary, the relationship between the play therapist and the child is a special one that has some specific limitations and some striking benefits. It is a relationship that focuses solely on improving the developmental functioning of the child and on helping him or her get his or her needs met more effectively and appropriately. It this sense it is not a reciprocal relationship because it is most effective when the play therapist suspends his or her needs to focus on those of the child. It is a relationship in which the sole purpose is to strengthen the child's relationships to others so that these take their appropriate place in the child's life, eliminating the need for the therapeutic relationship.

Role of Problem Solving

As we have stated repeatedly, the overarching goal of Ecosystemic Play Therapy is to assist children in finding ways to get their needs met consistently and appropriately. To do this on a day-to-day basis, persons must be able to engage in effective problem solving with respect to pragmatic, abstract, affective, and interpersonal difficulties. Most children who enter play therapy cannot get their needs met because they cannot solve the problems that interfere with the gratification of these. Through play therapy they can learn not only how to solve specific problems but also how to develop problem-solving strategies that will serve them for a lifetime. To ensure that child clients actually develop these skills, the play therapist may need to either teach and/or directly reinforce children's use of problem-solving strategies.

Problem Solving Steps

Although play therapy can be effectively completed without specifically teaching children a problem-solving approach or method, doing so can often facilitate both the play therapy process and generalization of gains made in treatment. One of the things that both play therapists and children often have difficulty doing is remaining problem-focused over both the course of a given session and the entire treatment. Working to solve problems is not necessarily fun and can even be downright unpleasant if the problem to be solved involves particularly painful content. In such cases, free play provides an easy, pleasant escape from the work of play therapy. This is not to say that every minute of every session needs to be more work than fun. On the contrary, helping children learn how to take a break from their problems can be very therapeutic in and of itself. However, it is important for both the client and the play therapist to keep in mind that what differentiates play therapy from playing is the therapeutic focus. In Ecosystemic Play Therapy that means using problem solving to help children find ways to get their needs met. Children are most easily engaged in this process if they are presented with an easy to follow model that is logically consistent and frequently rehearsed. A simple four-step strategy for problem solving is the Problem, Plan, Action, and Answer model (Nardone, Tyron, & O'Connor, 1986).

Problem   The first step is to operationally describe the problem. As with the initial treatment contracting, it is imperative that this description be framed in the child's experience. What does the child experience as problematic or unpleasant about the situation? Be sure to consider both emotional and physical comfort as potential problems, as children will work to avoid either one. Also consider long- versus short-term discomfort. Children are usually reluctant to tolerate short-term discomfort in order to prevent or undo longer range problems. Because children live in the here and now, they tend to see their present distress as more unpleasant than anything that might arise later. An example of this is the case example that follows the description of this problem-solving strategy.

Plan   Having identified the problem, the play therapist and child now engage in brainstorming potential solutions. A broad range of options should be generated, ranging from the fantastic to the pragmatic. The goal here is to help the child develop flexible thinking so that creative solutions can be derived. We have described one aspect of psychopathology as becoming struck in a habitual way of responding to problems that is no longer effective. If children are to become unstuck, they must be able to generate a variety of solutions to their difficulties so that they are prepared for any number of contingencies. For this reason, it is important to avoid critical thinking at this stage.

Action   In the action stage children evaluate the plans generated in the previous step and determine which one they would like to put into action. To accomplish this, they need to evaluate the degree to which each plan addresses the identified problem. They also need to identify any potential negative consequences that the plan might have for themselves or for others. One goal of this step is to select the plan that is most likely to resolve the problem and least likely to have negative consequences. In other words, the plan that will allow the child to get his or her needs met effectively and appropriately in ways that do not substantially interfere with the ability of others to get their needs met, the overarching goal of all Ecosystemic Play Therapy. Having identified the best plan, the child then implements the plan or puts it into action, which is the other goal of this step.

Answer   Once the child has implemented a plan in the action stage of the problem-solving process, the final step is to evaluate the plan by answering the question, How did my plan work? Did it resolve or begin to resolve the problem? If not, why not? Did it have any negative consequences? If yes, how could those negative consequences be avoided in the future. In other words, if the plan was not effective, the problem solving process starts over again in an attempt to generate a better solution.

Making a specific problem-solving strategy a regular part of every session is one way to ensure that the sessions are therapeutic and that the children are aware of the investment the play therapist has in finding ways to help them address their own real-life problems. To prevent every session from becoming a tedious cognitive exercise, the problem-solving strategy should be applied to a variety of problems, some of which are relatively light. A fun break can be created by using the problem-solving strategy to identify and address the child's desire to escape problem solving for that particular session.

Cara and her play therapist had spent about 15 minutes talking about strategies she might use to address some of her nighttime fears that were the posttraumatic result of abuse she had experienced. All of the sudden Cara said, "Let's play checkers."
"Oh, oh, I think I just discovered a new problem."
Cara rolled her eyes and looked frustrated, "No, I just want to play checkers."
"I think the problem is that you are sick and tired of talking about your abuse because it makes you nervous and kind of tired."
"Yeah, I get sick of talking about it. I want to do something else."
"OK. But I wasn't joking when I said let's try problem solving to see what to do next. The problem is that you are nervous and tired of talking about your abuse. What would be some good plans for fixing that problem."
"We could play CHECKERS!"
"I got it. What else? We could talk about something else. We could draw. We could run around the room. We could try the relaxation exercise I taught you the other day."
"We could play checkers!"
"OK, OK. But help me with the list of plans first in case we come up with a better idea."
"OK. I could never come back to play therapy and then I wouldn't have to talk about my abuse ever again."
"Good addition to the list. OK, now we have a bunch of plans. Let's see which one would best take care of the problem."
"Talking wouldn't make me feel better right now. I want to do something."
"Sounds like talking and relaxation are both out because they

aren't very active. But checkers isn't very active either. Maybe being rowdy would be the best way to get rid of those nervous feelings."

"What could we do that was rowdy?"

"Well we could run around, we could wrestle, we could have a paper wad fight?"

"Let's have a paper wad fight."

"Sounds like we have a winner. After we 'put that plan into action' and play for a while we'll stop and check to see if we made the right choice (answer). But before we start can we agree on one other thing?"

"What?"

"Can we agree that not coming back to play therapy or not ever talking about your abuse again wouldn't be a great plan? It would solve the problem of being nervous while talking but it wouldn't help the problem of the nightmares. So we'll take a break and come back to the nightmare problem in about 10 minutes."

"I know. I was just kidding. I really hate having nightmares but I hate talking about them too. I'll probably feel better after a break. Let's start."

Experiential Problem Solving

Although all of the discussion so far has focused on verbal problem solving, this is not the majority of what children do when left to their own devices. Most children attempt to solve their problems in the here and now by using trial and error learning. This does not mean that they will necessarily try out every option before being able to identify the best solution but rather that they will engage in a certain amount of experimentation much of which will most likely happen out of their conscious awareness.

The younger the child the more important it is to make problem solving an active, experiential process. Learning typically happens faster for all of us when we do things, rather than talk about them. It is can be very difficult to learn a new dance step by having someone describe it to you in words. However, if they show it to you once and then guide you through it physically once, you are much more likely to grasp what is required right away. Furthermore, for young children seeing is believing. You can tell them that a certain concentration exercise will minimize the pain they experience during a medical procedure, but they are much more likely to use it if they have even a brief experience with its effect or if they see another child using it effectively.

The play therapist should make every effort to incorporate experiential learning into every play therapy session. This is usually most easily done at the Action stage of the problem solving process by finding ways for the children to try out their plans in session. This can

be done through storytelling, role playing, puppet play, and many other types of pretend activities. In fact, the entire problem-solving process can be demonstrated for the child in the context of pretend activities. This can be done through blatant modeling in which a pretend character goes through the explicit steps of the problem-solving process by thinking out loud for the child. More often, however, it is demonstrated in a more natural way in the context of problems that occur in the play.

> Peter lost a baby animal in the sandbox and began searching for it.
>
> The play therapist took on the voice of the animal saying, *"Oh dear I'm very scared lost here in the sand. I don't know what I should do. My mommy told me that when you are lost you should stay put so that you don't accidentally wander away from the people trying to find you. But I still feel scared. Maybe I should sing because that makes me feel better. If I sang real loud and jumped up and down I bet it would be easier for Peter to find me."* At this point the play therapist began to sing loudly in a baby voice while helping the child find the animal in the sand.
>
> The play therapist found the animal first and made it jump up and down until Peter took it rather than handing it directly to Peter. Then the play therapist said, *"Whew, I was worried there but singing made me feel better and jumping up and down did make it easier for Peter to find me. I feel much better now so I'll have to remember to do that next time if I ever get lost again."*

The more closely the problem-solving demonstrations and experiences match the needs and concerns of the child, the more powerful and potentially therapeutic they will be. In the previous example, the play therapist could have used the same situation to focus on solving any number of problems. For a child prone to helplessness, the play therapist could have modeled seeking out a responsible adult for assistance. For the neglected child, the modeling could have addressed the feelings of always being lost and uncared for and fear that there was no real search under way. It is the therapist's role to determine how to use the play and play content optimally to address the goals of the treatment.

Cognitive/Verbal Problem Solving

Although experiential problem solving is both powerful and the natural way in which children learn, it does have its limitations. First, not all situations in the child's life can be readily brought into the playroom, even with great materials and acting skills. Second, experiential work takes a lot of time. Third, each situation is fixed in content so that the child's learning may be limited to a single variant of the experience. The play therapist and the child may develop an excellent strategy for helping the child cope with nighttime fears based on putting dolls to bed in the playroom. It is unlikely that the child would then use the same plan in an attempt cope with his or her fear of an injection at the doctor's office even though the strategy may have been effective. This leads us to the last problem, which is the tendency of experiential learning not to generalize well. The previous example showed how experiential learning may not generalize to similar situations. Conversely, traumatic experiential learning may generalize excessively. A child who is bitten by a particular dog is likely to become fearful of all dogs, at least for a while. Hopefully, the play therapy will not include such traumatic learning, but the point that the generalization of experiential learning is difficult to predict remains valid.

Language can be used to help the child understand both the concepts underlying a particular experience in session and the nature of the problem-solving process. Through language, the play therapist can help children refine their problem-solving plans to fit a variety of situations and help them to generalize what happens in session to their lives outside of the playroom. The play therapist can also help the child engage in hypothetical thinking. That is, a large number of scenarios can be covered without having to develop an experiential activity for each and every one of them. The play therapist and child might play out how the child is to respond the next time he or she feels picked on by a peer. Having completed this activity, the play therapist can then use language to enable the child to think about how he or she would modify their behavior if he or she felt picked on by a much older child, an adult, a teacher, or a caregiver. In such cases, refinement and generalization of the learning are accomplished very quickly.

Role of Education

The importance of education or teaching in the play therapy process was already alluded to in the previous discussion of intervention modalities. Clearly, the play therapist may need to teach the child both the concept of problem solving and the specific steps by which it is effectively implemented. This type of teaching can, however, be accomplished in a relatively indirect way that allows the play therapist to stay true to the role of play therapist rather than assume the role of teacher. In our model the essential difference between the two is the level of passivity the child assumes in response to one versus the other. When the play therapist stays in the play therapist role, the child is never a passive participant. The play therapist strives to keep the child actively engaged in the interaction and problem solving at all times, whether the tasks being used are purely experiential or largely cognitive in nature. When the play therapist shifts to the role of teacher, the child may be allowed to be a more passive learner. The play therapist

may not expect any immediate response from the client. The child is simply expected to acquire and store the information that the play therapist is providing. Because of the shift in the role of the child, the play therapist should be cautious about overusing an educational mode of intervention.

It is usually most important for the play therapist to shift into the role of teacher or educator when the child lacks specific knowledge or skills that are needed to engage in effectively problem solving a current issue or situation. Sometimes the lack of knowledge or skill is a problem in itself. More often, it is a contributor to children's inability to consistently and appropriately get their needs met in one or more situations. Therapists most often find themselves needing to take on the role of educator in one of five situations, these include teaching the child: (a) how to play, (b) about emotions and the expression of them, (c) about specific life events, (d) about various disorders or conditions, and (e) specific intra- and interpersonal skills. Before discussing each of these, let us look at way the play therapist might minimize the potential negative impact of assuming the role of teacher in a play therapy session.

It is often useful to bracket such interactions so that the child sees them as specifically different from the rest of the play therapy process. Saying something as simple as, "I want to take a minute to teach you something that may help both of us figure out some better ways to change some of the problems you are having," is often a sufficient signal. On a more blatant level, the play therapist might actually engage the child in a classroom style role play, complete with a desk and a blackboard, to ensure that the child is aware of the nature of the task at hand and the temporary shift in roles.

One way to engage in education while minimizing the negative aspects of the educator/student roles is to use books or other materials to distance both the play therapist and the child from the content. The educator becomes the author of the book or the creator of the audio or videotape. The play therapist can join the child in learning the information from an outside expert and can then assist the child in determining how well the material fits the child's situation and how it can be used in problem solving. A great way to implement this is by reading a book or showing a tape to a child in session while both of you engage in actively critiquing the work. The critique should focus on the realism and accuracy of the information presented and the degree to which it does or does not reflect the child's life experience. This is followed by one or more sessions in which the primary activity is the creation of a book or videotape that better represents the child's experience and depicts at least some problem solving relative to the child's issues. For those therapists and children who are not particularly artistically inclined, the play therapist can photocopy the pictures from the target text and block out the text. The child can then add in text he or she considers to be more appropriate and can even add in or delete pages as needed. This type of task introduces a variety of content without either imposing it on the child or disrupting the working relationship between the child and play therapist. This same style is useful when trying to convey information to others in the child's life. A book allows both the play therapist and the other adult to critique and adapt the information as needed without either of them losing face.

How to Play   As to the problems that may be best addressed through education, one of the most significant initial problems some children face when entering play therapy is that they do not know how to play. This is often seen in children who have been abused or neglected. Some children may not even know the names or uses of the toys and materials. These children cannot be expected to make much use of the play therapy materials or process until they have at least a basic understanding of play. Labeling the toys and demonstrating several ways in which each can be used can usually be accomplished in a relatively short period of time. Once this has been accomplished, the play therapist can then use more traditional therapeutic approaches to address the residual anxiety or discomfort the child may have about playing.

Understanding Emotions   Another important problem very common to children is a lack of understanding about emotions. Problems in this area can range from the inability to recognize emotional cues in themselves or others to the absence of a vocabulary sufficient to express their emotional experience. Although much of this type of learning can be accomplished through a variety of play activities, there may be times the play therapist needs to teach the child specific cues or vocabulary. For example, the child may need to be encouraged to look in the mirror and to label certain facial expressions as being consistent with various emotional states. That same child may need to watch the play therapist with various emotional states. That same child may need to watch the play therapist model different expressions to gain some ability to interpret the emotional responses of others. Many techniques have been developed to help children develop understanding and skills in this area. Among others, Harter (1983) has done quite a bit of work on strategies for teaching children the concept of ambivalence. The Color-Your-Life technique (O'Connor, 1983) was developed to teach children emotional concepts and vocabulary by using art materials.

Life Events   In the life events category, information can be presented to the child either before or after he or she has experienced the event. For example, it may be helpful if the child knows what to expect before experiencing, everything from a family move, to a divorce, to a tonsillectomy. For a child who has already experienced one of these events and who is having some difficulty coping, it may be useful to hear about the usual course of those events, the range of other children's reactions to those events, and their strategies for managing those reactions.

Information about group membership can be critical for children attempting to cope with issues of identity and being different. Relevant content might include information about the experiences of children in various ethnic, racial, or religious groups. This is also one of the best ways to take a culturally positive stance in play therapy by making books and materials available that both address the problems a particular group faces and portray the group in positive ways. If you cannot find materials about a specific group, it may still be useful to present material about a similar group and to encourage children (and/or the family) to gather information between sessions to create a book or tape that depicts important aspects of their own group.

Problem-Specific Information   Sometimes it is impossible for children to solve problems in their lives effectively because they lack information about the nature of the problem. There are many variations on this scenario. Children may not have been given adequate information about the nature of their own psychological or medical conditions. Parents may not talk to their child about the nature of ADHD because they are concerned the child will use it as an excuse to misbehave. Unfortunately, in the absence of such information, children often assume that the basic underlying problem is that they are inherently bad and consequently their self-esteem suffers terribly. Children suffering from catastrophic illnesses may not be told the nature of their problems either. In such cases, the children fill in what they do not know with fantasy, which prevents them from addressing the problem or increases their symptomatology. Conversely, the child may know much more than the adults suspect, but believe that because the adults are unwilling to discuss the problem, he or she should avoid it as well.

Many books have also been written to help children understand the nature of the problems being experienced by persons around them. Again, this might include information on medical and mental disorders. Parents are often reluctant to tell children about such things as serious illnesses of family members. One topic covered quite extensively in children's literature is parental alcoholism. The books help children understand both the dynamics of the disease and the stages of the recovery process. It is quite rate to encounter a child who is living with a mentally ill caregiver or sibling who has been given a comprehensive age-appropriate explanation of the nature of the problem. Again, in the absence of such knowledge, children are likely to fill in with their own information and explanations and these may involve significant and distressing distortions of reality.

It is also important to make sure both parents and children have good current information, as the mental health field has been making some rapid advances over the past 20 years. As a result, parents with problems and parents of children with problems are treated differently by mental health professionals. Parents are also expected to respond to their children's problems differently as the understanding of the nature of those problems changes.

There is also a larger problem that falls into this general category. These days it is common for children to be exposed, through the media, to the psychopathology of others in an intense and often frightening way. There is news coverage of parents who turn on their families, killing them and then themselves. There are stories of trusted adults who are discovered to have molested dozens of children with whom they interacted. And there are stories about random acts of violence to which children fall victim. As with many other unpleasant topics, there is a tendency on the part of adults to avoid discussing these with children. Although it is important for parents to monitor and to mediate the impact of these events on their children, it is also very important for therapists to keep abreast of events and to consider addressing those with which their clients may have a particular reason to identify in the context of play therapy.

Intra- and Interpersonal Skills   The last type of teaching discussed here is the need to teach some children specific intrapersonal and interpersonal skills so that they are better able to function in the world. One example of an intrapersonal skill is teaching a child a relaxation strategy. If overwhelming anxiety is part of the reason the child is unable to get his or her needs met consistently and appropriately, then he or she may greatly benefit both from learning how to manage that symptom and from the sense of empowerment that accompanies the acquisition of that skill. The vast majority of children who enter play therapy have some degree of interpersonal skills deficits. This is most obvious in the children who act out a great deal, who are often involved in fights at school, and who have very few friends. These deficits are less obvious in children

who tend toward being overcontrolled, who interact well with adults but who are shy, isolated, and virtually unable to engage in positive interactions with their peers.

An educational approach is often an effective way for teaching both children and others specific skills. Books and materials are available that cover parenting skills, behavior management, social skills, anger management, grief work, and so forth. When presenting skills information, it is important to help both children and adults translate the cognitive content into practice. It is one thing to hear about or think about the use of a particular skill, it is quite another to determine when and how to use that skill in one's own life. The play therapist should also provide opportunities for either the child or adult to practice the skills in a safe environment. Little will damage a client's motivation more than meeting with failure or, worse yet, a hostile response the first time they attempt a new skill. Role playing the use of the skill in session can be very useful especially if the play therapist demonstrates exaggerated, humorous errors in implementing the skill in a playful way. This desensitizes children to the seriousness of making mistakes and frees them up to adapt the skills to their own needs. This playful tone is useful for adults as well, as they often take the process of implementing important life skills with far too much seriousness. Parenting, teaching, medically caring for or even conducting play therapy with a child can become dreary, even painful experiences if the participants cannot play with roles at times and laugh at themselves in the process.

There are probably many other situations in which children might benefit from being provided with specific information by means of an educational intervention. The play therapist should always first determine whether there is someone in the child's environment who could take on the role of educator so that play therapy time need not be used. When it seems best to conduct the education in session, the play therapist should first attempt to provide the information in the context of the experiential or cognitive aspects of the therapeutic process. When this is not an option and direct education seems to be in order, then the play therapist should look for ways to bracket the educational elements to both emphasize their importance and separate them from the more cooperative problem-solving aspects of the play therapy process.

Role of Interpretation

Interpretation seems to be a process that is differentially defined by virtually everyone who writes about it, and one that is either abhorred or revered depending on one's theoretical orientation. The range of play therapist behaviors to which the term applies is vast. On the one hand, something as mild as a therapist's repetition of something the child has said or done, although most often called reflection, is also sometimes referred to as interpretation. On the other hand, something as intense as the therapist's connection of the client's current emotional experience to an earlier unpleasant interaction with someone important in the client's life is also called interpretation. Often, too, the purpose of interpretation seems unclear. Usually, interpretation is thought of as being used to provide clients with insight as to the nature of their problems, but it is sometimes construed as the play therapist imposing his or her own constructions of the problem onto the client's experience.

In Ecosystemic Play Therapy, we have attempted to clarify both the purpose and process of interpretation. The purpose of interpretation is to support the problem-solving process in play therapy by clarifying the exact nature of the problem being solved. This is accomplished by providing the child with information that he or she either did not know or could not access because of psychological interference (anxiety, defense mechanisms, and so forth). This information may or may not reflect "absolute truth." That is to say that the ability of the play therapist to provide the child with an alternative way of looking at the problem is more important than the accuracy of that viewpoint. The alternative understanding helps the child to break set and engage in renewed and creative problem solving, even if the content of the interpretation does not reflect a universal truth. Clients may improve with a Jungian, Freudian, Rogerian, or Buddhist reframing of their problems. Who is to say which explanation is the right one? Ecosystemic Play Therapy maintains a subject-dependent view that emphasizes the importance of the way the child experiences and resolves the problem over an external judgment of what the problem "really" is and the imposition of a single "correct" solution.

In Ecosystemic Play Therapy interpretation is not aimed at providing the client with insight for insight's sake. Self-knowledge is important but it is not the end goal of this model of play therapy. Rather the goal is to enable children to get their needs met consistently and appropriately and interpretation is used to achieve that end. To accomplish its purpose, interpretation must be used systematically and progressively, so that the child can accept and make use of the information and views being supplied by the play therapist. One way to ensure that the material is presented both systematically and progressively is to follow the five step model of interpretation (O'Connor, 1991), which is described in the following.

Reflection   This term is used in many descriptions of therapy in general and of play therapy in particular. Often it is used to describe a process by which the play therapist paraphrases something the child has said or puts descriptive words to what the child is doing, "Oh, look at you crashing those cars into the pile of blocks." Such statements may serve to demonstrate that the play therapist is paying attention to what the child is doing, but they do not seem to do much in the way of setting up the problem-solving process. These statements are not what are meant by the use of the term reflection in Ecosystemic Play Therapy.

Reflections are statements made by the play therapist that make explicit the affect or motives underlying the things the child says or does in session. If the child says, "I feel angry," the underlying affect has been made explicit and no reflection is needed. If, however, the child says, "I am going to throw this truck at you," the play therapist might make any one of several reflections:

- "You are certainly very angry at me."
- "You hope you can scare me into letting you do just what you want to right now."
- "You are really upset with me for forgetting to bring that game I said I would bring."

The play therapist could make the same string of reflections in response to a time when the child physically threatened to throw a toy truck or actually threw a truck. In either case, the point of the therapist's reflection is to expand the child's communication by adding a statement regarding the child's inner state. This provides the child with an element that will be useful in later problem solving. Over time, the play therapist will have identified a string of events and issues that the child finds pleasant and a string that the child finds unpleasant, and work can begin to increase the former while decreasing the latter.

Pattern   In a pattern interpretation the play therapist makes explicit repetitions in the child's behavior over time. These repetitions may be either behavioral or thematic. A pattern interpretation of behavior would simply be a statement noting that a current behavior has occurred on several previous occasions.

- "I just noticed that this is the third time you have changed the subject when I mention something about your mom."
- "That was the fifth fight over food you staged between those two puppets."

This last pattern interpretation actually conveys both a theme and a behavior. Pattern interpretations of themes identify similar content in what may be disparate behavior. The play therapist might first reflect, "Boy, you seem really angry today." The play therapist might then continue with a pattern interpretation, "I could hear you yelling at the receptionist before I came out, you knocked over a chair when you walked in the room, you drew a picture—tore it up—and then threw the pieces around, then you just started grumbling under your breath."

Pattern interpretations are useful for two reasons. One is that they let the child know that the play therapist has paid attention to what the child is doing over time. But, more importantly, they help the child see his or her behavior as connected rather than random or unrelated. Children, especially young children, have difficulty identifying realistic relationships between events. They tend to see events or behaviors that are superficially similar as related, often leading to odd conclusions. "Mom yelled at me yesterday morning and this morning when she was wearing her bright pink bathrobe; maybe it is uncomfortable and makes her cranky." They also tend to miss relationships between events that are not superficially similar, seeing no connection between the fact that yesterday they were yelled at for making a mess in the kitchen at breakfast and today they were yelled at for making a mess in the bathroom. Unless the mother is very clear in her use of the word *mess* to describe both situations, the child may miss the relationship between the yelling and his or her own behavior and may attribute the problem to something about mom's mood or bathrobe instead.

Pattern interpretations support the problem-solving process in two ways. One is that they provide the child with a string of examples of the problem situation. Conversely, these might be used to provide the child with a string of examples in which the problem does not occur. Pattern interpretations also tend to increase the child's investment in resolving the underlying problem. After all, one is much more likely to be motivated to work on resolving a recurring problem than to expend energy on something one perceives as a one-time event. Parents sometimes see the latter when they try to talk to their children about a specific negative behavior. The child, sensing a lecture coming on says "OK, OK, I won't do that again." The caregiver then makes a retroactive pattern interpretation saying, "But this isn't the only time you did it. You also did it at x, y and z." As feelings are now running high, the child is likely to reject the pattern interpretation saying, "Those times had nothing to do with this and I already said I won't do it again so what more do you want?" This example shows the importance of making the pattern interpretation in a relatively neutral tone well before attempting to initiate any potential problem solving.

Simple Dynamic   In a Simple Dynamic interpretation, the play therapist brings together a previously made reflection and a previously made pattern interpretation in order to make explicit the connection between the child's inner world and his or her behavior. "I'll bet the reason you quit block building, and drawing, and the game we were playing was because you decided you weren't doing well at any of them and that made you feel bad about yourself." The play therapist should have already reflected the child's negative self-evaluation, preferably in at least two of the three preceding events. The play therapist should also have already made a pattern interpretation noting the repeated quitting behavior. In the simple dynamic interpretation, the play therapist is just putting the two together.

Again, the point here is to support the problem-solving process by helping the child to see how feelings and motives drive behavior over time. The child's motivation to solve the problem at hand is increased and he or she has several examples with which to work. It is important that the play therapist not attempt to do all interpretive or problem-solving work with negative affects and experiences only. Good work can be done by focusing on times the child feels good and on problem solving ways to increase or enhance those situations.

It should also be noted here that, at least initially, the play therapist makes these first three levels of interpretation only in response to behavior or content he or she has actually seen or heard in session. The play therapist is cautious not to attempt interpretation of material reported by the child's parents or others in the child's environment. There are two reasons for this limitation. One is that the play therapist is more likely to misinterpret events that he or she has not directly witnessed. When a mother reports an event, no matter how objective she tries to be, she still reports what she saw and that report is colored both by the personal lenses through which she saw it and the limits of her ability to describe the event. The same is true of fathers, siblings, nurses, and everyone else. The other reason is that early interpretation of content reported by others tends to disrupt the process of building trust between the child and the play therapist. The child comes to believe that the play therapist gives great credence to what others say and, given that most of these reporters are probably adults, that the play therapist believes them rather than the child.

If the child reports an outside event, then it is perfectly reasonable for the play therapist to base interpretations on that content. The play therapist should still be cautious, however, especially when the child is reporting a misbehavior on his or her part. Sometimes children are told by their caretakers that they must tell the play therapist about a specific event or the caregiver will report it. In these situations the children usually report the event the way they think their parents would rather than the way they would and the play therapist is, again, put in the position of potentially taking sides with an adult against the child.

Generalized Dynamic   At the level of generalized dynamic interpretation, the play therapist moves beyond the content of the sessions to work with what he or she knows about the child's life outside of sessions. Now, the play therapist may begin to use material obtained from any source so long as it can be tied to work already done in the first three levels of interpretation. The child's negative self-evaluation and quitting behavior in session can now be tied to the way he or she approaches schoolwork or interactions with peers and so forth. Previous simple dynamic interpretations are merely generalized to events outside of play therapy.

Generalized dynamic interpretations also support the problem-solving process in two ways. One is that they help the child see the relationship between what occurs in session and his or her life in the real world. The process of generalizing the therapeutic gains is initiated. The other is that they often mark a transition in the play therapy process in which most of the problem solving is done relative to real life events and problems rather than through fantasy material or play. At this point, many children are already to shift to a problem-focused type of talking play therapy that does not look much different from that which might be conducted with adult clients.

Genetic   At this level, the play therapist connects previously made simple or generalized dynamic interpretations to the events or relationships that spawned them. Consistent with psychoanalytic tradition, these are usually events or interactions that occurred very early in the child's life, causing partial or complete regressions or fixations. The play therapist identifies that the child's fear of failure is the result of a long-held belief that if he or she failed to interpret and meet mom's needs consistently, then either abuse or abandonment would be the result. Or it may be when the play therapist notes that the child never seemed to regain a sense of importance in the family after the birth of a sibling. Although most genetic interpretations are based in the child's relatively early history, this is not always the case. A child may have become symptomatic in reaction to a relatively specific recent event or trauma. In such cases, the genetic interpretation identifies that event as the precipitant.

Usually a genetic interpretation facilitates the process of problem solving by beginning to identify that the origins of the problem are not particularly relevant to the present day difficulties. This is most often true in work with adults who no longer need to maintain intense dependent relationships with their caretakers in order to survive. If the genetic origins of a problem are discovered in the early primary relationship and that relationship is found to be an ongoing source of difficulty, then the adult client may choose to end or significantly modify that relationship. For children, however, this last part is usually not an option. Children are faced with the reality of their dependency and must be helped to find ways to get their needs met even in the context of a less than healthy relationship or family and regardless of whether or not the caretaker or family is able or willing to change. In some ways, this reality makes play therapy with children more difficult than therapy with adults, as a range of potential solutions is not available. This is the point at which family work, consultation, or advocacy may become a necessary course of action.

In some cases, the problem solving that needs to be done is that of finding ways to separate the child's past from the present. This is the case when the genetic event is no longer a problem or has changed significantly since it began. Children can be helped to see that whether their initial response was appropriate or not, the continuation of that response is no longer appropriate because the problem is gone or has changed. The child who became pseudo-mature in response to a period of time when the caretaker was depressed and emotionally unavailable can be helped to see that the caregiver has recovered, is now able to resume parenting, and is able to support the child in returning to being a child.

The previous list of interpretations is described in the order in which they would be presented to the child in session. There are several other points to keep in mind to use interpretation most effectively. These are frequency, intensity, timing and content or delivery.

The frequency with which interpretations should be delivered corresponds to the order in which they were previously described. That is, the play therapist should make regular and liberal use of reflections and make very few genetic interpretations. Typically, the play therapist will make several dozen reflections during a given session and no more than one or two genetic interpretations. In fact, it is unusual for the play therapist to make more than two or three genetic interpretations over the entire course of a child's treatment. Once made, however, a genetic interpretation may be repeated at regular intervals to identify its relevance across situations.

The intensity of the interpretations, that is, the impact they are likely to have on the child, also corresponds to the order in which they were described. Most children have little reaction to reflections or pattern interpretations. On the other hand, a well-timed genetic interpretation may cause the child to have an intense emotional reaction, accompanied by some degree of regression or even some level of acting out. Crying is one of the more common reactions to genetic interpretations, as the child is put in touch with the original hurt that has come to drive his or her behavior on a day-to-day basis.

The timing of the delivery of interpretations is critical to their effectiveness. The play therapy is more likely to be disrupted by an ill-timed interpretation than by a grossly inaccurate one. By sequencing the interpretations as described previously, timing errors will be greatly reduced. The play therapist will be sure to have presented each of the component parts of the genetic interpretation through the previous four levels by the time the painful material is presented. The only other matter is the timing of the genetic interpretations within sessions and within the course of the play therapy.

As a general rule, genetic interpretations should be delivered no sooner than half-way through a given session and no later than two-thirds of the way through. This ensures that the child has had time to settle into the session before the play therapist brings up intense material. It also means the play therapist has had time to observe and interact with the child to determine whether the child is ready to proceed. Leaving some time in the session after the genetic interpretation ensures that the child will have time to respond and recover from the material before having to leave the safety of the playroom. It is also the case that genetic interpretations are delivered one-half to two-thirds of the way through the course of treatment. That is, if a therapist is doing short-term work, say eight to ten sessions, he or she must plan on having the child ready for the interpretation by the fourth to seventh session. If the therapist has the luxury of doing long-term work, he or she knows that the course of treatment is one-half to two-thirds of the way through before making the key genetic interpretation. That is, if the therapist has seen the child for 6 months and he or she is able successfully to make a genetic interpretation, then the therapist can begin planning for termination within the next 3 to 6 months. The rationale for the timing across sessions is the same as for the timing of the delivery within sessions. The child needs to be adequately prepared and then needs time to respond to and resolve the issues the genetic interpretation uncovers.

The last technical issue to be considered is the context of the delivery of any interpretation. The impact of an interpretation can be minimized by making it completely within the child's play. It is not the child who is angry or whose mother hurt him, it is the puppet or doll or the figure in a drawing. This strategy allows children to take on the role of observer so as to see someone else's reaction to their feelings, thoughts, or experiences. The impact of an interpretation can be intensified somewhat by making it in an "as if" context. Here, the play therapist talks about how other children they know feel or think, or how other children the same age or gender as the client might feel, think, or behave. Such interpretations still allow the child to take on an observer role but increase the child's identification with the target of the interpretation. Finally, the play therapist should, at some point, interpret directly to the child so that the child is pushed to experience rather than simply observe the content of the interpretation.

Lastly, the play therapist should note that not all material that the child presents can or should be interpreted. During the treatment planning phase, the play therapist will have developed hypotheses about the etiology of the child's present difficulties and these will form the basis of later genetic interpretations. The play therapist should focus on making interpretations that lead to the planned genetic interpretation. If the child consistently rejects the preparatory interpretive work and the play therapist believes that his or her timing is good, then he or she must consider the possibility that the planned genetic interpretation was wrong and develop some alternative hypotheses. This is a different approach than that advocated within psychoanalysis.

In analysis, the analyst tracks the material the client presents in session and eventually is led to the genetic material. The analyst may have an idea of where the client is headed based on the client's history and symptoms, but this idea does not usually become a planned goal of the treatment process until the play therapy is well underway. In Ecosystemic Play Therapy, the most likely genetic interpretations are derived from the intake material and incorporated into the treatment plan as an explicit goal. The play therapist then develops experiential and cognitive activities that will lead toward the material needed to make the genetic interpretation explicit. There are pros and cons to both approaches. In psychoanalysis, one increases the chances that the play therapist will not get off on the wrong track by greatly increasing the length of the play therapy and the burden the client must bear for supplying content for the analysis. In Ecosystemic Play Therapy, one shortens the play therapy and decreases the burden on the client by increasing the chances that the play therapist will be off target with the genetic interpretation. The risks of the latter seem to be relatively easily managed if the play therapist is sensitive to early feedback from the child that his or her low-level interpretation does not fit the child's experience and if the play therapist is willing and able to make immediate adjustments to the treatment plan.

The process is similar to recent advances in computer technology. Older computers with linear processors followed a code that proceeded from A to B to C and on to the target end point be it K or Z. Each time, the computer followed the code in sequence from the beginning until it found the target end point. Newer computers use RISC processors that begin the sequence and, once a pattern is detected, jump to a "hypothesized" target end point. If that end point is not the one needed, it returns to where it left off of the sequence and starts again until another pattern is detected, at which point it jumps again.

Having determined the treatment goals and the degree to which the play therapy should be experiential and/or cognitive, the play therapist is ready to plan specific session activities that take into consideration the treatment goals, the phase of the treatment, and the developmental level of the child. In the next section we discuss interventions to address specific content and ones suited to the different phases of the treatment process. In Chapter 10, we present 25 sample session activities geared to children at different developmental levels.

INTERVENTIONS TO ADDRESS SPECIFIC CONTENT AREAS

Prevention and Inoculation

Using Ecosystemic Play Therapy to prevent the occurrence of psychopathology in children is probably one of the most rewarding and yet underutilized approaches. Children often face predictable stresses in their lives either as the result of routine life events, normal developmental changes, or predictable trauma. Even though many children come through these events unscathed, an unfortunate percentage suffer temporary or even long-term symptoms that may have been entirely preventable. As adults, we tend to forget how much children benefit from being prepared for the disruptions that will occur in their lives and how relatively easy it can be to teach them the coping skills they need ahead of time. Prevention has become commonplace with such problems as child physical and sexual abuse and potential abductions. It is also used somewhat regularly with children who face elective or long-term medical procedures. However, it is woefully underused for such common problems as the birth of a sibling, divorce, family moves or changes in school placement, medical emergencies, or even the onset of puberty.

The goal in any preventive or inoculating intervention is to present the child with relevant information about the stressful event and with an array of potential strategies for coping with specific aspects of the event. Just having knowledge of how the event is likely to proceed and why it will happen that way is often enough to enhance dramatically children's coping. This knowledge allows them to predict the course of the event and they often interpret that predictive ability as giving them a certain amount of control and power. Interestingly, children often want more information than adults, although they tend to want concrete, observable details rather than wanting to know a lot about what will be going on behind the scenes.

In addition to specific knowledge, the play therapist should help the child identify potential resources and strategies that might be helpful in managing the event. The resources identified can include both persons and objects. Many children survive a stressful event with the help of nothing more than a teddy bear. When specific strategies are identified or presented the child should be encouraged to practice these beforehand. Relaxation strategies or self-hypnosis can be used by even very young children to manage difficult medical procedures, but only when they have adequately mastered those skills before they are anxious or in pain.

One common event that occurs in most children's lives is some sort of family relocation, ranging from moving from one dwelling to another in relatively close proximity to moving cross country. Depending on the child's age, this can be a very stressful event, as he or she is separated from familiar people and places. There are many strategies that can be used by the parents and the children to make this event easier to tolerate. First of all just talking about it even with a very young child helps to decrease the level of surprise and, therefore, the helplessness the child experiences. Second, giving the child as much information about the new residence as possible helps make that place less frightening. Everything from brochures about the city or state to which the family is moving, to maps, to pictures of the new house or apartment, to actual photos of the child's new room are all very useful in helping the child to prepare. Third, helping the child prepare momentos of the current home is useful. Take pictures or make drawings of favorite activities and people. Create a scrapbook of the items collected. And, finally, do as many things as possible to set up some transitional activities. This could include collecting names, addresses, and phone numbers of favorite people and giving important people stamped post cards with the child's new address on them so that the child is sure to get at least some initial correspondence when they arrive at the new home. This type of anticipatory planning for various common (e.g., sibling births) and unusual (a caregiver requiring surgery) events, and even crises (a child requiring major medical interventions), can often be accomplished quickly and can be very powerful in preventing trauma and subsequent symptomatic behavior.

Person-Induced Difficulties

A very large proportion of the children seen in play therapy have become symptomatic as the result of previous or ongoing problems with specific persons in their lives. Child abuse is certainly the most serious of these difficulties. Most often the problematic relationship is between these children and their primary caretakers, but children who are suffering as the result of their parent's marital problems or problems with their siblings are by no means uncommon. In these situations, the play therapist needs to consider the systemic level at which intervention would be both most appropriate and possible. Even when the child's difficulties are clearly derived from his or her dyadic relationship with the primary caretaker, dyadic play therapy may not be the best starting point if either the child or the caretaker is so disturbed that joint sessions are likely to produce more unpleasant than pleasant interactions. Similarly, family play therapy may not be either clinically indicated or pragmatically possible for a child who is suffering because of intense parental conflict at the time of a divorce. In these cases, individual play therapy for one or more of the persons involved many need to precede any more systemic work. In the worse case scenarios, the work with the child may actually have to focus on helping the child to withstand a person or relationship that is unlikely to change.

Chronically Inadequate Relationships

One of the occasionally sad realities of childhood is the fact that children do not have choices about the families with which they must live. Although the social services system is often prepared to manage situations in which the child is suffering outright abuse or neglect, it is much more difficult for that system, the legal system, or the mental health system to address the problems faced by children whose caretakers or families are simply chronically inadequate. In the beset-case scenarios, these situations involve caretakers who are genuinely well meaning but who lack the cognitive or emotional skills needed for adequately addressing their children's needs. These family situations can usually be improved with education, play therapy, and support. In the worst case scenarios, the caretakers are uncaring or even hostile individuals who manage never to cross the line into severe abuse or whose functioning vacillates over time,

resulting in their children being removed from and returned to the home multiple times.

Irrespective of the eventual outcome of the changes made in the delivery of mental health services by managed care systems, the reality is that the majority of these cases require long-term interventions that serve to stabilize the children and families in a way that allows the children's needs to be met more consistently and appropriately. Every effort should be made to facilitate the child's development of coping skills that will allow him or her to flourish in spite of the family situation and without continuous play therapy, but this may be particularly difficult especially if the child is quite young at the time of the initial referral. Every effort should also be made to prevent the play therapy and the relationship with the play therapist from becoming a substitute for the child's relationship with his or her caretaker or family. As discussed previously, play therapy should be geared toward improving children's functioning in the context of their environments. This may mean that a lot of work needs to be done to identify appropriate resources for the child, but it should not mean that the play therapy becomes the child's only resource.

Time-Limited Interpersonal Crises

These include life events that many range from very positive to very negative. Some examples might be the death of a relative or having any member of the family undergo a specific stress. Play therapy for children who are reacting to these stressful events will generally be both content-focused and time-limited. A positive outcome will depend on the degree to which both the play therapist and the caretakers can anticipate which of the child's needs are likely to go unmet in the face of this crisis. It also usually depends on the availability of the other resources if, because of the crisis, one or more of the caretakers is physically or emotionally unavailable. Unfortunately, the very nature of a crisis tends to mean that the child's needs will not be addressed at the time and that treatment will not be initiated until well after the crisis has passed and the child has become symptomatic. Finally, if the crisis was one that could be anticipated and an intervention is begun beforehand, then a positive outcome is more likely.

Environmentally Produced Difficulties

When the ecosystemic play therapist determines that the environment is a significant cause of the child's difficulties, he or she should immediately consider the systems level at which an intervention or interventions would be best implemented. Individual play therapy may help children to understand their experience and to develop some coping strategies. Family or peer sessions may help them identify persons in the environment who can serve as resources in managing the problem system and may help the child feel less isolated and helpless. An advocacy or consultation approach may be needed to initiate the necessary systemic changes. It is particularly important in such cases for the play therapist to help the child, and often the family, externalize the source of the problem so that they can mobilize their efforts at correcting the environment rather than focusing on the child.

Problematic Systems

As just discussed, children who develop symptoms as the result of interactions with toxic systems are often best helped by a combination of therapeutic approaches. Although a wide range of approaches and combination of approaches are possible, the following example gives some idea of how a toxic school system might be addressed.

> James was a young African-American boy who was placed in a school that had serious gang-related difficulties. In this geographic area, gangs were divided along racial lines and James, who was not a gang member, experienced constant harassment and peer pressure to conform to antisocial gang behavior while at school. As the day-to-day stress increased, James became progressively more anxious and virtually school phobic. His mother was very concerned about the gradual decline in James' academic performance and brought him for treatment. The treatment plan involved a multipronged attack on the problem.
>
> James was seen in individual play therapy to focus on developing and maintaining his self-esteem in the face of peer pressure and reinforcing his interest in academics. He was also taught strategies he could use to ignore the peer harassment and to reduce his anxiety during stressful interactions. His family was encouraged to involve him in as many non-gang peer activities as they could identify, both in and out of school. James joined an after school sports program and began taking karate classes twice a week. The family was also involved in some play sessions aimed at intensifying their familial and ethnocultural identification as a way of counterbalancing the pull of potential gang affiliation. A consultation with the school helped to activate the administration to take steps to ensure the safety of the younger children on the campus and to consciously break up gang clusters by dispersing members into different classrooms.

Medical Crises

When helping a child to manage any type of crisis situation it is important to keep several things in mind. First, the play therapy will often need to occur at high frequency over a relatively short period of time. Depending on the nature of the crisis and the speed with which it will unfold or vary, sessions may need to occur more than once a day. When sessions are high fre-

quency, it is often better to keep them fairly short so that the child does not come to experience the play therapy as adding to rather than mediating the stress. Second, the play therapist may need to be quite directive so that the sessions stay content focused. In a crisis, the child may seek to avoid the content and many a play therapist, faced with the child's overwhelming anxiety, may go along with or even foster the avoidance. Although this may be an appropriate intervention strategy, it needs to be managed carefully. Finally, the play therapist needs to keep in mind that a crisis will often exacerbate or at least interact with problems that the child was already experiencing. It is usually not necessary to resolve these earlier difficulties to have a positive impact on the child's ability to cope with the present crisis. For example, a child who suffers from severe separation anxiety may be helped to cope with pain following an emergency medical procedure without resolving the underlying cause of the separation anxiety. The child may even be able to learn ways of coping with the immediate separation that resulted from being hospitalized without addressing the underlying separation issues.

Natural and Man-Made Disasters

Children who are exposed to disasters react in much the same way as children facing any other type of crisis. It is important to consider the exact dynamics of the disaster when planning the Ecosystemic Play Therapy. Natural disasters tend to have a broader scope of impact than other crises so that it is likely that more than one if not all of the family members have been exposed to the event. Natural disasters also tend to engender lots of feelings of helplessness because of the magnitude and unpredictability of the events. These can also be difficult to address because there is no person or group on whom to focus the problem solving. It is difficult to work out an understanding with nature. Man-made disasters can be attributed to specific people, and although that increases children's ability to focus blame, it can make them even more anxious than if they survived a natural disaster and their victimization seemed random. The response of the children who endured the Chowchilla bus kidnapping have been extensively studied and demonstrate just this type of long-term psychopathological response (Terr, 1981, 1990).

SESSION ACTIVITIES FOR EACH TREATMENT STAGE

The therapeutic relationship and the use of experiential and cognitive problem solving are embedded in the five treatment stages briefly described in the previous chapter. In that chapter we focused on the specific therapeutic goals to be accomplished in each stage of the process. In this chapter we focus more on the process and content of each stage.

Stage I: Introduction and Exploration

Excellent examples of activities that help the child negotiate the beginning of play therapy can be found in the Theraplay literature (Jernberg, 1979). Some of the activities we use quite frequently are variations on drawing the child's portrait. These allow the play therapist to focus fully on the child in a way that can be pleasant without having to activate distressing content. The play therapist can simply draw a picture of the child while making positive comments about the child's attributes. This allows for substantial physical distance with a high level of verbal interaction. On the other end of the spectrum, the play therapist can have the child lie on a large sheet of paper, trace the child's outline, and then engage the child in filling in the outline with some of the child's defining characteristics. Somewhere in between the two is having the child sit in a chair near a bright light that casts a distinct shadow onto a sheet of paper hung on the wall. The play therapist traces the profile and then either fills it in or engages the child in filling it in.

Stage II: Tentative Acceptance

"Simon Says" is a good game to play to operationalize the notion of tentative acceptance. Here, the child and the play therapist take turns being Simon and giving each other directions. The child's willingness to follow even the most bizarre or convoluted directions can be an excellent metaphor for the child's current willingness to tolerate just about anything the play therapist might do in session, at least for now.

Stage III: Negative Reaction

Any variation on an "Opposites Game" can be used to demonstrate and to help the child negotiate the negative reaction phase. In any of these games, the critical element is that the players do or say the opposite of what they are told or supposed to do. If "Simon Says" was placed in the previous phase, it can be reintroduced here with the rules changed so that the child either does the opposite of what Simon says or only follows the directions that are not preceded by the phrase "Simon says...." Alternatively, the play therapist might propose that the child say the exact opposite of whatever he or she is thinking or feeling. These types of games provide the child with a structured way of act-

ing out against the play therapy in a way that allows the interaction between child and play therapist to continue and remain relatively positive.

Stage IV: Growing and Trusting

Although the majority of this phase of the play therapy is focused on the problem-solving process, activities can be included that help the child focus on the notion of trust. Many of the activities commonly used in some trust groups or team-building activities can be adapted to play sessions. The play therapist and child might take each other on a trust walk around the room in which one is blindfolded and the other guides him or her to ensure that the blindfolded person remains safe. Similarly, the play therapist might encourage the child to fall toward the play therapist and allow the play therapist to catch him or her. Finally, this might be the point at which competitive games are introduced with the verbal comment that the play therapy relationship has progressed to the point that both the child and the play therapist are sure that the other will not cheat or hurt the other's feelings.

Stage V: Termination

The activity that we most often use to effect the actual termination is some form of a celebration or party at which the child's or family's progress can be reviewed and celebrated and good-byes said. This is another important point at which culture can be positively introduced by having the family bring specific foods or by incorporating ways of celebrating that are culture specific.

There are a number of activities that can be used to lead up to the actual termination that help to prepare the child for the separation. Including these is especially important for children who have had to cope with multiple separations and losses in the past. It is also important to emphasize the termination process with children who may seem oblivious or impervious to it. Children who have significant attachment difficulties or those who have moved through multiple foster placements often fall into this category. They may not protest the idea of termination at all and if they do it is usually a very brief protest, as they have learned that this has no real effect. Once they have accepted the reality of the termination they may immediately and completely sever any emotional connection they had to the play therapist or to the play therapy. They truly appear to be unaffected by the thought of leaving the relationship. In response to this emotional cold shoulder, therapists sometimes react by assuming that the child never made any sort of attachment and they, too, minimize the termination. Quite the opposite approach seems most appropriate. These children need to be reminded of the attachment and its value and then helped to grieve it in socially appropriate ways.

Simple games like "Hide and Go Seek" or "Peek A Boo" are actually good precursors to termination as they are fun ways in which to rehearse separations. Making a book about the play therapy can also be an excellent way to prepare the child for the end. If the child has produced artwork or stories along the way, these can be incorporated into the termination book. The book should include pictures and comments reflecting each stage of the child's progress through play therapy, and should include both positive and some negative experiences. Because all stories have natural beginnings and endings, the book format creates a concrete parallel to the play therapy process. For children who it is anticipated will have trouble terminating, the termination book might be started on the first day as a diary of play therapy that is added to at each session. The play therapist can use the book to keep the child abreast of the progress of the play therapy and to identify the point at which they begin working toward ending. The termination book then becomes something that the child takes with him or her after the last session as a concrete reminder of the process that was completed.

In the previous section we have tried to describe the process of Ecosystemic Play Therapy both within and across sessions. We have also given some examples of the types of activities that can be used to highlight and facilitate each of the treatment stages. These were included to stimulate creativity in designing and implementing goal-oriented Ecosystemic Play Therapy treatment plans. They are not meant to be recipes suitable for every occasion. Each will need modification to suit the needs of individual clients. They are reflective of the type of thinking that goes into the development of the Detailed Treatment Plan in Part VII of the Workbook.

SUMMARY

At this point, the reader has all of the pieces of the Ecosystemic Play Therapy Assessment, Treatment Planning, and Interventions model. Only two steps remain for the reader to integrate this information fully into his or her work. First, there is still the matter of designing specific session activities that meet the many theoretical, pragmatic, and case-specific issues and goals that have been described in this text. Designing these activities is really just a matter of creatively applying the principles we have presented. To get started, we present 25 examples of session activities for children at each of the first three developmental levels described in the Play Therapy Primer (O'Connor, 1991). The final step is to put all of the pieces we have presented together for yourself into a model that flows fairly easily. Reading through the case that is presented in its entirety without interruption in Chapter 10 should help with that process.

· **9** ·

SESSION ACTIVITIES

This chapter contains a collection of interventions that were designed to address specific developmental and content-related goals. The chapter is divided into three sections, one for each of the first three developmental levels through which children pass. These levels cover ages 0 to approximately 11, and probably represent, at least developmentally, the majority of children seen in play therapy.

GENERAL ISSUES

When planning session activities the therapist needs to take many factors into consideration. These include therapist-specific, setting-specific, and, of course, client-specific variables. The therapist variables include the therapist's theoretical orientation, training in various intervention strategies, and level of comfort with different styles of therapeutic interaction. The setting variables include such things as the degree of environmental control the therapist has, the specific features of the space available, and the types of materials available. Some activities are simply better suited for use in a small group convening in one corner of a classroom. This chapter focuses on the client variables that must be considered; specifically, the child's age, developmental level, specific psychopathology or unmet needs, and the type of content to be addressed.

A primary consideration in planning any session activity should be the child's current developmental level. However, developmental level cannot be considered out of the context of the child's chronological age and hypothesized optimal level of functioning. That is, all children who are functioning in Level I (ages 0 to 2) will display certain characteristics and will have certain developmentally based needs. However, there is a qualitative and quantitative difference in the issues faced by Level I children who are 18 months old versus 5 years old versus those who are 15 years old and still functioning at this level. Furthermore, there will be great differences between a 15-year-old who is in Level I as the result of neurologic impairment and one who is at that level because of catastrophic trauma in early life.

Two problems must be considered when planning sessions for children whose developmental level is below where it is assumed they are capable of functioning. One is the degree of "fixedness" the child seems to have acquired. For example, a healthy child who is early in Level II is likely to display temper tantrums and some acting out as he or she tests out the acquisition of mastery over self and others. If a child is 9 years old and has not yet acquired a sense of mastery to the point that temper tantrums and acting out are still manifest, these will typically be much more problematic than those displayed by a 2-year-old. After all, this child may have had as much as 7 years practice at being 2 and may have temper tantrums down to a veritable art form. These tantrums will be much more difficult to manage, both pragmatically and therapeutically, than would those of a healthy toddler.

The other problem that must be addressed in planning activities is the pervasiveness of the delays. Some children are delayed in all areas of development and as such their problems are usually easily recognized by all. Other children appear to be developmentally appropriate or even advanced, with delays in just one or two specific areas. For example, it is quite possible for a 10-year-old child who is doing well in school to have unresolved Level I developmental issues. This child may do well in school out of fear of abuse rather than a sense of secure attachment and desire to do well. The underlying attachment and trust problems may not be easy to recognize. Even more difficult is the fact that in some cases the delays may be both focused and situation-specific, making it even harder for others to accept that the child is delayed rather than acting out. As an example, many adults who were severely traumatized as children experience dramatic shifts in their functioning when exposed to something that triggers recall of the trauma. It is not at all uncommon for children to shift to much more concrete levels of thinking when they try to discuss a traumatic event that occurred earlier in their lives. In either case, the implications are that the therapist must often design treatment activities that address very early developmental issues for clients who otherwise appear to be functioning at a higher level. Our experience as supervisors suggests that the most common mistake made by novice and veteran play therapists alike is to begin therapy with activities and content geared toward too high a developmental level.

Besides very carefully considering the child's current developmental level and those developmental tasks that the child either never completed or resolved ineffectively, the therapist must also consider which other needs the child has that are not being adequately or appropriately met (psychopathology). As mentioned earlier, we believe all behavior to be children's best attempts to get their needs met. If the behavior does not appear to be functional from an outside perspective, then it is particularly important to try to understand what it accomplishes for the child. Therapy will not be effective if the child's needs are not met. Children have very little tolerance for frustration and cannot be expected to change their behavior for long if they do not experience the change as meeting their needs more effectively. Some aspect of every activity planned and implemented in session must directly address at least one of the child's needs. If the activity is

so stressful that it cannot be made to seem gratifying, then it is important to let the child know why it is being implemented and to find other ways to reinforce the child's participation. For example, some children find talking about abuse experiences so distressing that they cannot see that it may benefit them in any way. In such cases the therapist needs to find a developmentally suitable way of explaining such concepts as catharsis or systematic desensitization so that the child understands the point of enduring the pain. The therapist also needs to find ways to actively reinforce even the slightest participation on the child's part.

Finally, in planning session activities, the therapist must look for creative ways to incorporate significant content into the work. Although many children will spontaneously include distressing content in sessions, many more will avoid it for as long as possible. It is particularly difficult for children to see how distant, difficult experiences play a role in their present day-to-day lives. We do not advocate a "wait until the child is ready" approach to addressing difficult or traumatic content in sessions. Rather, we encourage therapists to find ways of introducing difficult content in small, manageable ways early in treatment, gradually progressing to more and more direct problem solving of the painful material.

Most of these client-specific issues are illustrated in the many examples included in the remainder of this chapter. Each section has a general description of the key developmental issues faced by children in that stage.[1] We focus on two areas that are critical to session planning. One is the way in which children in a particular developmental level acquire, process, store, and retrieve information. Understanding this helps us understand how a child may have responded to difficulties experienced during that level. The other is the interpersonal or social developmental task mastered by children as they progress through the level. Again, understanding this will help us identify the ways in which the child's development has been subverted by difficult or traumatic life experiences. Following these descriptions are specific session activities suited for use with children in that stage. Many of the specific intradevelopmental level tasks in these examples were derived from those listed on the Developmental Teaching Objectives Rating Form - Revised. We have tried to include examples that cover a wide range of client-specific content and the use of a variety of materials as well as some that are suited to various stages of the treatment

---

[1]For a more complete description of children's functioning at various developmental levels, see *The Play Therapy Primer* (O'Connor, 1991).

process. These are only examples, however, they will need to be modified in both content and form to suit the needs of specific clients. We do not advocate a cookbook type of approach to therapy, but rather, we emphasize subject-dependent thinking with respect to session planning to the same extent that we have emphasized its role in data gathering, case conceptualization, and treatment planning. We hope that these session descriptions will stimulate creativity and provide play therapists with the confidence to plan more directive and goal-oriented interventions in their play therapy work.

LEVEL I CHILDREN: DEVELOPMENTAL AND THERAPEUTIC ISSUES

For healthy children, Level I lasts from birth until about age 2. The end of this level is marked by the acquisition of at least a moderate amount of expressive language. Different developmental models focus on different aspects of the Level I child's development, such as social, moral, psychosexual, and so forth. As previously discussed, we view adequate cognitive development as a prerequisite to the child's development in other areas. Level I corresponds to what Piaget (1952, 1959, 1967) called the Sensorimotor phase, during which children learn from information they acquire through all of their senses.

Level I children experience their world in a way that is substantially different from the experience of older children or adults. Especially in the early part of this level, all information is of equal importance regardless of the sense through which it is acquired. A new smell is as important and potentially significant as a new food or the sight of a new person. Connections the child makes between these stimuli are based on their proximity not logic. That is, when a child experiences a new smell and a new person or event at the same time, these become connected and are stored together in memory. Later the smell can trigger memory of the person or event, and, vice versa, the person can trigger memory of the smell. These connections are often quite powerful, essentially having been classically conditioned, and may result in some behaviors or feelings that seem illogical or unpredictable to others. For example, a child who was hurt while there was a particular piece of music playing in the background may appear distressed later on whenever music that is even vaguely similar is played. Because the adult may not have even noticed the music, the child's responses seem unprovoked. One of the areas in which this phenomenon is most actively being explored is in the study of children's responses to sexual abuse; specifically, the con-

cept of "body memory," that is, trauma-related reactions that are triggered by stimuli the child or adult may not even consciously be able to identify. These memories or reactions are thought to be a manifestation of the power of abuse memories that are stored during the sensorimotor phase (Herman, 1992; James, 1989; Van de Putte, 1992).

The primary interpersonal or social task to be accomplished by Level I children is the development of bonding and attachment behavior (Mahler, 1967, 1972; Stern, 1995). In this context, we have defined bonding and attachment somewhat differently. Bonding is a near instinctual process by which the infant comes to associate an entire sensorimotor complex with the experience of being cared for. The infant rapidly learns to associate the caretaker's voice, smell, facial configuration, and way of moving with the gratification of basic needs such as feeding and soothing. Bonding probably begins before birth and is generally achieved in the first few days of life and is intensified over the course of the next few months. When anything occurs that prevents or disrupts bonding, the consequences, in terms of the child's development, are usually severe. Attachment is a more cognitive process in which the child adds cognitive and emotional elements to the image created during the bonding process. Eventually, attachment becomes a reciprocal interaction involving the exchange of positive feelings. Initially, the infant attaches to those responsible for its day-to-day care (primary caregivers), but over the course of Levels I and II the child begins to generalize attachment behavior to other adults in the environment who show any interest in interacting positively with him or her.

Trauma that occurs to children during Level I is likely to disrupt the attachment process between the child and the primary caregiver. This is due both to the nature of the role of the primary caregivers and to the attributions usually made by children at this level. By definition, the primary caregivers are the center of the child's universe and, as such, the source of all things both good and bad. Because Level I children can only respond to and understand that which they can readily experience, they have a difficult time conceptualizing forces or events beyond the control of their caregiver. Therefore, if the child and caregiver are in an automobile accident and the child is injured, he or she is likely to attribute the source or cause of the injury to the caregiver. If the caregiver is then the one who soothes the child, the child also attributes the rescue to the caregiver. Because Level I children are so stimulus-dependent, their attitude changes with their experience; they can hate you one minute and love you the next. However, if the balance of the child's experience shifts toward the unpleasant for any reason, then it is the relationship with the caregiver that is at risk.

When the child's attachment to the caregiver is disrupted or damaged, it is likely to result in one of two outcomes (James, 1994). The child may become obsessed with attachment and fear being out of contact with an attachment figure. Alternatively, the child may become detached and appear disinterested in or even afraid of social contact. In both cases, there may be great variability in the symptoms the child displays and in the intensity of those symptoms. In either case, the early attachment difficulties will interfere with the child's attaining adequate attachment during all future developmental levels. The child will not develop satisfactory relationships with other adults nor will he or she develop good peer relationships.

Regardless of the client's age, play activities geared toward remediating Level I difficulties have two characteristic features. One is that these are highly interactive and nurturing sessions in which many of the child's senses are stimulated. The use of toys is very limited, as the focus of the activity is on the interaction between the child and an adult. The other characteristic is that any content that needs to be addressed is usually introduced experientially and the verbal processing of that content is entirely or mostly completed by the therapist. For example, a therapist working with a violently abused 2-year-old who had yet to develop any language used small figures to act out the child's experiences while filling in all of the dialogue himself. The child watched these little plays with great interest and occasionally contributed to the action by moving figures. Although, the child never participated in the verbal processing and problem solving done by the therapist, the child's symptoms began to abate as he seemed to develop an understanding that his parent's had, indeed, not known that his baby-sitter was hurting him and had done everything they could to protect him once they found out.

One of the most comprehensive models of both attachment-related difficulties and the treatment of these can be found in *Theraplay* (Jernberg, 1979). The text presents models for conceptualizing, assessing, and treating problems triggered by poor attachment. Rather than attempt to replicate the broad range of techniques discussed, we refer the reader to the Theraplay Institute in Chicago. Furthermore, because interventions for children with problems originating in Level I are so well described in these sources, we present only five sample session activities in the next section.[2]

[2]All of the activities in this chapter were developed under the supervision of the authors by graduate students in the Ecosystemic Clinical Child Psychology Program at the California School of Professional Psychology, Fresno.

LEVEL I: ACTIVITY 1[3]

Case Synopsis

Ryan, age 4, was the oldest child in a family consisting of his mother, father, and a younger sister, age 1. Ryan was 14 months old when his mother miscarried a male child in her seventh month of pregnancy. At that time, she became severely depressed and withdrawn. Although Ryan's father attempted to take over the child care responsibilities, the demands of his job made his ability to do so sporadic. Ryan was, therefore, cared for by an array of people including baby-sitters, relatives, and nannies. Ryan became very quiet and withdrawn over a period of 6 months and, although he seemed to recover as his mother did, both of his parents report that he is still rather distant and does not particularly like to be held or touched.

Target Psychopathology and Session Goal

It appears that Ryan withdrew in response to the combination of his mother's unavailability during her depression and the lack of a consistent caretaking substitute in her absence. Upon his referral, his need for emotional contact was not being met and was being reflected in his desire to avoid physical contact. It seems he preferred to feel he was rejecting others rather than attempt to tolerate the pain of being rejected. The goal of this session was to provide Ryan with an experience that would foster both emotional and physical contact.

Treatment Phase

This activity could be used in either the Introduction and Exploration phase or the Growing and Trusting phase of therapy. It could be adapted for use in the Negative Reaction phase as a way of making manifest the degree to which the child is resisting, but it may very well trigger a response on the part of the child that will require significant limit setting if not outright physical restraint. In this case, the activity was introduced in the second session as a way of pushing interaction between Ryan and his mother who had engaged in parallel play during the first session.

Persons Attending the Session

The therapist, Ryan, and Ryan's mother.

Materials Needed/Preparation Required

None. An instant photograph camera might be useful for preserving specific moments in the activity and making these available to later processing.

[3]This activity was developed by James McCray, M.A.

Experiential Aspects of the Activity

This activity proceeded in rounds that demanded progressively more interaction between Ryan and his mother. The goal of the first round was simply to familiarize them with the activity and to get Ryan used to being touched. In subsequent rounds, emotional expression and communication were emphasized. For the first round the therapist identified Ryan's mother as "the blob of clay" and Ryan as "the sculptor." Ryan's mother was instructed to sit on the floor to allow the sculptor to position her as he saw fit. Because Ryan was reluctant initially to engage in the activity the therapist encouraged him by becoming relatively dramatic and pulling Ryan into a pretend scene in which they talked about the mother as though she was not there. Gradually, Ryan became more engaged and freer in moving his mother about and making her assume some silly positions. After about 5 to 10 minutes, the therapist had them switch roles.

Ryan relinquished control in the activity only reluctantly. He frequently moved out of position and verbally complained about what his mother was having him do. Again, the therapist helped Ryan's mother engage in the activity in such a way that they remained in control but were careful to address Ryan's needs. For example, when Ryan complained that a position was uncomfortable the therapist said to the mother, "you know I'm not sure the clay can stay in that position, our sculpture might fall apart, maybe we should move the arm down a little." In this way, Ryan could be assured that he was being attended to but his complaints were not allowed to control the activity to the extent that these interfered with its progress.

In the next round, Ryan was told to sculpt his mother doing something that made her happy. Ryan chose to show her taking care of his sister. Once Ryan had positioned her body the way he wanted it the therapist had him focus on molding her face to show the appropriate facial expression. When it was his mother's turn, she sculpted Ryan building with blocks. Again, the therapist had her mold Ryan's facial expression as well as his body. In the final round each molded the other doing something they did not like.

Cognitive/Verbal Aspects of the Activity

Because this activity was initiated very early in the therapy, the therapist focused on using interpretation to identify problematic issues and used problem solving to address only pragmatic issues that interfered with the progress of the session.

Focus of Problem Solving

The therapist used very brief problem solving with Ryan's mother each time that Ryan complained about the activity. As noted in the description of the activity, this was done in terms of problems in getting the clay to do what the sculptor wanted rather than in terms of Ryan's resistance or noncompliance. When Ryan was stiff, the therapist suggested the possibility that the clay was drying out and then suggested that the mother pretend to massage water into the affected part to see if it would soften up. This strategy allowed the therapist to begin modeling the use of problem solving with content that Ryan found nonthreatening.

Potential Interpretive Work

Because this was only the second session, the therapist did not move beyond the generalized dynamic level, but the sequence he had planned was as follows.

Reflections   When Ryan was molding his mother, the therapist noted how much fun he seemed to be having and his pleasure in being the "boss." When Ryan was the clay, the therapist verbalized Ryan's discomfort and the fact that he seemed particularly unhappy when his mother was molding his face.

Pattern   The therapist noted that both Ryan and his mother seemed to have trouble getting started when it was their turn and to have difficulty initiating contact with one another. The therapist also noted how much more eager Ryan was to be the sculptor than to be the clay.

Simple Dynamic   The therapist connected Ryan's reaction to being the clay with some underlying anxiety about being controlled and some anger at being made to do things he did not want to do. He also connected Ryan's pleasure at being the sculptor with a sense of power over his mother. Finally, he connected their difficulty initiating contact with one another to some anxiety about how the other person would respond and to a fear of alienating one another.

Generalized Dynamic   The therapist planned to mention the connection between the fact that both Ryan and his mother portrayed positive activities that did not involve interaction between them to their reports that they spent very little time playing together at home.

Genetic   The therapist's goal was eventually to point out that he believed this whole pattern of interaction got started back before Ryan could even remember what had happened. That Ryan's mother had been so sad when his little brother died that she did not feel like playing and that the two of them had, subsequently, forgotten how to play together. He was to frame the current problem as needing to get to know one another again and to have practice playing together.

Plan for Future Sessions   All of the sessions would involve direct play interactions. Additionally, the therapist planned to introduce more content over time. The role of the sibling's death in the course of Ryan's development was to be addressed in an art activity that was completed during part of each session. Specifically, the therapist had Ryan and his mother create a biography that included many family events from before Ryan was born to the present.

LEVEL I: ACTIVITY 2[4]

Case Synopsis

Beth was a 4-year-old child who had been hospitalized multiple times for severe asthma. She was referred for treatment because of her parents' concern that she was displaying increasing signs of anxiety that seemed to be generalizing beyond her experience of her illness and its treatment. Beth was having difficulty sleeping through the night and seemed reluctant to leave her house. She constantly questioned when she would have another attack. At these times she would ask questions about how far away she was from the hospital. Alternately, she also frequently asked if she would have to go to the hospital again.

Target Psychopathology and Session Goal

The therapist identified Beth's ambivalence about hospitalization as one of the more confusing and anxiety-producing aspects of her illness. On the one hand, Beth clearly felt safer when she was physically close to both her parents and to the hospital. On the other hand she was very much afraid of the various medical procedures and the separations from her parents that hospitalization entailed. Given her age she was unable to integrate these feelings and, instead, vacillated between them. Her need to feel safe and secure was thereby threatened. The goal of the session was to provide Beth with a concrete strategy for beginning to understand her feelings about her illness and her hospitalizations.

Treatment Phase

This task was introduced during the Tentative Acceptance phase of therapy to help provide a basis for future problem solving. It could easily be adapted for use

[4]This activity was developed by Sue Carroll, Psy.D.

at any point in therapy when the child is experiencing mixed feelings about either an outside event or even about the therapy itself.

Persons Attending the Session

The therapist and Beth.

Materials Needed/Preparation Required

Depending on the specific goals of the task and the child involved, the therapist either needs to have prepared two colors of pudding prior to the session or come prepared to make pudding in session with the child. If the pudding is to be made in session, an instant variety should be used so that it sets up quickly. The puddings could be of different flavors or simply colored with food coloring so that there is a significant contrast between the two. The two types of pudding need to be placed in separate containers. The technique also requires a flat baking pan or plastic container as well as several spoons.

Experiential Aspects of the Activity

The therapist can introduce the activity as a cooking task, an art activity, or a special treat. In this case, the therapist chose to prepare the pudding ahead of time and to focus in session on the affective elements of the task as a combined art and eating activity. The two types of pudding were introduced after the therapist had initiated a brief discussion of some of Beth's feelings about her asthma and going to the hospital. In previous sessions they had begun a list of good versus bad feelings about each. Beth was asked to label one color of pudding as the "the good stuff" and one as "the bad stuff." The therapist used vanilla pudding and intentionally mixed the colors in one to be a sort of olive green and the other one was colored a light pink. Beth immediately labeled the green pudding as bad and the pink as good.

The therapist then had Beth begin spreading a layer of the pink pudding over the bottom of an 8" × 8" × 2" baking dish. As each spoonful was added to the pan, they identified a good thought or feeling related to the combination of asthma, her parents, and the hospital. These included the fact that asthma sometimes got her out of doing things she did not like, that she trusted her parents to take good care of her, and that she liked the playroom at the hospital. The size of the spoonfuls added to the pan was matched to the intensity of the feeling being described. Getting out of things only warranted a small spoonful, whereas trusting her parents got a large spoonful. Once a number of feelings had been identified and there was about a $\frac{1}{2}$-inch layer of pudding in the container, the therapist switched the focus to the negative feelings Beth had about her asthma. As they identified items from the bad list they dropped spoonfuls of the greenish pudding onto the pink but did not mix them in.

During the next part, the therapist pointed out how the greenish pudding looked even uglier when it was on top of the pink just like the bad feelings did when they were compared with the good feelings. The therapist suggested they take out the greenish pudding and the therapist engaged her in some low-level problem solving as they did so. For example, as they removed the spoonful that represented Beth's fear of injections, the therapist listed several things Beth could do to make getting shots less scary. After all of the green pudding was removed, the therapist noted that traces of it were still left and compared these to Beth's leftover worries that persisted even on days that were going very well. The therapist had Beth taste the pink pudding. She reported that it tasted good. Then the therapist had Beth taste a section where there was a mix of green and pink. Beth was reluctant, saying that it looked gross, but agreed and admitted that it still tasted good. The therapist compared this to the fact that even though some of Beth's worries never went completely away, they did not always have to make everything else seem bad.

Cognitive/Verbal Aspects of the Activity

Because Beth was only 4, most of the verbal activity in this session was completed by the therapist who kept it moving along at a rather brisk pace. All of the verbal components were fully integrated with the experiential aspects of the session as noted in the previous discussion.

Focus of Problem Solving

The therapist worked on identifying brief solutions for two different issues. One was the degree to which Beth's good feelings sometimes got contaminated or even overshadowed by the bad feelings. The other was ways of eliminating or managing some of the bad feelings. The problems themselves had been identified in a previous session, although some were added and others expanded during this session. All of the solutions were generated by the therapist while Beth focused on the mechanics of the activity. Occasionally, the therapist left intentional pauses in the discussion to encourage Beth to add contributions of her own. Most of Beth's comments either expanded or modified things the therapist said so that they better matched Beth's experience.

Potential Interpretive Work

In this activity, the interpretive work was fully integrated with the activity.

Reflections   The therapist reflected a long list of both positive and negative thoughts and feelings that Beth experienced relative to many aspects of her illness. Some of these were things Beth had already reported, but many were derived from hypotheses the therapist had about Beth's internal process. The therapist constantly observed Beth for indications as to the accuracy of the reflections and interpretations she was making.

Pattern   The only pattern that was identified was the constant vacillation and interaction of the feelings Beth experienced both in session as these were discussed and in the real world.

Simple Dynamic   The therapist identified both the vacillation and the mix of feelings as a source of additional anxiety. "Sometimes you feel happy and then you have a little wheeze and you start to feel real scared. Then it goes away and you feel happy again. After a while you worry as much about feeling scared as you do about wheezing. You end up with two things to worry about."

Generalized Dynamic   Because all of the discussion focused on Beth's day-to-day experience both in and out of session, no specific Generalized Dynamic interpretations were made.

Genetic   At this level the therapist simply tied Beth's current confusion to the fact that she had experienced asthma her whole life and still was not sure she really understood what it was all about.

Plan for Future Sessions

The therapist planned to shift the focus of the sessions to more active problem solving strategies for reducing Beth's anxiety about both her illness and the unpleasant feelings associated with it. She also planned to do some further education with both Beth and her parents about the nature of asthma and the effects of the various medications on Beth's emotional state. Over time Beth's primary caretaker was included in many of the sessions so as to facilitate the Beth's generalization of the improvement she was making from her interactions with the therapist to her interactions outside of session.

LEVEL I: ACTIVITY 3[5]

Case Synopsis

Sam was a 2-year-old child who had already been diagnosed with significant learning problems that interfered with his ability to decode various cues in the environment. At the time of referral, he did not display any spoken language and often seemed to misunderstand things that were said to him. He often seemed to misread the emotional responses of others, including his primary caretaker. He was constantly frustrated and was beginning to avoid interactions with others. His physical and perceptual-motor development were within normal limits, suggesting the potential for average intellectual functioning.

Target Psychopathology and Session Goal

Because he so often misinterpreted other people's emotional and spoken messages, Sam's needs for positive interpersonal contact were not being consistently met. The goal of the session was to increase his focus on facial cues as a way of understanding affect, and also to train his mother to use exaggerated cues that would be easier for Sam to recognize.

Treatment Phase

This activity was one of several used in the very first session as a way of ensuring that Sam would find the sessions minimally frustrating and optimally rewarding. It is likely to be most effective early in treatment as a way of improving affective communication and establishing the basis for more positive interactions and future problem solving.

Persons Attending the Session

The therapist, Sam, and his mother. Sam's mother was included from the outset for two reasons. One reason was that Sam's difficulties were so pervasive that the therapist wanted his mother to be working with him between the scheduled therapy sessions to speed the rate and generalization of any changes that were accomplished. The other was the need to focus on improving the attachment relationship between the two, which was suffering in the face of their pattern of miscommunication.

Materials Needed/Preparation Required

An assortment of bite-size candies or other food items such as animal crackers.

[5]This activity was developed by Kellee Hom, M.A.

Experiential Aspects of the Activity

The activity was introduced to Sam and his mother as a variant on the "hotter-colder" game. Sam's mother hid an animal cracker somewhere on her person and gave Sam clues about where it was located. Instead of saying hotter or colder, she used facial expressions. She made exaggerated happy faces as he neared the cookie and exaggerated sad faces as he moved away from it. The therapist worked with Sam to help him focus on his mother's expressions and to guide him physically through the first couple of searches to minimize Sam's frustration with the task. As Sam seemed to get the idea of the task after several repetitions, the therapist gradually reduced the amount of assistance she gave to just occasional verbal cues. Sam's mother was instructed not to talk to Sam but to physically move his face toward hers if he seemed to be ignoring the faces she was making.

Cognitive/Verbal Aspects of the Activity

The therapist did all of the verbal work and did so in short, concrete sentences.

Focus of Problem Solving

The therapist actively used problem solving to address two aspects of the task. She constantly cued Sam to help him read his mother's facial expression and cued his mother to exaggerate her features even more if Sam seemed not to understand. She also helped Sam develop some strategies for finding the animal crackers.

Potential Interpretive Work

All of the interpretive work was geared toward the identification of affects and Sam's feelings about the task at hand.

Reflections "Look at that happy face your mom is making. That big smile sure looks happy. Look at mom's bright, happy eyes and how they crinkle up at the corners." "Look at that sad face. Now mom's mouth goes way down on the sides." "You look happy just like mom did." "You look like you're beginning to get sad."

Pattern The therapist simply identified Sam's tendency to search for the cookie without looking at his mother's face for cues.

Simple Dynamic Here the therapist connected Sam's pleasure at finding the animal crackers and his sadness when he was having trouble. She chose to use just the two feelings rather than introducing the concept of frustration or anger to keep the task as simple as possible. The therapist also made specific connections between the mother's happy faces and her desire to have Sam find the animal cracker as quickly as possible so that he could be happy too.

Generalized Dynamic   No connection between the activity and outside activities was made except to suggest that they play the game at home several times during the week.

Genetic   The therapist did not make any substantive genetic interpretations. She did identify the fact that Sam always had a difficult time identifying feelings, emphasizing the fact that this problem had existed as long as he could remember.

Plan for Future Sessions

The therapist planned to increase the number and variety of affective communications required as part of the different activities conducted during sessions. All of the initial focus was on improving Sam's ability to read his mother's affect. Later sessions were designed to help Sam communicate his own affect more effectively.

LEVEL I: ACTIVITY 4[6]

Case Synopsis

Rob was a 6-year-old boy who was referred to treatment after a history of aggressive behavior had caused him difficulty in both preschool and kindergarten. During Rob's first 2 years of life he lived with his mother and his father. Rob's father was very violent and frequently physically abused his wife in front of Rob. Rob's mother made few efforts to protect herself and remained in the relationship. When Rob was about 2 years old, his mother was severely beaten and the police were called to the home by a neighbor. His mother reports that seeing the terror in Rob's eyes during this incident was what finally motivated her to move out. Since that time, Rob has had sporadic contact with his father who usually shows up unexpectedly. These visits usually end because something happens to cause the father to become angry.

Target Psychopathology and Session Goal

The therapist hypothesized that, among other difficulties, Rob had some very negative beliefs about his

[6]This activity was developed by Beth Limberg, M.S., RPT.

mother and her ability and desire to protect him. She further hypothesized that these beliefs made him feel unsafe and that this anxiety interfered with their attachment to one another. Although she also hypothesized that Rob engaged in aggressive behavior as a way of fending off potentially dangerous interactions, this aspect of the problem was left to be addressed in later sessions. The goal of this session was to help Rob begin to identify both his anxiety and ways of feeling safe that would increase the frequency and intensity of positive interactions with his mother.

Treatment Phase

This activity is best suited for use very early in the treatment process as it focuses on problem identification and on the development of positive interactions.

Persons Attending the Session

The therapist and Rob.

Materials Needed/Preparation Required

Regular clay or pliable plasticine.

Experiential Aspects of the Activity

The activity proceeds in three phases. During the first phase, the child is introduced to the clay and asked to play with it and experience it without trying to make something. The child is encouraged to poke, pinch, throw, pound, smooth, and twist the clay as well as smell it and explore it visually. There are several goals to this part of the activity. First, by focusing on the child's sensory experience the therapist encourages a certain amount of regression. This can help children like Rob focus on the types of experiences they had during the sensorimotor stage of development. Second, the activity sensitizes the child to his or her own experience and bodily sensations. And, finally, the activity reduces the emphasis on the creation of a product so that the child can focus on thinking and feeling rather than on doing. Rob completed this portion of the activity although he did not seem particularly enthusiastic.

During the second phase, Rob was asked to think of a time when he felt safe, cared for, protected, or secure. The therapist did not insist that he talk about the episode, only that he have it firmly in mind before they proceeded. Once Rob seemed to have a specific situation in mind, the therapist instructed him to make something or someone out of the clay who was there with him when he felt safe. Rob began working immediately on making a human figure. Although he had not said anything about the event he had in mind initially, he began talking about several times when he had been very angry when his father ended a visit with an argument. He proceeded to make a figure of himself with very big muscles and to talk about how he could protect himself and his mother from his father anytime it was necessary. He talked about his own strength and fearlessness.

During the third phase of the activity, the therapist joined in to facilitate the creation of some corrective thoughts with respect to the problem Rob had presented. She took the clay and first made a figure of Rob's father. She took care not to make the representational quality of her figure any better than Rob's so that he did not feel the need to compete with her artistically. She made the figure of Rob's father much bigger than Rob's depiction of himself and made several comments about his size and angry-looking face as she proceeded. During this time, Rob appeared more anxious and added muscles to his own figure. The therapist then proceeded to make a figure representing Rob's mother. The therapist made this figure smaller than the father figure but larger than Rob and put it between the other two. As she put the mother figure down she noted that it was not much bigger than Rob and might not be all that good at protecting him from his dad, so they better give her some tools to help her with her job. The therapist then engaged Rob in making both realistic and fantasy tools for empowering the mother. At first Rob resisted and attempted to arm his own figure, but as the therapist increased the array of mom's weapons Rob was drawn into the task. They made mom everything from a magic sword to a cell phone she could use to call the police if dad got out of line.

Cognitive/Verbal Aspects of the Activity

Both problem solving and interpretation were done within the play and relative to Rob's real life experience. The mixture of fantasy and reality seemed to make it easier for him to tolerate the more anxiety-producing aspects of the discussion.

Focus of Problem Solving

The therapist simply identified Rob's size and age as a problem in having him defend himself against his father and suggested that mom might be better suited to the job if she could be made sufficiently powerful. The therapist focused on the notion that not only could this be accomplished, it could be accomplished in ways that did not involve Rob. At this stage, realistic problem solving was not the sole focus, rather the emphasis was on creating an initial sense of safety and security for Rob.

Potential Interpretive Work

The therapist used interpretation to identify the range of affects and motives each of the persons involved in their play scenario might be experiencing.

Reflections   At this level, the therapist focused on two elements. One was identifying Rob's anxiety about interactions with his father and the degree to which thinking of himself as powerful relieved that fear. The other was on interpreting the mother's motivation to protect Rob from all future problems and her willingness to do whatever it might take to make him feel better.

Pattern   Two patterns were identified. One was Rob's repeated shows of bravado. The other was his tendency to take over for his mother as they tried to push dad out of the picture.

Simple Dynamic   The therapist connected Rob's show of bravado to increases in anxiety about dad's aggressiveness and his desire to feel safe in these interactions. The therapist also connected Rob's tendency to take over for his mother as related to his belief that she was not really able to protect herself or him unless she had assistance.

Generalized Dynamic   Because all of the play was related to real-life events, little was done with Generalized Dynamic interpretation. At one point the therapist did relate the style of Rob's interaction in the face of fearing his father to the way he must interact with others who made him anxious or angry.

Genetic   All of the thoughts and feelings were related to earlier life events and Rob's thoughts and feelings about those events. The therapist also used this as an opportunity to disclose some of Rob's mother's thoughts and feelings regarding both the domestic violence and her past failures to protect Rob.

Plan for Future Sessions

The therapist planned to continue to address the domestic violence content over the course of future sessions. In addition, the therapist brought the mother into the sessions to work on two issues. One issue was some reparative attachment work that was done to make both her and Rob feel more positive about their interactions. The goal in this case was to begin to shift the balance from anxious times to warm and supportive times. The other goal was to create situations and experiences in which Rob had to rely on his mother's abilities to get his needs met in session.

LEVEL I: ACTIVITY 5[7]

Case Synopsis

Paulette was a 5-year-old girl whose mother brought her to treatment at the suggestion of Paulette's preschool teacher. The teacher noted that Paulette's affect rarely changed irrespective of the situations or interactions in which she was involved. Paulette always smiled and never argued with or contradicted either adults or peers even when she was genuinely being victimized. When treated badly she acted as if it was to be expected and did not protest. Her lack of affective variability was so extreme that the other children actually seemed to goad her in an attempt to get a reaction.

During the intake, Paulette's mother disclosed her own long history of chronic depressive episodes. These had begun long before Paulette was born and continued to the time of referral. Although Paulette's mother had been in treatment several times, the depression seemed to return. During these episodes, Paulette's mother was aware of being minimally available to Paulette and to have little tolerance for anyone else's negative affect. She reported that Paulette had always been the more emotionally stable one in their interactions.

Target Psychopathology and Session Goal

The therapist hypothesized that Paulette had come to expect her mother to be relatively unavailable at unpredictable intervals and had learned not to express her own negative affects for two reasons. One reason was that her mother reacted badly and withdrew even more if Paulette seemed angry or unhappy. The other was that if Paulette could remain positive in the face of her mother's moods, she stood a chance of reengaging her mother and eliciting a positive interaction. Over time, Paulette had come to see controlling her own moods as a way of controlling her mother's withdrawal and the anxiety that created. Unfortunately, Paulette had come to view the continuity of her relationship with her mother as being dependent on her ability to suppress all negative emotions to the point that it interfered with her functioning in other settings.

Treatment Phase

This activity would be suited to work during the Negative Reaction phase of treatment. During this phase, the child usually has begun to see that change is necessary but is resistant to the idea for any of a variety

[7]This activity and the related interpretive material was developed by Sharon Picard, M.S.

of reasons. This activity would allow Paulette to experiment safely with affective expression in a way that allowed her some distance from it. The actual activity requires a minimum of three sessions to complete.

Persons Attending the Session

The therapist and Paulette.

Materials Needed/Preparation Required

Session 1: Plaster-coated gauze strips of the type used by physicians for making casts (these are often available in craft stores as well). Petroleum jelly and soap and water for clean up. A hair dryer with a low heat setting to speed the drying of the plaster.

Session 2: Paints, beads, feathers, paintbrushes, glue, and so forth for decorating the masks created in Session 1.

Session 3: Completed masks from Sessions 1 and 2.

Experiential Aspects of the Activity

The first session followed several other sessions in which Paulette had been sensitized to the existence of different affects and had become somewhat aware of the relative lack of variability in both her own and her mother's affect. The new activity was introduced simply as one in which Paulette and the therapist would make masks that showed different feelings. Rather than using plain premade masks or cardboard, the therapist chose to cast simple plaster masks directly on Paulette's face for several reasons. First, the activity would allow substantial direct interaction between Paulette and the therapist, during which Paulette would have to trust the therapist's judgment. Second, the fact that Paulette would completely tolerate such an intrusive activity would provide the therapist an opportunity to comment on the fact that Paulette just seemed to accept such things without reaction. And, third, the therapist could have Paulette work at making faces reflecting different affects while the masks were cast.

To cast the mask, the therapist put a smock on Paulette and then spread a thin layer of petroleum jelly over most of her face. The therapist then demonstrated laying a dampened strip of plaster gauze on a doll to show Paulette what it would be like before proceeding. The therapist made a relatively simple cast of Paulette's face from mid-forehead, around both eyes and across her nose, to the middle of her cheeks. For the first mask, the therapist did not cast any of Paulette's lower face, although this was done with several subsequent masks. The therapist made the mask relatively thin and then used a small hairdryer set on low to speed the drying. The entire activity took only about 15 minutes, so she and Paulette decided to make one more so that they would have two to decorate during the second session. For the first mask, the therapist encouraged Paulette to try to look as happy as possible while the plaster set so they would have a good happy mask. During the drying of the second mask the therapist actually molded Paulette's features into a frown so that the mask would turn out "angry."

The second session focused on decorating the masks that had been made during the first session. This activity was accompanied by a discussion of the way in which the affects depicted could be exaggerated by emphasizing facial features and using color or other decorations. During this activity it became clear that Paulette was quite able to recognize affects in others and was indeed quite sensitive to these. It was only her own affects with which she had difficulty.

Over the course of the third and several subsequent sessions, Paulette and the therapist both used the masks as a way of role playing and practicing with affect. They also made additional masks to reflect the increasing complexity of Paulette's experience. To speed the process most of the subsequent masks began with a simple cardboard cutout rather than the plaster casts.

Cognitive/Verbal Aspects of the Activity

The amount of cognitive work increased steadily over the course of the sessions that included this activity. The focus was always on interpretation, with problem solving simply used to explore the ways in which Paulette's affect or lack thereof interfered with her day-to-day interactions at home and at school.

Focus of Problem Solving

As noted in the previous case, little problem solving was done over the course of this activity. Because Paulette was so compliant, her behavior did not elicit any problems to be addressed. Later, as Paulette became better at recognizing and expressing her own affect the use of problem solving was increased.

Potential Interpretive Work

The therapist's use of interpretation was very limited in the first session of this activity and gradually increased as the sessions progressed. Generalized dynamic and genetic interpretations were not made until the third session.

Reflections The therapist continuously reflected Paulette's affect as well as using reflections to identify a wide variety and intensity of affects in others. The therapist reflected anxiety especially when Paulette showed no overt signs of affect. The therapist identified the motive behind Paulette's lack of affect saying, "Oh, I get it. You use a smile to make me think everything is fine so I'll just go away." She also identified Paulette's ability to control her own responses and her desire to control the responses of others.

Pattern The therapist identified Paulette's constant acceptance of even the silliest demands such as having wet plaster strips laid across her face. She also identified that the few times Paulette was able to vary her affect all involved changing her face to look at the therapist with disbelief and mild annoyance.

Simple Dynamic The therapist drew a link between Paulette's persistent lack of affective display and her underlying anxiety. The therapist also drew a connection to Paulette's manifestation of internal control as a strategy for feeling in control of her life situation.

Generalized Dynamic At this level, the therapist identified the degree to which all of the previous interpretations applied to Paulette's interactions at home and at school.

Genetic Finally, the therapist identified the possibility that Paulette's ability to control her affect was developed as a response to her mother's inability to control her own affect.

Plan for Future Sessions

In future sessions, the therapist planned to increase the amount of time Paulette spent practicing, displaying, and expressing affects in a variety of situations. The therapist also planned to include Paulette's mother in sessions so that she could learn how to respond effectively and appropriately to her daughter's expression of affect, particularly negative affect.

LEVEL II CHILDREN: DEVELOPMENTAL AND THERAPEUTIC ISSUES

As children acquire progressively more expressive language they shift into Level II, which lasts from about age 2 to age 6. Piaget (1952, 1959, 1967) refers to this as the Preoperational phase, during which children acquire vast amounts of information but are limited in their ability to manipulate that information in their heads. Evidence of this can be found in measures as famous as Piaget's experiments to demonstrate that preoperational children are unable to see that the same quantity of water poured into containers of two different sizes remains the same amount even if it appears to be different. On a more subtle level, preoperational children are very susceptible to believing even the silliest information if they perceive the source of the information to be credible. Many a parent has been chastised by their preschooler for contradicting something the teacher had jokingly insisted was true. Even more subtle is preoperational children's susceptibility to mixed messages. They more often attend to the content of what is being said rather than the tone and are very likely to miss even the most obvious sarcasm. The end of this level is marked by the acquisition of the ability to conserve across many situations. That is, children are able to hold information in their heads and assess whether or not transformations they witness affect that information.

During Level II, memory storage and retrieval becomes more logical than it was in the sensorimotor stage, but it is still accomplished differently from the way it is in older children and adults. At this level, children are likely to continue to store complex sensory images of their experience, but these will often be overlaid with a cognitive conceptualization of the event. Whereas Level I children tend to store together in memory, any events that happen simultaneously, Level II children may break an event into components based on the labels they give the action. A Level I child would have put all the sights, sounds, tastes, and experiences of a birthday party together in memory as a cluster, with or without the label "birthday party." Labels play a much more significant role in a Level II child's memory. Now, that same birthday party may be separated into components and the experience of the cake may be stored in one cluster with other recent "pretty things," the best gifts go into a "good gifts" category with things the child received at Christmas, and the emotions experienced get distributed across a range of other categories. At the time, the child knows that these experiences are all the result of the same birthday party, but later, when asked to recall details of the event, related memories from the categories into which the event was distributed are likely to creep in and affect the child's thinking.

The impact of the variability in Level II children's recall skills can be seen in the literature on abuse and in the debates about the veracity of young children's memory for such highly traumatic events (Saywitz & Goodman, 1996). Many adults are aware that children this age, who must repeat descriptions of their abuse over and over again at widely separated intervals, do not always tell the same story. The abuser was wearing a green shirt in the first version and a red shirt in a subsequent version. This does not necessarily mean that the child is not telling the truth both times. There appear to be at least two possible explanations for this phenomenon. One is that the child stored the memory of the abuser's clothes somewhat away from the memory of the event, say with other memorable clothing items. Now when the child retrieves the abuse event it returns with any one of a number of important shirts that may or may not have belonged to the abuser. The other explanation is that more than one abuse incident has been stored so close together in memory that details of one seep readily into the other. Ironically, these changes in detail confound a legal system that is based on the consistency and congruency of evidence, when actually they reflect a normal part of Level II children's developmental experience and potentially attest to the veracity of the events described in ways that a perpetually congruent story does not. In any case, the end of Level II is marked, among other things, by a shift in children's thinking to ways that are considerably more similar to adult thinking with respect to their attention to detail.

The primary social task to be accomplished by Level II children is the generalization of their attachment to their primary caretakers to others. In this process, children first come to see adults other than those directly involved in their day-to-day care as potential sources of physical and emotional gratification. They seek out adult attention and revel in it when they get it. As their sphere of social interaction increases, Level II children become aware of the needs of adults and the interactions of adults with one another, and this awareness is not usually experienced as particularly positive. Suddenly, children realize that not all adults were put on this earth to meet their needs. In fact, they often seem to prefer meeting each others' needs over interacting with children. Level II children will typically go through a reactionary period in which they will try to regain possession of their primary caretakers and exclude other adults. This is often referred to as the Oedipal reaction or phase in psychoanalytic literature (Freud, 1933). It can be seen in something as simple as the fact that young Level II children seem almost driven to act out noisily when their parents are on the telephone. They know that the parent cannot attend to two things at once and they want to be the center of the parent's world. If Level II children feel safe in their interactions with their primary caretakers and continue to receive gratification from other adults, they quickly learn that there is more to be gained by interacting with other adults than by shutting them out and the generalization of their attachment behavior proceeds.

As children move through Level II they further generalize their social attachments to include peers. Again, peers tend to be first experienced as competitors for the resources held by adults and can only be accepted and valued by children who perceive that there are enough adult resources to go around. This phenomenon can be seen both in the home and at school. Sibling rivalry is likely to be most intense when one or more of the children believes that the resources (physical, but especially emotional) of the caretakers are limited for any reason. Many parents notice, for example, that their children fight more when the parent is feeling ill. Again, if these children feel secure in their earlier attachment relationships, they can tolerate the increased sense of competition and go on to form substantial peer relationships that enhance their day-to-day lives.

When Level II children experience a trauma they are likely to experience substantial cognitive confusion over the event and to regress in their social interactions. However, Level II children are more able than Level I children to sort out the exact nature of a trauma and its implications for their lives if they understand its nature. For Level I children, all traumas are roughly the same. Pain and unpleasantness are experienced as bad and the reasons for them or the intent of the persons involved in the trauma do not make much difference to the child. Level II children are more amenable to explanations of traumatic events and better able to use this information to make attributions that, in turn affect, their coping.

For the sake of simplicity, we divide trauma into three categories based on causality. One category is natural disasters; events over which no one has any control. This category includes hurricanes, floods, droughts, famines, and diseases. A second category is person-induced trauma, that is, events that another person caused that had a direct negative impact on the child. This category includes everything from automobile accidents to child abuse perpetrated directly against the child. The third category is events that the child experienced as physically or emotionally painful that were caused by or at least involved others but that were not intended to hurt the child. This last category includes everything from accidents in which no one intended to hurt the child or in which someone even tried to prevent an injury, such as taking the child for routine immunizations, or subjecting a child to chemotherapy. As was mentioned, most Level I children see all of these events as roughly similar, and their capacity for coping will largely depend on the availability of healthy adult caretakers. Level II children can grasp the differences but often need clear explanations if they are to understand and cope.

When an adult tells a Level II child that chemotherapy will help him or her get better, the child may perceive this to be, at best, a well-intentioned lie. Chemotherapy does not make you feel better. It makes you feel worse. If an adult tells the child that

chemotherapy will make him or her feel bad, the adult is now telling the truth but failing to help the child cope. If the adult takes the middle ground and says something such as, "In your body there is a disease that is taking over but is not making you feel sick yet. Let's think about the disease like soldiers marching across your room and taking your toys. Right now they have only taken a couple of toys and that does not seem so bad but we don't want to let them take over your room, then you would have nothing to play with! The medicine the doctor will give you is like soldiers who will fight on our side. They will take back your room (your body) and throw out the disease soldiers. But there is a problem. When they fight the battle you will feel sick. Battles never make anyone feel good. But once the battle is over for good you will feel better and the disease soldiers will be thrown out of your body." With such an explanation, the child understands the purpose of the trauma of chemotherapy in ways that are both concrete and manageable. Without such explanations, Level II children often misattribute the nature and causality of their traumatic experiences and, subsequently, have difficulty coping.

Regardless of the child's age, play activities geared toward remediating difficulties experienced by Level II children have several things in common. The first feature is something that is common to children at any level beyond Level I. That is, these children must be provided with sufficient support so that they do not regress developmentally. Many children who enter treatment have already begun to lose ground relative to the development of their peers and the goal of treatment must be to prevent further backsliding and to help the child resume normal development as soon as possible. For this reason, many therapists choose to include soothing, nurturing tasks early in the treatment of Level II children. In this way, they address the need for more primitive reassurance before it is even expressed and the child's regressive pull is neutralized.

Second, Level II play activities are designed to provide children with as much specific information about the nature of the problems they are facing as possible. As we have discussed, Level II children are susceptible to misunderstanding and misattributing their experiences, especially the negative ones, and cannot be expected to cope with things they do not understand. The therapist need not convey this increased understanding verbally or even cognitively. It can be conveyed through experiential activities as well. What is important is to make the child's definition of the problem as broad as possible so that there is room for creative problem solving.

Finally, Level II play activities foster the child's attachment to adults other than the child's caretaker, as this is the appropriate social developmental task for the child to undertake. The therapist is never likely to be as important to any client as he or she is valued by the Level II child. With this significance in the child's life goes enormous responsibility. The therapist will not be present in the child's life for long, and he or she must ensure that the child is able to identify and seek out other appropriate sources of adult support outside of the sessions. For this reason, although the primary caretaker will still have a central role in the play therapy of a Level II child, it is important for the therapist to involve other caretakers and teachers, if only indirectly, in the treatment plan.

The 10 sample activities for children experiencing difficulties associated with Level II developmental tasks were selected to reflect a range of developmental and experiential problems as well as the use of a variety of materials. The histories of many of the children described include problems that began before the onset of Level II development. In some of these cases, earlier treatment sessions geared toward earlier developmental issues may have been warranted and in some cases completed. These examples are designed to show how the therapist might address subsequent interference with Level II developmental tasks in the context of the child's history.

LEVEL II: ACTIVITY 1[8]

Case Synopsis

Paul, age 8, has never been able to concentrate or focus on school activities or to remain seated during snack time for more than 5 to 10 minutes. Although he is very bright intellectually, his attention difficulties have been diagnosed as resulting from neurologic defects. Both of Paul's parents attended college and, in spite of the fact that they understand the nature of his difficulties, they still place a great deal of emphasis on academic achievement.

Target Psychopathology and Session Goal

The combination of parental pressure and his attention difficulties has resulted in Paul constantly feeling he is incompetent. His difficulty in focusing on academic tasks has been compounded by the fact that he now believes he will fail at anything he attempts. He tends to attribute any difficulty he has to his own incompetence. The purpose of this activity is to provide him

[8]This activity and the related interpretive material was developed by Joan St. Louis.

with an experience that will help him make more accurate attributions. Specifically, this activity will help him differentiate between luck and skill in a game play situation.

Treatment Phase

This activity would be appropriate for use in either the Introduction and Exploration phase or the Growing and Trusting phase of treatment. In the former phase, it would provide a structure for some direct interaction. In the latter, the therapist would be able to do much more interpretation specific to the issue of attribution. Because of its focus on repeated competition, it would not be appropriate for use in the Negative Reaction phase. In this case it was used during the Growing and Trusting phase.

Persons Attending the Session

Therapist and Paul.

Materials Needed/Preparation Required

A pair of dice and a checkers game.

Experiential Aspects of the Activity

As mentioned, the goal of the activity was to give Paul multiple experiences in order to help him to differentiate his role in winning at luck versus skill games. The therapist began by engaging Paul in several quick dice games. They played to see who could get the highest single roll and who could get to 10 points first. The speed of the games made it easy for the therapist to keep Paul's attention. In spite of this, Paul tended to have significant reactions to both his wins and losses. He would jump around and gloat when he won and become self-critical when he lost. The therapist then suggested that they not keep score game by game but that they play 20 games and see how the score went. At this point, the therapist took a few minutes to explain the concept of chance and predicted that the score would be pretty close to 10 to 10. Because the games went so quickly, Paul and the therapist played about 50 games in less than 15 minutes and Paul was able to see the score shift back and forth as they went along. Gradually, his affective responses became less dramatic and he took both wins and losses more in stride. At this point the therapist suggested they switch to playing checkers.

The first checkers game went relatively quickly. The therapist played at her regular skill level and soundly defeated Paul. This triggered an immediate round of self-criticism on Paul's part. At this point, the therapist pointed out that checkers was a skill game and that it was typical for adults to do better than children at such games. She also said that in luck games everyone had the same chance of winning no matter how old or how smart they were, whereas in a skill game knowledge made a difference. Paul began to relax but said that if this was true, he did not want to play checkers with the therapist again. The therapist volunteered to teach Paul a secret skill that would make him a much better checkers player. Paul was immediately interested. The therapist made disclosing the secret to the game contingent on Paul agreeing to play another game. Paul agreed and the therapist told him that if he always moved his pieces toward the center of the board he would be much harder to defeat.

At this point, Paul and the therapist played another round during which the therapist constantly reminded Paul to move toward the center of the board even when another move seemed to look better. The game went much slower but was very even. Paul was very pleased with his new-found skill and bragged to his mother when he rejoined her in the waiting room.

Cognitive/Verbal Aspects of the Activity

This activity has more of an educational component than some others. In order for it to be optimally effective, the therapist must convey the difference between games of skill and games of chance and the impact that difference has on the outcome. This need not be a highly abstract explanation, but it does need to be sufficient for the child to (a) make a priori distinctions between games of skill and games of chance, (b) differentially attribute the outcomes of each type of game, and (c) maintain his or her self-esteem in the face of losses in games of chance.

Focus of Problem Solving

The problem solving in this activity was limited to two areas: Paul's willingness to return to an activity at which he was not being particularly successful, and maintaining his self-esteem in the face of losses at either type of game.

Potential Interpretive Work

Because the therapist wanted to focus on the educational and experiential nature of the task, the interpretive work was kept to a minimum. In the following sections are potential interpretations that address Paul's belief that he is not competent.

Reflections The therapist identified Paul's loss of self-esteem when he lost a game and his overly positive reaction to winning. "Just one bad roll of the dice and you look like you feel totally stupid." "Now you had a good roll and you look like you are on top of the world." In this case, the therapist tied the affect to a specific behavior even at the reflection level of interpretation in order to make explicit the degree to which Paul's affect was triggered by single, small events.

Pattern At this level, the therapist identified Paul's tendency to wander off whenever he lost a round of dice or made a bad move in checkers. She also noted his reluctance to return to a game that was not going well.

Simple Dynamic The therapist connected Paul's escapist and avoidant behavior to his feeling of incompetence and to the fact that losses seemed to threaten his self-esteem. "What you think of yourself seems to change a lot depending on how you are doing at these games. When you have good luck you feel great, but when you have bad luck you think you are stupid or bad." "Rather than risk feeling bad, it seems easier just not to play at all."

Generalized Dynamic "I'll bet the way you feel about these games is a lot like the way you feel about schoolwork. It seems better not to try any of it rather than to try something and end up feeling awful because it did not turn out well."

Genetic "I'll bet you don't even remember when you first started avoiding schoolwork. I'll bet that, for as long as you can remember, you have felt really stupid when you couldn't do something, so you just quit trying. Somewhere along the line you decided that the fact that you had trouble paying attention meant you weren't smart and that just didn't feel very good."

Plan for Future Sessions

In future sessions, the therapist would continue to expose Paul to games and activities that could be completed quickly and that would provide him with success opportunities. The frequent repetition of these tasks should prevent Paul from investing too much of his self image in any one game and eventually desensitize him to the impact of winning and losing. The therapist should also find ways to incorporate educational interactions into the sessions so that Paul's aversion to school-like situations is decreased.

LEVEL II: ACTIVITY 2[9]

Case Synopsis

Evan, age 12, constantly used toys to enact themes of destruction and chaos. He was reportedly physically abused by his father who had been out of the home for several years at the time of referral. Evan's fantasies of retribution against his father were subtly encouraged by his mother. Evan was often destructive and when he created something he usually was unable to leave it alone until he had destroyed it. He frequently talked about blood, gore, and dismemberment with apparent satisfaction.

Target Psychopathology and Session Goal

The therapist hypothesized that one of Evan's core beliefs was that his environment was extremely dangerous and that he would be attacked no matter what he did. His destructive behavior was viewed as his attempt to get his need for safety met by engaging in preemptory attacks that served to keep people at a distance and to increase his sense of personal power.

This intervention was designed to enhance the quality and appropriateness of Evan's pretend play and fantasy. In this context it was also designed to help him distinguish different types of play materials and to decrease the frequency with which he destroyed toys. This type of intervention could easily be adapted to children exhibiting perseverative and inappropriate play behaviors.

Treatment Phase

This activity could be used in any of the first three stages of treatment as it includes content, differential reinforcement, and some limit setting. The activity was used in the Introduction and Exploration phase to help structure Evan's expectations for the content and process of future therapy sessions.

Persons Attending the Session

Therapist and Evan.

Materials Needed/Preparation Required

Small table with miniature cars, trucks, animals, people, and clay. Sand tray with soldiers, military airplanes, and toy tanks.

---

[9]This activity and the related interpretive material was developed by Mary Nafpaktitis, M.A.

Experiential Aspects of the Activity

Because Evan generalized destructive behavior to all toys, the activity was designed to create a situation in which it was easy to discriminate between toys to be used for constructive play and those to be used to enact destructive themes. A small table was designated "our peaceful island" and furnished with clay, cars, trucks, civilian people, and farm animals. The sand tray was furnished with miniature soldiers, military planes, and tanks for enacting destructive themes. The therapist alternated play between the two areas beginning with 5 minutes at each and gradually extending the constructive play period.

Evan created a dynamic sand tray battle scene. He assigned one army to the therapist who followed Evan's lead in attacking and retreating. At the table, Evan attempted to engage in the same type of thematic play; however, the therapist intruded and took the lead enacting constructive themes. When Evan resisted he was allowed to return to the sand tray while the therapist continued on at the table until the 5 minutes was up and then rejoined Evan for 5 minutes at the sand tray. Evan was then encouraged to return to the table where he was able to play appropriately for about 3 minutes before needing to return to the sand tray. The therapist continued to alternate activities throughout the session.

Cognitive/Verbal Aspects of the Activity

Focus of Problem Solving

Having identified the underlying problem and its manifestation in the present, the therapist would later go on to engage Evan in both direct and fantasy problem solving. This problem solving would need to address both Evan's feelings about his abuse history and his father as well as his current feelings of both vulnerability and anger.

Potential Interpretive Work

All of the therapist's comments were geared toward identifying as many elements of the psychopathology underlying Evan's behavior as possible so that he could be engaged in constructive problem solving. The therapist outlined the following interpretations to make as the opportunity arose in session.

Reflections　　Fear, anger, desire to ward off attacks, view of the world as dangerous, safety associated with feeling powerful, and fear of competition with the therapist during the constructive play were affects and motives reflected by the therapist.

Pattern The therapist noted the repetitions of soldiers attacking others before they were attacked, Evan's need to return to the destructive play prematurely, and his repeated enactment of being the victorious attacker.

Simple Dynamic "Attacking play makes you feel powerful and safe, constructive play makes you feel scared and like you are competing with me. When you win a pretend battle it makes the feelings of being hurt or scared go away."

Generalized Dynamic "I'll bet that (previous simple dynamic reflection) is why you sometimes seem to beat up kids at school for no reason. You figure that they will attack you sooner or later so you might as well attack them first so that they know who is boss."

Genetic "It seems like most of your feelings of being in danger started when your father used to hurt you and your mother wasn't able to protect you."

Plan for Future Session

In subsequent sessions Evan's access to toys for enacting destructive themes would be gradually limited. The therapist might also need to teach Evan positive play skills. Evan's need for feelings of power would be met by introducing benevolent super heroes into his constructive pretend play.

LEVEL II: ACTIVITY 3[10]

Case Synopsis

April, age 7, was playing tag with her younger sister. During the course of the game her sister ran into the street in an attempt to avoid being tagged. She was hit by a car and killed. April continues to feel responsible for her sister's death. Since that time she has kept to herself and remained isolated from peers. The only activity in which she will engage is coloring. She refuses to play any active games and does not play basketball at recess as she had before the accident.

Target Psychopathology and Session Goal

April's belief that she was responsible for her sister's death is conscious and is frequently verbalized by her. It is clear that her needs to feel safe and good about herself are not being met. She has restricted her activity in

[10]This activity and the related interpretive material was developed by Daryl L. Hitchcock, M.A.

an attempt to reduce her fear that she could cause someone else to die and to reduce the related guilt. The degree to which she has restricted her activity is interfering with her development of peer social skills and is preventing her from receiving normal levels of peer reinforcement. The goal of the session is to begin reactivating April's play behavior.

Treatment Phase

Because the content of this activity is nonthreatening it could be used at any point in the treatment process. Because it did require April to shift what she experiences as an essential defensive behavior, the therapist did not use it until session four when he had established some rapport with April.

Persons Attending the Session

The therapist and April.

Materials Needed/Preparation Required

Coloring book containing pictures of children engaged in various active pastimes such as playing ball or jumping rope, crayons, an indoor basketball set with a foam ball.

Experiential Aspects of the Activity

The therapist structured the session so that two activities would alternate throughout. He told April that she would begin the session with 5 minutes of free coloring time and that she could earn more by playing basketball. Every minute of time she spent playing basketball earned her a minute of coloring time. Because this was a 50-minute session, the therapist told her she could earn up to 20 minutes of additional coloring time. April immediately stated that she did not want to play basketball. The therapist acknowledged this and suggested she might want to start with some of her free coloring time. April agreed and began coloring. The therapist warned her about the time every minute to minute and a half and, when the 5 minutes was up, took the crayons and put them in his pocket.

At this point April just sat and refused to do anything. The therapist allowed this to continue for about 5 minutes and then began to engage April in some problem solving aimed at breaking down the basketball task into parts that she could tolerate so that she could begin earning coloring time. April steadfastly refused to move or even to roll or throw the ball back to the therapist. At this point the therapist began tossing the foam ball at April hard enough that it would roll or bounce back to him. He repeatedly complimented her on her involvement and after a minute allowed her to return to coloring for 1 minute. Although April initially appeared annoyed, she began to smile as the therapist continued and was very pleased to return to coloring.

During the next round, April was willing to stand near the hoop but she was still unwilling to move, catch, or throw the ball. The therapist positioned April near the basket and began to throw the ball onto the top of her head trying to see if he could make it bounce into the basket. April tolerated this and smiled occasionally. At one point she bent down, picked up the ball and handed it back to the therapist. He complimented her profusely. Again, April earned a minute of coloring time.

With each round, the therapist increased the degree to which he expected April to be involved. During this session she was never actually willing to shoot a basket, but eventually she was willing to throw the ball to him so that he could make a shot. The therapist began to keep score. He earned a point if he retrieved and shot the ball. April earned a point if she retrieved the ball, handed or threw it to the therapist and he made a shot. By the end of the session April was moving about the playroom between coloring sessions. She was also willing to play for 2 minutes to earn 2 minutes of coloring time.

Cognitive/Verbal Aspects of the Activity

This is was a heavily experiential activity in which the cognitive work was kept relatively superficial. The genetic interpretation listed was not made because the therapist was concerned that it might disrupt April's play if made too early in the process.

Focus of Problem Solving

The only problem solving in which April was engaged focused on ways to break down the task of playing basketball into actions she could tolerate to earn more coloring time. April refused to participate verbally but was obviously listening to everything the therapist said. Given the fact that this was a relatively demanding activity, the therapist did all of the problem solving out loud without making any demands on April. He simply pretended to be her thinking out loud. When she would not engage at all he came up with his own silly solutions. It should be noted that such silly solutions often induce children to generate some solutions on their own if only to prevent the therapist from following through with his or her plan.

Potential Interpretive Work

Because of the very traumatic nature of the underlying content, the therapist chose not to address it in this early, active session. The reason for April attending play therapy had already been made clear and occasional references to her sister's death had been made in previous sessions.

Reflections   The therapist reflected April's fear, nervousness, and feeling unsafe when she even thought about engaging in active playing. He reflected her feelings of safety, control, and contentment when engaged in coloring. He also reflected her pleasure at being involved in interactive play even if the therapist was being awfully silly and childish.

Pattern   The therapist simply identified the degree to which April became immobile and quiet when active play was expected and her physical relaxation and increased verbal output when she was engaged in a quiet activity like coloring.

Simple Dynamic   The therapist connected the feelings of anxiety and fear to the movement required in the active play. He also noted her fear for both herself and others. In this case, the therapist also explicitly identified the safety of the playroom environment. Lastly, the therapist noted that when she could relax, April still seemed to harbor a love for basketball and other active play.

Generalized Dynamic   At this level the therapist connected April's resistance to being active in session to her resistance and anxiety both at home and at school. He used some specific examples from things he had been told by April's parents and some information that April herself had disclosed.

Genetic   Given April's overall level of anxiety with this sort of activity, the therapist chose not to make a genetic interpretation for fear of flooding April with affect she could not yet manage. If he had made such an interpretation he might have said something like, "Running around is still very scary because it was right in the middle of running around that your sister did not look where she was going, ran out in the street and got hit by a car." This interpretation not only identifies the source of the feeling but begins the process of correcting April's attribution and belief about the cause of her sister's death.

Plan for Future Sessions

The therapist would continue along two different lines. One line would gradually increase the demands for active play placed on April in each session. The goal would be to return her to her previous level of functioning. The other line would be the continued focus on identifying and managing the negative affect that April harbored regarding her sister's death.

LEVEL II: ACTIVITY 4[11]

Case Synopsis

Mark is a 6-year-old boy who lives with his mother and two older siblings. His father died unexpectedly 2 years before his referral to therapy. Since his father's death, Mark has displayed no specific symptoms; however, his mother has recently noticed that he is not playing as much as his siblings did at this age. The teacher supports this observation. In session, Mark has been unable or unwilling to demonstrate any imaginative play although he has been more than willing to sit and talk to the therapist.

Target Psychopathology and Session Goal

The therapist hypothesized that Mark responded to the anxiety created by his father's death by becoming more controlled and adult-like. He became one of his mother's primary sources of emotional support and began to identify with his father. He was receiving substantial reinforcement for his adult-like behavior and was gradually retreating from many age-appropriate activities. It appeared that his need for escape from the worries of a world in which one's father can die suddenly are not being met nor are his needs for peer social interaction and support.

The goal of this session was to begin making the transition from conversation as the primary form of therapeutic interaction to the incorporation of age-appropriate pretend play.

Treatment Phase

This activity was incorporated as a way of beginning to bypass the Negative Reaction phase of treatment. Mark's persistent refusal to play was interpreted as resistance to change, which he found threatening. The therapist hoped to begin breakup that defensive pattern.

Persons Attending the Session

The therapist and Mark.

[11]This activity and the related interpretive material was developed by Jessica Stone Phennicie, M.A.

Materials Needed/Preparation Required

An assortment of finger puppets depicting either humans or animals.

Experiential Aspects of the Activity

Mark made an initial approach to the puppets and began asking questions about them and describing their attributes. He then asked whether there was anything else available in the playroom that day, even though he could easily see that there was not. At that point he sat in a chair and began talking about some of the things he had done at school during the week.

Without comment, the therapist casually placed one finger puppet on Mark's finger and two on her own. She then began a dialogue between her puppet and Mark's in which she took both sides of the conversation. She used the dialogue to comment on Mark's behavior as if she were talking to another child. In this way she began introducing interpretive material through the medium of pretending. Mark did not engage in the play nor did he remove the puppet. He seemed fascinated by the therapist's behavior.

At one point, Mark moved his finger slightly and the therapist had her puppet react with an exaggerated startle response. She said (to Mark's puppet), "Oh, you scared me. You had been sitting so quietly I was wondering if you had fallen asleep and was surprised that you moved." At this, Mark moved his finger again and the therapist repeated an even more exaggerated response. At no point did the therapist acknowledge Mark's presence nor did she comment on his behavior. All of her behavior and verbalizations were directed at Mark's puppet. Slowly, Mark began to move more. He attempted to talk to the therapist directly but she ignored him and continued to interact with his puppet, still carrying on both sides of the puppet conversation. Eventually, Mark began to talk through the puppet as he realized that it was the only way he was going to get to do the thing with which he was most comfortable, talking.

Cognitive/Verbal Aspects of the Activity

Because this was an activity to transition Mark from the cognitive plain on which he tended to operate to a more experiential one, the therapist did a great deal of talking and only a little moving and pretending. The therapist made a great many interpretations through the dialogue and also modeled a little problem solving. She was careful to have Mark's puppet disclose most of the information about Mark that she used in the pretend dialogue. In other words Mark's puppet modeled

Mark's self-disclosure and the therapist was able to demonstrate the way she would react to such disclosures.

Focus of Problem Solving

At one point when Mark had not moved his puppet in a while, the therapist commented to the puppet that he must be getting stiff sitting so still. She had the puppet respond that he was dependent on the finger to which he was attached for movement and so felt relatively helpless. The therapist agreed and suggested that maybe she could help him initiate movement. The puppets discussed various options and finally agreed that the therapist's puppet should try to tickle Mark to get him to move. At this point, Mark made a slight movement and the two puppets rejoiced at how the mere threat of implementing their plan had been successful.

Potential Interpretive Work

This activity allowed for a substantial amount of interpretive work, all done within the context of the pretend play. Again, the reader should note that all of the following were comments made by the therapist in a dialogue between the therapist's and Mark's puppets.

Reflections   T: "The kid whose finger you are on seems frozen. Is he always like that or is he particularly worried right now?" M: "Well he does worry a lot. He likes to talk to grown ups more than play." T: "A kid who doesn't like to play? Weird." M: "He's not weird, he thinks you are weird." (At this point Mark smiled.) Besides his mom likes how well-behaved and grown-up he is." T: "You mean how boring he is, let's see if we can't get him to get a little rowdy."

Pattern   T: "OK. I know you said this boy was quiet but this has gone on for 10 minutes. Are you sure he is awake?" M: "Yeah, I told you he is always like this because he is always worrying about being good."

Simple Dynamic   T: "Oh, so he thinks if he is good all of the time everyone will like him." M: "Yeah, I also think he hopes that if he is good all of the time nothing will ever go wrong and then nothing bad will happen."

Generalized Dynamic   T: "You mean he is even like this at school?" M: "Oh yeah, he sits near the front and pays more attention to the teacher than to the other kids." T: "I'll bet he gets really good grades." M: "The teacher thinks he is great but even she worries that he doesn't ever seem to take a break or to have any fun."

Genetic   T: "Has he always been like this?" M: "No,

he used to play a lot before his dad died. That just seemed to take all of the playing out of him." T: "That is rough. Maybe you and I can put some of the playing back."

Plan for Future Sessions

The therapist would gradually increase Mark's involvement in the pretending by slowing the pace of her own activity and providing Mark with more openings to contribute to the activity. She could increase his involvement by using hand puppets, then masks, and then costumes in the sessions. Each would pull for progressively more activity on Mark's part. She would also proceed with extensive problem solving on strategies to assuage his anxiety and to enable him to play and eventually to interact with his peers in more age-appropriate ways.

LEVEL II: ACTIVITY 5[12]

Case Synopsis

Matt, age 7, was referred to a school-based treatment program as a results of his disruptive behavior in class. His teacher reported that Matt threw books and pencils and interrupted the other students' work as much as 25% of the day. What has proved particularly frustrating for his teacher is Matt's negative response to positive feedback. She notes that if she waits for a time when his behavior is acceptable and then praises him he becomes angry and acts out. As a result, she tends to ignore him when he is not causing problems. At this point, she believes he should be placed in a Special Education program for behavior problem children.

Matt's parents report no behavior problems of any kind at home. They are aware that school-based assessments have placed Matt in the high average range of intellectual functioning. They are also aware that for at least the past semester he has not earned any grades higher than a C. In spite of this, they do not seem concerned about either his academic performance or his school behavior. They seem to chalk it up to his "being a boy."

Target Psychopathology and Session Goal

The therapist's initial hypothesis was that Matt's need for reinforcement with respect to his academic performance was not being met in the home and, as a result, Matt was progressively devaluing anything re-

[12]This activity and the related interpretive material was developed by Barbara Hughes, M.A.

lated to school. This devaluing conflicted with his intellectual abilities and created an ongoing internal conflict. Matt believed his parents did not care about his performance, and the progressive deterioration of his schoolwork seemed to be an attempt to test the limits of their nonresponsiveness. In spite of himself, he sometimes did well and this proved frustrating.

The goal of this session was to set up a nonacademic situation in which Matt could gain experience at accepting reinforcement without becoming angry and acting out.

Treatment Phase

This activity would be suitable for use in any of the first three phases of treatment. In this case, it was used in the Negative Reaction phase because it turned Matt's oppositional behavior into a game, thereby neutralizing it.

Persons Attending the Session

The therapist and Matt.

Materials Needed/Preparation Required

Two or more foam balls and a plastic trash can. The room should be set up in such a way that no degree of acting out on Matt's part will necessitate limit setting on the therapist's part.

Experiential Aspects of the Activity

Matt was introduced to the play with the instruction that he was allowed to throw the balls anywhere in the room, but that he was not to let them go into the trash can. Matt immediately began to throw the balls, trying to be as wild as he could. The therapist actively reinforced Matt's actions, trying to create as much cognitive dissonance as possible. The worse he behaved, the more compliments he got. At this point, Matt began to throw the balls toward the trash can and the therapist said, "Oh I forgot to tell you what happens if they go in the can. If that happens then I start to play with you and we see who can get the most balls in the trash can the fastest." The therapist had now created a double bind for Matt. If he continued to throw the balls around he got compliments. If he was "noncompliant" and threw them in the trash can, he would trigger a game and break his pattern of isolation.

For a while Matt kept throwing the balls around. The therapist made comments such as, "Look how strong you are," "I can't believe you have such great aim," "You're being so good about avoiding the trash can."

Again, Matt threw a ball toward the can and accidentally hit it. Immediately, the therapist picked up a ball and said, "That was close enough to the can, now I'm going to throw some balls and I'll bet I get one in the can before you do." She began throwing the balls toward the can and Matt readily joined in the competition. At this point the therapist did not ignore the positive behavior but instead made a point of continuing to compliment Matt on his behavior at the same rate.

Throughout the entire session Matt rarely took his eyes off the therapist. He seemed to be waiting for her reaction to everything he did. He also seemed to gear his behavior to get the maximum response possible, no matter whether it was positive or negative. He seemed genuinely confused by the fact that the therapist remained positive in her comments and interactions no matter what he did.

Cognitive/Verbal Aspects of the Activity

Virtually all of the verbalizations made during this session were made by the therapist. She interpreted Matt's dilemma regarding compliance but did not problem solve the conflict during this session. She believed that introducing the problem solving too soon would reduce her chances of actually involving Matt in direct interaction, as she might sound too much like his teacher attempting to remedy a classroom behavior.

Focus of Problem Solving

No problem solving was done during this session. The plan was to introduce more problem solving over the course of the next few sessions.

Potential Interpretive Work

The therapist did interpret the conflict that Matt experienced over the course of this session. She used what we sometimes refer to as a hit-and-run technique. That is, interpretations were made in a casual, off-hand way, and then the therapist moved on to doing something else so that not too much emphasis was placed on what she had just said. This also made it clear that she did not expect Matt to respond to her statements at this time, although she did not prevent him from doing so.

Reflections The therapist verbalized the affects that corresponded to Matt's facial expressions and his behavior. She noted that he seemed angry, confused, happy, competitive, and proud at various points in the session. She also noted that no matter how he was feeling, it always looked to her as though he was in complete control of his behavior.

Pattern   The therapist identified Matt's tendency to do the opposite of what she told him to no matter what the outcome. She also noted his hesitation when he was faced with having to choose between being non-compliant and triggering her involvement in a game with him.

Simple Dynamic   "When you're doing the opposite of what you are told, you seem to feel happy and powerful." "When I don't scold you for doing wild things you look confused and a little annoyed, like things aren't turning out the way you planned." "I think you're surprised by how sneaky I can be at making it hard for you get in trouble." "I think that no matter how you behave you actually like it when people give you compliments and do fun things with you."

The therapist also made one low-level dynamic interpretation that was actually based on what she knew about Matt's school behavior rather than on what was occurring in session. Although this is usually reserved for the next level of interpretation, it was done here as an initial test of the validity of her hypotheses regarding the motives for Matt's behavior. "Sometimes getting in trouble is worth it if it gets people to leave you alone and do what you want to do."

Generalized Dynamic   "The difference between here and school is that, at school you can always find something to do that will actually get you in trouble." "At school you don't want to do well, you just want to be left alone." "From what I've heard, your teacher leaves you alone most of the time and yet you still do things in class that you know you're not supposed to do. That makes me think that what you do in class doesn't have much to do with your teacher or the schoolwork. I wonder if you're trying to find out how long it will take your parents to decide they actually care about what you do in school."

Genetic   "I think you kind of got stuck here. Your parents never cared about your schoolwork so you stopped trying. That made other people treat you like you're stupid which made you mad. So you started being bad because it was much better if people thought you were bad instead of stupid. Now your parents still don't care what you do at school and everyone is always mad at you. School must make you feel just generally lousy."

Plan for Future Sessions

The therapist wanted to proceed along two dimensions. One was to introduce school-like activities into the session gradually so that Matt could have positive experiences with these as well as with game play. The other was to engage Matt in more problem solving with respect to resolving the dilemma of forcing his parents to care about his school performance and about antagonizing teachers and peers at school. The parents would also be included in family play therapy sessions to help them become aware of and change their messages to him about his behavior and functioning at school.

LEVEL II: ACTIVITY 6[13]

Case Synopsis

Ann, age 5, was the youngest of six children in a family that was very socially active. The family was involved in several church-related activities a week and each of the older children were all involved in multiple after-school activities. Ann was referred for treatment by her parents who were concerned about the degree to which she did not act like her siblings. Specifically, they were concerned about her shyness and reluctance to interact with children outside of the family. They reported that Ann had always been different from her siblings but that her shyness seemed to have gradually increased over time.

Target Psychopathology and Session Goal

It appeared that Ann's temperament may have made her less comfortable in social interactions than her siblings. In this family that style did not bring her much reinforcement and because of this she believed that peer interactions would bring the same results. The combination of social anxiety and a belief that interactions would not bring reinforcement kept Ann from wanting, much less seeking, social contact. The goal of this session was to give her experience verbally interacting with peers in a safe setting.

Treatment Phase   This activity was used with Ann in the Growing and Trusting phase of therapy. With some modification it could also be used as a way of introducing group members to one another in the Introduction and Exploration phase.

Persons Attending the Session   Therapist, Ann, and the members of a peer social skills group (in this case, five other children).

Materials Needed/Preparation Required   A large sheet of cardboard, preferably something stronger than

---

[13]This activity and the related interpretive material was developed by Jessica Stone Phennicie, M.A.

posterboard, corrugated cardboard or foam core board would all work well. An assortment of magazines, scissors, glue, and markers.

Experiential Aspects of the Activity The group was instructed to create a large collage that depicted all of the members of the group. Each member of the group was to find a picture or word in the magazines that made them think of each of the other members of the group, including themselves. This meant that each member of the group would end up with six words or pictures representing them. The six items would be clustered on the cardboard sheet so that the end result was a "picture of the group." Before attaching the pictures to the cardboard, the person who selected it had to make a statement about why he or she had chosen it to represent the other group member. No limits were set on the type of pictures or words the children could select before the activity began. When several members began choosing pictures that made fun of another child, the therapist set out to use peer pressure to make them change their choices.

Cognitive/Verbal Aspects of the Activity

The therapist worked on three things as the children selected pictures. First, she compared and contrasted the pictures the children selected to represent themselves with those the other children selected to represent them. Second, she consistently reinforced any interaction the children had with one another. And last, she created peer pressure to prevent children from selecting negative depictions of each other.

Focus of Problem Solving

The therapist limited the use of problem solving to two problematic interactions. The children's choice of negative depictions of another child were identified as problems for the targeted children. Peer pressure was created by asking the target children how they could manage the behavior of those who were making fun of them. The targeted children suggested the option of revenge by selecting even worse pictures to depict those who had been mean to them. The therapist pointed out that this would result in a poster that made fun of all of the group members. For a while this seemed like the direction in which the group would go. Ironically, this was not necessarily malicious, rather it seemed to desensitize each of them to teasing as they began to laugh and joke. As selections proceeded, various members began to complain that the poster would turn out bad and, slowly, negative selections were replaced with positive ones. The therapist also triggered problem solving

whenever a member seemed reluctant or unable to say why he or she had selected a particular picture.

Potential Interpretive Work

The therapist used relatively little interpretation except to identify the affects that interfered with the children's ability to participate fully and appropriately in the activity.

Reflections The therapist identified Ann's anxiety about interacting with the other children. She identified Ann's fear of being either teased or ignored by the other children. She also identified the mixed feelings Ann had when she was ignored instead of teased during the time when the children were choosing negative depictions of one another. "This is really tough. I mean, which is worse, having kids tease you, which is looking kind of fun, or having them leave you alone?"

Pattern Ann's repeated tendency to wait until someone else initiated an interaction before saying or doing anything was noted.

Simple Dynamic "Sometimes you seem almost frozen. You seem so worried about what the other kids will do or say that you can't move until they move first." "Sometimes you look surprised when one of the other kids says something nice, like you didn't expect it."

Generalized Dynamic "I'll bet this is just what happens at school and church. You worry how other kids will react to you so you try not to do anything until they do. You're just sure they won't have anything nice to say."

Genetic "I'll bet you have always felt sort of the same way at home that you do with the kids at school. Like they aren't like you are, that they make you worry sometimes, and that they are nicer to each other than they are to you."

Having identified the degree to which Ann feels different from the rest of her family and perceives this as negative, the therapist would then go on to help her to develop strategies for minimizing both the feeling of difference and the negative self-evaluation.

Plan for Future Sessions

The therapist planned additional activities that would promote positive group interaction. The therapist also continued to help Ann develop strategies for managing her social anxiety and garnering positive peer responses.

LEVEL II: ACTIVITY 7[14]

Case Synopsis

Jeff, age 5, was referred to therapy shortly after he entered kindergarten because he seemed virtually phobic about initiating social interaction with other children in his class. Jeff had been very attached to both of his parents and his development was progressing very well until his younger sister was born when he was 4½ years old. After his sister's arrival, Jeff became very clingy and dependent in his interactions with both parents. He often refused to play out of their sight and wanted to be held whenever his sister was being held. He complained constantly about having to go to school and seemed generally unhappy.

Target Psychopathology and Session Goal

It appeared that the birth of a sibling caused Jeff to regress developmentally in response to anxiety that his parents would become more attached to his sister than they were to him. This anxiety seems to have caused him to focus on reestablishing his position as the center of his parent's world rather than making developmentally appropriate moves toward beginning peer friendships. The goal of this session was to introduce him to other children in a peer social group in a way that he would experience as safe and rewarding.

Treatment Phase

This activity would be best suited for use in the Introduction and Exploration phase of a play therapy group, as it was used in this case.

Persons Attending the Session

The therapist, Jeff, and six peers.

Materials Needed/Preparation Required

Paper and crayons or makers, as well as some small prizes or concrete reinforcers (plastic whistles, stickers, pencils, or the like).

Experiential Aspects of the Activity

During the first session, the children were asked to sit in a circle on the floor. Each child was given a piece of paper and a marker. They were asked to write their names on the paper, crumple it up, and throw it into the

[14]This activity and the related interpretive material was developed by Stamatoula Vagelatos.

center of the circle. The children were then told to take a crumpled paper, other than their own, from the pile. Once every child had someone else's name, the introductions began. In turn, each child was instructed to stand up, read the name on his or her piece of paper, walk to that child, and say, "Hello, my name is _____." The target child was instructed to reply, "It is very nice to meet you." If each child completed his or her single line they were given a reinforcer by the therapist.

Once the first round was completed, the therapist initiated a second round of the introduction game. This time the children were told to throw the wad of paper with their name on it at one of the other children in the group. The child who was hit had two seconds to say the thrower's name out loud in order to earn another reinforcer. This part of the game was played very fast, sort of like a game of "Hot Potato" so that the children were throwing paper wads and yelling each other's names in a very lively and playful way.

Cognitive/Verbal Aspects of the Activity

The therapist engaged in problem solving with the first two children who had to introduce themselves and who seemed very reluctant to do so. Interpretation was used to identify both the children's underlying anxiety and their responses over the course of the two introduction games.

Focus of Problem Solving

Jeff was one of the first children who had to introduce himself and he was very reluctant to say anything. The therapist identified this problem as feeling uncomfortable with this unfamiliar situation. She quickly identified the possible responses: Jeff could not comply, he could comply by saying his introduction very quietly, he could do something silly to feel more comfortable, or he could just comply. She then identified the responses that would earn him a sticker and pointed out that he could make his own choice. He said his introduction very quickly and quietly and then sat right down. The therapist verbally reinforced him and gave him a sticker as well.

Potential Interpretive Work

The therapist's interpretive work focused on identifying the nature and source of each child's social anxiety. For Jeff, she had planned the following series of interpretations. However, because this was only the first session, she did not move past the simple dynamic level.

Reflections "Boy do you seem nervous." "You seem a little worried about what the other kids will do when you introduce yourself." "Now that you finished your introduction you seem a lot more relaxed."

Pattern "Every time it is your turn to talk or do something it takes you awhile to get started." "You sure look happy when other kids talk to you and when you get a sticker."

Simple Dynamic "I think you get so worried about what the other kids will say that you have to take a second or two to get up the nerve to do or say anything around them. But when you finally say or do something you do have fun."

Generalized Dynamic "I'll bet you don't talk to the other kids at school either. Then they don't talk to you and you don't have much fun. Then you get home and you feel a lot better."

Genetic "I think you have always been happy at home and you want to make sure that doesn't change now that you have a little sister. You're not sure yet if other kids are really going to be as fun as your mom and dad so you worry quite a bit."

Plan for Future Sessions

Over the course of the early stages of the group, the therapist planned a number of activities that allowed the children to make brief, positive social contact with one another. She also gradually increased the depth of her interpretive work to identify Jeff's underlying separation anxiety and sibling rivalry. Once identified, the degree to which these interfered with his peer social interactions was the focus of the problem solving.

LEVEL II: ACTIVITY 8[15]

Case Synopsis

Sara, age 6, had lived with her mother who was drug and alcohol addicted. Six months ago, she was placed in foster care after her school filed a child abuse report with Child Protective Services. She was referred to therapy because she tended to remain relatively isolated all of the time. Early in the course of the treatment, the therapist noted that Sara preferred to play silently without interacting with the therapist. She rarely made eye contact. When the therapist attempted to interact with her, Sara would withdraw and stop playing altogether.

[15]This activity and the related interpretive material was developed by Janet E. Bucklin, M.A.

Target Psychopathology and Session Goal

Because Sara was abused and neglected she withdraws from interactive, sharing activities in order to keep control of the play situation and protect herself from being chastised for any mistakes she might make. Sara's mother would often punish her by taking away toys or putting her to bed without dinner. The therapist hypothesized that one of Sara's core beliefs was that the environment and adults were unpredictable, especially when she was not in control of the situation. By keeping others at a distance and keeping control over supplies she acquired like toys or food, she increased her chances of being both taken care of and safe. The goal of this activity was to provide Sara with a safe, positive sharing experience. Ideally, she would learn that she could actually get her needs met by sharing.

Treatment Phase

This activity could be used in any phase of treatment. It is very nonthreatening. It also promotes low-level interaction.

Persons Attending the Session

The therapist and Sara.

Materials Needed/Preparation Required

Small candies such as M&Ms, two bowls, a toy tea set, and two dolls.

Experiential Aspects of the Activity

Before Sara entered the playroom, the therapist made a trail of M&Ms from the door of the playroom to the table where the tea set was laid out. The therapist told Sara that they could each eat any of the M&Ms they picked up but there were three rules. One was that they could each only pick up one M&M at a time, the second was that they had to take turns doing so, and the third was that they could not eat any until they were all picked up.

When all of the candies were picked up, Sara and the therapist had equal numbers of M&Ms. The therapist then proposed they play a game in which they each stood a chance of ending up with more candies. Sara didn't seem too interested, but she did not withdraw. The therapist and Sara sat on the floor facing each other. The therapist put a bowl in front of each of them and instructed Sara to toss as many M&Ms into the bowl in front of the therapist as fast as she could. In the meantime, the therapist tossed candies into the bowl in front of Sara. The therapist did tell Sara that, at the end of the game, she would get all of the candies in the therapist's bowl. The game created the illusion of sharing or at least exchanging while in fact being self-serving. As they ran out of candies they used the ones in the bowl in front of them to continue the exchange. In trying to build up her own supply of candy, Sara worked as fast as she could putting candies into the therapist's bowl. Although she did not talk, she did smile a couple of times and was clearly engaged in the game.

As Sara's interest in the game began to taper off, the therapist initiated a tea party, using her candies as the food. Sara moved to the table and began eating her own candies but pretty much ignored the therapist. The therapist then set up the two dolls on the table and role played a tea party. Although Sara did not join in, she did sit and watch while she ate her candies.

Cognitive/Verbal Aspects of the Activity

Because Sara tended not to talk, the therapist modeled some problem solving geared toward keeping Sara involved in the interaction. The therapist also used interpretation to make some of Sara's internal processes explicit.

Focus of Problem Solving

The therapist identified Sara's reluctance to play the initial M&M tossing game as a problem. The therapist focused on the conflict the reluctance created. If Sara did not play, she would end up with fewer M&Ms, and if she did, she might feel anxious. The therapist mentioned a few things Sara could do to solve both problems, such as tossing the candies very quickly and not looking at the therapist. The therapist turned this suggestion into a lighthearted tease by constantly telling Sara not to look at her. Of course, Sara would glance up occasionally and the therapist would pretend to shriek and say, "Ahh, you're looking at me, don't do that." Then she would laugh. The therapist also verbalized how well Sara was doing at her candy tossing.

Potential Interpretive Work

Interpretations identifying Sara's beliefs about sharing and the unreliability of adults were made throughout the session. In the M&M exchange, the therapist interpreted directly. When the therapist was carrying out the role play with the dolls, she interpreted in the context of the play.

Reflections   "I can't tell which you want more, the M&Ms or to avoid having to play with me." "Right now wanting M&Ms seems to be winning out over wanting to play alone." "Now that you have enough

M&Ms you seem to have decided to stop playing with me." "I think you'd try just about anything to make sure you get the things you want." "You look a little worried when we play together and like you feel safer when you can play alone."

Pattern   "Every time I look at you, you look away." "You sure work hard to get the things you want." "In the last three sessions I think I've only heard you say one or two things." "The few times I have been able to get you to play you do seem to have fun."

Simple Dynamic   "I think you don't like to do things with other people because you worry it won't turn out well." "I think you work hard at getting the things you want because you think that's the only way you will get anything." "In a way, not talking makes you the boss because it make the other person have to do all the work of trying to figure out what you're thinking."

Generalized Dynamic   "I'll bet that the other kids at school pretty much ignore you when you don't talk or play with them and that is OK because that way you can feel safer." "I'll bet you don't like to share or exchange things at school because then you have to worry about whether or not you'll get everything you need."

Genetic   "I have an idea that you started feeling safer when you were alone, because with your mom you had to worry about being yelled at or hit when she was there but you were OK when she wasn't there. You also decided that your mom wasn't very reliable so you had to work hard to get things for yourself."

Plan for Future Sessions

The therapist wanted to increase the degree to which tasks pulled for interaction over the course of future sessions. She also wanted to increase the pull for verbal interaction. As Sara's level of trust increased, the therapist wanted to add tasks that allowed her to provide Sara with fairly direct nurturance.

LEVEL II: ACTIVITY 9[16]

Case Synopsis

Jack, age 7, was reportedly molested by his mother's boyfriend with whom he no longer has contact. Since

---

[16]This activity and the related interpretive material was developed by Daryl Hitchcock, M.A.

the molestation, Jack has been very aggressive with peers at school. He becomes very demanding and tries to control others during games. His mother reports that he currently has no peer friends because none of the other children can tolerate Jack's bossiness. The degree to which this is problematic is increased by the fact that Jack does not engage in much pretend play either, so he is left without much to do when other children will not play with him.

Target Psychopathology and Session Goal

It was hypothesized that Jack's aggressive and controlling behavior represented his best efforts at expressing his anger over the molest and at making sure that he was not victimized again. His needs for feeling safe were clearly not being met. The goal of the activity was to provide him with a successful, interactive play experience. The activity also encouraged his use of pretend play.

Treatment Phase

This activity was introduced during the Growing and Trusting phase of Jack's play therapy, although it could easily be adapted for use in the Introduction and Exploration phase or be used to prepare a child for Termination by role playing peer interactions once therapy ended.

Persons Attending the Session

The therapist and Jack.

Materials Needed/Preparation Required

Board game, dice, and a table with three chairs.

Experiential Aspects of the Activity

The therapist began the activity by asking Jack to name a peer he would like to have as a friend. Although Jack was initially resistant, he did mention a child in his neighborhood, Billy, who was OK. The therapist then said that for the rest of the session they were going to include Billy in their games because "some types of games are just more fun if more than two people play." The therapist moved Jack to the table and had him sit in one chair while Billy sat in another and the therapist took the third. (Note: the therapist controlled most of Billy's dialogue and behavior to ensure that the content needed for the session was made available and to ensure that the experience turned out positively no matter how controlling Jack might become.) The therapist

established his control by telling Jack that since Billy could not talk or move his game pieces on his own, the therapist would communicate for him as well as move the game pieces as Billy wanted.

The therapist started the game by having Billy ask Jack if he wanted to play a game. Jack agreed. The therapist had each one roll the dice to see who chose the first game to play. Billy won and chose checkers. Then Billy suggested that Jack take the first turn. During the checkers game Jack was able to keep ahead so he was not particularly controlling. When Jack won the game, Billy was very complimentary with respect to Jack's skills.

When the game was finished, Jack chose to play Candyland. Billy said he did not know how to play and asked if Jack would show him. Jack was clearly pleased with the opportunity to be the leader and was quite good at instructing Billy. The therapist played Candyland along with Jack and Billy, thereby doubling his opportunities to model appropriate game-playing behavior and to interpret and problem solve. Very quickly, however, Billy moved ahead in the game and Jack began to show anger. At first he just complained, but he gradually started knocking over Billy's game piece and attempted to change the rules. Although Billy was tolerant of Jack's behavior, he constantly stated how he felt in response to what Jack was doing. When Billy won the game, Jack was very angry and briefly refused to play any more. However, when Billy suggested they return to playing checkers because that was a game Jack seemed to like, Jack calmed down and agreed to play again.

Cognitive/Verbal Aspects of the Activity

The therapist mixed his use of both problem solving and interpretation into both his own dialogue and the dialogue he had Billy deliver.

Focus of Problem Solving

The therapist identified Billy's fear of losing the game as a problem to be solved. He did this during the checkers game because Jack was ahead most of the time. He also identified his own feelings about losing as a problem during Candyland so that he could demonstrate different approaches to managing the situation. When he role played Billy, he focused on the fact that this was only one game and that losing was not all that important because there would be other games. During Candyland, he focused on the fact that he was losing a game of chance and that at any time his luck might change. He also identified that the outcome of a game of chance was much harder to control. The therapist did not do any problem solving with respect to Billy's negative feelings in response to Jack's anger and control. He chose to save that more central and difficult problem for a future session.

Potential Interpretive Work

The therapist used interpretation to identify Jack's feelings during the course of the play as well as to provide Jack with information about how others might be reacting to his behavior.

Reflections   The therapist focused on this level of work to establish both the positive and negative affects and motives involved and to label the latter as problems to be solved. As previously stated, the therapist spent approximately equal amounts of time interpreting Billy's and Jack's feelings.

Pattern   The primary pattern identified was the increase in Jack's aggression and controlling behavior whenever he fell behind in a game.

Simple Dynamic   The therapist connected Jack's aggressiveness and controlling behavior as ways of managing his fear of losing or having his feelings hurt. The use of the phrase "have your feelings hurt" set up future interpretations that would compare feeling hurt emotionally with feeling hurt by the molest. The therapist also identified that Billy seemed more hurt when Jack was angry with him than he was when he was losing the game.

Generalized Dynamic   The therapist chose not to connect Jack's anger and control in session to his behavior in school at this time. Instead, the therapist identified that Jack's overresponse to winning was probably consistent with his behavior at school and that Billy's negative reaction to Jack's gloating was probably a lot like how the other kids at school felt as well.

Genetic   At this level, the therapist did not yet identify the molest as the source of Jack's fear of losing or of not being in control. Instead, the therapist identified the near universality of people's preference to win and to get things their way, and the fact that it was hard for most people not get angry or bossy when they felt threatened in any way.

Plan for Future Sessions

The therapist planned to work along three lines as the therapy progressed. First, the therapist wanted to introduce pretend activities in which Jack could play a more active role so that he could begin to use symbolic play as a way of addressing the molest content. Second, the therapist planned activities that more and more directly approached the molest content. And third, the therapist planned to move Jack to a peer play therapy group once the bulk of the individual work had been completed.

LEVEL II: ACTIVITY 10[17]

Case Synopsis

For many children like Sam, age 6, engaging in cooperative play activities is very difficult. Usually, these children tend to see peers as a source of competition for scarce resources rather than as either a potential provider of resources or at least as someone who can help them access supplies. In Sam's case, this view arose out of his experience as a middle child in a relatively large family. Although his difficulty cooperating with other children was not the primary reason for referral, it was sufficiently problematic to warrant intervention. Sam was seen in a peer play therapy group.

Target Psychopathology and Session Goal

As stated previously, Sam's need for peer social reinforcement was not being met adequately or appropriately. The goal of the activity was to provide him with an experience in which peer cooperation earned him rewards.

Treatment Phase

This activity could be used effectively in either the Introduction and Exploration phase or the Growing and Trusting phase of play therapy. The better the children know each other the more the therapist can focus on interpretation of their interactions as opposed to structuring the contact. In this case, it was used about two-thirds of the way through the course of a 12-week peer play therapy group.

Persons Attending the Session

Therapist, Sam, and five other children.

Materials Needed/Preparation Required

Three blindfolds, a paper cup for each child, three large balls, paper, and magic markers.

---

[17]This activity and the related interpretive material was developed by Barbara Hughes, M.A.

Prior to the session, the therapist needs to

- place six paper cups half-full of water on a table or near the sink in the playroom.
- put a masking tape line on the floor about 4 feet out from and parallel to one wall. The balls should be placed on the floor along the line.
- place a sheet of paper and markers at each of three chairs around a table.

Experiential Aspects of the Activity

The children in the group were divided into pairs and given the following instructions, "In this game there are leaders and there are followers. You will each have a turn being a leader and each have a turn being a follower. In each pair who wants to be the leader first?" This, of course, prompted every child to say "Me." The therapist identified this as a problem and asked for suggestions as to how they could decide who should go first. After some haggling they decided to draw lots. They tore a sheet of paper in half and put a colored dot on one half. Then, they folded the halves up and gave them to the therapist to hold in her closed fists. Each child in the pair chose a hand and then opened the paper he or she selected. The one who got the sheet with the dot was the first leader.

Once the leaders were selected, the following instructions were given. "Each pair is a team. I will be timing you to see which team can complete three things the fastest. First, the leader has to get the follower over to the sink and drink a glass of water without spilling any. Second, the leaders have to stand their partners against the wall and move out to this line where the balls are and get their partners to catch the ball once. And last, the leader has to help the follower draw a tree on one of the sheets of paper at the table." At this point the children were saying that this was going to be easy and were making fun of the therapist's choice of activities. The therapist then said that the team who finished the fastest got first choice of snacks at the end of the session. The children were now all bragging that they would finish first. It was at this point that the therapist said, "Oh, I almost forgot. Each follower will be wearing a blindfold and leaders can only tell them what to do. They cannot physically guide their follower except to get them from place to place." Although surprised by the change of events, the children were already so invested in winning the relay that they readily submitted to the additional rule.

The therapist blindfolded each follower to decrease the possibility of cheating or accusations thereof. She then lined up the pairs with the leaders in front and said, "Go." Once the leaders had their followers over at the sink, she reminded the leaders that they could now only guide with words as they told their followers where the cups of water were and tried to get them to pick the cups up without spilling the contents. Then she coached and problem solved with them as they led their partners through the remaining two tasks. After the first round, the therapist spent a few minutes telling the group what she had observed, what had worked well for some pairs and where others had had problems. Then the children switched roles and repeated the relay. The group actually had time for each pair to go four times so that each child had two opportunities to be the leader and the follower. The repetition increased both their individual skill at completing the tasks and their ability to guide their partner.

Sam appeared to enjoy this activity very much. He was much happier in the role of leader than follower but cooperated in both. He tended to be a somewhat critical leader, but improved once he had experience as a follower and found out how difficult it was to do these seemingly simple tasks while blindfolded. He included his partner in a "high five" hand slap when they won one of the rounds of the game. He also engaged his partner in some planning as to how they could do better in the next round.

Cognitive/Verbal Aspects of the Activity

The therapist focused the use of problem solving on developing strategies for completing the tasks. She used interpretation to identify those feelings the children were experiencing that interfered with optimal performance in the relay.

Focus of Problem Solving

Each time any of the pairs had difficulty with a task, the therapist identified this as a problem in that it prevented them from doing well. She tossed out ideas for both leaders and followers that might help them do better. Between rounds, she shared what she had observed with the group, providing them with information on how other pairs had accomplished the tasks and overcome various problems they encountered along the way. She also shared her evaluations of their problem solving simply by saying, for example, "Oh, that worked much better. Talking quietly right next to your partner helped him hear because the other leaders were just shouting directions." Whenever possible, the therapist referred to the pairs of children, rather than to an individual child, to heighten the children's sense of functioning as a unit.

Potential Interpretive Work

The therapist identified both Sam's doubts about fully involving himself in this cooperative venture and his pleasure when he and his partner did well.

Reflections "Before I mentioned the blindfolds you looked like you thought this was a silly, baby game, now you look pretty worried." "You look like you are super eager to start" (when Sam was going to be the leader). "Now you look like you are not so sure you want to do this at all" (when Sam was about to take his turn as a follower). "You look like you are going to explode you are so frustrated" (when Sam could not get his partner to catch the ball). "Now you look sort of embarrassed" (when Sam had missed the ball for the third time during his turn as a follower).

Pattern "That is the second time you have yelled at your partner for not listening to your directions." "I keep seeing you try things on your own and not really listening to the directions your partner is trying to give you."

Simple Dynamic "You feel good about being a leader and really don't see why your partner doesn't always trust you and listen to all of your directions." "When you're the follower you don't feel quite as good and then you're not sure you want to trust your partner and take all of *his* directions."

Generalized Dynamic "I'll bet all of you like being the leader more when you play with your friends at home." "It is hard to be a follower and trust that someone else will take good care of you and help you win."

Genetic "I'll bet your brothers and sisters tell you what to do a lot. Sometimes they probably tell you to do things that are good for you, but I'll bet that lots of times they want you to do things that are good for them. Since you're not sure you trust them you figure you'll just ignore them as much as possible even when they might be able to help you."

Plan for Future Sessions

As the group became more comfortable with cooperative tasks, the therapist wanted to introduce progressively more competitive tasks so that the children could learn to tolerate winning and losing without resorting to inappropriate behavior.

LEVEL III CHILDREN: DEVELOPMENTAL AND THERAPEUTIC ISSUES

As children acquire an increasing ability to manipulate information cognitively, they enter into Level III, which, as we describe it, lasts roughly from the ages of 6 to 11. This level corresponds to what Piaget (1952,

1959, 1967) refers to as the Concrete Operations stage. Whereas children in the Sensorimotor and Preoperational stages were preoccupied with acquiring information, the Level III child becomes preoccupied with organizing it. The rules governing mental processes that the child discovered in Level II are rigorously applied in Level III. Children at this level are interested in endless organization and categorization, it is often the time when they begin to collect things such as stones, coins, stamps, and baseball cards. They will sort and re-sort their collections, and then sort them again if new items are added. During this level, some children become relatively intolerant of change, preferring familiar friends, places, and routines. It is not until they approach the end of this stage that they become sure enough in their mental operations to take pleasure in testing those skills by adding new and progressively more abstract information.

Level III children's capacity for acquiring, storing, and retrieving information about their experience rivals that of an adult, and yet some fundamental differences remain. Level I children acquired all sensory data about an experience regardless of its relevance, stored all of the data together in memory, and retrieved it in total as well. For them, gifts received are a collection of sights, sounds, tastes, and feelings, and, indeed, the box is every bit as important as its contents. Level II children were able to minimize some of the sensory data occurring during an experience as unimportant, to break the event into component parts based on labeled as opposed to perceived similarities, and to store the information acquired with similar ideas previously acquired. The problem created for many Level II children is that when they attempt to retrieve an experience, they can sometimes only access a portion of it; the experience may be mixed with other experiences stored similarly. For them, gifts received are valued for what they contain, the experience of the packaging these came in is cognitively banished to the general memory category of "trash" and recall of a specific box is difficult to extract from the trash heap. Ironically, the gift may be cognitively assigned to the broad category of gifts and it too may be difficult to recall as separate from other gifts in the child's memory. Level III children are able to engage in more sophisticated cognitive processing of events, more organized storage of those events in memory, and, therefore, more efficient retrieval of those memories at future dates. The primary difference between Level III children's experiences and memories and those of adults is that during Level III, time still does not play a major role in the lives of children.

Again, we can look to the child abuse literature for an example of the clinical importance of the Level III child's lack of temporal attunement. We noted that Level II children may change significant details of the story of their abuse each time they tell it, and we tied this to the fact that they may not have stored all aspects of the event together or that, if they did, their recall may be contaminated by other abusive experiences stored with the one they are attempting to recall. Most Level III children experience recall difficulties that are somewhat similar to those of the Level II child. If Level III child abuse victims are asked to tell the stories of their victimization repeatedly, most of the concrete details will remain the same. Unlike Level II children's stories, the perpetrator will not be wearing a green shirt in one story and a red shirt in a later version. However, a Level III child may report that the abuser removed his shirt before the molest in one version and after or during the molest in a later version. If the child experienced more than one abuse event, he or she may put them in different order each time the sequence is recited. Although this seems illogical and even impossible to members of the legal profession, it reflects Level III children's focus on contents over sequence or time as they acquire information. It is only as they near the end of this phase that time will take on the powerful organizing significance that it has for adults and become, therefore, the benchmark against which all experience is organized. Even the assumption that time will necessarily become central to children's experience may be culturally biased in that many non-Western cultures seem less bound by it than do Westerners. In this context, however, we will consider the acquisition of both a firm sense of the temporal order of things and the ability to engage in progressively more abstract thinking as hallmarks signaling the end of Level III.

The primary social task of Level III children is, for the most part, an extension of work begun in Level II. During that level, children generalized the attachment they developed with their primary caretakers to include, first, other adults and then peers. At the close of Level II, peers are important to children but they are still easily viewed as a source of potential competition for the resources held by adults. That is, Level II children tend to have their most satisfying peer relationships when they are embedded in positive, supportive relationships with other adults. Secure children will even do well with peers when no adults are present. Many an adult has walked in on two preschoolers who had been playing happily together in their room for hours only to find themselves embroiled in sudden interchild complaining or fighting. Over the course of Level III, children come to see their peers as possessing resources in their own right separate from what adults have to offer. Under significant stress the child is still more likely to seek out an adult than a peer, but the balance is slowly shifting. By adolescence, the balance has most often shifted and a peer may be viewed as the preferred source of solace when the child is in distress. Level III has been referred to as the Latency phase within the psychoanalytic literature (Freud, 1933), referring to the assumed calm of this period of development. In fact, it seems to be quite the opposite. Level III children are learning a complex array of cognitive and social skills that will affect the quality of their self-esteem and their interpersonal lives from this point forward.

Level III children are usually much better able to cope with trauma than are children at either of the previous levels. In fact, their coping often amazes adults who see the child as doing better than they might in the same situation. Besides depending on these children's developmental level, their capacity for coping will also depend on what, if any, trauma they have experienced in the previous stages and the degree to which the child coped with or resolved those experiences. Remember that in most cases when faced with a crisis, children will move back to the lowest developmental level over which they had mastery. Level III children who are new to the developmental phase or who feel unsure about their newly developing skills are likely to manifest Level II or even Level I behavior in the face of trauma. Many times adults are surprised to see a seemingly high functioning child whining and clinging when stressed, but this is not at all uncommon. Whereas Piaget (1952, 1959, 1967) believed that children's development proceeded in steps that prevented backsliding to earlier levels of functioning, we now know that is not the case. Children's development is more fluid, and optimal functioning at any one point in time is very much tied to the experience of an optimal environment.

Under good conditions, Level III children will display a good understanding of their experience. They are able to sort trauma based on causality and are much less likely to misattribute events than are Level II children. Typically, they still require much more direct, specific information about what has happened to them than will adults. They do not easily take someone else's word for things and may need to hear similar explanations from several people they trust before they accept what they have heard. At this level, they are also much more responsive to input from their peers. Whereas a Level I child's response is likely to be a direct mirror of that of his or her caretaker, the Level III child's response may mirror that of peers. If other children are distressed, he or she will be distressed, if they are not, he or she is not. In some situations, a peer's response may even outweigh the caretaker's response. Many a 10-year-old boy has been mortified when his mother fussed over his bleeding lip in front of the other boys on his baseball team. Many the mother of a 10-year-old boy has been confused when, a half hour later, when the teammates are out of sight, her son begins to cry about his hurt lip. This situation is a clear depiction of the mixed pull in social demands experienced by the Level III child, and later by adolescents (and their parents as well).

Finally, adults need to remember that Level III children are not always as well grounded in time as we think and to provide them with additional temporal anchors when they are under distress. When you are 8 or 9 years old, 6 weeks with your leg in a cast while a break heals can seem like an endless period of time. The child may complain that things are taking much longer than he or she expected and become frustrated by the parent's seeming lack of sympathy. When a trauma extends over time, even Level III children are better able to cope when provided with a calendar on which they can mark off the days to signal movement toward the end of their distress.

Regardless of the child's age, play activities geared toward remediating difficulties experienced by Level III children have several things in common. First, as with Level II children, the therapist's primary goal is to prevent regression to earlier levels of developmental functioning and subsequently to promote the child's normal developmental progress. As with Level II children, this may mean beginning the treatment with some activities that address earlier developmental needs in order to block the regressive pull experienced by children in distress. Second, effective play therapy with Level III children requires that the therapist provide the children with as much information about the nature of their problems as possible. This does not differ at all from the goal of play sessions with Level II children. What does differ is the relative balance between the use of cognitive versus experiential activities to convey that understanding. With Level II children, cognitive understanding is important, but most of their day-to-day learning and problem solving still happens through their experiences in the world. They do more than they think. As children pass through Level III, they are supposed to begin to think if not more than do, than at least before they do. For this reason, the therapist is likely to accompany even the most experiential interventions with progressively more complex cognitive and verbal processing as the play therapy proceeds. In fact, many older Level III children are quite capable of engaging in a talking-based therapy either from the outset or after some preparation through play sessions.

Finally, Level III play activities need to enhance the children's development of peer relationship skills and emotional investments. Whereas the therapist treating a Level I child included the child's primary caretaker and the therapist working with a Level II child included other adults important in the child's life, the therapist working with a Level III child is well advised to consider including peers in the child's play sessions. Peer inclusion can be accomplished in many ways. At the simplest level, they can be included in the form of pretend activities and role plays. Another possibility is to include one or more of the child's peers in the later sessions of an overall plan. Some play therapist's allow the child to bring a friend to the last session or two, for example. Many Level III children should also be considered for inclusion in a peer play therapy group. Unfortunately, there are often many fewer groups available than there are children who would benefit from these so that therapists are left to come up with creative alternatives.

The following 10 descriptions of a variety of cases and play activities illuminate the role that consideration of Level III developmental issues plays in the design of the intervention and draws attention to the impact of this developmental level on the child's response to the play activity. As with many of the Level II case examples, the histories of many of the children described in connection with the activities include problems that originated in earlier stages. However, in these activities it is the developmental tasks specific to Level III that are being addressed, rather than any potentially important earlier developmental issues.

LEVEL III: ACTIVITY 1[18]

Case Synopsis

David, 12 years old, lives with his parents. He has two adult sisters who do not live in the home. According to school personnel David has been exhibiting signs of hyperactivity, but David's parents are reluctant to place him on medication until all other interventions have been attempted.

During the intake David was able to relate appropriate expectations for classroom behavior in response to a number of situations the therapist presented, although he did display some impulsive behavior. Reports from other sources indicate that David is unable or unwilling to refrain from unacceptable behavior when others in the classroom begin acting out. David's teachers report that he does well in school in most academic tasks and generally seems to be developmentally on target. Although he was not thrilled with the idea of coming to therapy he agreed to it because he admitted to being sick of having his teachers yelling at him.

[18]This activity and the related interpretive material was developed by Michael Watson, M.A.

Target Psychopathology and Session Goal

It was hypothesized that David probably does have some degree of ADHD and that he requires more structure than most children his age in order to function optimally. It appeared that his need for social reinforcement during academic activities was not being met. It also seemed possible that David sought peer reinforcement because he believed he was unlikely to be reinforced by adults. The goal of the session was to assess his need for and response to structure, to assess his response to reinforcement from adults, and to begin helping him create some internal structures to maintain his behavior when others are acting out.

Treatment Phase

This activity was used in the first session of David's treatment.

Persons Attending the Session

Therapist and David.

Materials Needed/Preparation Required

Playmobil classroom set or other materials that could be used to set up a pretend classroom. Figures should include one to represent a teacher, David, and two of his peers.

Experiential Aspects of the Activity

David initially resisted becoming involved in pretend play, saying it was babyish. The therapist proceeded to dramatize some of the classroom incidents that were reported over the course of the intake. David rapidly became annoyed with the therapist's portrayal of the events saying, "No, no, no. That is not what happened. The other kids always start it. Let me show you." The therapist allowed David to take control of the teacher and David figures while the therapist retained control of the two peer figures and continued to have them act out. During this phase of the play, David exhibited many of his characteristic responses by choosing to join the peers in acting out and virtually ignoring the teacher figure.

After a short while the therapist traded figures with David. David greatly enjoyed taking on the role of the two who were acting out. The therapist created a scenario in which the David and teacher figures were allies who were going to resist every attempt on the part of the other children to engage them in acting out. The therapist then dared David to find a pretend acting out activity that the David and teacher figures could not withstand.

As David began to have his figures act out, the therapist enacted the teacher actively supporting the fact that the David figure was not being sucked into the action. The therapist verbalized strategies that the David figure might try to help prevent himself from joining in the acting out. The therapist portrayed David receiving elaborate rewards in terms of reduced schoolwork and extra free time because he was able to resist the peer acting out. Slowly, David began to lose interest in having the peer figures act out and wanted to resume play with the David and teacher figures. The therapist then allowed David to take control of all four figures while the therapist moved to interpret the action of the play.

Cognitive/Verbal Aspects of the Activity

The initial focus of the therapist's comments was on obtaining more information about how David experienced the problem situations at school.

Focus of Problem Solving

Direct problem solving was not attempted in this initial session on the topic of David's difficulties with self-control. Instead, the therapist modeled several potential solutions to David's problem during the time he had control of the David and teacher figures. The therapist also modeled the type of reinforcement David might expect from his teacher for these alternative behaviors.

Potential Interpretive Work

The following interpretations might be made as the opportunity arose and if David seemed receptive.

Reflections The therapist consistently reflected David's feelings of anxiety, anger at being punished, anger at peers for getting him in trouble, desire to fit in with peers, pleasure at receiving positive reinforcement, and attempts to dismiss the hurt he experienced when he did get in trouble.

Pattern Only two patterns were pointed out to David. One was his repeated demonstrations of going along with his peers in their acting out and the negative consequences that followed. The other was his increased ability to resist his peers when he was getting reinforcement from adults.

Simple Dynamic At this level, the therapist identified David's desire to fit in as one of his motivations for going along with his peers. The therapist also identified the degree to which David actually seemed to enjoy resisting temptation and receiving positive reinforcement from his teacher.

Generalized Dynamic   Because this activity was such a blatant re-creation of events in David's day-to-day life, no Generalized Dynamic interpretations were needed.

Genetic   Two potential genetic interpretations could be made if David seemed ready this early in the treatment. One would be to identify that David has probably always had difficulty staying on task when things around him got hectic. This would serve as a lead into later discussing the nature of his actual deficits. The other interpretation is that David has never really felt like he fit in with peers and that he would very much like to have more peer friends. This would set up working to enhance David's positive peer social skills.

Plan for Future Sessions

The therapist's aim was to engage David in some additional direct role playing in which strategies for managing his problem behavior in the classroom could be developed directly. The therapist planned to consult with the school about ways to support and reinforce any attempts David might make to resist becoming involved in others' acting out. The therapist planned to do some education with David regarding ADHD should this prove necessary. Finally, the therapist also planned to refer David to a peer therapy group to facilitate his development of improved peer social skills so that David could more effectively meet his needs for positive interactions with peers.

LEVEL III: ACTIVITY 2[19]

Case Synopsis

Aaron is a 9-year-old boy who lives with his single mother. His mother reported that Aaron had very few peer friends because he tended to be very controlling in his interactions. School personnel reported that Aaron had verbal outbursts in class, would not listen to his peers, and had difficulty sharing and cooperating in classroom activities. Because Aaron's mother worked an evening shift, he was home alone a great deal and was not used to having to interact with other children. Aaron's mother reported that he was able to engage in

[19]This activity and the related interpretive material was developed by Emily Piper, M.A.

elaborate pretend play by himself for sustained periods of time.

Target Psychopathology and Session Goal

It was hypothesized that Aaron viewed peers as both competition for the attention of adults and interfering with his ability to engage in activities he uses to meet his own needs. The goal of the session was to encourage Aaron to identify the needs of others and to begin to view peers as a potential resource for getting his own needs met.

Treatment Phase

This session was conducted several weeks into Aaron's treatment once he had become comfortable in engaging in some pretend play with the therapist.

Persons Attending the Session

Therapist and Aaron.

Materials Needed/Preparation Required

The main part of this activity requires a simple container that could be used as a pretend rocket ship. The therapist could construct something from a cardboard box before the session or could engage Aaron in building the craft himself in an earlier session.

The materials needed for the session may be as elaborate or simple as the therapist desires. The object is to include both some items that would be necessary in a survival situation and some that would be very appealing to a child Aaron's age. The following list is suggested: 2 pillows, 2 small blankets, small first-aid kit, 2 small boxes of animal crackers, 2 boxed servings of juice, 2 walkie-talkies, 2 space helmets, a teddy bear, magnifying glass, comic book, candy, pail and shovel, and a small jar of confetti labeled "Magical Moon Dust."

Experiential Aspects of the Activity

The activity was presented as a very important moon mission that Aaron would undertake with an imaginary friend to try to retrieve the Moon King's lost gold. Aaron was shown the array of items available to him for stocking his spaceship and was told that to prevent the rocket from being too heavy to take off he could only choose 10 items to take along. Aaron was reminded that he must plan carefully, thinking of possible emergencies and selecting the most potentially useful items. As Aaron selected items, the therapist periodically reminded him that he was packing for two. She even suggested that Aaron take on the role of the imaginary friend while he selected a few of the items. She also mentioned that once Aaron reached the moon there would be some surprises and that if he did not have the right equipment he and his imaginary friend would fail in their mission. Once Aaron had chosen the 10 items these where checked and discussed by the Moon Trip Inspector (therapist).

Cognitive/Verbal Aspects of the Activity

Because Aaron was quite bright and used to interacting with adults, a great deal of this activity was conducted on a verbal level.

Focus of Problem Solving

The primary problem solving focused on identifying basic needs and the difficulties of sharing. Actual problem solving was completed relative to each item that Aaron selected for the trip. To prevent this from becoming boring and repetitive, the Moon Trip Inspector (MTI) engaged in as much joking as possible and even used some occasional sarcasm. For example, when Aaron chose the comic book, the MTI said, "I can certainly see where you will need that. Might run across some cartoon-deprived monsters and then you'll be able to read them to sleep and get past them." The therapist worked hard to ensure that Aaron did not feel demeaned at any time and yet kept the activity light enough that Aaron did not mind the continuous problem solving in which they were engaged. At several points, the therapist chose to take on the role of the imaginary friend to push Aaron to recognize the needs of his peer.

Potential Interpretive Work

In this role play the problem solving was the central focus of the work. Interpretation was used to support and expand the problem-solving process.

Reflections The therapist identified the conflict Aaron experienced over taking things he liked as opposed to taking things he might need. She also reflected his feelings that taking along another person was a burden and his fear that the rocket ship would not hold everything they needed. Lastly, she reflected his annoyance with her for setting the 10-item limit.

Pattern The primary pattern identified was Aaron's tendency to make selections of single items rather than choosing two of anything. The therapist also noted that he tended to gravitate toward interesting as opposed to

practical items and that he frequently became heavily involved in the pretend aspect of the play.

Simple Dynamic "Traveling or playing alone is more fun because you don't have to worry about what the other person wants." "It is frustrating and a little scary when you have to worry that you might not have everything you need." "Boy, you sure do love pretending."

Generalized Dynamic "I'll bet it is easier to play alone at school because you don't have to worry about what the other person wants or needs." "I think that sometimes you don't like to share or play with other children because you worry that there won't be enough to go around." "Pretending is a lot of fun because then everyone else always does what you want and you can always have everything you need."

Genetic "It seems like one of the reasons you worry about not having everything you need is because you have spent a lot of time worrying if your mom will be there when you need her." "It seems like it's hard to learn to play with and consider other kids when you have gotten to be so good at taking care of yourself when your mom is not at home."

Plan for Future Sessions

The actual trip to the moon could take place later in the same session or during the next session. Once there, he and his imaginary friend would begin the process of locating the gold (a number of gold-colored items such as chocolate coins, a pen, or stickers that the therapist hid prior to the session). The therapist would encourage Aaron to role play having problem-solving discussions with his imaginary friend as the search proceeded. In this case, the therapist took on the role of creating various forms of interference that required Aaron and his friend to use some of the materials they brought along to solve the crisis. For example, the therapist took on the role of a moon monster that could only be rendered friendly by the "Magical Moon Dust." Because this was not one of the items Aaron chose to bring, he and his friend had to come up with an alternate plan (they decided to feed the monster animal crackers). When a number of gold items were located, Aaron was given his choice of two to take back to earth. One item was to be for him and one for his imaginary friend.

In subsequent sessions there was more emphasis on cooperative interactions with the therapist, and eventually Aaron was to be included in a peer group to learn and practice needed social skills and to provide him with experiences in which he saw his peers as potential resources.

LEVEL III: ACTIVITY 3[20]

Case Synopsis

Rochelle is an 11-year-old girl who is the middle child of five siblings. There was a family history of neglect and abuse. Rochelle showed signs of an insecure attachment to her mother and only minimally interacted with other children. She was much more likely to interact with adults. Her life had been quite chaotic to this point, involving several moves and two out-of-home placements. She was frequently self-critical.

Target Psychopathology and Session Goal

It was hypothesized that Rochelle had come to view the world as a hostile and unpredictable place and that she did not expect to have her needs for safety or nurturance met consistently. It was also hypothesized that she had developed an autoplastic way of responding to this by believing that she was generally a bad child who somehow brought all of this unpleasantness upon herself. This gave her some sense of control in that it meant her life could change if she could change. It also tended to reduce the degree to which others criticized her because she beat them to it. Unfortunately, the strategy cost her any ability to engage in positive self-evaluation. The goal of the session was to facilitate Rochelle's development of a more positive self-image and to enable her to impose some sense of structure or order on her life to this point. It was hoped that the sense of organization would satisfy Rochelle's need for control and allow her to begin evaluating herself more positively.

Treatment Phase

This activity would be suitable for use early in treatment, during either the Introduction and Exploration phase or the Tentative Acceptance phase. It could be repeated during the Growing and Trusting phase and even potentially used as a termination activity that would provide the client with a souvenir or summary of her treatment experience. In Rochelle's case, it was used repeatedly throughout the therapy, occupying 10 to 20 minutes of several sessions.

Persons Attending the Session

Therapist and Rochelle.

[20]This activity and the related interpretive material was developed jointly by Sharon Picard and Janet E. Bucklin, M.A.

Materials Needed/Preparation Required

Sheets of $8\frac{1}{2}'' \times 11''$ paper, pencils, pens and crayons, markers, or paints.

Experiential Aspects of the Activity

The actual activity is to make a book reflecting two things. One is the sequence of events in Rochelle's life and the other is Rochelle's positive personal characteristics. The session was very structured to establish the necessary order and sequencing. The idea of an autobiography was introduced as an activity that would be completed over parts of the next several sessions and was begun by having Rochelle draw a self-portrait that was used for the initial cover of the book. (As Rochelle's self-esteem improved over the course of treatment, a later, more vibrant self-portrait was substituted for the original cover, which became one of the pages in the book showing her at the beginning of therapy.) Over a number of weeks, pages where added to the book that included both events from Rochelle's life and positive things she had said, done, or reported to the therapist. The therapist focused on having Rochelle complete at least one picture of an event in her life during each session. These pictures were completed in order, beginning with Rochelle's earliest memory and moving in sequence to her present living situation and school. The maintenance of the sequence was important to enhance Rochelle's sense of organization and control. When there were doubts about details of her life or the sequence of particular events, Rochelle was encouraged to consult her mother for additional information so that she and the therapist could be sure they were getting the autobiography down just right.

Initially, the therapist worked alongside Rochelle, completing additional pages for the book. These pages depicted Rochelle's special attributes. One was a picture of just her eyes showing how blue they were and comparing them to other pleasant blues such as the sky and a flower. Another showed Rochelle on a swing with a simple statement about how high she was able to swing. The therapist was careful to keep these pictures simple and to include a variety of things that were both innate aspects of Rochelle's person as well as behaviors and skills. Over time, the therapist switched tasks with Rochelle. The therapist would add life event pages under Rochelle's direction while Rochelle completed the positive self-image pages.

The skeleton of the book was completed in the first few sessions by using much of the history that the therapist had obtained. It was then expanded over sessions to include progressively more detail and to focus on things that Rochelle thought were important. As termination approached, a section was added to depict the history of the therapy relationship.

Cognitive/Verbal Aspects of the Activity

Although the therapist commented frequently on both the content and process of the activity, it was the nature of the task itself that was believed to be the most therapeutic.

Focus of Problem Solving

Early problem solving focused on how Rochelle might find out more about her life and how she could balance the parts that seemed painful with more pleasant thoughts or experiences. As the treatment progressed, problem solving focused on things Rochelle could do that made her feel good about herself and how she could be more assertive in complaining when things at home or school became chaotic.

Potential Interpretive Work

Interpretation was used to support and expand the problem solving that Rochelle did with respect to separating her feelings about her family, especially her parents, from how she felt about herself.

Reflections   The therapist consistently reflected the feelings of all of the characters depicted in Rochelle's drawings. She reflected all positive and negative feelings Rochelle displayed relative to any aspect of herself. She made a special effort to point out times when an action or event made someone in the situation feel differently from the way Rochelle felt. The idea was to identify occasions when others felt sad or angry but in ways that did not involve Rochelle. The therapist also reflected the notion that one of the motives behind Rochelle's self-criticism was to elicit compliments from those around her. Lastly, the therapist reflected Rochelle's anxiety whenever she (the therapist) criticized Rochelle's parents or their past behavior in any way.

Pattern   The therapist identified two patterns. One was Rochelle's tendency to criticize her own drawings while complimenting the therapist's drawings. The other was Rochelle's tendency to make excuses for the unpleasant things that her parents did or that happened in her family.

Simple Dynamic   "I think you really like compliments but you are afraid that if you ask for them directly you won't get them, so instead you say bad things about yourself trying to get me to contradict

you." "It seems very scary for you to hear me say that something your parents did was not OK."

Generalized Dynamic   Because this task directly involved content from Rochelle's life, there was not much need for generalized dynamic interpretation. The therapist did, however, repeatedly point out that the way Rochelle interacted with her was probably very similar to the way she interacted with other adults, as well as with her peers. The therapist also noted, "I'll bet you are pretty good at keeping other kids from saying bad things about you because you are always saying them first."

Genetic   "I think you very much want to love your parents in spite of the bad things they sometimes do, but that has always been a pretty hard thing to do. After a while it just got easier to think you were bad and deserved what happened rather than to try and make up an excuse for every new bad thing they did. That way you could love them no matter what. The problem is now you're stuck thinking you're bad even when you're not and you don't love yourself very much."

Plan for Future Sessions

In future sessions Rochelle would be encouraged to continue her autobiography and to expand it to depict more of the therapy process and her own growth. The therapist will continue to have Rochelle include both self-descriptive pictures and ones that show both positive and negative events in her life and family. Simultaneous consultation with Rochelle's parents would be important to help them manage those times when Rochelle might become critical of their behavior. Consultation with the school to involve them in supporting and reinforcing the development of Rochelle's self-esteem would also be important.

LEVEL III: ACTIVITY 4[21]

Case Synopsis

Linda is a 10-year-old girl with a history of neglect virtually from birth. She was abandoned by her mother and now lives in a foster home. She was very shy and reserved. Because of her low self-esteem she had difficulty interacting with peers, although she was more comfortable with adults. She even had difficulty when peers took the initiative and approached her and when she felt she was being observed, such as when reading aloud in class.

---

[21]This activity and the related interpretive material was developed by Sharon Picard.

Target Psychopathology and Session Goal

The therapist hypothesized that Linda believed it was very unlikely that other adults would meet her needs for nurturance and even less likely that peers would or could do so. She responded to this by withdrawing to avoid disappointment. This withdrawal was so severe that it prevented Linda from receiving enough feedback to develop an adequate sense of herself, thereby continuously decreasing her sense of self-worth to the point of diminishing her sense of self. It was almost as if Linda believed that if she just disappeared it would eliminate the reality of her abandonment. The goal of the session was to begin developing Linda's sense of self in ways that brought her positive responses from both adults and peers. It was hoped that Linda could use this positive feedback to counteract the devastating effects of her history of neglect and abandonment.

Treatment Phase

This activity was designed to be repeated at intervals throughout Linda's therapy. It served as an excellent orientation activity. The session described is from the Growing and Trusting phase of treatment.

Persons Attending the Session

Therapist and Linda.

Materials Needed/Preparation Required

Large piece of paper (butcher, easel pad sheets, etc.), crayons or markers, and a mirror.

Experiential Aspects of the Activity

The therapist began the session by tracing Linda's outline on the paper. The therapist worked slowly and commented on attributes of each of the parts of Linda's body she was tracing. Next, the therapist and Linda filled in the outline based on Linda's description of herself. The description included both physical and intrinsic traits. The mirror was used whenever Linda seemed to falter in her attempts to describe herself physically, especially relative to facial details. Abstract attributes were depicted with symbols or slogans. For example, Linda said she was enjoying the activity with the therapist so they drew her with a smiling mouth. When Linda said she liked to do well in school, the therapist added the slogan "Hardworking Student" to the T-shirt they had already drawn. Whenever Linda seemed stuck in her description, the therapist added an obser-

vation so that the activity did not drag. At the end of the session Linda wanted to take the picture home and was allowed to do so.

Cognitive/Verbal Aspects of the Activity

Most of the verbal activity consisted of comments made by the therapist to support Linda's sustained involvement.

Focus of Problem Solving

The problem solving focused on developing strategies by which Linda could come to know herself and her attributes better. Most of the initial work was done by using the mirror as one potential solution to the problem of self-observation. Because Linda tended to be so withdrawn, the therapist did most of the problem solving herself while talking out loud.

Potential Interpretive Work

The therapist covered a wide variety of content in the course of completing the activity with Linda.

Reflections   The therapist reflected Linda's anxiety both when she could not think of a characteristic to add to the picture and when she felt uncomfortable verbalizing those things she had thought of. Also reflected were Linda's fear of criticism, her feelings of being ignored, her enjoyment of some parts of the task, and her difficulty identifying any characteristics beyond her physical appearance.

Pattern   The therapist noted that Linda seemed to wait to be spoken to before she spoke and noted her intermittent withdrawal from interaction with the therapist.

Simple Dynamic   "Not speaking until spoken to makes you feel safer because there isn't much chance you will say something I might disagree with." "Sometimes you seem to worry about what I'm thinking or doing so much that you sort of leave. You're body is still here but it seems like your head took a vacation."

Generalized Dynamic   Each of the preceding interpretations was connected to specific events that occurred at school. "I'll bet you don't like to play with other kids because they might make fun of you and you already feel bad enough." "So long as people don't know you they can't hurt you."

Genetic   "I think all of this started when you were just a little kid. You found out that your mom was nicer to you if you stayed real quiet and out of her way. Now you just want to make sure that you don't upset anyone so that they don't bother you and so they don't have any reason to leave you. The problem is you seem to have stayed quiet so long that you stopped noticing yourself and it seems like you have forgotten who you are."

Plan for Future Sessions

The therapist added activities that further enhanced Linda's self-awareness and self-image. These included other self-portraits and an autobiography, as described in another activity in this text. As Linda came to know herself better, the sessions focused on identifying her needs and developing strategies for getting those needs met.

LEVEL III: ACTIVITY 5[22]

Case Synopsis

Mike was a 7-year-old boy who had grown up in a household in which both parents were substance abusers. Although both parents cared for him and were not abusive, their lives tended to be chaotic, with frequent moves and changes of employment. Similarly, his parents' moods tended to be rather erratic depending on their substance use. Mike was referred to treatment because his own behavior in school tended to be rather erratic. He had some peer friends but tended to be moody and change "best friends" often. Mike's sister had died when she was 10 months old and Mike was 6 years old. Since that time, he became progressively more anxious and had difficulty concentrating in school.

Target Psychopathology and Session Goal

It was hypothesized that Mike's needs for nurturance were not consistently met and that this led to his moody responses. It was also hypothesized that his sister's death increased his separation anxiety as his parent's became quite depressed and even less available. Mike did not talk about himself because he feared the complaints would create even more distance between himself and his parents. On some level he also believed that his parent's should have prevented his sister's death and feared that they might not be able to prevent his. There may also have been some fear on his part that he contributed to his sister's death should he have had

[22]This activity and the related interpretive material was developed by Stamatoula Vagelatos.

any feelings of sibling rivalry when she was born. The goal of the session was to increase his self-expression so as to provide the therapist with information that could be used in future problem solving.

Treatment Phase

This activity would be suited for use at any stage except for the Negative Reaction phase. As described, it was used during the Tentative Acceptance phase.

Persons Attending the Session

Therapist and Mike.

Materials Needed/Preparation Required

Large cardboard bricks.

Experiential Aspects of the Activity

The therapist introduced the activity as simply building the house in which Mike lived. They started by attempting to construct the basic layout of his house but then focused on re-creating the layout of his own room, which he had shared with his infant sister. Mike made a bed for himself and his sister. He laid down and pretended to be asleep and insisted that the therapist do the same. He then pretended to wake up and check on everyone in the household, including his sister. He then pretended to wake everyone up and prepare them breakfast. He repeated this entire scenario four different times.

Cognitive/Verbal Aspects of the Activity

Because this activity was initiated very early in the therapy, the focus of all of the verbal components was on the identification of Mike's thoughts and feelings regarding his parents and his sister's death.

Focus of Problem Solving

Very little problem solving was attempted other than to identify the degree to which Mike's feelings of responsibility made it difficult for him to sleep through the night.

Potential Interpretive Work

Again, because this activity was used early in the treatment the interpretations were limited. The primary goal was the identification of Mike's underlying feelings and the degree to which these posed a problem or were unpleasant.

Reflections The therapist identified Mike's anxiety, feelings of responsibility, desire to re-create a scene in which his sister was still present, his fear of other people in his family dying, and Mike's own fear of dying. "Pretending that your sister is still alive is part fun part yucky. It is fun because, for a little while, it seems like it never happened. It's yucky because each time you remember that she really is dead." Mike's positive affect in response to checking on others was also noted. "Now that you know everyone is OK you feel better."

Pattern The repetition of the sleeping, waking, and checking on other's health and safety was simply stated. "That is the fourth time you've gotten up and checked to see if everyone was OK before you could go back to sleep."

Simple Dynamic The therapist identified a relationship between the repeated checking on the health and safety of others as a way of reducing Mike's anxiety by giving him a sense of control. "When you wake up in the night you get scared that maybe everyone isn't OK. Then you get up and check on them. When you are sure they are all right then you feel better and can go back to sleep."

Generalized Dynamic Although this content might not be used in the first session, the therapist would have created a good lead into discussing Mike's anxiety about the welfare of his family whenever they were out of his sight. This could be applied to situations in which he was separated for any reason, such as going to school or even playing with friends in the yard.

Genetic The therapist might wish to go ahead and make at least one connection to the extremely painful content underlying Mike's separation anxiety even though a secure therapeutic relationship has not been developed. In this case, the therapist simply said, "This kind of pretending must be hard for you since your sister died not too long ago." This statement served several functions. One, it let the child know that the therapist already knew the painful content and was able to address it without undue discomfort. Second, it demonstrated the degree to which the therapist empathized with the child's distress and saw the impact of that distress on the present situation. And finally, it set the stage for future discussions of the painful content.

Plan for Future Sessions The therapist planned activities that continued to pull for themes of separation and death anxiety. The interpretive work focused more on the genetic origins of these feelings and then began to shift toward engaging Mike in additional problem solving that provided him with alternative strategies for addressing his feelings of guilt and anxiety without taking on undue responsibility. Additionally, the focus of the genetic work widened to include identifying the degree to which Mike's chaotic life situation and his parents' substance use interacted with the reality of his sister's death to intensify whatever negative feelings he was experiencing.

LEVEL III: ACTIVITY 6[23]

Case Synopsis

Jane was an 11-year-old girl who constantly engaged in impulsive and aggressive play. She had been abused by her mother, had been removed from that home, and was placed with her maternal grandmother at the time of treatment. Eventual reunification was planned but not imminent. Jane was defiant at home and school and seemed not to understand the importance or value of following rules. Her grandmother often felt sorry for Jane and gave in to her demands. Jane's teachers were less sympathetic and often threatened or carried out punishments for disruptive or aggressive behavior.

Target Psychopathology and Session Goal

It appeared that Jane's needs for safety and consistency and predictability in her environment had not been met by her mother and that she had come to see the world as a dangerous place where adults were untrustworthy. Because of this, Jane acted out aggressively in order to maintain control over situations and to attempt to meet her own needs instead of relying on others. Jane saw rules as obstacles that stood in the way of her getting her needs met. Her behavior was maintained by the intermittent successes she achieved. The goal of this session was to create an experience in which Jane would learn the value of rules.

Treatment Phase

This activity would be suited to any treatment phase but seems particularly appropriate for the Introduction and Exploration or early Growing and Trusting phases. In this case is was used in the Negative Reaction phase.

Persons Attending the Session

Jane and the therapist.

---

[23]This activity and the related interpretive material was developed by Janet E. Bucklin, M.A.

Materials Needed/Preparation Required

The plastic floor mat from the game Twister. The mat is a large white plastic sheet with four columns each containing four circles (about 9 inches in diameter) of a particular color. There is a red, green, yellow, and blue column. The activity also requires paper cups and jellybeans in colors to match the circles on the mat (red, green, yellow, and blue). Prior to the session, the therapist assigned a domain in Jane's life to each of the colors on the mat (blue, interactions with mom; yellow, school; green, interactions with peers; red, life with grandma). The therapist then made up three questions for each domain and taped these to each of the circles on the mat. One circle in each column was left empty. All of the questions required the player to identify why a rule in that particular domain should be followed (e.g., Why should you tell your friends the truth?)

Experiential Aspects of the Activity

The game was introduced as one that required reading and responding to questions that were taped to each circle on the Twister mat. Jane and the therapist were to take turns stepping onto a circle and then asking the other person the question taped to that circle. If the other person answered correctly both received a jellybean of the color corresponding to the dot on which the player was standing. A response that simply identified avoiding negative consequences as a rationale was rewarded with a single jellybean. A response that gave a prosocial rationale earned two jelly beans. Stepping onto an empty circle allowed the player to ask any question they desired of the other person. The object of the game was to obtain six jellybeans of the same color.

Initially, Jane was eager to play the game. In spite of this, she gave a completely inappropriate response to the first question and did not earn any jellybeans. As the therapist went to take her turn, Jane said that she did not want the therapist to play and that she, Jane, should get another turn. The therapist acknowledged Jane's objections but took her turn anyway while modeling both a one- and a two-jellybean response to her question. Jane took her next turn and intentionally gave a one-jellybean response. The therapist praised her and took a turn, again modeling both levels of response. Realizing that the therapist now had four jellybeans Jane escalated her noncompliance. She ate her only jellybean and refused to answer any more questions, saying the game was stupid. The therapist took a turn, earned two jellybeans, and declared herself the winner of that round. The therapist then replaced the questions on the mat and suggested Jane go first this time.

Jane refused to take the first turn in the second game.

However, just as the therapist bent over to pick up her first question Jane interrupted and said, "You said I could go first," and grabbed the question from the therapist. The therapist moved away slightly and acted as if the confrontation had not occurred. Instead of setting limits, she simply allowed Jane to go first. Although Jane continued to pout she became progressively more engaged and won the next round.

Cognitive/Verbal Aspects of the Activity

This activity provided the therapist with multiple opportunities to interpret Jane's feelings, thoughts, and behavior, as well as providing repeated openings to introduce both abstract and concrete problem solving.

Focus of Problem Solving

Jane was engaged in problem solving at two levels. The therapist modeled problem solving relative to the questions that were included in the game. She stated out loud both the rationale for a given rule and potential negative outcomes that could result from not following the rule. She identified consequences that would be negative, for the person breaking the rule as well as the impact of the violation on others. All of this problem solving was sufficiently distant and abstract that Jane did not see it as particularly threatening.

The therapist also problem solved each situation in the session in which Jane was not getting her needs met. She focused primarily on Jane's desire to be in control and the degree to which that need interfered with fulfilling her need for primary reinforcement (jellybeans). Where possible, the therapist differentiated between gaining control by controlling oneself and controlling others. That is, Jane did not earn jellybeans by attempting to bully the therapist. Jane did earn jellybeans when she was able to control her own behavior and respond to questions, no matter how frustrated she was with the therapist.

Potential Interpretive Work

All of the interpretive work focused on identifying those elements that were needed to complete the various stages of the problem solving process.

Reflections   The therapist worked to identify Jane's desire to

• Be the boss, "Boy, you don't want to follow my rules at all." "You sure seem happier when you do things the way you want to rather than the way I want you to."
• Maximize her rewards, "You want to make sure

you have as many, or more, jellybeans than I do." "Now that you have the hang of this game it sure is important to you to earn two jellybeans on every turn."

• Avoid depending on others, "I can tell that you are not happy with the fact that I get to hand out the jellybeans in this game."

• Be angry when rewards were withheld, "Even though you knew you wouldn't get a jellybean if you didn't answer the question you sure are mad at me for not giving in and letting you have one anyway." "The way you are looking at me makes me think that you have decided I'm just a mean person."

Pattern   The primary pattern the therapist identified was the degree to which Jane's desire for control interfered with, rather than increased, her ability to maximize the rewards she received. "Every time you decide not to follow the rules you win because you do what you want, but you lose because you don't get any jellybeans."

Simple Dynamic   Again, the therapist emphasized the pros and cons of control versus compliance. "Not following the rules make you feel powerful and like you are the boss but it keeps you hungry." "Following the rules means you are the boss of yourself and not me and it gets you fed."

Generalized Dynamic   "I'll bet you're trying to see who I'm going to act like, your grandma or your teacher. Grandma gives in if you fight hard enough. Your teachers punish you when you fight the rules." The therapist then went on to identify a third possibility, "I don't do either. I don't give in but I don't punish if you don't want to play by the rules of the game. Here you get to decide whether or not you want to play. I will make sure you always get a reward if you follow the rules."

Genetic   "I think you decided that it was important to be the boss a long time ago when your mom used to hit you. When she was the boss you didn't get taken care of very well and you got hit. I think you figured if you were the boss you could make sure you were safe and that you got what you needed, and sometimes it works but sometimes it actually causes more problems."

Plan for Future Sessions

As Jane was engaged in the problem-solving process, the focus was on developing strategies so that she felt both safe and able to get her needs met without re-

sorting to aggressive control. The therapist continued to engage her in activities that required Jane to make a choice between compliance and reward. All activities also required that Jane interact directly with the therapist, as part of Jane's difficulties had to do with trusting adults. As the treatment progressed, the complexity of the rules of the games and activities were increased, and Jane was involved in developing the rules and rewards to increase her sense of control and her investment in problem solving geared toward preventing problems.

LEVEL III: ACTIVITY 7[24]

Case Synopsis

Susan is a 10-year-old girl who is also an only child. She grew up in a rural area where she was relatively isolated from peers up until she began attending school. Once in school, she was so shy and withdrawn that her social problems seemed to increase rather than decrease. At this time, she seems to have trouble identifying the thoughts and feelings of other children so that she tends to be somewhat inappropriate both when she initiates or responds to interactions.

Target Psychopathology and Session Goal

Susan's need for positive social contact with her peers was not being met. The therapist hypothesized that Susan's difficulties identifying emotions in others stemmed from lack of contact rather than from either cognitive deficits or trauma. The goal of the session was both to teach Susan to use cues to identify the thoughts and feelings of others and to provide her with some safe practice.

Treatment Phase

This activity would be suitable for use in the early Growing and Trusting phase of treatment. It does not require a strong working relationship between the child and the therapist, but the child does have to be ready to work on their peer social problems fairly directly. The weaker the working relationship the more the content of any interpretation or problem solving that was done would need to avoid specific reference to the child client. In this case, it was used during the early Growing and Trusting phase.

---

[24]This activity and the related interpretive material was developed by Michael Watson, M.A.

Persons Attending the Session

Susan and the therapist. This activity could also be readily adapted for the early stages of a peer play therapy group.

Materials Needed/Preparation Required

This activity is based on the Color-Your-Life technique (CYL) (O'Connor, 1983). In that activity, the child is taught to pair colors and feelings to provide the child with a way of communicating feelings directly through art. To use this activity successfully, the therapist should either use the CYL with the child in a previous session or should use the CYL introduction to set up this activity. The introduction simply teaches the child color–emotion pairs common in the target culture. Common color–emotion pairs in Anglo- and Euro-American cultures are red = angry, purple = rage, blue = sad, black = very sad, yellow = happy, green = jealous, and brown = bored. Many children also seem to pair orange with excited.

This activity requires a coloring book or black and white story book that has no words. The therapist could use a commercial book with suitable pictures or could create one. The pictures should not be so complex that the process of coloring overshadows the process of identifying the thoughts and feelings of the characters in the pictures. The child will also need crayons or colored pencils in red, purple, blue, yellow, green, orange, brown, and black, or whatever seems suited to the child and the cultural context in which the child is embedded.

Experiential Aspects of the Activity

Susan had completed the CYL technique in a previous session. She had readily grasped the concept and was able to use it to depict quite a lot of detail about her own emotional experience. The therapist introduced this task as an extension of the CYL, which seemed to draw Susan right into the activity. The therapist presented the coloring book and told Susan that their job would be to create a story to go with the pictures and to color them in. She was also told that in a future session, they would fill in the empty balloons over the character's heads with dialogue. (The creation of dialogue was deferred to prevent Susan from avoiding the character's affect by addressing only the cognitive elements of the task.) She was told that in addition to the regular coloring she would need to give each character an "aura" that let others know how that character was feeling.

Susan's anxiety visibly increased when the idea of identifying the character's affects was introduced. The therapist identified this and chose to engage in some problem solving to structure the activity. With Susan, he decided that they should make the task smaller and complete it in stages. First, the therapist reduced the number of pictures to just three. These were the equivalent of a beginning, middle, and end to a story. Then the therapist and Susan took turns making up a segment of the story to go with each picture. The therapist went first so that Susan only had to make up one segment and so that he could structure the story in a way that it would be appropriate no matter how Susan misinterpreted the affect of the character in the middle segment. The therapist and Susan then worked together coloring in each picture. With this much structure, Susan was willing to risk taking turns with the therapist identifying the feelings of the characters and adding a suitable aura.

Cognitive/Verbal Aspects of the Activity

This activity involves more teaching than many of the other activities presented so far. The potential for this to make the child passive in the session is countered by keeping her actively engaged in all phases of its completion.

Focus of Problem Solving

In this session, the therapist used problem solving to structure the session itself to better meet Susan's needs. This allowed the therapist to demonstrate the utility of problem solving in day-to-day life. Problem solving was also used to help Susan uncover cues in each of the pictures that she could use to identify the character's thoughts and feelings.

Potential Interpretive Work

Interpretation in this session was limited because of the educational nature of the task. The therapist used interpretation to identify Susan's anxiety about trying to identify other people's affects. He also used it to draw comparisons between Susan's feelings and those of the various characters.

Reflections "Boy, does this whole thing seem to make you nervous." "You seem really worried that you will make a mistake." "You didn't seem this nervous when we did the CYL last week."

Pattern "Every time we start to talk about the pictures you switch to talking about something you did."

"I just noticed that you are talking more about what we did last session than what we are doing this session."

Simple Dynamic   "Figuring out other people's feelings seems to make you a lot more nervous than looking at your own feelings."

Generalized Dynamic   "I'll bet that what is going on in here is a lot like what happens when you get around other kids. You don't always know what is going on and that makes you nervous. The more nervous you get the less you know what is going on and so you try to talk about something else."

Genetic   The therapist chose not to make a genetic interpretation given that there was no seminal event or conflict in this case. However, a genetic interpretation might serve to alleviate any feelings Susan may have that she is defective because of the peer difficulties she is having. For example, the therapist might say, "I think this is hard for you because you have spent most of your life with grown-ups and not kids, so you never got much practice figuring out what other kids are all about."

Plan for Future Sessions

The therapist gradually increased the complexity and reality base of the tasks presented. The stories created became longer, with content progressively more similar to Susan's day-to-day life. Puppet plays and role plays were substituted to facilitate generalization of Susan's learning to real-life situations. Finally, Susan was transferred to a short-term, peer socialization group once she had acquired some basic skills and had learned to manage her anxiety.

LEVEL III: ACTIVITY 8[25]

Case Synopsis

Gerald was an 8-year-old child who was the second of three children in an intact family. Both parents worked full time outside of the home at very demanding professional careers. At the time of referral, both parents were experiencing substantial job-related stress that left them minimally available to the children or each other after work. Gerald was a bright child who competed with his siblings for his parents' attention and did not share or take turns. He intruded on others and pushed when anyone else got something he wanted.

[25]This activity and the related interpretive material was developed by Mary Nafpaktitis, M.A.

ed. His mother was afraid that Gerald might injure his younger sibling if the rivalry continued.

Target Psychopathology and Session Goal

Gerald's need for emotional supplies from his parents was not being met. It was likely that the origins of the problem lay in his being a middle child who may have always felt he did not get as much as the older or the younger child. The problem appears to have been compounded by his parents' present unavailability. Furthermore, Gerald did not seem to see his siblings as potential sources of emotional supplies. He competed with his siblings for what he viewed as limited parental supplies. He viewed sharing and turn taking as interfering with his access to those supplies. The goal of the session was to provide Gerald with an experience in which his needs were met as the result of sharing and turn taking.

Treatment Phase

This activity would lend itself to any phase of treatment. It may be particularly well suited to the Negative Reaction phase, as it allows for a certain amount of structured acting out. It will probably prove most effective relatively early in treatment. The level of interpretation should be kept relatively low so as not to prevent the child's direct interaction with the therapist. It was used during the Negative Reaction phase of Gerald's play therapy.

Persons Attending the Session

Gerald and the therapist.

Materials Needed/Preparation Required

Several competitive games that can be played relatively quickly and that require turn taking. An indoor basketball game or ring toss game would be particularly well suited to the activity and the interests of a child this age. The focus on the rules can be enhanced if they are written on a large sheet of paper hung on the wall as they are developed. The therapist should also have primary reinforcers (such as small candies, chips, or pretzels) available in case they are needed to initiate or maintain the child's involvement.

Experiential Aspects of the Activity

The therapist chose an indoor basketball game as the activity for this session. The therapist then asked Gerald to participate in making up rules for the game. The rules were written on an easel pad that the therapist had hanging on the wall. Their rules were as follows:

- Each person could shoot a maximum of four times in any one turn
- Shots could be made from anywhere in the room
- The defensive player could get rebounds, in which case that person became the offensive player
- No score would be kept

The therapist helped Gerald identify several spots from which he was usually successful in making shots and the game began. As the game progressed, the therapist became more intrusive and challenging by guarding Gerald, making eye contact, bumping into him, and trying hard to get rebounds. She also worked to make the game more interactive and fun by laughing and by minimizing her own focus on scoring. Instead of trying to make a basket, she would intentionally shoot the ball over Gerald's head and then dive for the rebound. She also spent more time between shots daring him to try and get the ball from her.

Whenever Gerald became the least bit aggressive, the therapist immediately switched her tone and style of interacting. Instead of laughing she immediately became serious, stopped talking, broke eye contact, and made every effort to score points or get the ball away from Gerald. Each time, this resulted in Gerald focusing on the game instead of the therapist, thereby decreasing his aggression. After scoring a point or two, the therapist would then shift back to a more light-hearted style. This pattern of social rewards and consequences was effective in maintaining the interaction and preventing aggression without necessitating the use of the primary reinforcers. Toward the end of the session, the therapist congratulated Gerald on having played a good game and gave him a handful of pretzels. At this point, they laid on the floor and recalled their favorite shots and portions of the game.

Cognitive/Verbal Aspects of the Activity

The structure of the task involved Gerald in the problem solving from the outset by having him help determine the rules of the game. Although all levels of interpretation are described here, the actual work was limited to maintain the focus on the interaction.

Focus of Problem Solving

The therapist constantly asked Gerald whether a particular rule or behavior would actually get him the response he wanted. She did this relative to both his desire to score and his desire to have fun as the intensity of their interaction increased. She tried to alternate between the two types of problems to set the stage for later discussions of the degree to which competition interfered with having fun with peers and siblings. Whenever Gerald hesitated before responding to the therapist's questions, the therapist would state the outcome she expected the rule or behavior to produce and the fact that some of these did not seem to be what Gerald actually wanted to have happen.

For example, when the therapist made several baskets in a row, Gerald proposed adding a rule that all players had to shoot from behind a line down the middle of the room. The therapist noted that Gerald wanted to decrease the number of baskets she was making and increase the number he was making so that he would feel like he was coming out ahead. Gerald agreed and said that the therapist had to shoot from behind the line but he did not. The therapist noted that this would solve the problem of the difference in the rates of scoring but would not really improve Gerald's view of himself because the rule simply handicapped the therapist. She also pointed out that when Gerald tried to interfere with her scoring by becoming angry or aggressive, she actually became more focused and her shooting improved. At this point Gerald became frustrated, so the therapist suggested that instead of changing the rules or getting angry, Gerald focus on distracting the therapist by doing silly things to block her shots so that she would laugh and get distracted. This solution took the emphasis off the competition and placed it on nonaggressive strategies that would result in Gerald's need to maintain the emotional interaction being met.

Potential Interpretive Work

The following interpretations were made as the activity was completed over the course of the play therapy session.

Reflections The therapist reflected Gerald's anger when he missed a shot, when the therapist got the ball, or when the therapist scored. She pointed out his reluctance to take turns and the fun he had when they focused more on interacting than on scoring.

Pattern The therapist identified two patterns. At the beginning of the session, Gerald became at least a little bit aggressive every time the therapist got the ball or made a shot. Toward the middle of the session, Gerald laughed almost every time he blocked one of the therapist's shots and rarely became aggressive.

Simple Dynamic The therapist identified the fact that feeling in the one-down position tended to make Gerald angry and to trigger aggression. The therapist also identified that when Gerald was able to set the competition aside for even a few moments he genuinely seemed to have fun in spite of himself.

Generalized Dynamic   The therapist cited the similarity between the types of problems they had in session and the fights he got into with his siblings at home. She also identified the probability that the times that Gerald actually had fun with his siblings were few and far between.

Genetic   In future sessions the therapist wanted to identify the fact that Gerald's sense of needing to compete with his siblings was a common, although not inevitable, problem faced by middle children. She also suggested that his parents' present distress and subsequent unavailability probably contributed to the problem by making all of the children feel like there just was not enough of the parents' energy and attention to go around.

Plan for Future Sessions

The therapist hoped to accomplish two things in future sessions. One was to move from such primarily experiential activities to ones that required more cognitive problem solving and verbal interaction. The use of progressively less competitive and more cooperative games facilitated this. The therapist also wanted to ensure that Gerald's growing sense of the value of non-competitive and nonaggressive interaction was one way of getting his needs met generalized to interactions with his siblings. This was accomplished in two ways. The therapist consulted with the parents on strategies for promoting and reinforcing positive interactions between the children. A simple reward system through which they earned a group reward such as going to the zoo or a movie proved sufficient. The therapist also worked toward including the siblings in Gerald's sessions so that she could directly reinforce cooperative interaction with them and structure ways in which they could reinforce one another.

LEVEL III: ACTIVITY 9[26]

Case Synopsis

Billy was a 10-year-old boy whose parents had divorced recently. He reportedly had a long-standing, positive relationship with his mother. By report, he had never developed much of a relationship with his father and seemed to be afraid of him. His father had a histo-

ry of antisocial behavior including violent crime. At the time Billy was referred to therapy his father was incarcerated, serving a 5-year term for robbery. Billy was referred for difficulties he had in his interactions with his peers. He did not communicate effectively with peers, tended to be impulsive, and had difficulty taking turns in group activities. He also tended to isolate himself in groups, avoiding both the roles of follower and leader.

Target Psychopathology and Session Goal

The therapist hypothesized that Billy had an adequate attachment relationship with his mother that he had been unable to generalize to his interactions with his father because of the father's antisocial style. As a result of having been unable to generalize his attachment to his primary caretaker to include his father, Billy seems to have been unable to generalize his attachment behavior to peers as well. He seemed to trust no one other than his mother. He did not see his peers as a potential source of social reinforcement. The goal of this activity was to enhance Billy's ability to express and communicate affect to his peers, to have him take turns, and to take a leadership role. The activity was also designed to provide him with a positive and safe peer interaction.

Treatment Phase

This activity would be appropriate for either the Introduction and Exploration phase or the Growing and Trusting phase of peer group therapy. During either phase, the activity pushes for interaction and low-level emotional communication. It would not be appropriate during the Negative Reaction phase because the level of disclosure involved would make it likely that the children would resist or use the information to tease each other. It was used during the Growing and Trusting phase of Billy's play therapy.

Persons Attending the Session

Therapist, Billy, and a group of his peers. Given his age, Billy would probably do best in a group of five to six same-gender peers.

Materials Needed/Preparation Required

Index cards, markers, mirror, and an instant photo camera.

Experiential Aspects of the Activity

The point of this activity is to play a game during which the children take turns demonstrating an affect

---

[26]This activity and the related interpretive material was developed by Sharon Picard.

for the group. Each child named an affect and then showed the group how he looked when experiencing that affect. Children who had difficulty were given a mirror to help them gauge their own expression and they could get help from others in the group. The therapist assisted as needed. After each child had taken a few turns, the group selected the group members who they thought had made the best faces when demonstrating a particular affect. The therapist then took an instant photo of these children making their prize-winning faces. The pictures were posted on a bulletin board in the room to serve as cues for future demonstrations.

The therapist then wrote each of the affects on an index card with a stylized drawing of a face expressing the affect. The therapist then had the group play charades with the emotions on the cards. Each child took turns going to the front of the group, drawing a card, and acting out the affect. The other children attempted to guess the affect being demonstrated. If the group could not guess, the therapist encouraged the child doing the demonstration to look at the posted photos or to use the mirror in order to enhance his or her performance.

Cognitive/Verbal Aspects of the Activity

Because of the intensity of the experiential aspect of this activity, the therapist limited the cognitive/verbal work that was done.

Focus of Problem Solving

The therapist limited the use of problem solving to helping the boys improve their strategies for communicating the target affects by facial expressions. When they could not enact an affect or could not do it in a way that the group could identify it, then the therapist would identify this as a problem and encourage the group to brainstorm ideas that could improve the actors performance. These ideas were then critiqued, the best ones implemented, and their effect evaluated.

Potential Interpretive Work

For this session, the therapist decided to limit her interpretations to those having to do with Billy's reluctance to engage with the group, particularly in a leadership role.

Reflections   The therapist identified Billy's anxiety and distrust of others. She identified his very positive reactions when he got any sort of positive feedback from the group. She also noted that he seemed to enjoy acting out negative affects.

Pattern   The therapist noted that Billy refused to take a turn whenever instructed to do so by the thera-

pist, but did so quite readily if another child asked him. She pointed out his reluctance to enact positive affects in front of the group. She also identified the fact that Billy tended to stop talking or interacting with the other boys in the group as soon as he was out of the role of demonstrator.

Simple Dynamic   The therapist made two interpretations at this level. She stated that it appeared that Billy was most anxious when in a role that did not have clear expectations and structure. That is, he was anxious when trying to be just another member of the group. She also stated that he seemed genuinely to enjoy getting encouragement and positive feedback from his peers and that this was easiest when what they expected of him was clear.

Generalized Dynamic   The therapist did no more than identify the fact that it was probably easiest for Billy to interact with peers at school when they approached him and asked him to do something specific rather than either approaching them or joining in unstructured activities.

Genetic   At this level, the therapist noted that Billy's reluctance to interact with peers came from his general feeling that other people were not trustworthy, a belief that stemmed from the fact that he never really trusted his own father.

Plan for Future Sessions

In the next session, the above activity was repeated with the added requirement that each child describe a time he had experienced the affect he was demonstrating. The plan was to increase gradually the amount of time Billy spent in direct interaction with his peers. The therapist planned to introduce activities that called for more cooperative and then competitive interaction among the members. She also planned to ensure that the boys continued to provide each other with support and positive feedback.

LEVEL III: ACTIVITY 10[27]

Case Synopsis

Andrew is a 9-year-old boy who lives with his mother. His parents were divorced years ago and he has had virtually no contact with his father. His primary social and emotional support system has been his mother. He has never had many friends and has tended toward be-

---

[27]This activity and the related interpretive material was developed by Emily Piper, M.A.

ing socially isolated in school. Recently he had been involved in therapy to help increase his peer social interaction. His mother reported that some children were beginning to approach Andrew to initiate social interactions, but that Andrew still seemed very uncomfortable in these situations.

Target Psychopathology and Session Goal

The therapist hypothesized that Andrew was made anxious by peer social interactions and that this anxiety prevented him from initiating or developing peer friendships. The lack of peer friendships, in turn, limited the amount of social reinforcement he was receiving. The goal of this session was to help him begin to identify what he liked about interacting with other children and to begin defining and describing potential friendships.

Treatment Phase

This activity was used in the Growing and Trusting phase of treatment. It requires that the child already be comfortable in interactions with the therapist, as well as being ready and willing to discuss topics from his or her daily life outside of the session.

Persons Attending the Session

Therapist and Andrew.

Materials Needed/Preparation Required

Colored construction paper, hole punch or stapler, yarn or ribbon to hold the book together, items to decorate the book (markers, crayons, old magazines, stickers, macaroni, tempera paint, and so forth), scissors, glue, and paintbrushes. If the therapist has access to a laminator, the book can be given a special finishing touch.

Experiential Aspects of the Activity

The therapist began the session by telling Andrew that they were going to begin a collection of drawings and collages that reflected fun things Andrew did with other children, which would be called his "Friendship Book." The therapist then initiated a discussion of friendship. What made someone a friend? What did one do with friends? What were the pros and cons of having friends? At this point Andrew began to talk about his imaginary friend and the therapist used this to discuss the pros and cons of having real versus imaginary friends. Andrew then drew a picture of his imaginary friend and this became the first entry in his book.

He and the therapist then added a list of the good and bad things about this friend.

At this point the therapist became concerned that the activity itself created so much anxiety that Andrew could not get past the imaginary content to discuss real children in his neighborhood or classroom. To structure the session in such a way that this anxiety was bypassed, she decided to put some distance between Andrew and the content of the session. To do this, she suggested they look through magazines and find some pictures of people (of all ages) being friends. As they found pictures that showed people engaged in pleasant interactions they worked at identifying the cues that let one know the people were friends. This seemed to make the task much easier for Andrew and produced a few new pages for the "Friendship Book," including one that said you can tell people are friends when they are having fun doing something together.

The therapist then gave Andrew a homework task to be completed before the next session. He was to identify something he had either done or would like to do with another child from his classroom or neighborhood.

Cognitive/Verbal Aspects of the Activity

A substantial amount of this activity ended up involving cognitive work because Andrew seemed to find discussion of friendships much less threatening than actually operationalizing friendships. The discussion remained fairly abstract and educational in nature, again because of Andrew's overall anxiety.

Focus of Problem Solving

Because this was the first session in which they had broached the subject of Andrew's peer friendships, the therapist chose to engage in very little problem solving with Andrew. Instead, she determined ways in which to change the structure of the task to decrease Andrew's anxiety and enhance his ability to benefit from the content of the discussion and experience.

Potential Interpretive Work

All of the interpretive work focused on identifying Andrew's anxiety about interacting with peers and the potential reasons for those feelings.

Reflections   The therapist reflected Andrew's feelings of safety relative to his comments about playing alone. She also noted his feelings of control and safety when discussing interactions with his imaginary friend. She noted his anxiety whenever they talked about his interacting with other children.

Pattern   The therapist identified the many times Andrew attempted to change the course of their discussions about friendships. She also pointed out the fact that Andrew was never able to identify or discuss any interactions he had with peers.

Simple Dynamic   The therapist connected Andrew's sense of safety in discussing and interacting with his imaginary friend to his ability to control what that friend thought, did, and said. She then connected his anxiety about interacting with other children to the uncertainty those interactions involved.

Generalized Dynamic   This level of interpretation was embedded in the Simple Dynamic interpretation because all of their discussions focused on material and examples drawn from outside of the session.

Genetic   The therapist identified the source of Andrew's anxiety about peer interactions to his lack of experience and his belief that adults (like his mother) were more predictable and reliable sources of social and emotional supplies.

Plan for Future Sessions

As indicated from the homework the therapist assigned Andrew, the goal of future sessions was to de crease Andrew's anxiety and increase the quantity and quality of his peer interactions.

SUMMARY

In this chapter the authors discussed three content areas relevant to planning individual activities for use in play therapy. First, the developmental experience of children in first three stages of life, Level I (ages 0–2), Level II (ages 2–6), and Level III (ages 6–11), was described. The focus of these descriptions included the way in which these children obtain, process, store, and retrieve information, as well as the primary social task they face during each stage. In this developmental context, the way in which children at each level may respond to traumatic events was also discussed. This led, in turn, to the second area: a discussion of the primary therapeutic issues to be considered when planning a play therapy intervention for children at each of these developmental levels. Finally, examples were given of session activities and related interpretations that could be used to facilitate the process of the therapy. As we have stated repeatedly, we do not believe in a cookbook approach to therapy. Rather, therapists must consider the specific developmental task to be addressed, the specific therapeutic content to be included, and both their own and their clients' personalities when planning effective play therapy interventions.

· 10 ·

JENNIFER M.

This chapter contains a completed Workbook. The client described is Jennifer M., an 8-year-old girl who was sexually abused by a man outside of her family. The case is presented without any explanatory material so that the reader can get a good sense of the flow of the Workbook. However, at the beginning of each section there are page numbers that refer to the pages in this text where explanatory material for that particular section can be found.

The reader may follow the case as it is presented either by passively reading it or by developing his or her own treatment plan for the case as the data are presented. To do the latter, we suggest reading the case through to the end of Part III: "Assessment Data." After which the reader should complete the Workbook: Appendix (a blank one is included at the end of this text) using the information obtained from the case to that point. The reader may also attempt to complete the Workbook: Parts IV–VII before reading them as they are completed in this chapter. In presenting this case we are not asserting that either the case formulation or play therapy treatment plan are necessarily the only or the best ones that could have been developed. Therefore, the reader should be aware that it is very likely that the

work he or she generates will deviate, perhaps substantially, from what is contained herein. Therapists with different theoretical orientations might conceptualize this case very differently; and, therapists with different intervention styles might plan a very different course of treatment. As was mentioned in Chapter 1 we do not view therapy as a process of finding and implementing the "one true" formulation and treatment plan. Rather, what is critical to the practice of good play therapy is that both the formulation and the treatment plan are internally consistent so as to maximize the chances that child clients will become better able to get their needs met more effectively and appropriately.

Throughout the case some abbreviations are used that are not noted in the Workbook itself.

NA Not applicable. The item does not apply to the case under review.

UK Unknown. The client or reporter did not remember or know the information.

NR None Reported. The client or reporter did not disclose any information on the topic.

RD Refused to Disclose. The client or reporter chose not to disclose information on a particular topic to the therapist.

PLAY THERAPY TREATMENT PLANNING WORKBOOK
The Ecosystemic Model

Clinician's Name: Dr. K.   **Work Site Name:** Child's View Center

Address: Main Street

City: Center City   **State:** CA   **Zip:** 99998   **Phone:** 666-666-6666

I. IDENTIFYING INFORMATION   CASE NAME: JENNIFER M.

INTAKE, ASSESSMENT & CONTRACTING CONTACT RECORD   (see pp. 30–31)

DATE	PERSON(S) ATTENDING	TASK COMPLETED	PERSON(S) COMPLETING
1	Mrs. M. and Mr. J.	Intake, CBCL and DTORF	Therapist
2	Mrs. M. and Jennifer.	Intake and contracting	Therapist
3	Mrs. L. (Jennifer's teacher)	DTORF	Therapist, telephone contact
4	Mrs. M. and Jennifer	MIM	Therapist

Client Name: Jennifer M.   **Gender:** F   **Birthdate:**

Home Address: 2020 Windward

City: Fresno   **State:** CA   **Zip:** 99999   **Phone:** 666-666-6666

RESPONSIBLE ADULT(S) INFORMATION   (see p. 31)

Adult 1 Name: Mrs. M   **Relationship:** Mother

Home Address: Same as above.

City: **State:**   **Zip:**   **Phone:**

Employer: Grocery Chain   **Position:** Cashier

Work Address: 9878 Main

City: Fresno   **State:** CA   **Zip:** 99998   **Phone:** 666-444-4444

Insurance Carrier & Number: Good Deal Medical

Adult 2: Name: Mr. M.   **Relationship:** Stepfather

Home Address: Same as above.

City: **State:**   **Zip:**   **Phone:**

Employer: Auto Service Station   **Position:** Mechanic

Work Address: Corner of Main and Automotive Dr.

City: Fresno   **State:** CA   **Zip:** 99998   **Phone:** 666-777-7777

Insurance Carrier & Number: None.

FAMILY CONSTELLATION (Include all persons named above. For all persons mentioned here and throughout the workbook be as specific as possible about their relationship(s) to the child, e.g. Maternal grandmother, half-sibling through mother, step-parent, etc.) (see pp. 31–32)

Name	Relationship	HH	%H1	%H2	BD	Age	Ethnicity	Grade/Work
Client	**Self**		100			8	Anglo-American	3
Mrs. M.	Mother	1	100			35	Anglo-American	Cashier
Mr. M.	Step father		100			25	Anglo-American	Mechanic
Mark	Mr. M.'s bio-son		100			8	Anglo-American	3
Mr. L.	ex-stepfather	2		100		27	Mexican-Amer.	Farm worker
David	half brother			100		16	Mexican-Amer.	10
Mr. J.	father	3				29	Anglo-American	Unknown

[In column HH put a 1 for the Head of Household 1, a 2 for the Head of Household 2, etc. Put 0 if not Head of Household. In column %H1 put the % of time each individual spends in Household 1, repeat for time spent in Household 2.]

PRESENTING PROBLEM (Define in behavioral terms, including onset, frequency and severity. Be sure to include reporters affect regarding the problem.) (see pp. 32–34)

Child's View: Jennifer is very distressed by her severe symptoms that include: nightmares, visual and auditory hallucinations, agoraphobia, self-mutilation and suicidal ideation. All of these are directly related to her abuse.

Parent's View: Mrs. M's concerns are similar to Jennifer's. In addition she is distressed by her own feelings of helplessness in addressing Jennifer's escalating difficulties.

Other's View: The school personnel were surprised to hear that Jennifer was having difficulty. They reported that she is a generally low average student who has some difficulty attending in class but who is otherwise developmentally on target.

HISTORY OF PRESENTING PROBLEM (Define precipitants, impact on/reaction from environment, situations variations, attempts to resolve problem and results, and changes in problem over time.) (see pp. 34–35)

Jennifer's symptoms began following disclosure of repeated sexual abuse that was perpetrated by a non relative. The symptoms were exacerbated by multiple court appearances including one at which her perpetrator threatened to "get her" when he was released from prison. The frequency and intensity of the symptoms have been gradually increasing over time.

II. INTAKE: SYSTEMS REVIEW

INDIVIDUAL SYSTEM: DEVELOPMENTAL HISTORY

(see pp. 35–38)

Pregnancy

Planned: ☐ No ☒ Yes, **Describe:** Mrs. M and Mr. J had been married for about a year when Jennifer was conceived.

Discomfort/problems: ☒ No ☐ Yes, **Describe:** _____

Drugs/Alcohol during pregnancy: ☒ **No** ☐ **Yes, Describe:** <u>Mrs. M denied using substances during her</u> <u>pregnancy but given her current daily consumption of 1-3 beers it seems likely that she drank some at least early in</u> <u>her pregnancy.</u>

Stressors/Complications with the pregnancy: <u>NR</u>

Support System: <u>Mr. J.</u>

Labor & Delivery: WT: <u>UK</u> **APGAR:** <u>UK</u> **Who present at delivery:** <u>Mr. J.</u>

How long/how difficult/problems: <u>UK. No problems reported</u>

If problems - what happened: _____

Developmental Milestones: Walk: <u>UK</u> **Talk:** <u>UK</u> **Words:** <u>UK</u> **Sentences:** <u>UK</u>

Age Toilet Trained: Bladder: <u>UK</u> **Bowel:** <u>UK</u>

Problems: ☒ **No** ☐ **Yes, Describe:** _____

Developmental Delays

Language: ☐ **No** ☒ **Yes,** ☒ **Expressive** ☐ **Receptive** ☒ **Articulation** ☐ **Auditory Processing**

Describe: <u>Jennifer's articulation has always been below age expectancy.</u>

Motor: ☒ **No** ☐ **Yes, Describe:** _____

Adaptive Behavior: ☒ **No** ☐ **Yes, Describe:** _____

Other: ☒ **No** ☐ **Yes, Describe:** _____

Gender Identity, Gender Role Behavior and Sexual Orientation

Gender identity divergent from biologic gender: ☒ **No** ☐ **Yes, Describe:** _____

Client experiences divergence as problematic: ☐ **No** ☐ **Yes, Describe:** _____

Others experience divergence as problematic: ☐ **No** ☐ **Yes, Describe:** _____

Gender role behavior divergent from socio-cultural norms: : ☒ **No** ☐ **Yes, Describe:** _____

Client experiences divergence as problematic: ☐ **No** ☐ **Yes, Describe:** _____

Others experience divergence as problematic: ☐ **No** ☐ **Yes, Describe:** _____

Sexual Orientation Development

☒ **Client's sexual orientation not behaviorally evident at this time.**

Client experiences sexual orientation as problematic: ☐ **No** ☐ **Yes, Describe:** _____

Others experience client's sexual orientation as problematic: ☐ **No** ☐ **Yes, Describe:** _____

INDIVIDUAL SYSTEM: MENTAL STATUS EXAMINATION (see pp. 38–50)

Behavioral Observations

Appearance: <u>Jennifer was dressed in an age appropriate manner. She was somewhat dirty and disheveled.</u>

Motor Activity: <u>Jennifer's gross motor activity was within normal limits for a child her age. Her level of fine</u> <u>motor activity tended to be quite high, especially when discussing emotionally loaded material.</u>

Speech: (Content and Productivity) <u>Jennifer spoke more during the intake session than many children her age and</u> <u>was consistently focused on the topic at hand.</u>

Emotions

Mood: Jennifer's overall mood was very anxious, however, she relaxed considerably over the course of the interview and even seemed to be enjoying herself.

Affect: (Range, Reality Base, Control) Her range of affect was from extreme anxiety to clear pleasure. Her ability to express anger seemed limited. Given the intensity of the topics she was discussing her affect seemed based in reality although her anxiety tended to exceed that expected in such a protected setting as the intake. Her ability to control her affect was very limited especially when it came to her anxiety.

Attitude: Jennifer was initially very reluctant to come into the intake session as she had told her mother she did not want to talk to anyone about the abuse anymore. After the first 10 minutes she relaxed visibly and seemed genuinely pleased to be in the session.

Relatedness: After her initial reluctance passed Jennifer became overly attached to the therapist. She did not want to leave the intake session and wanted to return for another appointment in less than the scheduled week's time.

Cognitive Processes (*WNL = Within Normal Limits for Age)

Estimated Developmental Level: WNL: ☐ Yes ☒ No, **Describe:** Jennifer's speech and overall manner of social interaction make her seem more like a child of 5 or 6 than an 8 year old.

☐ **Sensorimotor** ☐ **Pre-operational** ☒ **Concrete Operations** ☐ **Formal Operations**

Orientation:.......WNL: ☒ **Yes** ☐ **No, Disoriented:** ☐ **Time** ☐ **Place** ☐ **Person** ☐ **Purpose**

Memory:............WNL: ☒ **Yes** ☐ **No, Impaired:** ☐ **Immediate** ☐ **Intermediate** ☐ **Long Term**

Concentration:..WNL: ☐ **Yes** ☒ **No, Difficulty is:** ☐ **Severe** ☒ **Moderate** ☐ **Minimal**

Abstraction:......WNL: ☒ **Yes** ☐ **No, Thinking is:** ☐ **Overly Concrete** ☐ **Overly Abstract**

Intellect:............WNL: ☐ **Yes** ☒ **No, Intelligence is:** ☒ **Below Average** ☐ **Above Average**

Judgment:.........WNL: ☒ **Yes** ☐ **No, Impaired:** ☐ **Severe** ☐ **Moderate** ☐ **Minimal**

Insight:..............WNL: ☐ **Yes** ☒ **No, Insight is:** ☐ **Absent** ☐ **Limited** ☒ **Above Average**

Organization:....WNL: ☒ **Yes** ☐ **No, Thinking is:** ☐ **Chaotic** ☐ **Loose** ☐ **Rigid**

If No, Describe: _____

Hallucinations:............ ☐ **No** ☒ **Yes, Type:** ☒ **Visual** ☒ **Auditory** ☐ **Other:** _____

If Yes, Describe: Jennifer complains of hearing her abuser's voice during the daytime while she is at school. The voice is intrusive and interferes with her ability to concentrate. Jennifer complains of seeing her abuser in her room at night before she goes to sleep. It is unclear if these are hypnagogic experiences. She knows he is not really there but she sees him anyway.

Delusions:.................. ☒ **No** ☐ **Yes, Type:** ☐ **Persecutory** ☐ **Grandiosity** ☐ **Other:** _____

If Yes, Describe: _____

Trauma Symptoms: .... ☐ **No** ☒ **Yes, Type:** ☒ **Nightmares** ☐ **Flashbacks** ☐ **Alexithymia** ☐ **Reenactment Behaviors** ☒ **Disassociative Phenomena** ☒ **Other:** _____

If Yes, Describe: Jennifer reports severe nightmares that recreate her sexual abuse and her court experiences. She worries constantly about her abuser getting out of prison and coming to get revenge on her for testifying against him in court. She has used self-injury to induce disassociative states so as to have a break from her anxieties.

Subjective Experience

Self-Concept: Jennifer's self-concept was moderately distorted. She saw herself as a good student and as generally trouble free. She was able to say that her symptoms greatly exceeded those of her peers. She reports feeling ashamed that she was abused and is clear that she does not want her peers to know about it for fear that they will reject her.

View of World: Jennifer sees the world as a dangerous place that contains many things she would like to have such as friends. She is distressed by the fact that her fear of the danger keeps her from what she wants.

3 Wishes: I don't want to have no more nightmares. I want to be able to go outside to play. I want Mr. X (molester) to stay in jail forever.

Reality Testing: Jennifer's reality testing is actually quite good in spite of the intrusive auditory and visual hallucinations she is experiencing.

Dangerous Behavior

Self Injurious Behavior or Ideation: ☐ **No** ☒ **Yes, Describe:** Jennifer thinks about hurting herself on a regular basis. She is stopped by recall of the degree to which these injuries hurt later on. She will use whatever is at hand when the desire to self-injure strikes. She has no preferred plan or consistent ideation.

Prior Acts or Ideation: ☐ **No** ☒ **Yes, Describe:** Jennifer has self-inflicted multiple cigarette burns on the tops of her feet. She has also made scratches on her wrist with a razor blade. She reports that when she does these things she can no longer hear her abuser's voice and doesn't feel as anxious.

Suicidal Behavior or Ideation: ☒ **No** ☐ **Yes, Describe:** (Include: imminence, plan, means, reality base, dangerousness, etc.): _____

Prior Attempts or Ideation: ☒ **No** ☐ **Yes, Describe:** _____

Family History of Suicide: ☒ **No** ☐ **Yes, Describe:** _____

Support/Response Plan: _____

Aggressive Behavior or Ideation: ☒ **No** ☐ **Yes, Describe:** _____

Target(s): ☐ **Property** ☐ **Animals** ☐ **Children** ☐ **Adults. Describe:** _____

Prior Acts or Ideation: ☐ **No** ☐ **Yes, Describe:** _____

Homicidal Behavior or Ideation: ☒ **No** ☐ **Yes, Describe:** (Include: imminence, plan, means, reality base, dangerousness, etc.): _____

Target(s): _____

Prior Attempts or Ideation: ☒ No ☐ Yes, Describe: _____

Family History of Violence: ☐ No ☒ Yes, **Describe:** Mrs. M reports that her first husband, Jennifer's father, was occasionally abusive toward her. She says that their arguments were usually verbal and that he threatened physical violence. He did slap her a few times.

Support/Response Plan: _____

History of Sexually Inappropriate Behavior: ☒ No ☐ Yes, Describe: _____

History of Fire Setting: ☒ No ☐ Yes, Describe: _____

Observations of Play Behavior

Jennifer's behavior was very appropriate throughout the intake session. She displayed signs of anxiety and seemed distressed when discussing her symptoms: these included nail biting and hand wringing. She became very verbal as the session progressed and vocalized an inappropriate level of attachment to the therapist. During free play she interacted directly with the therapist using the limited number of play materials in age appropriate ways.

DYADIC SYSTEM: FIRST THREE YEARS   (see pp. 50–53)

Primary Caretaker(s): Mrs. M. _____

Significant Disruptions in the Primary Relationship: ☒ No ☐ Yes, Describe: _____

First Year

Type of Baby: Very easy. Generally happy and quiet. _____

Description of Bonding (Parental experience of relationship to the child)**:** Good. Mrs. M reports that she was pleased that Jennifer was easier to care for than her first child (son) had been.

Affective Responsiveness of Child to Parent: Mrs. M reported that Jennifer always liked to be held, responding with smiles and coos. She also noted that Jennifer also seemed very contented when left alone.

Second & Third Years:

Type of Toddler: Moderately oppositional but easily redirected. _____

Description of Relationship to Caretaker: Mother and daughter remained close although Mrs. M's responses give one the sense that she never much noticed Jennifer one way or another. When Mrs. M was attuned things seem to go well, when she wasn't, Jennifer seems to have either occupied herself or at least faded from Mrs. M's awareness.

Description of Relationship to Other Family Members: Jennifer responded very well to anyone who paid attention to her. She seems to have become very attached to her older brother early in her toddlerhood.

Description of Child's Exploratory Behavior: Jennifer did not engage in a great deal of exploratory behavior. Mrs. M reports that she did not have to do much "baby proofing" of the house as Jennifer seemed content to play wherever she was placed.

How was toilet-training implemented? UK. Mrs. M reports that Jennifer's toilet training seemed fairly spontaneous.

What was child's response? _____

What type of discipline was used? <u>Mrs. M used mostly verbal discipline (yelling) and an occasional "swat on the behind."</u>

    What was child's response? <u>Jennifer immediately altered her behavior and would attempt to coax her mother back into positive interactions.</u>

Separations/Reunions

    Attended Daycare/Preschool: ☒ **No** ☐ **Yes, Describe:** _____

    Child's Reaction to Separation & Reunion: <u>Never seemed to mind separations. She was always happy and seemed not to notice when Mrs. M was not there so long as some adult was present.</u>

    Parent's Response to Child's Reaction: <u>Mrs. M was always satisfied with Jennifer's behavior and took her easygoing nature to be a great gift.</u>

Observations of Child-Caretaker Interactions

<u>During the intake Jennifer made frequent physical contact with her mother, smiled at her and tended not to move too far away. Mrs. M seemed somewhat oblivious to Jennifer's behavior. Intermittently, she would become more aware of Jennifer's presence and to smile at her or stroke her hair. Several times Mrs. M brushed away Jennifer's hand as one would brush away a fly.</u>

FAMILY SYSTEM

(see pp. 54–60)

Genogram [Complete by Hand]

Jennifer M's family (Current family unit consists of shaded members.)

Family Functioning & History

    Current Family Relationships & Dynamics: <u>The current household consists of Mr. and Mrs. M, Jennifer and Mr. M's son, Mark, who is the same age as Jennifer. Mr. and Mrs. M have only been married for about six months although he has lived in the home for about a year. During the intake he acted more like Mrs. M's parent than her spouse in that he tended to respond for her and to protect her from any unpleasant topics. He seemed to relate the</u>

family history much more accurately than Mrs. M was able to in spite of his being a newcomer. Jennifer appeared to like Mr. M very much and referred to him as "Dad." While Jennifer is reported to get along well with Mark she never mentioned him during the intake interview.

Family History: (Include changes in family membership &/or home location, major events, significant losses, and support system) Mrs. M has moved frequently and has had multiple male partners aside from the men to whom she was married. It appeared, from the history, that she has never spent more than a couple of weeks without a live-in partner since before she was first married. On one occasion less than 24 hours elapsed between the departure of one partner and the arrival of the next. Jennifer has had no contact with her father for over 2 years. Jennifer's half brother, David, is often in the home, usually as a result of disagreements with his father. He and Jennifer have virtually no relationship. Jennifer does not have any contact with her former stepfather.

Extended Family History: None reported.

Sibling Sub-System

> **Relationships with Siblings:** Jennifer followed her older brother around all the time when he still lived in the home. He tended to ignore her. Since he has been living with his father though she shows little sign of missing him. She reverts to her old behavior when he visits.

> **Role of Siblings in the Presenting Problem:** NR

> **Impact of the Presenting Problem on Siblings:** Little to none.

Spousal Sub-System

> **Persons in Spousal System:** Mr. and Mrs. M.

> **Current Problems:** ☒ **No** ☐ **Yes, Describe:** _____

> **History of Problems:** ☐ **No** ☒ **Yes, Describe:** This is Mrs. M's third long-term relationship. She was married to Jennifer's father and then lived with another man before meeting and marrying Mr. M. Mr. M very casually mentioned that Mrs. M might not be keeping him around for long. He did not seem particularly distressed by this and she did not acknowledge hearing him.

> **Role of Spousal Difficulties in the Presenting Problem:** The tentativeness of the spousal relationship seems to mirror some of the apparent superficiality in Mrs. M's interactions with Jennifer.

> **Impact of the Presenting Problem on Spousal Relationship:** Mr. and Mrs. M disagree on how to manage Jennifer's behavior. Mr. M tends to view Jennifer's symptoms as bids for attention and strategies for avoiding doing work both at home and at school. Mrs. M is much more sympathetic and worries a great deal about her daughter's mental stability.

Significant Adults' Current Occupational Functioning

> **Adult 1:** Mrs. M. _____ **Employed:** ☐ **No** ☒ **Yes, Describe:** Part-time cashier for a grocery store chain.

>> **Occupational History/Problems:** Mrs. M has held multiple lower level positions in various food stores.

>> **Role of Occupational Difficulties in the Presenting Problem:** None.

Impact of the Presenting Problem on Occupational Functioning: <u>Mrs. M occasionally stays home from work because she has not slept much the night before staying up to keep Jennifer from additional nightmares.</u>

Adult 2: <u>Mr. M.</u>   **Employed:** ☐ **No** ☒ **Yes, Describe:** <u>Auto mechanic.</u>

   Occupational History/Problems: <u>Mr. M has been employed at the same service station since he was 18.</u>

   Role of Occupational Difficulties in the Presenting Problem: <u>None.</u>

   Impact of the Presenting Problem on Occupational Functioning: <u>None.</u>

Social Network

   Social Support: <u>Mrs. M's extended family and Mr. M's friends from work serve as the primary social contacts for this family. None of the ties seem very close.</u>

   Problems in Social Network: <u>NR</u>

Family Development

<u>This family is in mixed stages of development. Mr. and Mrs. M have only been married about 6 months so they are still in the process of defining their relationship as a couple. They are responsible for raising two elementary school children (1 biologically related to each of them). They are also, somewhat prematurely, beginning to adjust to having grown children move out of the home as Mrs. M's son David has moved out to live with extended family members.</u>

Familial Identification

   Familial Ethnocultural Identification: <u>The family self-identifies as Anglo-American although they observe virtually no specific traditions. They do celebrate Christmas and Easter.</u>

   Familial Religious Affiliation (Identification and degree of involvement): <u>None.</u>

Observations of the Family System

<u>Mr. M tended to do most of the talking during the intake interview but made it clear that Mrs. M was the head of the household. In many ways his status appeared to be that of a guest invited in by Mrs. M. Jennifer was physically clingy with both Mr. and Mrs. M. Mrs. M was very willing to let Mr. M be the primary reporter of the family history even though they have only been together about a year. He seemed better able to recall details and the sequence of events in Jennifer's life than did Mrs. M. Mr. and Mrs. M's relationship seems to mirror the relationship between Jennifer and her mother. Mr. M paid a great deal of attention to Mrs. M and was very active in the intake interview process while she seemed to only intermittently acknowledge his attentions.</u>

SOCIAL SYSTEM

(see pp. 61–62)

Current Social Functioning

   Close Friends: ☐ **No** ☒ **Yes, Describe** (Number/Duration): <u>Jennifer relates well with female peers. She has one friend who lives in her neighborhood and who goes to the same school with whom she is close.</u>

   Problems with Peers: <u>NR</u>

Problems with Adults: Mr. M saw Jennifer's behavior as oppositional and difficult to manage.   Most of the examples he gave included being demanding or not doing her chores without constant reminders.   Mrs. M did not view Jennifer's behavior as problematic and tended to frame any difficulties as being the result of Jennifer's unhappiness and PTSD. Mr. M saw this as making excuses for Jennifer.

Past Social Functioning

Problems with Peers: Jennifer has always had female friends both at home and at school.   She enjoys playing with peers and seems to miss not having more friends now that her agoraphobia keeps her isolated.

Problems with Adults: NR

Interpersonal/Sexual History

Involved in Significant Intimate Relationship: ☒ **No** ☐ **Yes, Describe:** _____

Problems in Sexual Relationship: _____

Problems in Previous Relationships: _____

Observations of Peer Interactions

Jennifer was not observed in direct interaction with her peers.

EDUCATIONAL SYSTEM   (see pp. 62–64)

Current School Circumstances

Grade: 3 **School/District:** Central Elementary/Central Unified Schools   **Telephone:** 666-333-3333

Teacher(s): Mrs. L.   **Counselor:** Mrs. R.

Special Education or Support Services: ☐ **No** ☒ **Yes, Describe:** Intermittent speech therapy.

Specific Problems: Jennifer's language articulation problem was diagnosed when she was in second grade.

School History

School Placement History: Jennifer has attended multiple schools, consistent with Mrs. M's frequent moves.

Problems (Especially note adjustment to K, 1st, 3rd and 6th grades)**:** None reported. Although Jennifer has been a C or D student since beginning school neither Mrs. M or the school seems to view this as a particular problem. Even Jennifer seems to see herself as a good student.   The language articulation problem does not interfere with her school performance.

Interventions/Outcomes: Jennifer has received intermittent speech therapy for the past year.

Family History of Learning Problems

NR. However, Mrs. M's cognitive functioning appears to be quite low.

Site Visit Information/Observations

A site visit was not made although school records were obtained. The records showed nothing other than the evaluation for the language articulation problem.

LEGAL SYSTEMS (see pp. 65–71)

Child Abuse/Domestic Violence

Current: ☐ **No** ☒ **Yes:** ☐ **Physical** ☒ **Sexual** ☐ **Emotional** ☐ **Neglect** ☐ **Witnessed Violence**
Perpetrator(s): <u>Mr. X</u>   Victim(s): <u>Jennifer</u>
Relationship to Child: <u>None</u>   Relationship to Child: <u>Self</u>

Description: <u>Beginning at age 6, Jennifer was repeatedly molested by the school janitor over 6 months. These</u> <u>occurred in a minimally supervised after school program Jennifer attended when her mother's shift at the store</u> <u>ran late. The first molest occurred when Jennifer happened to encounter the janitor in the bathroom. The</u> <u>molestation escalated over time eventually resulting in attempted vaginal and anal penetration. The janitor gave</u> <u>Jennifer money after some of the episodes, if she cooperated. He also threatened her and her family with</u> <u>physical violence if she ever disclosed. The abuse was uncovered when a friend of Jennifer's disclosed to her</u> <u>own mother that she was being molested.</u>

Report Filed: ☐ **No** ☒ **Yes, When:** <u>Upon discovery, 18 months prior</u>   **CPS Involved:** ☐ **No** ☒ **Yes**
Caseworker: <u>UK</u>   **Telephone:** _____

CPS Response and Long Term Plan: <u>Perpetrator was arrested, tried and convicted of sexually abusing</u> <u>Jennifer and at least one other girl. He was sent to prison and served all of a two year sentence.</u>

Impending Court Appearance: ☐ **No** ☒ **Yes, Date:** _____

   Purpose: <u>Mrs. M filed a civil suit against the school district to obtain funds for Jennifer's mental health</u> <u>treatment. (During therapy the suit was settled out of court preventing Jennifer from having to testify.</u> <u>The settlement proceeds were put in a trust for Jennifer to which the parents had no access.)</u>

Domestic Violence Shelter: ☒ **No** ☐ **Yes, Describe:** _____

Caseworker: _____   **Telephone:** _____

Orders of Protection: ☐ **No** ☒ **Yes, Describe:** <u>Upon his release from prison (shortly after therapy was</u> <u>initiated) an order was obtained which barred Mr. X from living within 500 miles of Jennifer.</u>

Previous: ☒ **No** ☐ **Yes:** ☐ **Physical** ☐ **Sexual** ☐ **Emotional** ☐ **Neglect** ☐ **Witnessed Violence**
Perpetrator(s): _____   Victim(s): _____
Relationship to Child: _____   Relationship to Child: _____

Description: _____

Report Filed: ☐ **No** ☐ **Yes, When:** _____   **CPS Involved:** ☐ **No** ☐ **Yes**

Caseworker: _____   **Telephone:** _____

CPS Response and Long Term Plan: _____

Impending Court Appearance: ☐ **No** ☐ **Yes, Date:** _____

   Purpose: _____

Domestic Violence Shelter: ☒ **No** ☐ **Yes, Describe:** _____

Caseworker: _____   **Telephone:** _____

Orders of Protection: ☒ **No** ☐ **Yes, Describe:** _____

Intergenerational History of Child Abuse/Domestic Violence: ☒ No ☐ Yes, Describe: _____

Legal System (Non-Criminal) (For all persons mentioned be as specific as possible about their relationship(s) to the child.)

Divorce: ☐ No ☒ Yes, **Describe:** Mrs. M divorced Mr. L (David's father) about 1 year before Jennifer was born. Mrs. M divorced Mr. J, Jennifer's father, when Jennifer was about 2 years old. He has had no contact with the family since.

Current Custody Proceedings: ☒ No ☐ Yes, **Describe:** Children have continued to live with their mother without any court proceedings having been initiated by any of the adults.

Mediator/Attorney: _____ **Telephone:** _____

Past Custody Proceedings: ☒ No ☐ Yes, Description/Outcome: _____

Foster Placement: ☒ No ☐ Yes, Describe: _____

Adoption: ☒ No ☐ Yes, Describe: _____

Law Enforcement System (For all persons mentioned be as specific as possible about their relationship(s) to the child.)

Contact(s) <u>Not</u> Leading to Arrest: ☒ No ☐ Yes, Describe: _____

Arrest(s) <u>Not</u> Leading to Court Proceedings: ☒ No ☐ Yes, Describe: _____

Juvenile Offender System (For all persons mentioned be as specific as possible about their relationships(s) to the child.)

Arrests for Statutory Violation(s): ☒ No ☐ Yes, Description/Outcome: _____

Arrests for Misdemeanor(s): ☒ No ☐ Yes, Description/Outcome: _____

Arrests for Felony(s): ☒ No ☐ Yes, Description/Outcome: _____

Juvenile Hall Placement(s): ☒ No ☐ Yes, Describe: _____

Probation: ☒ No ☐ Yes, Describe: _____

Probation Officer: _____ **Telephone:** _____

Family Members Involved in Juvenile Justice System, Past or Present: ☒ No ☐ Yes, **Describe:** __

_____

_____

Legal System (Criminal) (For all persons mentioned be as specific as possible about their relationship(s) to the child.)

Court Appearances for Misdemeanor(s): ☒ No ☐ Yes, Description/Outcome: _____

Court Appearances for Felony(s): ☐ No ☒ Yes, **Description/Outcome:** Jennifer's molester was arrested, tried and convicted to 5 years in prison. Jennifer was required to testify in open court and to face her abuser. During her testimony she decompensated and had to be carried, sobbing from the courtroom. She reports that she could not cope with her abuser constantly staring at her. In court her abuser threatened to "get her" when he got out of prison.

Probation/Parole: ☒ No ☐ Yes, Describe: _____

Probation/Parole Officer: _____ **Telephone:** _____

MEDICAL SYSTEM (see p. 71)

Allergies: ☒ No ☐ Yes, Describe: _____

Serious Accidents: ☒ No ☐ Yes, Describe: _____

Head Injury w/ Loss of Consciousness: ☒ **No** ☐ **Yes, Describe:** _____

Serious Illness: ☐ **No** ☒ **Yes, Describe:** Jennifer was hospitalized for a series of seizures just prior to being referred for psychotherapy. The origin of the seizures was unknown

Chronic Illness: ☐ **No** ☒ **Yes, Describe:** Jennifer has had several addtional seizures since her hospitalization.

Hospitalizations: ☐ **No** ☒ **Yes, Describe:** See above.

Other Medical Problems: ☒ **No** ☐ **Yes, Describe:** _____

Present Medications: ☐ **No** ☒ **Yes, Physician:** Dr. R.

   Type, Dose, Frequency: Tegritol (for seizures). Mrs. M was unsure of the dose.

Eating Pattern: Within normal limits and unchanged.

Sleeping Pattern: Jennifer has difficulty going to sleep at night due to her tendency to hallucinate her abuser standing in the room as she is trying to fall asleep. She awakens frequently during the night in response to nightmares.

Family History of Medical Problems: NR

MENTAL HEALTH SYSTEM

(see pp. 71–72)

Concurrent Outpatient Treatment: ☒ **No** ☐ **Yes, Describe:** _____

   Diagnosis: _____

   Facility/Therapist: _____

Previous Outpatient Treatment: ☐ **No** ☒ **Yes, Describe:** Jennifer was referred for short-term group therapy immediately after her abuse was discovered. At the end of the 8 week treatment period the clinician reported that Jennifer was symptom free and in need of no further treatment.

   Diagnosis: Adjustment Disorder secondary to Sexual Abuse.

   Facility/Therapist: Specialized program for sex abuse victims.

Previous Inpatient Treatment: ☒ **No** ☐ **Yes, Describe:** _____

   Diagnosis: _____

   Facility/Therapist: _____

Psychotropic Medications: ☒ **No** ☐ **Yes, Describe:** _____

   Current Medications: Type, Dose, Frequency: None

   Prescribing Physician: _____

   Previous Medications: Type, Dose, Frequency: None

   Prescribing Physician: _____

Current Mental Health Difficulties and Treatment of Other Family Members: (For all persons mentioned be as specific as possible about their relationship(s) to the child.) NR, however, Mrs. M appears to be moderately depressed. Her affect is flat with only very slight variability. She displays little interest in events or the people around her other than her genuine concern that Jennifer's symptoms are worsening. She is not well oriented to time.

History of Mental Health Difficulties and Treatment of Other Family Members: (For all persons mentioned be as specific as possible about their relationship(s) to the child.) NR _____

Current Substance Abuse: ☒ None ☐ Mild ☐ Moderate ☐ Severe: _____

    Substances Used/Frequency/Intensity: _____

    In Treatment: ☐ No ☐ Yes, Describe: _____

Previous Substance Abuse: ☒ None ☐ Mild ☐ Moderate ☐ Severe: _____

    Substances Used/Frequency/Intensity: _____

    Treatment: ☐ No ☐ Yes, Describe: _____

Current Substance Abuse and Treatment of Other Family Members: (For all persons mentioned be as specific as possible about their relationship(s) to the child.) NR, however, Mrs. M reports drinking 1-3 beers every day.

History of Substance Abuse and Treatment of Other Family Members: (For all persons mentioned be as specific as possible about their relationship(s) to the child.) NR _____

     Note: The following 4 sections should be completed if the therapist has any reason to believe that these systems may have played a role in the origin of the presenting problem or that they are playing a role in maintaining the problem.

REGIONAL CULTURAL SYSTEM
(see p. 73)

Mr. and Mrs. M are part of a lower socio-economic community that seems to see themselves as disenfranchised from the world around them. They do not appear hostile towards those whose lives are different from theirs rather they act as if the rest of the world does not exist or is completely irrelevant. For example, they seem unaware of local, national or world events. They also tend not to question authority figures at all. Mrs. M did not question the decision to have her daughter testify in open court in spite of her concerns about how Jennifer would react. Mrs. M does not know what type of financial settlement was reached with the school system, only that there is money Jennifer will receive when she turns 18.

DOMINANT/NATIONAL OR POLITICAL SYSTEM
(see pp. 73–74)

In the same way that Mr. and Mrs. M seem to ignore the systems in which they are embedded so the systems seem largely oblivious to their difficulties. Jennifer has had trouble in school for years and yet no one in that system sees this as a problem. Their attorney responds to the entire family with a level of caretaking that would be appropriate if working with a five-year-old.

WORLD COMMUNITY
(see p. 74)

No significant role.

HISTORICAL TIME

(see p. 74)

Jennifer's court experience is a remnant of a legal system that puts the rights of the accused ahead of the best interests of the child. In other states and at other times in the recent past children have been protected from such confrontations. Although it does not seem to play a large role in this specific case Jennifer's abuse occurred during a period in time where there is a growing sentiment that sexual abusers should be severely punished.

III. ASSESSMENT DATA

DATA SOURCES

(see p. 79)

Tests and/or Measures Administered: Developmental Therapy Objectives Rating Form-Revised (DTORF-R), Rorschach, Thematic Apperception Test (TAT), Kinetic Family Drawing (KFD), Weschler Intelligence Scale for Children-Revised (WISC-R), Marschack Interaction Method (MIM). This last was administered jointly to Mrs. M and Jennifer.

Other Data Sources: Interview and observation.

INDIVIDUAL DATA

(see pp. 79–85)

List the source of the data reported in each of the following sections. For example: Data regarding a child's intellectual functioning may have been obtained from an intelligence test, school records and their scores on various projective instruments.

Cognitive Functioning (Including, if relevant, intelligence, learning styles, language and all academic skill areas.): Jennifer's WISC-R scores were: VIQ - 94, PIQ - 93 and FSIQ - 92. She functioned poorest in the areas of Arithmetic and Block Design. Her other subscale scores were in the average range. Her overall thinking appears more concrete than one would expect for a child her age. Her thinking with respect to her emotional experience is more insightful and abstract than one would expect. On the DTORF-R she scored in Stage III although she missed item 15. Her first ceiling item was 23.

Emotional Functioning: Subsequent to her abuse Jennifer became preoccupied with oral dependency issues. She sees her mother as unable or unwilling to care for her in the ways she needs. Jennifer sees her mother as having been unable to protect her from the sex abuse. In addition it appears that Jennifer's attachment to her mother was fairly minimal prior to the abuse. It appears that basic attachment is there but that Jennifer learned that her mother was not particularly good at meeting her day to day needs. She seems to have partially generalized her attachment to her father but then he left and has not maintained contact. Fortunately, Jennifer seems to have gone on to generalize her attachment to peers and to have had very positive relationships since she was quite young. Unfortunately, her current problems are too severe for her peers to manage and her symptoms prevent her from accessing her friends. At this point her affect has become very labile in a manner similar to much younger children. She appears to be experiencing "stranger danger" in much the same way as a one-year-old and this seems to have generalized to all men except those that her mother has moved into the father role. Jennifer is clingy, whiny and demanding but cannot seek out peers for comfort because of the interference caused by her symptoms.

Behavioral Functioning: Based on Mr. M's report Jennifer's behavior seems oppositional in the manner of a 5-year-old in that she tends to be purposefully unresponsive or noncompliant when she is not getting her needs met. On the DTORF-R she scored in Stage III. She missed items 16 and 17 but regularly did items 19-21.

Physical Functioning and Motor Development: Because of her articulation difficulties Jennifer seems somewhat younger than 8. It is possible that her seizure disorder is interfering with her cognitive functioning and that it exacerbates her sense of helplessness and fear of sudden and traumatic hospitalizations. There were also indications that Mrs. M may have been told that Jennifer's seizures were psychogenic and induced by the stress of the sex abuse.

INTERPERSONAL DATA (see p. 86)

List the source of the data reported in each of the following sections. For example: Data regarding a child's peer social functioning may have been obtained from a parent rating scale, a sociogram and the child's responses to projective instruments.

Dyadic Functioning (Specify dyads assessed.): The MIM completed by Mrs. M and Jennifer was striking in its lack of positive interaction. Initially, Mrs. M responded by reading all of the cards, saying "I do that with you," and moving to the next card. Only when she came to the card that read, "Have Jennifer tell you something about her abuse that still bothers her," did Mrs. M become active in the task. At that point she pressured Jennifer verbally in spite of the fact that Jennifer became increasingly agitated. When Jennifer refused to disclose Mrs. M referred to other disclosures that Jennifer had made and Jennifer readily agreed that those still applied. In spite of this Mrs. M continued and as Jennifer became more distraught said, "After I bought you ice cream on the way here you can't do this for me. That's not very nice." Jennifer continued to protest and then finally said she did not like the fact that Mr. X had given her money. After this Mrs. M went back and read the cards she had moved to the bottom of the pile as if she were reading them for the first time. At this point she was able to minimally comply with the directions although she significantly limited the degree to which she allowed Jennifer to make physical contact with her. While Jennifer giggled a great deal during some of the tasks Mrs. M's affect did not change from her muted and rather depressed tone.

Family Functioning: No assessment completed.

Social Functioning (Including, if relevant, both extrafamilial and peer interactions.): Jennifer desperately wants to resume her same sex peer friendships. Both her symptoms and her fear of rejection should they find out about the abuse interfere with her pursuing contacts. Jennifer will play with younger children as it increases her sense of safety and control. She has regressed developmentally to the point where most of her socialization energies are directed toward the relationship with her mother. On the DTORF-R she scored in Stage III. Her ceiling items were 26 & 27.

NOTE: Before completing the rest of the workbook complete the APPENDIX**

IV. DIAGNOSIS
(see p. 103)

Axis I (Clinical Disorders): <u>309.81 Post Traumatic Stress Disorder, Chronic. 315.00 Mathematics Disorder. 315.39 Phonological Disorder.</u>

Axis II (Personality Disorders & Mental Retardation): <u>None.</u>

Axis III (General Medical Conditions): <u>Seizure Disorder</u>

Axis IV (Psychosocial & Environmental Problems): <u>History of sexual abuse.</u>

Axis V: Current GAF: <u>40</u> **Highest GAF in past year:** <u>40</u>

V. CASE FORMULATION (This should be an integration of the case data and a description of the primary hypotheses to be addressed in treatment.)
(see pp. 103–104)

<u>Jennifer was a generally functional child who has regressed to an earlier developmental level in response to severe trauma, namely, repeated, intense sexual abuse and threats of violence. Her vulnerability to that trauma was enhanced by her mother's limited cognitive and emotional functioning which appears to have prevented her from consistently responding to Jennifer's needs. It also appears that Mrs. M is powerfully dependent on the men in her life and that this may further interfere with the stability and consistency of her relationship with Jennifer. In response to the above Jennifer seems to have developed primarily autoplastic response strategies. She does not see others as able or willing to help her address either her relationship problems or her symptoms. Unfortunately, while she sees herself as her only hope for change she also seems to see herself as relatively powerless hence the self destructive and suicidal reactions. The severity of her symptoms is an indication of the extent to which the trauma of her abuse remains unresolved. Jennifer's symptoms cause her mother to have some awareness of Jennifer's needs and to provide some basic caretaking. Jennifer's symptoms prevent her from seeking out the peer relationships and support upon which she relied in the past. The primary indicator of a positive prognosis is Jennifer's desire to regain her previous level of functioning.</u>

VI. TREATMENT: CONTRACT & GENERAL PLAN
(see pp. 110–112)

Contract with Child: <u>An immediate contract was established with Jennifer in which the therapist agreed to do everything possible to provide symptom relief if Jennifer would agree to come to sessions and remain engaged even if she found some of the discussions or activities threatening.</u>

Contract with Caretaker(s)/Family: <u>Mrs. M agreed to a contract that focused on reducing Jennifer's symptoms while initially ignoring any behavior problems she might be exhibiting. Mr. M agreed reluctantly.</u>

Treatment Objective(s): <u>Reduction of Jennifer's self-mutilating behavior was the initial focus of the therapy.</u>

Treatment Modality(ies): <u>Individual, Dyadic, Family and Peer Group Play Therapy.</u>

Anticipated Number of Sessions: <u>Individual and Family: 27-35. Peer Group: 8-16.</u>

Collaborative Interventions (Evaluation, Education, Consultation, Advocacy, etc.): <u>Consult with school. Advocate in civil court for limiting Jennifer's contact with the proceedings. Advocate in the Criminal Court for an Order of Protection barring Jennifer's perpetrator from contacting her once he is released from prison.</u>

Signature: _____ **Position:** _____ **Date:** _____

Signature: _____ **Position:** _____ **Date:** _____

| **VII. DETAILED TREATMENT PLAN** | **CASE NAME:** JENNIFER M. | (see pp. 113–119) |

Stage I: Introduction & Exploration: (Anticipated Number of Sessions: **1**)

Stage Goal(s): To provide immediate symptom reduction so that Jennifer experiences adults as able to respond to her needs and becomes more available to the work of the therapy.

Participants: Jennifer

Materials: Interactive nurturant toys like a baby blanket, baby bottles, baby doll, toy telephones.

Experiential Component(s): Jennifer will need to experience direct, positive interaction with the therapist in a manner that is focused entirely on her needs. This will assure her that she will be the focus of the sessions and that this is not just another relationship in which adult needs take precedence over her own.

Verbal Component(s): Jennifer will be taught a verbal relaxation program with guided imagery to use whenever she feels her anxiety is becoming unmanageable. Jennifer will also be guided through strategies designed to desensitize her reaction to abuse-related content discussed in the session. At this stage reflections will be used heavily to help Jennifer identify her feelings, motives and underlying needs.

Collaborative Component(s): (Advocacy, Consultation, Education, Evaluation) Jennifer needs a psychiatric evaluation to determine if psychotropic medications might relieve some of her severe anxiety symptoms and improve her reality testing. In addition the school needs to be made aware of the degree to which Jennifer's symptoms are interfering with her ability to function in school and provided with some strategies for helping her to remain focused in class. Jennifer will need to be educated as to the way in which therapy can benefit her.

Stage II: Tentative Acceptance: (Anticipated Number of Sessions: **5**)

Stage Goal(s): Increased symptom relief. Improving Jennifer's ability to identify and verbalize her own needs.

Participants: Jennifer

Materials: Art materials, hand puppets, anatomically correct dolls, sand tray and animal families, toy dishes, miniature dolls and doll house.

Experiential Component(s): If the therapist is able to provide Jennifer with initial symptom relief it is anticipated that Jennifer will move rapidly and solidly into this stage of treatment. During this phase the emphasis will be on promoting direct interaction between Jennifer and the therapist in ways that address her needs for nurturance without activating her anxiety with respect to the dangers of intimacy. Since the therapist is male this will need to be very carefully monitored.

Verbal Component(s): Because Jennifer is likely to be very open during this stage the therapist will make extensive use of interpretation in order to make all of the information needed for effective problem solving available to Jennifer before she enters the Negative Reaction phase of treatment. The overall goal would be to identify the degree to which Jennifer's reactions to and defenses against her abuse experience have invaded all parts of her life and how they affect all of her internal and external transactions. This will have to be done carefully so that Jennifer sees that the problem is certainly large and invasive enough to work to resolve but not so large as to be overwhelming. Without this, Jennifer is likely to try to avoid any in-depth discussion of the abuse once the most severe symptoms begin to abate.

Collaborative Component(s): (Advocacy, Consultation, Education, Evaluation) During this stage it will be critical to keep Mrs. M aware of Jennifer's response to treatment. Like Jennifer, Mrs. M is likely to begin minimizing the severity of Jennifer's problems once initial symptom reduction takes place. If she becomes too comfortable with Jennifer's improved functioning she is likely to pull Jennifer from treatment so as to avoid the more painful aspects of the treatment (such as discussing her own feelings of guilt regarding Jennifer's experience).

Stage III: Negative Reaction: (Anticipated Number of Sessions: **3**)

Stage Goal(s): Having identified some of Jennifer's underlying needs in the previous stage it will be important to develop strategies by which she can get those needs met and then to have her implement and refine those strategies.

Participants: Jennifer and maybe Mrs. M.

Materials: Art materials, hand puppets, anatomically correct dolls, sand tray and animal families, toy dishes, miniature dolls and doll house.

Experiential Component(s): Again, if there is initial symptom relief it is highly likely that Jennifer will make very rapid gains in the first portion of the treatment and be willing to do and talk about anything the therapist initiates. However, given her history of less than satisfactory interactions with her mother and the trauma of her abuse it is likely that she will be very resistant to attempting to initiate any sort of change outside of the sessions. She is least likely to be willing to approach others in order to get her needs met for fear of rejection or that disclosing such vulnerability will put her at risk for further abuse. As a result this portion of the treatment will focus on rehearsing the implementation of the strategies developed in the previous stage. This will be done initially through pretend play, later through role plays using dolls or puppets and still later in role plays between Jennifer and the therapist. If Jennifer is ready the final step will be to have Jennifer begin telling Mrs. M how she feels about her role in the abuse and its aftermath.

Verbal Component(s): It is likely that little new information will be uncovered at this time. The focus will be on identifying those things that interfere with Jennifer's ability to approach others in order to get her needs met. Additional problem solving will be engaged in as needed to address these interferences.

Collaborative Component(s): (Advocacy, Consultation, Education, Evaluation) Again it will be critical that Mrs. M be kept abreast of Jennifer's progress in treatment. It is likely that some of her symptoms may return at this time, triggered by her anxiety about approaching others in her environment. It is also likely that Jennifer will begin to experience some anger at Mrs. M initially for Mrs. M's failure to protect her and later for her chronic unavailability. She may either withdraw from interactions with Mrs. M at this time or become more clingy and dependent. It is likely she will vacillate between the two. Mrs. M will need substantial support if she is to withstand the interaction of her own feelings of guilt and inadequacy and Jennifer's anger. Similarly, the school may need to be informed should Jennifer's resistance result in either withdrawal or oppositional behavior in that setting.

Stage IV: Growing & Trusting: (Anticipated Number of Sessions: **13-21**)

Stage Goal(s): To foster generalization of the symptom reduction made in the initial phases of treatment. To facilitate transfer of Jennifer's dependency needs from the therapist to Mrs. M. To enhance Jennifer's relationship with Mr. M and his son.

Participants: Initially just Jennifer for a period of 5-8 sessions. Then a series of sessions with Jennifer and Mrs. M consisting of 5-8 sessions. And, finally, a series of about 3-5 sessions with Jennifer and Mr. M.

Materials: Art materials, hand puppets, anatomically correct dolls, sand tray and animal families, toy dishes, miniature dolls and doll house. Fewer materials will be made available as Mrs. M becomes more involved in the sessions so as to promote interaction between her and Jennifer rather than between each of them and the toys. During these sessions the more nurturant toys like those provided in the first session will be reintroduced. As normal play development resumes the toys made available will be chosen to facilitate developmental progress.

Experiential Component(s): The sessions with Jennifer will be structured so as to provide her with the experience of gaining a positive response to any expression of her needs. Over time she will be required to interact in progressively more age-appropriate ways but initially every attempt will be made to gratify any need directly expressed. Should Jennifer's dependency needs become very primitive Mrs. M will be called into the sessions to assist with providing direct nurturance and will be encouraged to continue these activities outside of session. It is quite possible that Jennifer will seek infantile nurturance and want to be held and even fed without talking. As this phase continues Jennifer will likely proceed through the normal play development stages in rather rapid progression moving from nurturance and cuddling, to active or even rough play to simple and then complex pretending and finally to more organized games. Mr. M will not be involved in the sessions until Jennifer is at least at the rough and tumble play stage.

Verbal Component(s): The therapist will use every opportunity to translate Jennifer's attempts to communicate her needs into language and activities appropriate for a child her age. The primary focus of the verbal work will be problem solving strategies that increase Jennifer's ability to get her needs met more effectively and consistently.

Collaborative Component(s): (Advocacy, Consultation, Education, Evaluation) This stage should involve the least work outside the sessions. It may be helpful for the therapist to keep the school informed of Jennifer's newly emerging strategies for getting her needs met so that they can attempt to reinforce her progress and meet some of her needs more directly.

Stage V: Termination: (Anticipated Number of Sessions: **5**)

Stage Goal(s): To foster generalization of the gains made in treatment. To facilitate transfer of Jennifer's dependency needs from the therapist to her peers.

Participants: <u>One session with Jennifer alone to review her gains and her newly developed strategies for getting her needs met. One session with Jennifer and Mrs. M, again, to review gains. Finally, 3 sessions with Jennifer, Mrs. M, Mr. M and his son to facilitate positive family interactions. In these last few sessions no reference would be made to the abuse unless it was directly raised by one of the family members. When this series of sessions is completed Jennifer will be referred for a short-term course of peer group therapy aimed at reestablishing her peer social interactions. While this could be a group for sexually abused children it does not necessarily need to be one as the focus will be socialization rather than abuse recovery.</u>

Materials: <u>For the session with Jennifer alone and the one with Jennifer and her mother the only materials would be paper, crayons and markers. For the family session there would be a mixture of art materials and some toys for promoting gross motor activity.</u>

Experiential Component(s): <u>During the session with Jennifer the goal is simply review and celebration of her gains. She would be allowed to pick a favorite activity from a previous session to be included toward the end of this session. This session would end with a farewell party to which both Jennifer and the therapist will have contributed some treat foods and drinks. The session with Jennifer and Mrs. M will be structured much the same way except that there will not be a party at the end. The family sessions will focus much more on interaction rather than content. Any activity that promotes direct, positive interaction between the family members may be used. The last session of the three will include a termination party planned by the family.</u>

Verbal Component(s): <u>During Jennifer's last session and the last session with her and Mrs. M there will be substantial focus on verbal as opposed to experiential activities since the goal is to promote review, consolidation and generalization. No new content will be elicited by the therapist. During the family session the focus will be on experience rather than verbalization. The therapist will simply identify the degree to which various family members are engaged in and enjoying the activities and assist the family in problem solving strategies for maximizing each member's participation and pleasure.</u>

Collaborative Component(s): (Advocacy, Consultation, Education, Evaluation) <u>At this time it will be important for the therapist to alert Mrs. M to one of the common problems seen in children who have been sexually abused. That is the potential recurrence of some symptomatology as the child enters adolescence. She should be assured that this does not mean Jennifer will definitely become symptomatic, only that the burgeoning of adolescent sexuality may trigger some new difficulties. If this occurs another round of short-term therapy should be initiated as soon as possible so that the problems do not crystallize. Beyond this, Jennifer will be referred to a short-term peer socialization group.</u>

Stage I-V: Peer Group Therapy: (Anticipated Number of Sessions: **8-12**)

<u>For a complete discussion of one model of peer group therapy that would be well suited to Jennifer's needs, see Chapters 14 and 15 of The Play Therapy Primer (O'Connor, 1991).</u>

Signature: _____ Position: _____ Date: _____

Signature: _____ Position: _____ Date: _____

APPENDIX:
Data Integration and Hypothesis Formulation

(see p. 90)

A1.　DEVELOPMENTAL INTEGRATION OF INTAKE INFORMATION

Age	Cognitive Stage	Individual History	Family	Social
<Birth			Mrs. M divorced Mr. L and later married Mr. J.	
Birth			Brother, Mark, age 8	
1				
2				
3				
4			Mrs. M divorces Mr. J	
5			Mrs. M marries Mr. M. He and his son join the household.	
6		Sex abuse occurs. Six months later, sex abuse disclosed.		
7				
8	Concrete Operations		David moved out of the home to live with maternal extended family members	
9				
10				
11				
12				

Age	Educational	Legal	Medical	Mental Health
<Birth				
Birth				
1				
2				
3				
4				
5	Kindergarten			
6	1nd grade			
7	2nd grade	Criminal proceedings against Mr. X, molest perpetrator		Jennifer enters 8 week sex abuse group therapy program.
8		Civil suit against Mr. X	Onset of seizure disorder. Emergency hospitalization.	Referred for treatment.
9		Mr. X due for release from prison		
10				
11				
12				

A2. DEVELOPMENTAL DESCRIPTION OF THE CHILD

Describe the child's present functioning in each of the following areas.

DEVELOPMENTAL LEVEL

(see p. 90)

General: (What is your overall impression of this child's current functioning? Do you think others would perceive him or her to be developmentally on, above or below age level?) Jennifer impresses as a somewhat younger child, maybe 5 to 6 years old. She is so manifestly needy that it seems likely others would perceive her as either very immature or very difficult.

Interpersonal: (Does this child's functioning change depending on the developmental level of the person(s) with whom he or she is interacting?) Jennifer seems to become more immature, quiet and clingy when her mother is present but she resorts to this behavior whenever her needs are not being met. It seems likely that she is not like this when she interacts with unfamiliar adults.

COGNITIONS

(see pp. 91–92)

Functional Level: (Describe overall cognitive functioning as well as any changes that occur when the child is working with emotionally loaded material versus more concrete material.) Jennifers's overall cognitive functioning is at age level although an IQ of 92 may be the cause of her chronic poor school performance. She seems to have specific problems with arithmetic that will require specialized remediation. Her cognitive functioning and reality testing become severely impaired in response to any stimulus that triggers abuse-related content. On the other hand Jennifer shows remarkable ability to understand and use emotional information when she can tolerate her anxiety.

Significant Organizing Beliefs:

1. My mother cannot or will not meet my current needs.
2. Men are dangerous unless they are in the role of "father."
3. Peers will reject me if they find out that I was sexually abused.
4. I know I am missing out on life and social interactions because of my symptoms but there is nothing I can do to change that.
5. There is nothing anyone can do to relieve my symptoms.

EMOTIONS

(see pp. 92–94)

Type: Jennifer's mood is a mixture of anxiety and depression. The latter seems to be, in part, a response to the pervasiveness of the former.

Repertoire: Jennifer has a full repertoire of affects available to her although she only rarely relaxes enough to truly enjoy herself. At best she appears to briefly distract herself from her anxiety for short periods of time.

Range: Jennifer is still able to experience a full range of emotions but mild to powerful negative affects predominate.

Reality Base: Jennifer's negative affects far exceed the reality of her current situation. Often she is responding to quasi-hallucinatory stimuli. While she knows these are not real she cannot control her emotional response to them.

PSYCHOPATHOLOGY

(see pp. 94–95)

Individual (Client) Need(s) Not Being Met Effectively

Jennifer is unable to feel safe in her environment either within or outside her home. She is unable to manage the negative feelings she still experiences as a result of her abuse and uses self-destructive and disassociative strategies that interfere with her own safety and her ability to function academically and socially. She is unable to get the amount or type of nurturance she would like from her mother. She is unable to get her needs for nurturance met through a positive, stable relationship with an adult male caretaker. She is unable to get her needs for nurturance met through adequate peer relationships. She is unable to develop adequate self-esteem.

Individual (Client) Need(s) Not Being Met Appropriately in That These Interfere with Other's Getting Their Needs Met

Jennifer's attempts to meet her need for control through temper outbursts results in Mr. M not getting his need for a peaceful household met. Jennifer's attempts to manage her symptoms result in behavior (such as cutting or burning herself) which greatly interfere with Mrs. M's need to feel like a competent parent and her need to minimize the anxiety in her life. Additionally, Jennifer's need to seek out her mother for reassurance in response to her nightmares is likely to be interfering with Mr. and Mrs. M's needs for intimacy.

Others' Need(s) Not Being Met Appropriately in That These Interfere with Child's Needs Being Met

Mrs. M's need for a relationship with an adult male in spite of the fact that these relationships do not last very long has resulted in significant turnover in the men who function as Jennifer's father. This seems to have contributed to Jennifer's sense of adults as unreliable.

RESPONSE REPERTOIRE

(see pp. 95–96)

Dominant Approach to Problems: ☒ **Autoplastic** ☐ **Alloplastic**

Autoplastic: (Describe those situations to which the child is most likely to make an autoplastic response.)

Jennifer is likely to respond autoplastically to virtually every situation. When she encounters a supportive or nurturing adult she is likely to become very demanding but she does not expect them to provide for her except under duress. Unfortunately, Jennifer does not see herself as particularly comptent so that she does not hold out much hope of getting her needs met in reality.

Alloplastic: (Describe those situations to which the child is most likely to make an alloplastic response.)

When pushed beyond her capacity to function Jennifer is capable of acting out. Mr. M reports that Jennifer will have brief tantrums when he pushes her to complete household chores immediately. She can become particularly demanding when she perceives adults to be intentionally withholding. However, she gives up easily and retreats into helplessness and depression.

A3. HYPOTHESIS DEVELOPMENT: ETIOLOGIC FACTORS

Develop hypotheses regarding the bases for the child's present level of function/dysfunction.

CHILD FACTORS

(see pp. 97–98)

Endowment: Jennifer's slightly below average intellectual capacities have made it difficult for her to use an autoplastic response style effectively.

Developmental Response: Because Jennifer's parents were divorced when she was four years old she may not have developed as complete an attachment to men as she might have if they had divorced later in her life. Because Mrs. M remarried soon after the divorce from Jennifer's father Jennifer may have come to believe both that men are replaceable and that it is important to have one in one's life. Because there were no traumas as Jennifer entered school she was able to develop positive peer attachments. Because Jennifer was abused at the age when peer relationships are becoming more significant for children her own relationships have been disrupted. Because she developed a seizure disorder at about the same time that her PTSD symptoms became very problematic Jennifer may believe that her entire "self" is falling apart under the strain of the abuse.

ECOSYSTEMIC FACTORS

(see pp. 98–99)

Family: Because of Mrs. M's apparent cognitive and emotional limitations, Jennifer seems to have reacted by believing that all adults have limited ability and/or desire to meet her needs. Jennifer seems to feel that her mother will put her own needs over Jennifer's needs in most situations. Interestingly, she does not seem angry about this but rather she seems to have accepted it as the norm. The high turnover of adult males in the house may have made Jennifer feel that men are unstable and untrustworthy.

Peers: Peers do not seem to have played a significant role in the etiology of Jennifer's problems.

Other: Educational, Medical, Legal, Cultural, Historical: Jennifer's school contributed to the current problem by leaving Jennifer in a situation where she has been chronically less than successful and not providing her with any assistance. In addition the school personnel's obliviousness to the problem must contribute to Jennifer's sense that all adults are unwilling or unable to address her needs. The mental health system contributed by failing to recognize the severity of Jennifer's symptoms, again making it appear that adults are blind to her needs. The legal system contributed by forcing Jennifer to face her abuser in court, adding significantly to the trauma she has experienced. Ironically, she is aware that her testimony is largely responsible for his conviction and this has reinforced her tendency to believe that she is the only one who can do anything about her problems. The fact that her abuser will only spend two years in jail has contributed to Jennifer's sense of helplessness and victimization.

A4. HYPOTHESIS DEVELOPMENT: MAINTAINING FACTORS

Develop hypotheses regarding factors maintaining the child's present level of function/dysfunction.

CHILD FACTORS (see pp. 99–100)

Endowment: Jennifer's average IQ may make the development of new coping strategies somewhat more difficult.

Developmental Response: Now that Jennifer has regressed to a very early developmental level of emotional and social functioning she is unable to engage in effective problem solving with respect to getting her needs met. This leaves her prone to repeating earlier negative developmental responses.

COST/BENEFIT ANALYSIS OF BELIEFS, EMOTIONS AND BEHAVIOR (see pp. 100–101)

Jennifer's symptoms cost her a great deal in terms of emotional pain and isolation. She suffers most from the loss of peer interactions and this will serve as her primary motive to return to health. Her symptoms protect her from the anger she harbors towards her mother for failing to protect her from her abuse. This anger is intolerable because she has become physically and emotionally dependent on her mother in a manner consistent with a much younger child. Her symptoms serve both to solicit support from her mother and to punish her mother both literally and figuratively. Mrs. M is experiencing sufficient guilt and anxiety about Jennifer's symptoms to seek out mental health services. In addition Jennifer's nightmares and sleep disruption is so severe that it is quite effective in preventing Mrs. M from getting a full night's sleep. The degree to which Jennifer is able to use autoplastic strategies to care for herself masks the severity of her underlying disturbance.

ECOSYSTEMIC FACTORS (see pp. 101–102)

Family: Jennifer's family experience makes her prone to believing that adults are essential but unreliable, so she attaches easily and then does not expect much of a return. Mrs. M's limited cognitive and emotional skills make her a poor resource for Jennifer to use in the course of her treatment.

Peers: Peers may prove to be a good source of support for Jennifer and eventually placing her in a peer group may greatly enhance her progress in treatment.

Other: Educational, Medical, Legal, Cultural, Historical: Jennifer's school maintains her sense of being minimally competent and their failure to respond to her distress maintains her sense of hopelessness and distrust. The legal system is about to exacerbate Jennifer's symptoms substantially by releasing her abuser so soon after the final trauma of the court appearance. These events increase Jennifer's belief that adults are unable or unwilling to take care of her.

A5.　GOAL DEVELOPMENT/SYNTHESIS AND TREATMENT PLANNING

A. Develop goal statements specific to the factors identified in Section VI and VII.　　　(see pp. 105–110)

B. Indicate the category into which the goal falls
　　S = Safety/Crisis, **SB** = Secure Base, **D** = Developmental, **PC** = Problem/Content, **C** = Coping, **Sy** = Systemic

C. Check those goals to be addressed in context of psychotherapy.

D. Number the goals in order of priority.

E. Determine the system or context in which each of the treatment goals should be addressed.
　　I = Individual, **F** = Family, **P** = Peer, **S** = School, **M** = Medical Setting, **MH** = Mental Health Setting, **C** = Community, etc.

F. Determine the interventions to be used in the course of the treatment.
　　R = Referral, **IP** = Individual Psychotherapy, **FT** = Family Therapy, **PG** = Peer Group Therapy, **Fi** = Filial Therapy, **C** = Consultation, **Ed** = Education, **Ev** = Evaluation, **A** = Advocacy, etc.

	A: Comprehensive Goal List	B	C	D	E	F
1.	B-15: Is able to complete short, individual tasks with familiar materials independent of any adult intervention.	D	X	4	I/S	IP/C
2.	B-23: Indicates flexibility in modifying procedures to satisfy the changing needs of the group.	D	X	4	I/S/P	IP/C/ PG
3.	B-24: Participates in new experiences with verbal and physical control. (Child) participates with or without verbal support from an adult.	SB/D	X	4	I/S	IP/C
4.	C-16: Uses words or gestures to show appropriate positive and negative feeling responses to environment, materials and people or animals. Adult uses activities to elicit responses.	PC/D	X	4	I	IP
5.	C-18: Uses words or nonverbal gestures spontaneously to show pride in own work or to make positive statements about self.	PC	X	4	I/S	IP/C
6.	C-22: Uses words spontaneously to show pride in group achievements. (Child) indicates identification with the group's success and conveys this through the use of plural and possessive pronouns.	PC	X	4	S/P	PG
7.	S-26: Seeks assistance or praise from a peer spontaneously.	D	X	4	P	S/PG

8. S-27: Assists others spontaneously in conforming to group rules.	D	X	4	P	S/PG
9. Decrease frequency and intensity of PTSD symptoms	S/PC	X	1	I	IP
10. Self-mutilation and suicidal ideation	S	X	1	I	IP
11. Nightmares	PC	X	1	I	IP
12. Visual and auditory hallucinations	PC	X	1	I	IP
13. Agoraphobia	SB/ PC	X	1	I	IP
14. Increase behavioral compliance	D	X	4	F	FP
15. Increase number and quality of peer interactions	D	X	4	P	PG
16. Increase Jennifer's cognitive understanding of the molest experience	PC	X	2	I	IP
17. Who was at fault	PC	X	2	I	Ed
18. What was "wrong" about her experience	PC	X	2	I	Ed
19. What her mother's role was in both her original and current experience	PC	X	2	I	IP
20. The role of the legal system	PC	X	2	I	Ed
21. Activate Jennifer's anger at her mother for failing to protect her from the abuse.	PC	X	2	I	IP
22. Increase Jennifer's awareness of her intrapsychic and interpersonal needs.	D	X	2	I	IP
23. Decrease Jennifer's feelings of guilt relative to having been an abuse victim.	PC	X	2	I	IP
24. Improve ability to ask to have needs met.	D	X	3	I/F/P	IP/FP /PG
25. Enhance and stabilize Jennifer's relationship with her mother so that both are able to get their needs met.	SB	X	3	F	FP
26. Enhance and stabilize Jennifer's relationship with her stepfather so that both are able to get their needs met.	SB	X	3	F	FP
27. Improve school performance.	D		5	S	C
28. Enhance sense that she will continue to be safe after her abuser is released from prison.	C		5	Legal	C/A

Note: Goals that are preceded by a letter/number code from the DTORF-R (Developmental Therapy Institute, 1992) completed by Mrs. M.

◆ REFERENCES ◆

Abney, V. (1966). Cultural competency in the field of child maltreatment. In J. Briere, L. Berliner, J. Bulkley, C. Jenny, & T. Reid (Eds.), *The APSAC handbook on child maltreatment* (pp. 409–419). Thousand Oaks, CA: Sage.

Ainsworth, M.D.S., Blehar, M. D., Waters, E., & Wall, S. (1978). *Patterns of attachment.* Hillsdale, NJ: Erlbaum.

American Psychiatric Association. (1994). *Diagnostic and statistical manual of mental disorders* (4th ed.). Washington, DC: Author.

American Psychological Association. (1992). Ethical principles of psychologists and code of conduct. *American Psychologist, 47,* 1597–1611.

Ames, L. B., & Ilg, F. L. (1976). *Your three-year-old: Friend or enemy.* New York: Dell.

Ammaniti, M. (1991). Maternal representations during pregnancy and early infant-mother interactions. *Infant Mental Health Journal, 12*(3), 246–255.

Ammen, S. A. (1990). A phenomenological hermeneutic investigation of Maturana's biological systems theory and its implications for the theories of family therapy. Doctoral dissertation, California School of Professional Psychology, 1989. *Dissertation Abstracts International, 51,* 1483B.

Ammen, S. (1993). The Good Feeling—Bad Feeling Game: A technique to facilitate attachment, communication, and therapeutic process between foster parents (and parents) and children. In K. J. O'Connor & C. E. Schaefer (Eds.), *Handbook of play therapy: Vol. 2. Advances and innovations* (pp. 283–294). New York: John Wiley & Sons.

Anderson, H., & Goolishian, M. A. (1992). The client is the expert: A not knowing approach to therapy. In K. J. Gergen & S. McNamee (Eds.), *Therapy as a social construction* (pp. 25–39). Newbury Park, CA: Sage.

Apgar, V. (1953). A proposal for a new method of evaluation in the newborn infant. *Current Research in Anesthesia and Analgesia, 32,* 260.

Ariel, S. (1992). *Strategic family play therapy.* New York: John Wiley & Sons.

Ashby, W. R. (1956). *An introduction to cybernetics.* London: Chapman & Hall.

Atwood, G., & Stolorow, R. (1984). *Structures of subjectivity: Explorations in psychoanalytic phenomenology.* Hillsdale, NJ: The Analytic Press.

Axiline, V. (1947). *Play therapy.* Boston: Houghton Mifflin.

Bandler, R., & Grinder, J. (1975). *The structure of magic I.* Palo Alto, CA: Science and Behavior Books.

Barbaree, H. E., Marshall, W. L., & Hudson, S. M. (Eds.). (1993). *The juvenile sex offender.* New York: Guilford Press.

Barker, P. (1990). *Clinical interviews with children and adolescents.* New York: W. W. Norton.

Bateson, G. (1972). *Steps to an ecology of mind.* New York: Ballantine Books.

Belsky, J. (1980). Child maltreatment: An ecological integration. *American Psychologist, 35,* 320–335.

Bertalanffy, L. von. (1968). *General system theory.* New York: George Braziller.

Bird, H. R., & Kestenbaum, C. J. (1988). A semistructured approach to clinical assessment. In C. J. Kestenbaum & D. T. Williams (Eds.), *Handbook of clinical assessment of children and adolescents* (Vol. 1, pp. 19–30). New York: New York University Press.

Bixler, R. (1949). Limits are therapy. *Journal of Consulting Psychology, 13,* 1–11.

Bornstein, B. (1945). Clinical notes on child analysis. *Psychoanalytic Study of the Child, 1,* 151–166.

Bowlby, J. (1973). *Attachment and loss: Vol. 2. Separation: Anxiety and anger.* New York: Basic Books.

Bowlby, J. (1980). *Attachment and loss: Vol. 3. Loss: Sadness and depression.* New York: Basic Books.

Bowlby, J. (1982). *Attachment and loss: Vol. 1. Attachment* (2nd ed.). New York: Basic Books.

Bowlby, J. (1988). *A Secure Base: Parent–child attachment and healthy human development.* London: Routledge.

Brassard, M. R., Germain, R., & Hart, S. N. (Eds.). (1987). *Psychological maltreatment of children and youth.* Elmsford, NY: Pergamon.

Braun, B. G. (1984). Towards a theory of multiple personality and other dissociative phenomena. *Psychiatric Clinics of North America, 7*(1), 171–193.

Bretherton, I. (1987). New perspectives on attachment relations in infancy: Security, communication and internal working models. In J. D. Osofsky (Ed.), *Handbook of infant development* (2nd ed., pp. 1061–1100). New York: Wiley.

Bretherton, I. (1993). Theoretical contributions from developmental psychology. In P. G. Boss, W. J. Doherty, R. LaRossa, W. R. Schumm, & S. K. Steinmetz (Eds.), *Sourcebook of family theories and methods: A contextual approach* (pp. 275–297). New York: Plenum.

Bronfenbrenner, U. (1977). Toward an experimental ecology of human development. *American Psychologist, 32,* 513–531.

Bronfenbrenner, U. (1979). *The ecology of human development: Experiences by nature and design.* Cambridge, MA: Harvard University Press.

Bubolz, M. M., & Sontag, M. S. (1993). Human ecology theory. In P. G. Boss, W. J. Doherty, R. LaRossa, W. R. Schumm, & S. K. Steinmetz (Eds.), *Sourcebook of family theories and methods: A contextual approach* (pp. 419–448). New York: Plenum.

Bulkley, J. A., Feller, J. N., Stern, P., & Roe, R. (1996). Child abuse and neglect laws and legal proceedings. In J. Briere, L. Berliner, J. A. Bulkley, C. Jenny, & T. Reid (Eds.), *The APSAC handbook on child maltreatment* (pp. 271–296). Thousand Oaks, CA: Sage.

Canino, I. A., & Spurlock, J. (1994). *Culturally diverse children and adolescents: Assessment diagnosis and treatment.* New York: Guilford.

Cantlay, L. (1996). *Detecting child abuse: Recognizing children at risk through drawings.* Santa Barbara, CA: Holly Press.

Caplan, F. (1973). *The first twelve months of life: Your baby's growth month by month.* New York: Bantam.

Caplan, F., & Caplan, T. (1977). *The second twelve months of life: Your baby's growth month by month.* New York: Bantam.

Caplan, R., & Sherman, T. (1991). Kiddie Formal Thought Disorder Rating Scale and Story Game. In C. E. Schaefer, K. Gitlin, & A. Sandgrund (Eds.), *Play diagnosis and assessment* (pp. 169–202). New York: John Wiley.

Caplan, T., & Caplan, F. (1983). *The early childhood years: The 2 to 6 years old.* New York: Bantum.

Cappelletty, G. G. II. (1987). Factors affecting psychological distress in the Hmong refugee community. Doctoral dissertation, California School of Professional Psychology, 1986. *Dissertation Abstracts International, 48,* 257B.

Carson, M., & Goodfield, R. (1988). The children's garden attachment model. In R. W. Small & F. J. Alwon (Eds.), *Challenging the Limits of Care.* Needham, MA: Trieschman Center.

Cattell, R. B. (1971). *Abilities: Their structure, growth, and action.* Boston: Houghton-Mifflin.

Cipani, E. (1989). *The treatment of severe behavior disorders: Behavior analysis approaches.* Washington, DC: American Association of Mental Retardation.

Cipani, E. (1993). *The Cipani Behavioral Assessment and Diagnostic (C-BAD) System.* Visalia, CA: Cipani & Associates.

Cohen, R. J., Swerdlik, M. E., & Smith, D. K. (1992). *Psychological testing and assessment: An introduction to tests and measurements, Second edition.* Mountain View, CA: Mayfield Publishing.

Conners, C. K., & Barkley, R. A. (1985). Rating scales and checklists for child psychopharmacology. *Psychopharmacology Bulletin, 21,* 809–815.

Conoley, J. C. (1981a). Advocacy consultation: Promises and problems. In J. C. Conoley (Ed.), *Consultation in schools: Theory, research, procedures* (pp. 157–178). New York: Academic Press.

Conoley, J. C. (Ed.). (1981b). *Consultation in schools: Theory, research, procedures.* New York: Academic Press.

Cramer, B., Robert-Tissot, C., Stern, D. N., Serpa-Rusconi, S., De Muralt, M., Besson, G., Palacio-Espasa, F., Bachmann, J. P., Knauer, D., Berney, C., & d'Arcis, U. (1990). Outcome evaluation in brief mother–infant psychotherapy: A preliminary report. *Infant Mental Health Journal, 11*(3), 278–300.

Crittenden, P. M., & Ainsworth, M.D.S. (1989). Child maltreatment and attachment theory. In D. Cicchetti & V. Carlson (Eds.), *Child maltreatment: Theory and research on the causes of child abuse and neglect* (pp. 432–463). New York: Cambridge University Press.

Dana, R. H. (1993). *Multicultural assessment perspectives for professional psychology.* Boston: Allyn & Bacon.

Davidson, M. (1983). *Uncommon sense: The life and thought of Ludwig von Bertalanffy (1901–1972), Father of General Systems Theory.* Los Angeles: J. P. Tarcher.

Developmental Therapy Institute. (1992). *Developmental teaching objectives for the Developmental Teaching Objectives Rating Form-Revised: Assessment and teaching of social emotional competence* (4th ed.). Athens, GA: Author.

Elliott, R. (1984). A discovery-oriented approach to significant change events in psychotherapy: Interpersonal process recall and comprehensive process analysis. In L. Rice & L. Greenberg (Eds.), *Patterns of change: Intensive analysis of psychotherapy process.* New York: Guilford Press.

Erickson, M. F., & Egeland, B. (1996). Child Neglect. In J. Briere, L. Berliner, J. A. Bulkley, C. Jenny, & T. Reid (Eds.), *The APSAC handbook on child maltreatment* (pp. 4–20). Thousand Oaks, CA: Sage.

Eron, J. B., & Lund, T. W. (1996). *Narrative solutions in brief therapy.* New York: Guilford.

Exner, J. (1993). *The Rorschach: Vol. I: Basic Foundations* (3rd ed.). New York: John Wiley & Sons.

Exner, J., & Weiner, I. (1994). *The Rorschach: Vol. III. Children & Adolescents* (2nd ed.). New York: John Wiley & Sons.

Ferenczi, S. (1919). The phenomena of hysterical materialization. Thoughts on the conception of hysterical conversion symbolism. In *Further contributions to the theory and technique of psycho-analysis.* London: Hogarth, 1926.

Fischer, J., & Corcoran, K. (1994). *Measures for clinical practice: A sourcebook: Vol. 1. Couples, families and children* (2nd ed.). New York: Free Press.

Flavell, J. H. (1963). *The developmental psychology of Jean Piaget.* New York: D. Van Nostrand.

Folse, H. J. (1985). *The philosophy of Niels Bohr: The framework of complementarity.* New York: North-Holland.

Freud, A. (1928). *Introduction to the technique of child analysis.* L. P. Clark (Trans.). New York: Nervous and Mental Disease Publishing.

Freud, S. (1909). Analysis of a phobia in a five-year-old boy. In *Standard edition* (Vol. 9). London: Hogarth.

Freud, S. (1933). *Collected Papers.* London: Hogarth Press.

Friedman, N., & Sherman, R. (1987). *Handbook of measurement for marriage and family therapy.* New York: Brunner/Mazel.

Friedman, W. (1982). *The developmental psychology of time.* New York: Academic Press.

Gil, E. (1994). *Play in family therapy.* New York: Guilford.

Giorgi, A. (1979). Phenomenology and psychological theory. In A. Giorgi, R. Knowles, & D. L. Smith (Eds.), *Duquesne studies in phenomenological psychology* (Vol. III, pp. 60–80). Pittsburgh: Duquesne University Press.

Giorgi, A. (1983). Concerning the possibility of phenomenological psychological research. *Journal of Phenomenological Psychology, 14*(2), 129–169.

Giorgi, A. (1985). The phenomenological psychology of learning and the verbal learning tradition. In A. Giorgi (Ed.), *Phenomenology and psychological research* (pp. 23–85). Pittsburgh: Duquesne University Press.

Goodman, J. D., & Sours, J. A. (1994). *The child mental status examination* (softcover). Northvale, NJ: Jason Aronson. (Original work published 1967)

Goolishian, M. A., & Anderson, H. (1987). Language and systems and therapy: An evolving idea. *Psychotherapy, 24,* 529–538.

Greenspan, S. I. (1992). *Infancy and early childhood: The practice of clinical assessment and intervention with emotional and developmental challenges.* Madison, CT: International Universities Press.

Greenspan, S. I. (with Greenspan, N. T.). (1991). *The Clinical Interview of the Child* (2nd ed.). Washington, DC: American Psychiatric Press.

Grotevant, H. D., & Carlson, C. I. (Eds.). (1989). *Family assessment: A guide to methods and measures.* New York: Guilford.

Guerney, L. F. (1976). Training manual for parents: Instruction in filial therapy. In C. E. Schaefer (Ed.), *Therapeutic use of child's play* (pp. 216–227). New York: Jason Aronson.

Guerney, L. F. (1983a). Client-centered (nondirective) play therapy. In C. E. Schaefer & K. J. O'Connor (Eds.), *Handbook of play therapy* (pp. 21–64). New York: John Wiley.

Guerney, L. F. (1983b). Introduction to filial therapy: Training parents as therapists. In P. A. Keller & L. G. Ritt (Eds.), *Innovations in clinical practice: A sourcebook* (Vol. 2, pp. 26–39). Sarasota, FL: Professional Resource Exchange.

Guerney, L. F., & Guerney, B. G., Jr. (1987). Integrating child and family therapy. *Psychotherapy, 24,* 609–614.

Gurman, A. S., Kniskern, D. P., & Pinsof, W. M. (1986). Research on the process and outcome of marital and family therapy. In S. L. Garfield & A. E. Bergin (Eds.), *Handbook of psychotherapy and behavioral change.* New York: Wiley.

Hart, S. N., Brassard, M. R., & Karlson, H. C. (1996). Psychological maltreatment. In J. Briere, L. Berliner, J. A. Bulkley, C. Jenny, & T. Reid (Eds.), *The APSAC handbook on child maltreatment* (pp. 72–89). Thousand Oaks, CA: Sage.

Harvey, S. (1994). Dynamic play therapy: Creating attachments. In B. James (Ed.), *Handbook for treatment of attachment-trauma problems in children* (pp. 222–233). New York: Lexington.

Harter, S. (1983). Cognitive-developmental considerations in the conduct of play therapy. In C. E. Schaefer & K. J. O'Connor (Eds.), *Handbook of play therapy* (pp. 95–127). New York: John Wiley & Sons.

Hathaway, S., & McKinley, J. (1991). *Minnesota Multiphasic Personality Inventory-2.* Minneapolis: University of Minnesota Press.

Hempel, C. G. (1966). *Philosophy of natural science.* Englewood Cliffs, NJ: Prentice-Hall.

Herman, J. L. (1992). *Trauma and recovery.* New York: Basic Books.

Hesse, M. (1980). *Revolutions and reconstructions in the philosophy of science.* Bloomington, IN: Indiana University Press.

Hinde, R. A. (1979). *Towards understanding relationships.* London: Academic Press.

Holman, A. M. (1983). *Family assessment: Tools for understanding and interventions.* Beverly Hills, CA: Sage.

Irwin, E. C. (1991). The use of a puppet interview to understand children. In C. E. Schaefer, K. Gitlin, & A. Sandgrund (Eds.), *Play diagnosis and assessment* (pp. 617–635). New York: John Wiley.

James, B. (1989). *Treating traumatized children: New insights and creative interventions.* Lexington, MA: Lexington.

James, B. (1994). *Handbook for treatment of attachment-trauma problems in children.* New York: Lexington.

Jernberg, A. (1979). *Theraplay.* San Francisco: Jossey-Bass.

Jernberg, A. (1988). Promoting prenatal and perinatal mother–child bonding: A psychotherapeutic assessment of parental attitudes. In P. Fedor-Freybergh & M.L.V. Vogel (Eds.), *Prenatal and perinatal psychology and medicine: Encounter with the unborn* (pp. 253–266). Park Ridge, NJ: Parthenon.

Jernberg, A. (1991). Assessing parent–child interactions with the Marschak Interaction Method (MIM). In C. E. Schaefer, K. Gitlin, & A. Sandgrund (Eds.), *Play diagnosis and assessment* (pp. 493–515). New York: John Wiley.

Jernberg, A., & Jernberg, E. (1993). Family Theraplay for the family tyrant. In T. Kottman & C. Schaefer (Eds.), *Play therapy in action: A casebook for practitioners* (pp. 45–96). Northvale, NJ: Jason Aronson.

Johnson, O. G. (1976). *Tests and measurements in child development* (Vols. 1 & 2). San Francisco: Jossey-Bass.

Kalichman, S. C. (1993). *Mandated reporting of suspected child abuse.* Washington, DC: American Psychological Association.

Karen, R. (1994). *Becoming Attached: Unfolding the mystery of the infant–mother bond and its impact on later life.* New York: Warner Books.

Karpel, M. A., & Strauss, E. S. (1983). *Family evaluation.* New York: Gardner Press.

Katz, K. (1992). Communication problems in maltreated children: A tutorial. *Journal of Childhood Communication Disorders, 14*(2), 147–163.

Kaufman, A. S. (1994). *Intelligent testing with the WISC-III.* New York: Wiley.

Kazdin, A. E. (1987). *Conduct disorders in childhood and adolescence.* Newbury Park, CA: Sage.

Kestenbaum, C. J., & Williams, D. T. (Eds.). (1988). *Handbook of clinical assessment of children and adolescents* (Vols. 1 & 2). New York: New York University Press.

Kilpatrick, A. C., & Holland, T. P. (1995). *Working with families: An integrative model by level of functioning.* Boston: Allyn & Bacon.

Krystal, H. (1988). *Integration and self-healing: Affect, trauma, alexithymia.* Hillsdale, NJ: Analytic Press.

Landreth, G. L. (1991). *The art of the relationship.* Muncie, IN: Accelerated Development.

Landreth, G., Homeyer, L., & Bratton, S. (1993). *The world of play therapy literature.* Denton, TX: The Center for Play Therapy, University of North Texas.

Linder, T. W. (1993). *Transdisciplinary play-based assessment: A functional approach to working with young children.* (rev. ed.). Baltimore: Paul H. Brookes.

Lyons-Ruth, K., & Zeanah, C. H., Jr. (1993). *The family context of infant mental health: I. Affective development in the primary caregiving relationship.* In C. H. Zeanah, Jr. (Ed.), *Handbook of infant mental health.* New York: Guilford.

Mahler, M. (1967). On human symbiosis and the vicissitudes of individuation. *Journal of the American Psychoanalytic Association, 25,* 740–763.

Mahler, M. (1972). On the first three subphases of the separation–individuation process. *Journal of Psycho-Analysis, 53,* 333–338.

Maslow, A. (1970). *Motivation and personality.* New York: Harper and Row.

Maturana, H. R. (1978). Biology of language: The epistemology of reality. In G. A. Miller & E. Lenneberg (Eds.), *Psychology and biology of language and thought* (pp. 27–63). New York: Academic Press.

Maturana, H. R. (1980). Introduction. In H. R. Maturana & F. J. Varela, *Autopoiesis and cognition: The realization of the living* (pp. x–xxx). Boston: Reidel.

Maturana, H. R., & Varela, F. J. (1980). *Autopoiesis and cognition: The realization of the living.* Boston: Reidel. (Original work published in 1973)

Maturana, H. R., & Varela, F. J. (1987). *The tree of knowledge: The biological roots of human understanding.* Boston: New Science Library (Shambhala).

Mayes, S. D. (1991). Play assessment of preschool hyperactivity. In C. E. Schaefer, K. Gitlin, & A. Sandgrund (Eds.), *Play diagnosis and assessment* (pp. 249–282). New York: John Wiley.

McArthur, D. S., & Roberts, G. E. (1982). *Roberts Apperception Test for Children manual.* Los Angeles: Western Psychological Services.

McGoldrick, M., & Gerson, R. (1985). *Genograms in family assessment.* New York: Norton.

Morgan, G. A., Maslin-Cole, C. A., Biringen, Z., & Harmon, R. J. (1991). Play assessment of mastery motivation in infants and young children. In C. E. Schaefer, K. Gitlin, & A. Sandgrund (Eds.), *Play diagnosis and assessment* (pp. 65–86). New York: John Wiley.

Moustakas, C. (1959). *Psychotherapy with children.* New York: Harper & Row.

Nader, K., & Pynoos, R. S. (1991). Play and drawing techniques as tools for interviewing traumatized children. In C. E. Schaefer, K. Gitlin, & A. Sandgrund (Eds.), *Play diagnosis and assessment* (pp. 375–390). New York: John Wiley.

Nardone, M., Tryon, W., & O'Connor, K. (1986). The effectiveness and generalization of a cognitive-behavioral group treatment to reduce impulsive/aggressive behavior for boys in a residential setting. *Behavioral and Residential Treatment, 1*(2), 93–103.

National Center for Clinical Infant Programs. (1994). *Diagnostic Classification: 0–3. Diagnostic Classification of Mental Health and Developmental Disorders of Infancy and Early Childhood.* Arlington, VA: Zero to Three/National Center for Clinical Infant Programs.

Nichols, M. P. (1984). *Family therapy: Concepts and methods.* New York: Gardner Press.

O'Connor, K. J. (1983). The Color-Your-Life technique. In C. E. Schaefer & K. J. O'Connor (Eds.), *Handbook of play therapy* (pp. 251–258). New York: John Wiley & Sons.

O'Connor, K. J. (1991). *The play therapy primer: An integration of theories and techniques.* New York: Wiley.

O'Connor, K. J. (1993a). Child, protector, confidant: Structured group ecosystemic play therapy. In T. Kottman & C. Schaefer (Eds.), *Play therapy in action: A casebook for practitioners* (pp. 245–280). Northvale, NJ: Jason Aronson.

O'Connor, K. J. (1993b). Ecosystemic play therapy. In K. J. O'Connor & C. E. Schaefer (Eds.), *Handbook of play therapy: Vol. 2. Advances and innovations* (pp. 61–84). New York: John Wiley.

O'Connor, K. J. (1997). Ecosystemic play therapy. In K. J. O'Connor & L. M. Braverman (Eds.), *Play therapy and practice: A comparative presentation* (pp. 234–284). New York: John Wiley.

O'Neill, R. E., Horner, R. H., Albin, R. W., Storey, K., & Sprague, J. R. (1990). *Functional analysis of problem behavior: A practical assessment guide.* Sycamore, IL: Sycamore Publishing Company.

Orvaschel, H. (1988). Structured and semistructured psychiatric interviews for children. In C. J. Kestenbaum & D. T. Williams (Eds.), *Handbook of clinical assessment of children and adolescents* (Vol. 1, pp. 31–42). New York: New York University Press.

Othmer, E., & Othmer, S. (1989). *The clinical interview using DSM III-R.* Washington, DC: American Psychiatric Press.

Pedersen, P. (1988). *A handbook for developing multicultural awareness.* Alexandria, VA: American Association for Counseling and Development.

Pfeffer, C. R. (1979). Clinical observations of play in suicidal latency age children. *Suicide and Life-Threatening Behavior, 9,* 235–244.

Phares, E. J. (1976). *Locus of control in personality.* Morristown, NJ: General Learning Press.

Phares, E. J. (1984). Locus of control. In R. J. Corsini (Ed.), *Encyclopedia of psychology* (Vol. 2, pp. 316–318). New York: Wiley.

Piaget, J. (1952). *The origins of intelligence in children.* New York: International Universities Press.

Piaget, J. (1959). *The language and thought of the child.* London: Routledge & Kegan Paul.

Piaget, J. (1967). *Six psychological studies.* New York: Vintage.

Pope, A. W., & Bierman, K. L. (1991). Play assessment of peer interaction in children. In C. E. Schaefer, K. Gitlin, & A. Sandgrund (Eds.), *Play diagnosis and assessment* (pp. 553–578). New York: John Wiley.

Roopnarine, J. L., Johnson, J. E., & Hooper, F. H. (Eds.). (1994). *Children's play in diverse cultures.* Albany, NY: State University of New York Press.

Ross, P. (1991). The family puppet technique: For assessing parent–child and family interaction patterns. In C. E. Schaefer, K. Gitlin, & A. Sandgrund (Eds.), *Play diagnosis and assessment* (pp. 609–616). New York: John Wiley.

Rubin, P. B., & Tregay, J. (1989). *Play with them—Theraplay groups in the classroom.* Springfield, IL: Charles C. Thomas.

Sacks, H., & Reader, W. D. (1992). History of the juvenile court. In Workgroup on Psychiatric Practice in the Juvenile Court of the American Psychiatric Association, Handbook of psychiatric practice in the juvenile court (pp. 5–11). Washington, DC: American Psychiatric Association.

Satir, V. (1972). *Peoplemaking.* Palo Alto, CA: Science and Behavior Books.

Saywitz, K., & Goodman, G. (1996). Interviewing children in and out of court: Current research and practice implications. In J. Briere, L. Berliner, J. Bulkley, C. Jenny, & T. Reid. *The APSAC handbook on child maltreatment* (pp. 297–318). Thousand Oaks, CA: Sage.

Schaefer, C., & Carey, L. (Eds.). (1994). *Family play therapy.* Northvale, NJ: Jason Aronson.

Schaefer, C. E., Gitlin, K., & Sandgrund, A. (1991a). Annotated bibliography: Projective play assessment. In C. E. Schaefer, K. Gitlin, & A. Sandgrund (Eds.), *Play diagnosis and assessment* (pp. 637–639). New York: John Wiley.

Schaefer, C. E., Gitlin, K., & Sandgrund, A. (Eds.). (1991b). *Play diagnosis and assessment.* New York: John Wiley.

Siegel, B. (1991). Play diagnosis of autism: The ETHOS play session. In C. E. Schaefer, K. Gitlin, & A. Sandgrund (Eds.), *Play diagnosis and assessment* (pp. 331–374). New York: John Wiley.

Simon, R. (Ed.). (July/August, 1994). Multiculturalism [special issue]. *Family Therapy Networker, 18*(4).

Smith, D. (1991). Parent–child interaction play assessment. In C. E. Schaefer, K. Gitlin, & A. Sandgrund (Eds.), *Play diagnosis and assessment* (pp. 463–492). New York: John Wiley.

Smith, G. (1991). Assessing family interaction by the collaborative drawing technique. In C. E. Schaefer, K. Gitlin, & A. Sandgrund (Eds.), *Play diagnosis and assessment* (pp. 599–608). New York: John Wiley.

Solomon, B. B. (1993). Ethnocultural issues in child mental health. In H. C. Johnson (Ed.), *Child mental health in the 1990s: Curricula for graduate and undergraduate professional education.* Rockville, MD: U.S. Department of Health and Human Services, Public Health Service, Substance Abuse and Mental Health Services Administration, Center for Mental Health Services.

Southworth, L. E., Burr, R. L., & Cox, A. E. (1981). *Screening and evaluating the young infant: A handbook of instruments to use from infancy to six years.* Springfield, IL: C. C. Thomas.

Stern, D. N. (1985). *The interpersonal world of the infant: A view from psychoanalysis and developmental psychology.* New York: Basic Books.

Stern, D. N. (1995). *The motherhood constellation: A unified view of parent–infant psychotherapy.* New York: Basic Books.

Stollak, G. E., Crandell, L. E., & Pirsch, L. A. (1991). Assessment of the family in the playroom. In C. E. Schaefer, K. Gitlin, & A. Sandgrund (Eds.), *Play diagnosis and assessment* (pp. 527–548). New York: John Wiley.

Sue, D. W., & Sue, D. (1990). *Counseling the culturally different: Theory and Practice* (2nd ed.). New York: John Wiley & Sons.

Sullivan, K. (1996). *Children's projective drawing battery.* Unpublished manuscript.

Teglasi, H. (1993). *Clinical use of story telling: Emphasizing the TAT with children and adolescents.* Boston: Allyn & Bacon.

Terr, L. (1981). Forbidden games: Post-traumatic child's play. *Journal of the American Academy of Child Psychiatry, 20,* 741–760.

Terr, L. (1990). *Too scared to cry: Psychic trauma in childhood.* New York: Harper & Row.

Thorndike, R. L., Hagen, E. P., & Sattler, J. P. (1986a). *Guide for administering and scoring the fourth edition of the Standford-Binet Intelligence Scale.* Chicago: Riverside Publishing.

Thorndike, R. L., Hagen, E. P., & Sattler, J. P. (1986b). *Technical manual for the Standford-Binet Intelligence Scale, Fourth Edition.* Chicago: Riverside Publishing.

Touliatos, J., Perlmutter, B. F., & Straus, M. A. (Eds.). (1990). *Handbook of family measurement techniques.* Newbury Park, CA: Sage.

Tronick, E. Z. (1989). Emotions and emotional communication in infants. *American Psychologist, 44*(2), 112–119.

Vaihinger, H. (1924). *The philosophy of "As If."* London, UK: Routledge, Kegan, & Paul, Ltd.

Valdés, M. J. (1987). *Phenomenological hermeneutics and the study of literature.* Toronto: University of Toronto Press.

Van de Putte, S. J. (1992). Sexual abuse of male children: A phenomenological investigation. Doctoral dissertation, California School of Professional Psychology. *Dissertation Abstracts International, 53,* 12B.

Van de Putte, S. J. (1993). A structured activities group for sexually abused children. In K. J. O'Connor & C. E. Schaefer (Eds.), *Handbook of play therapy: Vol. 2. Advances and innovations* (pp. 409–427). New York: John Wiley.

Van Fleet, R. (1993). Filial therapy for adoptive children and parents. In K. J. O'Connor and C. E. Schaefer (Eds.), *Handbook of play therapy: Vol. 2. Advances and innovations* (pp. 371–385). New York: John Wiley.

Van Fleet, R. (1994). *Filial therapy: Strengthening parent–child relationships through play.* Sarasota, FL: Professional Resource Press.

Verny, T. R. (1981). *Secret life of the unborn child.* New York: Summit Books.

Webster's Seventh New Collegiate Dictionary. (1967). Springfield, MA: Merriam.

Weaver, S. J. (Ed.). (1984). *Testing children: A reference guide for effective clinical and psychoeducational assessments.* Kansas City: Test Corporation of America.

Wechsler, D. (1989). *Wechsler Preschool and Primary Scale of In-*

telligence—Revised. San Antonio, TX: The Psychological Corporation.

Wechsler, D. (1991). *WISC-III: Wechsler Intelligence Scale for Children—Third Edition manual.* New York: The Psychological Corporation.

Westby, C. E. (1991). A scale for assessing children's pretend play. In C. E. Schaefer, K. Gitlin, & A. Sandgrund (Eds.), *Play diagnosis and assessment* (pp. 131–161). New York: John Wiley.

Wiehe, V. R. (1990). *Sibling abuse: Hidden physical, emotional, and sexual trauma.* New York: Lexington.

Weiner, N. (1961). *Cybernetics or control and communication in the animal and machine* (2nd ed.). Cambridge: M.I.T. Press.

Willi, J. (1987). Some principles of an ecological model of the person as a consequence of the therapeutic experience with systems. *Family Process, 26,* 429–436.

Winnicott, D. W. (1965). *The maturational processes and the facilitating environment.* New York: International Universities Press.

Wirt, R. D., Lachar, D., Klinedist, J. E., Seat, P. D., & Broen, W. E. (1977). *Personality Inventory for Children.* Los Angeles: Western Psychological Services.

Wood, M., Combs, C., Gunn, A., & Weller, D. (1986). *Developmental therapy in the classroom* (2nd ed.). Austin, TX: Pro-Ed.

Wood, M. M. (1992a). *Developmental Teaching Objectives Rating Form-Revised technical report.* Athens, GA: Developmental Therapy Institute.

Wood, M. M. (1992b). *Developmental Teaching Objectives Rating Form-Revised user's manual.* Athens, GA: Developmental Therapy Institute.

Wood, M. M. (with Davis, K. R., Swindle, F. L., & Quirk, C.). (1996). *Developmental therapy—Developmental teaching: Fostering social–emotional competence in troubled children and youth* (3rd ed.). Austin, TX: Pro-Ed.

Worden, M. (1996). *Family therapy basics.* Pacific Grove, CA: Brooks/Cole.

Workgroup on Psychiatric Practice in the Juvenile Court of the American Psychiatric Association. (1992). *Handbook of psychiatric practice in the juvenile court.* Washington, DC: American Psychiatric Association.

Young, T. M. (Spring/Summer, 1987). Therapeutic case advocacy: A summary. *Focal Point: The Bulletin of the Research and Training Center to Improve Services for Seriously Emotionally Handicapped Children and Their Families, 1*(3), 1–5.

Zilbach, J., & Gordetsky, S. (1994). The family life cycle: A framework for understanding family development and play in family therapy. In C. Schaefer & L. Carey (Eds.), *Family play therapy* (pp. 165–183). Northvale, NJ: Jason Aronson.

◆ **Index** ◆

PLAY THERAPY TREATMENT PLANNING WORKBOOK

PLAY THERAPY TREATMENT PLANNING WORKBOOK
The Ecosystemic Model

Clinician's Name: _____   Work Site Name: _____

Address: _____

City: _____ State: _____ Zip: _____ Phone: _____

I. IDENTIFYING INFORMATION ‖ CASE NAME: _____

INTAKE, ASSESSMENT & CONTRACTING CONTACT RECORD

DATE	PERSON(S) ATTENDING	TASK COMPLETED	PERSON(S) COMPLETING

Client Name: _____   Gender: _____   Birthdate: _____

Home Address: _____

City: _____ State: _____ Zip: _____ Phone: _____

RESPONSIBLE ADULT(S) INFORMATION

Adult 1 Name: _____   Relationship: _____

Home Address: _____

City: _____ State: _____ Zip: _____ Phone: _____

Employer: _____   Position: _____

Work Address: _____

City: _____ State: _____ Zip: _____ Phone: _____

Insurance Carrier & Number: _____

Adult 2: Name: _____   Relationship: _____

Home Address: _____

City: _____ State: _____ Zip: _____ Phone: _____

Employer: _____   Position: _____

Work Address: _____

City: _____ State: _____ Zip: _____ Phone: _____

Insurance Carrier & Number: _____

FAMILY CONSTELLATION (Include all persons named above. For all persons mentioned here and throughout the workbook be as specific as possible about their relationship(s) to the child, e.g. Maternal grandmother, half-sibling through mother, step-parent, etc.)

Name	Relationship	HH	%H1	%H2	BD	Age	Ethnicity	Grade/Work
Client	Self							

[In column HH put a 1 for the Head of Household 1, a 2 for the Head of Household 2, etc. Put 0 if not Head of Household. In column %H1 put the % of time each individual spends in Household 1, repeat for time spent in Household 2.]

PRESENTING PROBLEM (Define in behavioral terms, including onset, frequency and severity. Be sure to include reporters affect regarding the problem.)

Child's View: _____

_____

_____

Parent's View: _____

_____

_____

Other's View: _____

_____

_____

HISTORY OF PRESENTING PROBLEM (Define precipitants, impact on/reaction from environment, situations variations, attempts to resolve problem and results, and changes in problem over time.)

_____

_____

_____

_____

_____

_____

_____

_____

_____

II. INTAKE: SYSTEMS REVIEW

INDIVIDUAL SYSTEM: DEVELOPMENTAL HISTORY

Pregnancy

Planned: ☐ No ☐ Yes, Describe: _____

_____

Discomfort/Problems: ☐ No ☐ Yes, Describe: _____

_____

Drugs/Alcohol during pregnancy: ☐ No ☐ Yes, Describe: _____

_____

Stressors/Complications with the pregnancy: _____

_____

Support System(s): _____

Labor & Delivery: WT: _____ APGAR: _____ Who present at delivery: _____

How long/how difficult/problems: _____

_____

If problems - what happened?: _____

_____

_____

Developmental Milestones: Walk: _____ Talk: _____ Words: _____ Sentences: _____

Age Toilet Trained: Bladder: _____ Bowel: _____

Problems: ☐ No ☐ Yes, Describe: _____

_____

_____

Developmental Delays

Language: ☐ No ☐ Yes, ☐ Expressive ☐ Receptive ☐ Articulation ☐ Auditory Processing

Describe: _____

_____

Motor: ☐ No ☐ Yes, Describe: _____

_____

Adaptive Behavior: ☐ No ☐ Yes, Describe: _____

_____

Other: ☐ No ☐ Yes, Describe: _____

_____

Gender Identity, Gender Role Behavior and Sexual Orientation

Gender identity divergent from biologic gender: ☐ No ☐ Yes, Describe: _____

_____

Client experiences divergence as problematic: ☐ No ☐ Yes, Describe: _____

_____

Others experience divergence as problematic: ☐ No ☐ Yes, Describe: _____

_____

Gender role behavior divergent from socio-cultural norms: : ☐ No ☐ Yes, Describe: _____

_____

Client experiences divergence as problematic: ☐ No ☐ Yes, Describe: _____

_____

Others experience divergence as problematic: ☐ No ☐ Yes, Describe: _____

_____

Sexual Orientation Development

☐ Client's sexual orientation not behaviorally evident at this time.

Client experiences sexual orientation as problematic: ☐ No ☐ Yes, Describe: _____

_____

Others experience client's sexual orientation as problematic: ☐ No ☐ Yes, Describe: _____

_____

INDIVIDUAL SYSTEM: MENTAL STATUS EXAMINATION

Behavioral Observations

Appearance: _____

_____

Motor Activity: _____

_____

Speech: (Content and Productivity) _____

_____

Emotions

Mood: _____

_____

Affect: (Range, Reality Base, Control) _____

_____

_____

Attitude: _____

_____

Relatedness: _____

_____

Cognitive Processes (*WNL = Within Normal Limits for Age)

    Estimated Developmental Level: WNL: ☐ **Yes** ☐ **No, Describe:** _____

_____

    ☐ **Sensorimotor**   ☐ **Pre-operational**   ☐ **Concrete Operations**   ☐ **Formal Operations**

Orientation: .... **WNL:** ☐ **Yes** ☐ **No, Disoriented:** ☐ **Time** ☐ **Place** ☐ **Person** ☐ **Purpose**

Memory: .... **WNL:** ☐ **Yes** ☐ **No, Impaired:** ☐ **Immediate** ☐ **Intermediate** ☐ **Long Term**

Concentration: .. **WNL:** ☐ **Yes** ☐ **No, Difficulty is:** ☐ **Severe** ☐ **Moderate** ☐ **Minimal**

Abstraction: ...... **WNL:** ☐ **Yes** ☐ **No, Thinking is:** ☐ **Overly Concrete** ☐ **Overly Abstract**

Intellect: .... **WNL:** ☐ **Yes** ☐ **No, Intelligence is:** ☐ **Below Average** ☐ **Above Average**

Judgment: .... **WNL:** ☐ **Yes** ☐ **No, Impaired:** ☐ **Severe** ☐ **Moderate** ☐ **Minimal**

Insight: .... **WNL:** ☐ **Yes** ☐ **No, Insight is:** ☐ **Absent** ☐ **Limited** ☐ **Above Average**

Organization: .... **WNL:** ☐ **Yes** ☐ **No, Thinking is:** ☐ **Chaotic** ☐ **Loose** ☐ **Rigid**

    If No, Describe: _____

_____

Hallucinations: .... ☐ **No** ☐ **Yes, Type:** ☐ **Visual** ☐ **Auditory** ☐ **Other:** _____

    If Yes, Describe: _____

_____

Delusions: .... ☐ **No** ☐ **Yes, Type:** ☐ **Persecutory** ☐ **Grandiosity** ☐ **Other:** _____

    If Yes, Describe: _____

_____

Trauma Symptoms: .... ☐ **No** ☐ **Yes, Type:** ☐ **Nightmares** ☐ **Flashbacks** ☐ **Alexithymia**

    ☐ **Reenactment Behaviors** ☐ **Disassociative Phenomena** ☐ **Other:** _____

    If Yes, Describe: _____

_____

Subjective Experience

    Self Concept: _____

_____

    View of World: _____

_____

    3 Wishes: _____

_____

    Reality Testing: _____

_____

_____

Dangerous Behavior

   Self Injurious Behavior or Ideation: ☐ No ☐ Yes, Describe: _____

_____

_____

      Prior Acts or Ideation: ☐ No ☐ Yes, Describe: _____

      _____

   Suicidal Behavior or Ideation: ☐ No ☐ Yes, Describe: (Include: imminence, plan, means, reality base,

dangerousness, etc.): _____

_____

_____

      Prior Attempts or Ideation: ☐ No ☐ Yes, Describe: _____

      _____

      Family History of Suicide: ☐ No ☐ Yes, Describe: _____

      _____

      Support/Response Plan: _____

      _____

   Aggressive Behavior or Ideation: ☐ No ☐ Yes, Describe: _____

   _____

      Target(s): ☐ Property ☐ Animals ☐ Children ☐ Adults. **Describe:** _____

      _____

      Prior Acts or Ideation: ☐ No ☐ Yes, Describe: _____

      _____

   Homicidal Behavior or Ideation: ☐ No ☐ Yes, Describe: (Include: imminence, plan, means, reality base,

dangerousness, etc.): _____

_____

      Target(s): _____

      Prior Attempts or Ideation: ☐ No ☐ Yes, Describe: _____

      _____

      Family History of Violence: ☐ No ☐ Yes, Describe: _____

      _____

      Support/Response Plan: _____

      _____

   History of Sexually Inappropriate Behavior: ☐ No ☐ Yes, Describe: _____

   _____

   History of Fire Setting: ☐ No ☐ Yes, Describe: _____

   _____

Observations of Play Behavior

_____

_____

_____

_____

_____

DYADIC SYSTEM: FIRST THREE YEARS

Primary Caretaker(s): _____

Significant Disruptions in the Primary Relationship: ☐ No ☐ Yes, Describe: _____

_____

_____

First Year

    Type of Baby: _____

    Description of Bonding (Parental experience of relationship to the child)**:** _____

    _____

    Affective Responsiveness of Child to Parent: _____

    _____

Second & Third Years

    Type of Toddler: _____

    _____

    Description of Relationship to Caretaker: _____

    _____

    _____

    Description of Relationship to Other Family Members: _____

    _____

    Description of Child's Exploratory Behavior: _____

    _____

    How was toilet-training implemented? _____

    _____

        What was child's response? _____

        _____

    What type of discipline was used? _____

    _____

        What was child's response? _____

        _____

Separations/Reunions

Attended Daycare/Preschool: ☐ No ☐ Yes, Describe: _____

_____

Child's Reaction to Separation & Reunion: _____

_____

Parent's Response to Child's Reaction: _____

_____

Observations of Child-Caretaker Interactions

_____

_____

_____

_____

_____

FAMILY SYSTEM

Genogram [Complete by Hand]

KEY: Male: ☐   Female: ○   Deceased: ⊠ or ⊗   Client: ☐ or ◎

Married: ☐—○   Living Together: ☐⋯○   Separated: ☐⁄○   Divorced: ☐⫽○

Children
(List by birth order starting on left)   Miscarriage/Abortion: Twins: Adoption:

Family Functioning & History

Current Family Relationships & Dynamics: _____

_____

_____

_____

_____

Family History: (Include changes in family membership &/or home location, major events, significant losses, and support system) _____

_____

_____

_____

_____

Extended Family History: _____

_____

_____

_____

Sibling Sub-System

Relationships with Siblings: _____

_____

Role of Siblings in the Presenting Problem: _____

_____

Impact of the Presenting Problem on Siblings: _____

_____

Spousal Sub-System

Persons in Spousal System: _____

Current Problems: ☐ No ☐ Yes, Describe: _____

_____

_____

History of Problems: ☐ No ☐ Yes, Describe: _____

_____

_____

Role of Spousal Difficulties in the Presenting Problem: _____

_____

_____

Impact of the Presenting Problem on Spousal Relationship: _____

_____

Significant Adults' Current Occupational Functioning

    Adult 1: _____ **Employed:** ☐ **No** ☐ **Yes, Describe:** _____

        Occupational History/Problems: _____

        _____

        Role of Occupational Difficulties in the Presenting Problem: _____

        _____

        Impact of the Presenting Problem on Occupational Functioning: _____

        _____

    Adult 2: _____ **Employed:** ☐ **No** ☐ **Yes, Describe:** _____

        Occupational History/Problems: _____

        _____

        Role of Occupational Difficulties in the Presenting Problem: _____

        _____

        Impact of the Presenting Problem on Occupational Functioning: _____

        _____

Social Network

    Social Support: _____

    _____

    Problems in Social Network: _____

    _____

    _____

Family Development

_____

_____

_____

Familial Identification

    Familial Ethnocultural Identification: _____

    _____

    Familial Religious Affiliation (Identification and degree of involvement)**:** _____

    _____

Observations of the Family System

_____

_____

_____

_____

_____

_____

SOCIAL SYSTEM

Current Social Functioning

Close Friends: ☐ No ☐ **Yes, Describe** (Number/Duration): _____

_____

Problems with Peers: _____

_____

_____

Problems with Adults: _____

_____

Past Social Functioning

Problems with Peers: _____

_____

Problems with Adults: _____

_____

Interpersonal/Sexual History

Involved in Significant Intimate Relationship: ☐ No ☐ **Yes, Describe:** _____

_____

Problems in Sexual Relationship: _____

_____

Problems in Previous Relationships: _____

_____

Observations of Peer Interactions

_____

_____

_____

_____

_____

EDUCATIONAL SYSTEM

Current School Circumstances

Grade: _____ **School/District:** _____ **Telephone:** _____

Teacher(s): _____ **Counselor:** _____

Special Education or Support Services: ☐ No ☐ **Yes, Describe:** _____

_____

Specific Problems: _____

_____

_____

School History

    School Placement History: _____

_____

_____

    Problems (Especially note adjustment to K, 1st, 3rd and 6th grades)**:** _____

_____

    Interventions/Outcomes: _____

_____

Family History of Learning Problems

_____

_____

_____

Site Visit Information/Observations

_____

_____

_____

_____

_____

LEGAL SYSTEMS

Child Abuse/Domestic Violence

    Current: ☐ No ☐ Yes: ☐ Physical ☐ Sexual ☐ Emotional ☐ Neglect ☐ Witnessed Violence
    Perpetrator(s): _____ Victim(s): _____
    Relationship to Child: _____ Relationship to Child: _____

    Description: _____

_____

_____

    Report Filed: ☐ No ☐ Yes, When: _____ **CPS Involved:** ☐ No ☐ Yes

    Caseworker: _____ **Telephone:** _____

    CPS Response and Long Term Plan: _____

_____

    Impending Court Appearance: ☐ No ☐ Yes, Date: _____

        Purpose: _____

    Domestic Violence Shelter: ☐ No ☐ Yes, Describe: _____

_____

    Caseworker: _____ **Telephone:** _____

    Orders of Protection: ☐ No ☐ Yes, Describe: _____

_____

Previous: ☐ No ☐ Yes: ☐ Physical ☐ Sexual ☐ Emotional ☐ Neglect ☐ Witnessed Violence

Perpetrator(s): _____ Victim(s): _____

Relationship to Child: _____ Relationship to Child: _____

Description: _____

_____

_____

Report Filed: ☐ No ☐ Yes, When: _____ **CPS Involved:** ☐ No ☐ Yes

CPS Response and Long Term Plan: _____

_____

Impending Court Appearance: ☐ No ☐ Yes, Date: _____

Purpose: _____

Domestic Violence Shelter: ☐ No ☐ Yes, Describe: _____

_____

Caseworker: _____ **Telephone:** _____

Orders of Protection: ☐ No ☐ Yes, Describe: _____

_____

Intergenerational History of Child Abuse/Domestic Violence: ☐ No ☐ Yes, Describe: _____

_____

_____

Legal System (Non-Criminal) (For all persons mentioned be as specific as possible about their relationship(s) to the child.)

Divorce: ☐ No ☐ Yes, Describe: _____

_____

_____

Current Custody Proceedings: ☐ No ☐ Yes, Describe: _____

_____

_____

Mediator/Attorney: _____ **Telephone:** _____

Past Custody Proceedings: ☐ No ☐ Yes, Description/Outcome: _____

_____

Foster Placement: ☐ No ☐ Yes, Describe: _____

_____

Adoption: ☐ No ☐ Yes, Describe: _____

_____

Law Enforcement System (For all persons mentioned be as specific as possible about their relationship(s) to the child.)

Contact(s) <u>Not</u> Leading to Arrest: ☐ No ☐ Yes, Describe: _____

_____

Arrest(s) <u>Not</u> Leading to Court Proceedings: ☐ No ☐ Yes, Describe: _____

_____

Juvenile Offender System (For all persons mentioned be as specific as possible about their relationship(s) to the child.)

Arrests for Statutory Violation(s): ☐ No ☐ Yes, Description/Outcome: _____

_____

Arrests for Misdemeanor(s): ☐ No ☐ Yes, Description/Outcome: _____

_____

Arrests for Felony(s): ☐ No ☐ Yes, Description/Outcome: _____

_____

Juvenile Hall Placement(s): ☐ No ☐ Yes, Describe: _____

_____

Probation: ☐ No ☐ Yes, Describe: _____

_____

Probation Officer: _____   **Telephone:** _____

Family Members Involved in Juvenile Justice System, Past or Present: ☐ No ☐ Yes, Describe: _____

_____

_____

Legal System (Criminal) (For all persons mentioned be as specific as possible about their relationship(s) to the child.)

Court Appearances for Misdemeanor(s): ☐ No ☐ Yes, Description/Outcome: _____

_____

Court Appearances for Felony(s): ☐ No ☐ Yes, Description/Outcome: _____

_____

Probation/Parole: ☐ No ☐ Yes, Describe: _____

_____

Probation/Parole Officer: _____   **Telephone:** _____

MEDICAL SYSTEM

Allergies: ☐ No ☐ Yes, Describe: _____

_____

Serious Accidents: ☐ No ☐ Yes, Describe: _____

_____

Head Injury w/ Loss of Consciousness: ☐ No ☐ Yes, Describe: _____

_____

Serious Illness: ☐ No ☐ Yes, Describe: _____

_____

Chronic Illness: ☐ No ☐ Yes, Describe: _____

_____

Hospitalizations: ☐ No ☐ Yes, Describe: _____

_____

Other Medical Problems: ☐ No ☐ Yes, Describe: _____

_____

Present Medications: ☐ No ☐ Yes, Physician: _____

    Type, Dose, Frequency: _____

Eating Pattern: _____

Sleeping Pattern: _____

Family History of Medical Problems: _____

_____

_____

_____

MENTAL HEALTH SYSTEM

Concurrent Outpatient Treatment: ☐ No ☐ Yes, Describe: _____

_____

    Diagnosis: _____

    Facility/Therapist: _____

Previous Outpatient Treatment: ☐ No ☐ Yes, Describe: _____

_____

    Diagnosis: _____

    Facility/Therapist: _____

Previous Inpatient Treatment: ☐ No ☐ Yes, Describe: _____

_____

    Diagnosis: _____

    Facility/Therapist: _____

Psychotropic Medications: ☐ No ☐ Yes, Describe: _____

    Current Medications: Type, Dose, Frequency: _____

    Prescribing Physician: _____

    Previous Medications: Type, Dose, Frequency: _____

    Prescribing Physician: _____

Current Mental Health Difficulties and Treatment of Other Family Members: (For all persons mentioned be as specific as possible about their relationship(s) to the child.) _____

_____

_____

History of Mental Health Difficulties and Treatment of Other Family Members: (For all persons mentioned be as specific as possible about their relationship(s) to the child.) _____

_____

_____

Current Substance Abuse: ☐ None ☐ Mild ☐ Moderate ☐ Severe: _____

_____

Substances Used/Frequency/Intensity: _____

In Treatment: ☐ No ☐ Yes, Describe: _____

_____

Previous Substance Abuse: ☐ None ☐ Mild ☐ Moderate ☐ Severe: _____

_____

Substances Used/Frequency/Intensity: _____

Treatment: ☐ No ☐ Yes, Describe: _____

Current Substance Abuse and Treatment of Other Family Members: (For all persons mentioned be as specific as possible about their relationship(s) to the child.) _____

_____

_____

History of Substance Abuse and Treatment of Other Family Members: (For all persons mentioned be as specific as possible about their relationship(s) to the child.) _____

_____

_____

Note: The following 4 sections should be completed if the therapist has any reason to believe that these systems may have played a role in the origin of the presenting problem or that they are playing a role in maintaining the problem.

REGIONAL CULTURAL SYSTEM

_____

_____

_____

_____

DOMINANT/NATIONAL OR POLITICAL SYSTEM

_____

_____

_____

_____

WORLD COMMUNITY

_____

_____

_____

_____

HISTORICAL TIME

_____
_____
_____
_____

III. ASSESSMENT DATA

DATA SOURCES

Tests and/or Measures Administered: _____
_____
_____

Other Data Sources: _____
_____
_____

INDIVIDUAL DATA

List the source of the data reported in each of the following sections. For example: Data regarding a child's intellectual functioning may have been obtained from an intelligence test, school records and their scores on various projective instruments.

Cognitive Functioning (Including, if relevant, intelligence, learning styles, language and all academic skill areas.): _____
_____
_____
_____
_____
_____
_____
_____
_____

Emotional Functioning: _____
_____
_____
_____
_____
_____
_____
_____

Behavioral Functioning: _____
_____
_____
_____
_____
_____

Physical Functioning and Motor Development: _____
_____
_____
_____
_____
_____

INTERPERSONAL DATA

List the source of the data reported in each of the following sections. For example: Data regarding a child's peer social functioning may have been obtained from a parent rating scale, a sociogram and the child's responses to projective instruments.

Dyadic Functioning (Specify dyads assessed.)**:** _____
_____
_____
_____
_____
_____

Family Functioning: _____
_____
_____
_____
_____
_____

Social Functioning (Including, if relevant, both extrafamilial and peer interactions.)**:** _____
_____
_____
_____
_____

NOTE: Before completing the rest of the workbook complete the APPENDIX

IV. DIAGNOSIS

Axis I (Clinical Disorders): _____

Axis II (Personality Disorders & Mental Retardation): _____

Axis III (General Medical Conditions): _____

Axis IV (Psychosocial & Environmental Problems): _____

Axis V: Current GAF: ___   **Highest GAF in past year:** ___.

V. CASE FORMULATION   (This should be an integration of the case data and a description of the primary hypotheses to be addressed in treatment.)

_____

_____

_____

_____

_____

_____

_____

_____

_____

_____

_____

_____

_____

_____

_____

_____

_____

_____

_____

_____

_____

_____

_____

_____

_____

_____

_____

VI. TREATMENT: CONTRACT & GENERAL PLAN

Contract with Child: _____
_____
_____
_____
_____

Contract with Caretaker(s)/Family: _____
_____
_____
_____
_____

Treatment Objective(s): _____
_____
_____
_____

Treatment Modality(ies): _____
_____
_____

Anticipated Number of Sessions: _____

Collaborative Interventions (Evaluation, Education, Consultation, Advocacy, etc.)**:** _____
_____
_____
_____
_____

Signature: _____ **Position:** _____ **Date:** _____

Signature: _____ **Position:** _____ **Date:** _____

VII. DETAILED TREATMENT PLAN ‖ CASE NAME:

Stage I: Introduction & Exploration: (Anticipated Number of Sessions:)

    Stage Goal(s): _____

_____

_____

    Participants: _____

    Materials: _____

_____

    Experiential Component(s): _____

_____

_____

_____

    Verbal Component(s): _____

_____

_____

_____

    Collaborative Component(s): (Advocacy, Consultation, Education, Evaluation) _____

_____

_____

Stage II: Tentative Acceptance: (Anticipated Number of Sessions:)

    Stage Goal(s): _____

_____

_____

    Participants: _____

    Materials: _____

_____

    Experiential Component(s): _____

_____

_____

_____

    Verbal Component(s): _____

_____

_____

_____

    Collaborative Component(s): (Advocacy, Consultation, Education, Evaluation) _____

_____

_____

Stage III: Negative Reaction: (Anticipated Number of Sessions:)

   Stage Goal(s): _____

   _____

   _____

   Participants: _____

   Materials: _____

   Experiential Component(s): _____

   _____

   _____

   _____

   Verbal Component(s): _____

   _____

   _____

   _____

   Collaborative Component(s): (Advocacy, Consultation, Education, Evaluation) _____

   _____

   _____

Stage IV: Growing & Trusting: (Anticipated Number of Sessions:)

   Stage Goal(s): _____

   _____

   _____

   Participants: _____

   Materials: _____

   Experiential Component(s): _____

   _____

   _____

   _____

   Verbal Component(s): _____

   _____

   _____

   _____

   Collaborative Component(s): (Advocacy, Consultation, Education, Evaluation) _____

   _____

   _____

Stage V: Termination: (Anticipated Number of Sessions:)

    Stage Goal(s): _____

_____

_____

    Participants: _____

    Materials: _____

_____

    Experiential Component(s): _____

_____

_____

_____

    Verbal Component(s): _____

_____

_____

_____

    Collaborative Component(s): (Advocacy, Consultation, Education, Evaluation) _____

_____

_____

Signature: _____ **Position:** _____ **Date:** _____

Signature: _____ **Position:** _____ **Date:** _____

PLAY THERAPY TREATMENT PLANNING WORKBOOK
APPENDIX: Data Integration and Hypothesis Formulation

A1. DEVELOPMENTAL INTEGRATION OF INTAKE INFORMATION

Age	Cognitive Stage	Individual History	Family	Social
<Birth				
Birth				
1				
2				
3				
4				
5				
6				
7				
8				
9				
10				
11				
12				

Age	Educational	Legal	Medical	Mental Health
<Birth				
Birth				
1				
2				
3				
4				
5				
6				
7				
8				
9				
10				
11				
12				

A2.   DEVELOPMENTAL DESCRIPTION OF THE CHILD

Describe the child's present functioning in each of the following areas.

DEVELOPMENTAL LEVEL

General: (What is your overall impression of this child's current functioning? Do you think others would perceive him or her to be developmentally on, above or below age level?) _____

_____

_____

_____

Interpersonal: (Does this child's functioning change depending on the developmental level of the person(s) with whom he or she is interacting?) _____

_____

_____

COGNITIONS

Functional Level: (Describe overall cognitive functioning as well as any changes that occur when the child is working with emotionally loaded material versus more concrete material.) _____

_____

_____

_____

Significant Organizing Beliefs:

1. _____

2. _____

3. _____

4. _____

EMOTIONS

Type: _____

_____

Repertoire: _____

_____

Range: _____

_____

Reality Base: _____

_____

PSYCHOPATHOLOGY

Individual (Client) Need(s) Not Being Met Effectively: _____

_____

_____

Individual (Client) Need(s) Not Being Met Appropriately: _____

_____

_____

Others' Need(s) Not Being Met Appropriately in That These Interfere with Child's Needs Being Met: ____

_____

_____

RESPONSE REPERTOIRE

Dominant Approach to Problems: ☐ Autoplastic   ☐ Alloplastic

Autoplastic: (Describe those situations to which the child is most likely to make an autoplastic response.)

_____

_____

Alloplastic: (Describe those situations to which the child is most likely to make an alloplastic response.)

_____

_____

A3. HYPOTHESIS DEVELOPMENT: ETIOLOGIC FACTORS

Develop hypotheses regarding the bases for the child's present level of function/dysfunction.

CHILD FACTORS

Endowment: _____

_____

_____

Developmental Response: _____

_____

_____

_____

ECOSYSTEMIC FACTORS

Family: _____

_____

_____

_____

_____

Peers: _____

_____

_____

Other: Educational, Medical, Legal, Cultural, Historical: _____

_____

_____

_____

_____

A4.   HYPOTHESIS DEVELOPMENT: MAINTAINING FACTORS

Develop hypotheses regarding factors maintaining the child's present level of function/dysfunction.

CHILD FACTORS

Endowment: _____

_____

_____

Developmental Response: _____

_____

_____

_____

COST/BENEFIT ANALYSIS OF BELIEFS, EMOTIONS AND BEHAVIOR

_____

_____

_____

_____

_____

_____

_____

_____

_____

_____

ECOSYSTEMIC FACTORS

Family: _____

_____

_____

_____

_____

_____

Peers: _____

_____

_____

_____

Other: **Educational, Medical, Legal, Cultural, Historical:** _____

_____

_____

_____

_____

_____

A5.   GOAL DEVELOPMENT/SYNTHESIS AND TREATMENT PLANNING

A. Develop goal statements specific to the factors identified in Section VI and VII.

B. Indicate the category into which the goal falls
S = Safety/Crisis, **SB** = Secure Base, **D** = Developmental, **PC** = Problem/Content, **C** = Coping, **Sy** = Systemic

C. Check those goals to be addressed in context of psychotherapy.

D. Number the goals in order of priority.

E. Determine the system or context in which each of the treatment goals should be addressed.
I = Individual, **F** = Family, **P** = Peer, **S** = School, **M** = Medical Setting, **MH** = Mental Health Setting, **C** = Community, etc.

F. Determine the interventions to be used in the course of the treatment.
R = Referral,   **IP** = Individual Psychotherapy ,   **FT** = Family Therapy,   **PG** = Peer Group Therapy,   **Fi** = Filial Therapy,
C = Consultation,   **Ed** = Education, **Ev** = Evaluation, **A** = Advocacy, etc.

A: Comprehensive Goal List	B	C	D	E	F
1.					
2.					
3.					
4.					
5.					
6.					
7.					
8.					
9.					
0.					

A: Comprehensive Goal List (Continued)	B	C	D	E	F
11.					
12.					
13.					
14.					
15.					
16.					
17.					
18.					
19.					
20.					
21.					
22.					
23.					
24.					
25.					
26.					
27.					
28.					
29.					
30.					